Making social lives

Making social lives

Edited by Stephanie Taylor, Steve Hinchliffe, John Clarke and Simon Bromley

The paper used in this publication contains pulp sourced from forests independently certified to the Forest Stewardship Council (FSC) principles and criteria. Chain of custody certification allows the pulp from these forests to be tracked to the end use (see www.fsc.org).

The Open University Walton Hall, Milton Keynes MK7 6AA

First published 2009

Edited and designed by The Open University

Typeset in India by Alden Prepress Services, Chennai

Printed and bound in the United Kingdom by Latimer Trend & Company Ltd, Plymouth.

ISBN 978 0 7492 1641 2

1.1

Contents

Preface

Making Social Lives is the course textbook and main source of course content for the first part of *Introducing the social sciences* (DD101 and DD131). As with other Open University texts, *Making Social Lives* has been produced by a 'course team' of academic and production staff that included the authors and editors named in this book but many others besides. This wider course team played a vital role in shaping the book as a whole as well as in helping to refine successive drafts into a coherent text. Our external assessor, Professor Alan Warde, provided critical and supporting advice on how to improve the text and we are very grateful for his careful work on our behalf.

The academic staff at the Open University are especially fortunate in being able to draw on the expertise and patience of excellent production and administrative colleagues. Our Course Co-ordinators, Lesley Moore and Annette Portlock, worked on successive drafts with efficiency and goodwill and provided great support to the course team. Our Editorial Media Developers, Emma Sadera and Richard Jones, oversaw the editing and composition of the book and the course with a reassuring attention to detail, care and good humour, creatively shaping the final results along the way. Thanks too to Paul Hillery and Howie Twiner, Graphics Media Developers, for the excellent work on the design and artwork of the book. Last, but definitely not least, thanks to Matt Staples, Caitlin Harvey and Lucy Smith, and then Eileen Potterton and Lucy Morris, who successively worked as Course Managers on *Introducing the social sciences*. Together, they oversaw the production of *Making Social Lives*, as well as the course as a whole, with such unflappable efficiency, energy and all-round goodwill that even the difficult bits were easy.

Making Social Lives is divided into three strands of course content – Material lives; Connected lives; and Ordered lives. Each of these strands is introduced and concluded by the strand editors, respectively, Steve Hinchliffe, Stephanie Taylor, and John Clarke. Working with the rest of the course team, they have played a key role in shaping and refining this text and we are very grateful to them all.

Georgina Blakeley and Simon Bromley
Co-chairs of the *Introducing the social sciences* course team

Introduction: Material lives

Steve Hinchliffe

Introduction: Material lives

This book is about how society is made and repaired. It asks what kinds of activities make society today. In the chapters that follow, you will learn about contemporary UK society and the special insights that the social sciences can give you as you develop an understanding of how society is made. The book will introduce both the ideas and the forms of investigation developed by social scientists. Each chapter starts with or refers to the contemporary UK, and involves you reading about a street or streets. You will soon realise, however, that the street is only a starting point. Some chapters travel back in time to understand how contemporary society is coloured and even partly produced by its past. Some extend well beyond the conventional boundaries of the UK (in other words, the land area shown on maps) in order to understand how societies are made in part through their connections to other people and places.

The chapters in this book have been arranged into three strands – 'Material lives', 'Connected lives' and 'Ordered lives'. You will read more about the second and third strands in the introductions that precede each group of chapters. This first strand, 'Material lives', looks at *how* people live, their material existence, and how these ways of life have consequences for their own and other people's welfare, for society and for the environment.

In order to start you thinking about how people live today, the kinds of things many of them do, one particular feature of contemporary UK society which all three chapters in this strand share as a focus and starting point is consuming and shopping.

Why choose consuming and shopping? One answer is that for some people and for many social scientists, contemporary UK society differs from societies in the recent past in that people tend to define themselves less by their jobs and more by what they consume. Another answer is that, as at the time of writing the UK enters a deep recession, the state of the high street and the amount of shopping people do has become a key issue in economic and social recovery. Jobs, welfare, urban renewal, social order; these all seem to be dependent on where and how people shop. So, in Chapter 1 Kevin Hetherington notes that, in the past, much of the UK could be considered an industrial society, marked that is by its factories and its workers, and with lifestyles organised to a large extent around working lives. Today, social life seems to revolve as much if not more around what people buy and what they do with their possessions. We are, at least in part it seems, what we wear, what we eat, watch, listen to, live in. Indeed, we are what we consume is a common enough claim (see Figure 1). No longer simply defined by our jobs (teacher, nurse, office worker, shop worker), we also tend to define ourselves and others by what, as Hetherington puts it, 'we are into' (cycling, music, clubs, cars, collecting, clothes…). The opening chapter reflects upon this possible shift in emphasis in how social life is organised. It looks at what is sometimes called a *consumer society*.

Figure 1   *I shop therefore I am* – a screen-print by Barbara Kruger, 1987. The artwork plays on the phrase 'I think therefore I am' which has often been taken to be a defining statement of human being

As you read Chapter 1 you will notice that Hetherington traces an image of a consumer society which is awash with material goods, where choice seems to be the order to the day. Faced with this range of goods and services offered from many different shopping outlets, he asks us to think about the role of shopping and consumption and what we buy in terms of who we would like to be. But, he notes, this is not all about equal choice. Not everyone is equally able to consume. There are people who are better placed than others to join the consumer society. There are divisions between young and old, the employed and the unemployed, able-bodied and less able, 'in'-crowds and 'out'-crowds. A consumer society is, then, a divided society.

As you read the chapters, and engage with shopping and consumption, it's useful to bear the key questions for this course in mind. To help you, I have extended these questions and rephrased the first two of them so that they apply to the content of the chapters in this part of the course. We shall return to these questions in the conclusion for this strand.

1 How are differences and inequalities produced? Or, who are the winners and losers in a consumer society?

First of all, as already stated, a consumer society implies a shift in emphasis away from what people do for a living to how people live their lives. This can seem liberating (as well as being a policewoman, carer or office worker, a person can also be a car owner, proud homeowner or into collecting rare dolls …). But it can, as Hetherington argues in Chapter 1, make divisions in society just as, if not more, apparent. 'Old' divisions between rich and poor may now be intensified. Participating in consumer society quite clearly favours those who have plenty of money over those who have little. But, as Hetherington also tell us, consumer society seems to favour an 'in'-crowd who have particular lifestyles, bodies and abilities to consume in the right way. Meanwhile, as John Allen argues in Chapter 2, consumer society is also characterised by some big players, the Tescos and other major retail organisations, who not only play a role in shaping the high streets of the UK but also influence how, where and what people buy and how the things they buy are grown, produced and manufactured. Whether these large organisations are a force for the good of society or for the impoverishment of parts of that society is a question that Allen poses. And in order to answer the question he introduces the important social science concept of *power*, asking you to consider the ways in which power is understood and used in social science and other accounts. Finally, this issue of who wins and loses in a consumer society is picked up again in Chapter 3, where Vivienne Brown asks us to focus on the part of consumption that most of us choose not to think about – rubbish. Consumption is not just about buying things, it is also about disposal – finding somewhere for all the waste that goes with consumption (the food that isn't eaten, the packaging that isn't needed, the old radio that becomes obsolete once a new digital one has been purchased, and so on). Thinking about where all this stuff goes provides another sense of winners and losers, and prompts Brown to consider not only the plight of people who receive all the rubbish (which is increasingly exported from the UK to China, India and elsewhere) but also the effects of a 'wasteful' society on the environment.

2   How is society made and repaired? Or, what role do materials play in a consumer society?

The title of this strand, 'Material lives', suggests we live in a world that is dependent on material things. This may have always been so. Society is not just about people, it is also about people and the materials, objects and environments that help to make that society and which in turn are made by society. But what is different about a consumer society? A consumer society suggests that people are not just dependent on things for life's necessities. They also consume for pleasure, fun, out of habit, to be part of a group, to look different … and, many people consume inordinate amounts of items in today's society in a way that they did not sixty years ago. While it has always been important for social scientists to study people and the things that surround them (indeed if you study past societies it is necessary to focus on the things that people left behind in order to understand their society – you probably already do this when you visit museums, for example), contemporary consumer society is clearly shaped by people's relations to material things. In Chapter 1, for example, Hetherington shows how luxury goods are used by people as a mark of status and therefore as a way of saying something about who they are. He also describes how, in the nineteenth century, department stores became adept at selling the image of luxury to people through the goods that they displayed and sold. In Chapter 3, the relationships between people and the things they value, and conversely those which they want to get rid of, become a key element for understanding contemporary society. In short, to understand society, we need to think about people's relations not just to each other but also to the vast array of goods, technologies and wastes that surround them.

How many of our modern possessions do we need?

3 How is society made and repaired? Or, is consumer society sustainable?

The consequences of all this consumption are more and more matters for concern. From the sheer volume of materials that go to make an average life in the UK to the amount of waste that this often involves, a question arises as to the sustainability of all this consuming. From the polluted skylines of Chinese cities where a good deal of consumer goods that find their way to the UK are manufactured, to the waste incinerators and landfills where old items and packaging end up, the downside of consumer UK is evident. Can current patterns of consumption continue for long without devastating effects on social and environmental life, now and further into the future? All three chapters touch on this issue, and give us greater understanding of the difficulties we face in trying to think about the consequences of consumption – for in helping us to understand consumption they give us a real insight into what needs to be done if we want to start to change how society consumes.

In sum, all three chapters take shopping and consumption as starting points to understand many aspects of contemporary society. They will help you to learn more about contemporary social life and develop your

The waste mountains: a consequence of and cause for concern for consumer societies

social science understanding. In each chapter you will also learn important skills and start to explore how social scientists approach issues and topics of social concern. The focus is on social science understanding, something which includes practices such as describing a social scene or how a society does things, offering explanations as to why things are this way and then formulating arguments, using concepts, theories and models, to inform that understanding. Towards the end of each chapter there is a 'How do we know?' section, which asks you to reflect on the approaches social scientists use to understand the world. We shall return to the lessons for social science understanding in the Conclusions for these chapters.

Chapter 1

Consumer society? Shopping, consumption and social science

Kevin Hetherington

Contents

Introduction

Shopping and the street

There is an inner-city high street near to where I live and where I sometimes shop that provides an interesting illustration of some of the recent developments in shopping practices (see Figure 1). At one end, among the housing, churches, a mosque and a Sikh temple, there's a range of outlets that are mostly now dominated by bars, clubs, restaurants and a few convenience stores. At the other end, out near a major motorway junction, there is a large retail park or shopping mall, two hotels and two supermarkets. In between, on a two-mile stretch of road, are a few older shops and lots of housing, Victorian terraces giving way to 1930s' semi-detached houses the further you move out from the city centre. This street is in an old part of the city that had been run-down for a long time but which started to revive in the late 1990s and early 2000s, mainly due to new consumer outlets opening up at each end. In some ways it is typical of the contemporary UK shopping scene. A brief **description** in this introductory section will provide a snapshot of what happened and also a starting point for thinking about a range of social science issues associated with consuming that provides an opportunity for further explanation.

Shopping seems to have become a major preoccupation for many in our society – something that is often thought about in terms of being a leisure or lifestyle activity and not just something that is done to purchase the essentials of life. Shopping is a part of what social scientists call consumption and many social scientists suggest we now live in a **consumer society**.

This chapter looks at why the use of the term consumer society might be a good way of describing society, how this has come about and how social scientists try to explain it. To begin that process I start with a description of an example – the high street near where I live in the Midlands. It may share some similarities with other streets you will have come across, but there are differences too, as no two places are exactly the same.

A changing street scene

The city centre end of this street has developed into a socially mixed area with an ethnically diverse community of local residents. It has continually changed as new migrants from different parts of the world

Description
A written or sometimes visual depiction of a social scene, situation or event. Descriptions are attempts to represent something without necessarily trying to explain or account for it. Descriptions are always selective in that they can't tell a reader everything about a place or issue. They attempt to answer 'what?' questions.

Consumer society
A label used to refer to a society which is defined as much by how and what people purchase and use as by what they make or do.

Consuming
The acquisition, use and disposal of goods and services.

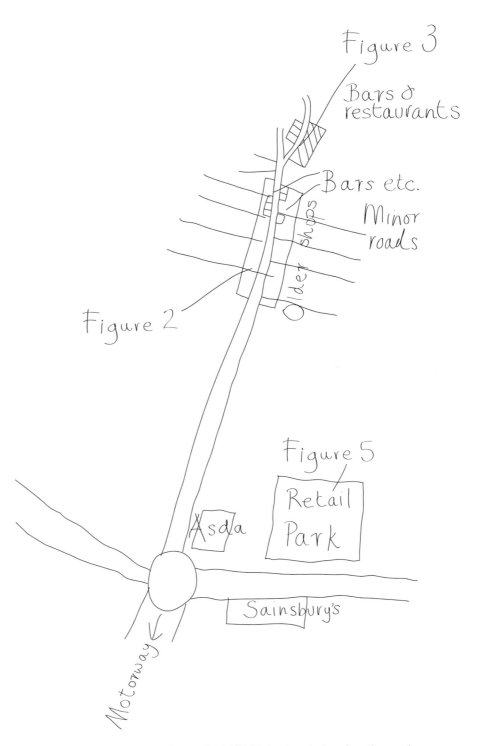

Figure 1   A sketch map of a typical UK high street showing the main areas described in the text

Figure 2   Older shops on what is often seen as the more run-down part of the high street

have arrived and continue to move in. It is also an area with many university students who live there for part of the year while they are studying nearby. A visitor coming here some years ago, before the late 1990s, might have thought the street was rather shabby as this area, like many British inner cities, had seen little investment for years and had become rather run-down. At that time it was full of cheap second-hand shops, clothing warehouses, the occasional fast-food place and lots of run-down Victorian housing, most of which had been rented out as cheap bedsits.

While some of these uses remain, things began to change in the late 1990s and early 2000s, with a more prosperous tone to the street emerging. An **explanation** for this is that change was mostly driven by many of those cheap terraced houses being bought by young people who couldn't afford to buy in more expensive areas of the city. They moved in and began to renovate and improve the housing. As an indicator of this house prices rose, though they continue to fluctuate, and in the recent past have started to fall. Nevertheless, as people with more money at their disposal moved into the area, so the new

Explanation
An attempt to give reasons for society taking on particular characteristics or qualities. Explanations attempt to answer 'why?' questions.

A high street pound shop

consumer outlets like shops and bars arrived too. More money in an area meant a bigger market and an opportunity to make a profit for store owners. So these bars and shops were set up by business people looking to benefit from the growing market for the sort of consumption that students and the under-35s are typically interested in.

At the city-centre end of the street the junk shops, charity shops and clothing warehouses that had come to dominate this area in the past have now mostly gone and in their place are bars, clubs and restaurants instead. Some of these bars have been purpose-built but most have been renovations of these previous retail outlets. At this end of the street, near to a university, the selling of food and drink is what dominates – there are outlets that specialise in fish and chips and takeaways (fried chicken, kebabs, pizzas and burgers, but not the big chain brands), as well as a couple of more upmarket and expensive restaurants. There are also many curry houses around here that are particularly popular. But it is the approximately two dozen bars within a five-minute walking distance of each other that are the most prominent feature of the retail environment. As might be expected, this area forms an important part of the night-time economy, serving in particular the many students and young people who live nearby, and it is heaving with people on a Friday and Saturday night. Though fairly quiet during the day, at these times the area has a buzz about it.

Figure 3   Bars and restaurants on the high street

A little further along the street, where there has been less investment in these kinds of outlets, other shops begin to appear – older shops that have been there for some years: a few surviving wholesale clothing warehouses, often serving the local Asian community who were migrants to the area in the 1960s and 1970s; a surviving second-hand bookshop for students; and a variety of all-night grocers – Turkish, Pakistani and a Polish food store – to cater for the most recent group of migrants to arrive into the area. One can find a halal butcher, a couple of convenience stores, a shop selling Asian sweets, newsagents, massage parlours and numerous second-hand furniture shops. There are also a number of empty shops but not many. There will be more, no doubt; every time there is an economic recession and people have less money to spend, then shops and bars go out of business. This part of the street resembles more how the whole area used to be a few years ago before the improvements, so it still has something of a run-down feel to it. Rents may be cheaper here. It is here where there is the one remaining traditional shop that a visitor from fifty years ago might still recognise – an ironmonger selling just about everything for home and garage.

Further out, the shops mostly give way to houses, though there is a newly opened Tesco Express, part of a petrol station, there to serve motorists leaving town after work in the city and on their way to the nearby motorway and surrounding dormitory villages. A mile or so further on one reaches the large edge-of-town retail park and also two very large supermarkets: an Asda and a Sainsbury's. While there is a bus service, the car parks here are huge and always seem to be full. This is where people really come to shop these days. This is the great temple of contemporary consumption where people indulge not just in the purchase of essentials but, some would argue, seek to fulfil their dreams and fantasies of how they want to live.

Every high street is similar but also has its differences due to the local situation. But the big question, the one that goes beyond a description of the street, is why might social scientists be interested in all this? What might they have to say about it? So far, this is mostly description – a snapshot of a changing area in which consumer practices are becoming more important – but what social scientists are really interested in is identifying the issues this raises for thinking not only about consumer activity but about society in general. This chapter explores this issue, first by seeking, in the next section, to understand more about the practice of consumption, and how social scientists have approached this issue. Section 2 examines the growth of consumption and investigates how it has changed over time. The final section considers how consumption has moved away from the high street and looks at some of the ways that it is contested in society. Throughout, the chapter looks at social science understanding of consumption, exploring the concepts that social scientists have used to explain the activity and understand its effects.

Activity 1

Social science often starts with description but it doesn't end there. Write a brief 200-word description of a shopping street or complex that you know and/or where you have shopped. (This can be quite quick and rough, in the form of a note to yourself. Alternatively, or as a way to reduce the words, draw a sketch map like the one in Figure 1.) Social scientists call this empirical detail. What social science often goes on to do is try to explain what is going on within that detail. It tries to answer the question 'Why are things like this?' Try to formulate three or four questions that you might want to ask about the area you have just described, as if you were planning to study it further.

Tips: When thinking about why your street is like this, think about the composition of people who live there, the range and type of typical retail outlets, the rents they pay, where the street is located (city centre, suburb, small town or village) and possibly how it has changed over time. Think about who is mainly being catered for by this location and who might feel excluded from shopping there.

Summary

- Shopping occurs in a variety of different places and, as it changes, those places change too and so do the lives of the people who live there.
- Social scientists talk about consumption when they refer to shopping activity and the use to which things are put.
- Consumer society is a society which is defined as much by what people buy and use as by how they are employed.
- Social scientists use description and explanation in order to answer what and why questions.

1   Understanding consumption

1.1   Individual and social issues in consuming

Stepping away from this particular description of a street for a moment and thinking about what people do when they go shopping, an activity that many take for granted, that some people love doing and others hate, then the reason for this focus on consumption at the start of an introductory course in social science might start to become apparent. Consuming has never been simply a matter of necessity to meet basic bodily needs. It raises a whole range of important questions that social scientists might want to find some answers for. Some would argue that consuming has become all about individual identity and self-expression; others that families and communities are important to understanding the practices of consuming. Whether as individuals or as groups, what people buy and what they do with those things once they have them provide an important indicator of who they are. Certainly, those with something to sell – advertising agents and brand consultants as much as the retailers themselves – would like people to believe that through consumer activity people are able freely to create a **lifestyle** that reflects their personalities and their individual identities.

Though individuality might be an important issue, consuming is a social activity as much as a personal one and is understood by social scientists to reveal broader questions about society as much as it does about consumer practices themselves. People need to feed and clothe themselves and their families in order to survive, but what they buy, the options on offer, the choices they make, the restrictions and constraints placed upon them, the influences they respond to and what they do with something once they have bought it are all complex issues that involve more than responding to basic human needs. After all, people live in societies where others, family, friends, authority figures, have an influence on them in the form of peer pressure. Consuming is a form of **socialisation** and most people want to feel they belong and are a part of something when they consume – whether that may be to the idea of society as a whole, a minority ethnic community, a subculture based on particular, exclusive interests, or to a social group that has a particular status within society. Consuming is one of the ways that people can feel they belong or are part of something.

Aspirational fantasies that are associated with celebrity lifestyles, lifestyle magazines or fashions might also be an influence for some. A concern

Lifestyle
A shared set of activities and forms of identification that can be recognised as being part of a distinctive way of life (e.g. luxury lifestyle, hippy lifestyle, retired lifestyle). People's ability to adopt a particular lifestyle will often depend on both choices and constraints such as their access to key knowledge, economic and social resources and the chances in life associated with that way of life.

Socialisation
A term used by social scientists to refer to the ways in which people become social beings by conforming to the beliefs, norms and values of their society.

for family might be important for others. Others might make environmental concerns or their carbon footprint uppermost in their considerations before they consume anything. These all provide a diverse social context of attitudes, values and senses of belonging for people that will influence how they act when they consume. People are also socialised by the culture industries like the media and advertising into thinking of themselves as individuals with choices who can shape their own lifestyles.

Social scientists would suggest, then, that a variety of social factors have to be taken into consideration in order to understand what consuming is about, whether consuming out of choice or necessity. The following would be a useful list of factors to consider:

- income
- education
- family and peer-group pressure (our friends and associates)
- social expectations
- media influence (including advertising)
- the role of retailers
- the nature of the goods themselves.

Such factors provide the context for the seemingly individual choices people make when they walk down a street on a Saturday afternoon intent on acquiring something they want.

These are some of the issues that need to be considered when understanding how social scientists look at shopping and consuming. You will see in the next chapter, for example, that supermarket shopping raises questions about power in society, and, in the chapter after that, that disposing of rubbish raises a whole series of economic and social questions about the consequences of getting rid of what is left over after consuming activities have taken place. Here, this chapter is asking you to think about the detail, going beyond the description of shopping on the street in order to think about some of the explanations that social scientists have given for what consumption entails.

1.2   Consumption and social science

The previous section started to tease out why consumption matters generally and why it matters to social scientists. One of the things that this chapter is asking you to think about is why consumption might be a good way to introduce you to what social science is all about. In the last couple of decades consumption has been one of the most significant areas of interest within social science. It is now an important area of social investigation and of interest to a range of different social sciences:

- Economists are interested in issues of markets and personal finance.

- Sociologists are interested in questions of how consumption shapes society and how it can be a source of both empowerment and social exclusion.

- Psychologists are interested in how people relate to both things and others through consumer activity and how they construct an identity through that process.

- Geographers are interested in the distribution and patterns of consumer activities across different regions, how a sense of place can be made and experienced through consumption and the social and environmental consequences of consumer society.

- Consumption can also be of interest to those who study politics, in that different political ideologies look on consumption in different ways. Consuming or not consuming is often thought of as a political act (buying some goods rather than others, boycotting goods from a particular place), and how people vote can often be influenced by their experiences as consumers in changing economic conditions.

Consumption is now seen by many social scientists as just as important as production and work when thinking about what modern societies are all about and the kinds of social identities they produce. Thirty years ago it was common to hear social scientists talking about society in the UK and similar areas as an industrial society defined by class divisions. Then, in the 1980s, they began talking about a post-industrial society after many traditional manufacturing industries went into decline, working-class communities changed and class identities became less clear, and more jobs were created within the traditionally middle-class service sector. As society became characterised by what it consumed rather than what it made, many social scientists began to speak of a consumer society or culture to reflect how important issues of consumption had become in shaping society as a whole.

But just like the street described in the introduction to this chapter, the old does not completely disappear as change happens. It is still common to encounter the question 'What do you do?' when people meet for the first time, and most people still think in terms of the idea of work or career as saying something very important about who they are. But quickly browsing any of the social networking internet sites or looking at lifestyle magazines in the newsagent will reveal that the question people are increasingly trying to answer, and are perhaps more interested in, is 'What are you into?' Issues of consumption, identity and lifestyle are inextricably linked to such a question because those are the sorts of issues that matter to many people when they think about who they are and how they can relate to others around them. Who we think we are and how we relate to others are important social science questions. Meanwhile, to move beyond the description of different patterns of activity social scientists will want to come up with explanations of what they see.

What people buy, why and how they use things, and how they relate to them once they have bought them tell us a good deal about contemporary society. Social science is not just interested in individuals and their activities, it is also often interested in broader social, political, geographical and economic questions – opportunities and inequalities, changes and conflicts, power and freedom, for example. Social scientists have always been very much interested in these broader questions and they have come to recognise that they can be studied by looking at issues associated with consuming.

1.3   'You spent how much?'

Look at Figure 4. It provides some recent data collected by the Office of National Statistics (ONS) on what households spend their money on during a typical week. A household can be anything from a single person to a large, extended family group. Have a look at some of the figures and what people typically consume. Such statistical analysis might be seen as typical of the kind of data that social scientists collect and use.

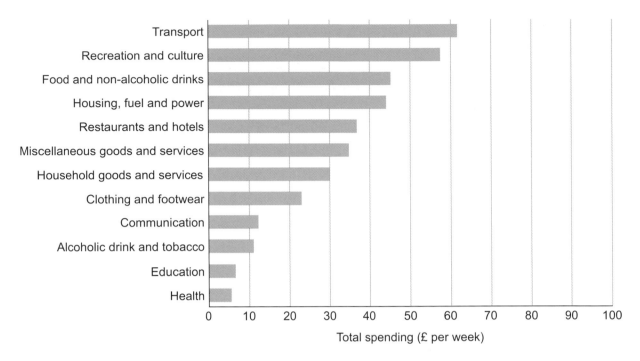

Figure 4   Average weekly household expenditure on main commodities and services, 2007, UK (Source: ONS, 2008)

Activity 2

Summarise the main features of Figure 5 in no more than two sentences. Are the bar chart and your summary descriptions or explanations of family spending?

Summaries should find a way of capturing some of the detail of a figure in a few words. For example, you could say the bar chart shows that the majority of the average weekly spend is on transport, leisure activities, household bills (fuel and other), and food. Rather less is spent on health, education, alcohol and smoking. You could add more detail to these summaries by stating figures read off from the bar chart.

For many people the biggest weekly expenditure is on their rent or their mortgage. That is not included in this figure. Rather, the figure shows what people spend their money on, using what they have left after that major expense has been paid. It is concerned with what economists call disposable income. What this figure reveals is that people spend their money on a mix of things but that it shouldn't be assumed that necessities always top the list. It is noteworthy, for example, that a typical household spends more on recreation and culture (luxuries) than it does on food and non-alcoholic drink (essentials – though these can also be fashionable luxuries as much as necessities). The biggest category here though is transport – that includes car costs, petrol and public transport. It is unlikely that that is all leisure travel; much of it might be associated with commuting to work – an essential.

Consumer habits change. Different things become important. Things once seen as a novelty for the wealthy might come to be seen as an everyday essential for the majority a few years later. For example, in the 1980s very few people owned a mobile phone, a new and expensive novelty then. Now the majority of people do and it has become a major item of weekly expenditure – something that many people might say they could not be without as it has become an integral part of their lives, allowing them to connect to others in an easy and convenient way.

This figure provides some basic and very interesting data but it is also limited in what it can tell us. It is a form of numerical description based on a survey where a number of people have been asked to say what they consume on a regular basis. We do not get a breakdown of what people spend money on within those categories and the figure certainly doesn't tell us why people spend their money on the things they do. The why answer isn't always apparent in the data. Any explanation will involve trying to answer how and why questions based on studies like this but also by making use of theories and concepts. To consider how social scientists go about explaining consumer activity the chapter will now look at the work of one leading and influential social scientist who has tried to do just that.

1.4   The seduced and the repressed

According to the social scientist Zygmunt Bauman (1988), people in contemporary Western societies can be broadly divided into two groups of consumers that he calls, in deliberately loaded terms, the seduced and the repressed. Bauman believes we now live in a consumer society rather than an industrial society, but that it is not an equal society just as the industrial society before it wasn't equal either. But, he believes, the forms of inequality and freedom in a consumer society differ from what went before. A consumer society promises choice and freedom to those who, because of their financial and social circumstances, are in a position to consume effectively. In industrial society it was really only the very wealthy – the aristocracy whose wealth was based on land ownership, or rich merchants and factory owners (capitalists who profited from factory production) and a few well-paid professionals like bankers, doctors and lawyers, who could have defined themselves as consumers and lived lives defined by a luxury lifestyle. The idea that consumption should become available to the many rather than the few, for good economic as much as social reasons, began to develop in the latter years of the nineteenth century and has continued to develop up to the present time.

In contemporary society there are still aristocrats, capitalists and professionals who can afford to consume to a greater degree than others, but they are now joined by many others who have access, in varying degrees, to the trappings of a consumer lifestyle. These others would include wealthy people, certainly, but also people with a good, steady income and a secure job who have enough money, or disposable income, and those who have access to relatively cheap credit, to allow them to buy things beyond the basic necessities of life. Bauman calls these people the seduced – the reason for his use of this term will become clear a little later. For Bauman that group does not only include people with surplus income to spend on things that they want but also people in a position to buy into the ideals of a consumer society which, he suggests, are based on a number of key features:

- the idea that markets offer people freedom of choice and that market freedom is the defining freedom in society
- the idea that consumer activity can be a means to creative self-expression, a sense of self-worth and an identity that people wish to have
- the idea that creating consumer lifestyles is the means to a sense of belonging, acceptance and membership within society.

Status
A common, shared and recognised position that some people hold in society. Having a particular status is determined by a person's access to social resources that convey, in different degrees, recognition, honour and prestige on the status holder. Consumer goods and services can be used as signs of belonging to a particular status group. Their absence can lead to a lack or loss of status.

In an industrial society, political freedoms like the right to vote or the right to join a trade union might have been seen as the most important freedoms. A sense of self-worth and identity would typically have been created through having secure employment and skilled and satisfying work or through citizenship rights. Not everyone had these, indeed many didn't, but a sense of social belonging and inclusion was often defined by following the forms of accepted behaviour appropriate to a person's class and **status**, which were often determined by the job that they did and the occupational community in which they lived. For Bauman, these forms of freedom, expression and membership have faded into the background as industry has become less dominant in

Western societies. In their place, consumer freedoms have become more dominant in the present time.

The seductive appeal of consumption, for Bauman, is that it offers not just goods and services that people want but also a sense of both self-expression and social membership to those who are able to consume effectively. Buying something in a shop and taking it home and using it offers more than the satisfaction that that good or service can provide as something with a use. It offers entry into the social realm of shared meanings where one's identity can be established and displayed to others. It offers the promise of allowing people to create, through what they consume, a personality that they aspire to have and that they can use to communicate to others their membership and position within society.

In the past people might have done this through work and a limited range of leisure activities rather than activities like how one decorates one's home, the car one drives, the holidays one takes or the hobbies and pastimes that one has. A person is no longer limited to describing themselves as a mechanic, painter or domestic servant. Rather, they might use terms like classic car enthusiast, a punk, or someone who is into horse riding. Certainly, it is visibly apparent that the patterns of our industrial work-dominated past have not altogether disappeared from society. The UK is still a capitalist society and most people below retirement age have to find an income to support themselves based on a wage, state benefits and credits or a combination of these. But those like Bauman who argue that we now live in a consumer society are making the point that it is principally consumption that is the dominant feature in shaping identities rather than production and work.

The seduced, then, in Bauman's terms are those who can participate in this consumer society. They are included as members with a positive identity. The seduced include not only those with enough money to buy goods and services but also those who are seen as valued members of a consumer society both by other consumers and by those with something to sell to a lucrative market: the employed, the young, older people with good pensions and savings, those in a position to achieve their aspirations through such things as talent, good looks, or a particular skill that is valued and financially rewarded within society. In sum, the seduced in Bauman's terms are those in a position to be admitted to membership in society because they are able to consume effectively in the eyes of others. The pressures to conform are strong because not doing so can easily lead to social exclusion and a devalued identity. Someone who does not have a car can be socially excluded in certain areas – notably ones where public transport is rather limited. An adolescent who does not have a mobile phone might quickly find themselves socially excluded as friendship networks are often established and maintained by regular texting and phone calls. A person with mobility difficulties might find themselves physically excluded from some places. Increasingly, as many consumer services are provided online (or are cheaper online), not having ready access to a computer and the internet might lead to forms of social exclusion. All of these activities involve the ability, or not, to consume things like cars, phones or computer services.

The physical exclusion of people with disabilities by virtue of the design of the built environment is one means through which social divisions are made

In this account, the seduced doesn't include everyone, and neither is membership of the seduced necessarily a permanent or fixed thing as a person's life circumstances can change. There is another group in Bauman's terms who are excluded from this consumer society or who are pushed to its margins. These people he calls the repressed. This group would typically include the unemployed, the low paid, those in insecure or casual employment, recently arrived migrants, or those often not in a position to participate fully in a consumer society – some people with disabilities, the chronically sick, older people on basic state pensions, for example. It might also include people from ethnic minorities who experience other forms of social exclusion and discrimination as well.

Clearly, income matters a lot in defining whether a person belongs to the category of the seduced or the repressed, but it is not the only factor. For example, a young person with little money might find it much easier to participate in consumer activities than a person with a similar income who also has disabilities or is in a different age group. They might be in a better position to buy into the acceptance of others though having fashionable clothes, being able to go to the right clubs, listening to whatever music happens to be popular, being fit and healthy, or by having a large network of friends with whom they can share similar interests. They can often speak the lingo of consumption in a knowledgeable way and read its trends. In contrast, an older person or a person with a disability might be excluded from this world, either because they have to spend what money they might have on basic foods, care, prescriptions, clothing and heating, or because they are more socially isolated, less mobile and less valued as target consumers with spending power by the companies that sell things. Their opportunities for self-expression and social membership in a consumer society, unless they can compensate for a disadvantaged status by having some wealth or other skill, are likely to be more restricted. They are more likely to be excluded from some aspects of this society and seen as somehow failed members of society, just as, to use the terms of the period, the slum-dwelling poor, debtors, criminals, the 'idle' (unemployed) or those confined to the workhouse were a hundred years ago in a more industrial society.

Activity 3

The street that I described at the beginning of this chapter could be divided into three retail sections:

1   newly arrived bars, clubs and restaurants in a once run-down area that was now becoming more prosperous

2   an area still marked by cheap, second-hand stores, shops for recently arrived migrant groups and ethnic minorities, and convenience stores

3   a large edge-of-town retail park with big-name supermarkets and hotels.

Describe who each of these areas might cater for as its typical consumers. Give an explanation for why you think this would be the case. Think about such things as income, age, ethnic identity, access to different forms of transport, ability to move around easily, and so on. Is it possible to map Bauman's categories of the seduced and the repressed onto these different areas of the street?

It is easy to see why Bauman might call these people the repressed and why he might suggest that society excludes and marginalises them because of their inability to participate in consumer activity beyond its most basic forms – treating them as social outcasts. What he is doing is observing that there are different patterns of consumer activity within society. He is basing his argument on observation and description. What he then does is try to offer an explanation, or theory as to why things are how they are, and to use concepts, terms that act as a kind of shorthand for the description that can then be used to explain what he sees. There are several points of explanation that Bauman is trying to get across in his argument:

- Consuming is the defining feature of capitalist societies like the UK.
- Membership and a valued identity within society are determined by the degree to which someone can participate in consumer activities.
- Society remains unequal and divided in terms of inclusion in and exclusion from the activities of consumption.
- Consumption is a key means for establishing and maintaining status within society.

He uses the terms seduced and repressed as concepts to convey this explanation. These are simplified terms, used to provide clarity to his argument. Whether they convey the full complexity of society is debatable, just as the division between capitalists and workers was a rather simplified picture of industrial society. There may be a more varied set of positions that might exist in society, people may be able to move between these categories at different times and in different places. However, as an explanation Bauman is not looking to provide an accurate classification of every position that might exist within society; rather, he is trying to use his explanation as an argument about consumer society in general. It is important to his explanation that he provides a simplified picture so that the main points of his argument can be communicated clearly.

It may be apparent why the term repressed could be applied to those who cannot participate in consumer activity because their lack of resources or ability to participate might further their exclusion and marginalisation in society as a whole, but the question remains as to why he calls those who are socially included the seduced. The reason for this has something to do with the history of consumption.

1.5   Consumer society and its seductions

When social scientists speak of consumption they refer to a broad range of social issues that influence and shape our way of life – or culture. The idea of society having a culture shaped by consumption is not entirely new. Historians have argued that eighteenth-century British society could be described as being shaped by consumption. The aristocracy and a growing number of middle-class people of that time enjoyed buying fine things – luxuries like porcelain, silver, tea and fine clothes, for example. They did so not only to enjoy such things for what they were in terms of their use but also because having luxury things was often seen as a mark of rank and status within society. This is still true today. An expensive car, camera or mobile phone can be desirable not just because of its functionality but because of how it is perceived by others as a mark of distinction and status. Some consumer items, therefore, are status symbols that convey a message to others about their owner.

In contemporary society people sometimes measure a person, their status in particular, by the consumer trappings that they surround themselves with: where they live, the size of their house, cars, holidays, clothes, gadgets, jewellery, watches, and so on. The concept that social scientists have developed to try to explain this is conspicuous consumption.

Conspicuous consumption

One of the first social scientists to write about the culture of consumption in this way was the American sociologist Thorstein Veblen in his book *The Theory of the Leisure Class* that was first published in 1899. He studied the consuming habits of the new rich, the successful industrialists and their families, in America at the end of the nineteenth century. He found that they often bought things for a particular reason: they wanted the things they bought to make a positive impression and to demonstrate to others their newly acquired wealth and rising status within society. A big house, quality furnishings, clothes

An example of luxury, high-status goods

in the latest fashion, expensive jewellery and antiques were the sort of high-status luxury items that they often bought and put on display in their homes so that guests who came to visit for dinner parties, for example, would see the trappings of success on display. Those things became an extension of the people who owned them. Veblen used the concept of conspicuous consumption to try to explain this. He used this term to explain this process of visibly displaying status to others through what had been acquired – especially when a person had newly gained wealth and wanted to make an impression in wealthy circles. Buying luxury things and showing them off to others through display is what he meant by this concept. Conspicuous consumption is a shorthand way of saying that. These people were the seduced of the nineteenth century.

Luxury items and the trappings of wealth were an important means of displaying character and status at that time. For the wealthy, the conspicuous consumption of luxury goods is important in being able to convey one's status as a prosperous person. Today people most commonly associate conspicuous consumption with highly paid celebrities who have made their name in the music or entertainment industries, with sporting stars, city traders who could earn six-figure bonuses by being successful on the stock market, or with big lottery winners. But the likelihood is that in more limited ways many people engage in acts of conspicuous consumption without fully realising it, even if they are not particularly wealthy or their lifestyles are not defined by luxury. The reason why people do this is not simply because

Conspicuous consumption then and now – the trappings of an ostentatious lifestyle in the nineteenth century and today

they want to show off but because they want to fit in, impress their friends, and be accepted into social networks where they feel they ought to belong. Things like a luxury car, membership of a prestigious golf club, serving fine wines at a dinner party or taking holidays in an exclusive resort can all send such a message about status and inclusion.

1.6 Consuming uses or meanings?

What this concept of conspicuous consumption suggests is that people often consume things for social reasons as much as personal ones. But displaying status to others is not the only reason why people might want to own something. There is a whole range of social issues that social scientists might consider when looking at the practices of consumption. Clearly people consume things – stuff – of various kinds: food, petrol, clothing, electrical goods, ornaments to decorate their homes, for example. But people also consume services such as those offered by a hairdresser, bank or window cleaner. People can consume experiences as well as things or services – experiences like a holiday, a hot-air balloon ride or attendance at a major sporting event, for example.

Sometimes people will simply consume something for its usefulness. A plain, mass-produced dishcloth is unlikely to be bought for any reason other than for its usefulness for cleaning purposes. But it is not impossible for people to find other uses for mundane things. For example, in the 1970s punks became famous for using bin-bags as clothing and safety pins as jewellery. However, this is an extreme example of using something for very different purposes from those typically associated with an item. But what about something like a pair of shoes? Shoes certainly have a useful purpose, but it is unlikely that people always buy them only for the use and comfort they provide, important though those qualities are. Other issues like style and fashionability (or anti-fashion) might be important as well. So might the brand or the name of the designer associated with them. Signs, the social messages associated with a thing, service or experience, can be consumed too. Sometimes consuming the messages attached to a thing or a service – messages that are encoded into the commodities through design and logo – might be more important than consuming the thing itself that we buy and make use of. For example, a thing might be part of a brand. There is a difference, for example, between a burger bought from one of the local fast-food places on the road I described to you in the Introduction compared with one bought from a large and recognisable chain, even though what we do with them is the same. What a person does with the burger, eat it, is the same. But the message associated with the brand of burger being consumed, its meaning, can be different. The same sorts of issues could apply to other goods too – mobile phones, beer, cars, washing powder, toys – or to services and experiences. Consider, for example, the image associated with a particular kind of holiday, such as a luxury cruise on a liner or skiing holiday at a luxury resort, compared with two weeks in a cheap hotel in Benidorm, Ibiza or Faliraki.

These signs and messages mean different things to people. They can suggest things like wealth or the lack of it, luxury or functionality, daring novelty or established tradition, sophisticated taste or trashy entertainment. Different people want different things when they consume: they all want a lifestyle but what they value, their tastes, will vary considerably depending on such things as income, education, exposure to different cultures, and so on. Issues of status and image impression – the impression that someone might want to give about themselves to others – are important aspects of a consumer society that are expressed through the ways in which people consume the messages associated with **commodities**.

Commodities
A commodity is a good or service that is produced for exchange and sold in a market with the intention of generating a profit for the seller.

Someone buying their weekly shopping, focusing on organic produce, at a local farm shop or farmers' market is saying something different from someone buying the less expensive, basic range at a supermarket like Tesco or Asda, as each of these outlets conveys a different social message because of associations with things like: who typically shops there, price, items available, the status of the items available, and so on. We can observe this and describe the activity involved, but to offer an explanation of it we need to develop theories and use concepts to try to explain why.

A farmers' market – a place to buy useful things or to consume meanings?

This is where the issue of seduction comes in and why Bauman describes those who are able to engage in consumption effectively within society as the seduced. What he is suggesting is that people are seduced not so much by the use that a good or service will provide them but with what it means, the image conveyed through having it, the allure it has, the associations that they can make through that good or service to images of certain types of lifestyle and status associated with it. It is this, the signs of consumption – what things like image, brand and logo associated with particular goods and services come to mean to sections of society that a consumer might like to feel they belong to and where they can express who they are – that provide the basis for the seductive character of a consumer culture. Being skilled in being able to read these things, often in a tacit rather than a knowing way, is key to being a successful consumer. Even young children can be observed to be skilled in knowing that certain items, certain brands, mean more, have a higher status than others. What this shows is that consuming is associated with how people relate to things as useful objects, but it is also about how they relate to each other through what those things mean socially – and that involves understanding the messages they convey. What is apparent here is that people consume things because those things, services or experiences come to mean something to them and allow them to express a sense of their identity to others through what they consume. One of the first types of retail outlet to do this and to promote these ideas to the public as a whole was the department store.

Summary

- Consumption is about more than buying things for their use.
- The well off with status aspirations engage in the display of their wealth to others through conspicuous consumption in order to try to produce a good image of themselves in they eyes of others.
- Consumer societies contain new social divisions and new groups of included and excluded people: the seduced and the repressed.
- Consuming influences broader issues within our culture and the lifestyles associated with it.
- When we consume a commodity we consume a range of social messages associated with it as well as employing it for its use as a thing or a service. This is the reason why successful consumers can be described as the seduced.

2 Mass consumption and the department store

As mentioned in Section 1.5 above, a society shaped by consuming is not something entirely new. Most social historians would say that a consumer culture was a prominent part of social life in Britain in the eighteenth century, if only for the rich. The places that first bought this consumer culture to the majority of the people (often referred to, somewhat unfavourably, as the masses) were department stores, that first began to appear in Europe in the 1860s. They did so principally by extending the idea of luxury to a wide range of consumers and by creating an environment where shoppers could engage in consumption as if it were a seductive, imaginary fantasy world of abundance and availability.

A department store in the 1890s

2.1 Understanding the importance of department stores

This type of all-purpose shop, which we take for granted today, and perhaps even see as just a bit old-fashioned, was a real novelty in the nineteenth century. The first purpose-built department store was the

Bon Marché in Paris, founded in 1869. Department stores contained a whole range of goods under one roof that might previously all have been sold by different stores. In the UK, department stores either evolved out of existing specialist shops (such as grocers or drapers), including places like Fortnum & Mason, Harrods, and Debenhams that are still household names today, or from indoor markets and bazaars like the one on Deansgate in Manchester that later became Kendals. There were also a whole host of other department stores in larger towns and cities across the UK that emerged between about 1880 and 1930. What was different about these stores was not just that they were large and carried a widely varied stock but that they sold in volume mass-produced goods that were the product of industrial rather than handmade or craft production. As such, they were often cheaper than other kinds of shops and were very much at the centre of promoting consumption to a widening section of the public within what was still very much an industrial society.

It might seem at first glance that this is the opposite of the luxury end of the market – catering for less wealthy consumers (though not the very poorest) and providing them with relatively inexpensive mass-produced items – and yet the idea of luxury was at the very centre of all that department stores stood for. Department stores were made possible not only because of a growing market for consumer items but because industrial technology, the supply of raw materials and factory production allowed for things to be made in volume by machine more cheaply than before when things were made by hand. The railway, then a new system of transportation, allowed goods to be moved around the country quickly and more cheaply than by earlier routes such as unreliable roads and slow canals. This also helped to make department stores profitable and efficient in selling large volumes of goods to the public.

The department store was not really a place designed for selling many genuine, high priced luxury items; rather, it was geared up to selling high volumes of cheaper goods and making a profit out of the economies of scale that came with selling lots of things at a small profit rather than a few things for a large profit. However, the idea or image of luxury was something that department stores sought to promote. They used the idea of luxury as a tool of seduction. It was a key message that they conveyed to shoppers who became skilled in being able to read it. They sought to create the idea of being a space of luxury within the public imagination. That was the social message that department stores associated with the goods that could be bought there. This was done through how the shops were designed and how their goods were displayed to the public. People could not only see what was for sale but could also browse as they shopped. The stores presented an image of abundance, dazzle, luxury and availability through the departmental layout of large volumes of goods and by having goods available to handle (a novel idea, as previously many things would have been kept behind the counter in most shops), through attractive window displays with the latest fashions, and through the use of new and exotic forms of lighting (first gas and later electric). In other words, department stores became as much sites of spectacle and entertainment – key forms of seduction – as places for the routines of shopping itself.

A department store interior

The storeowners were astute too; they recognised that the majority of their clientele would be women – a new group of shoppers in what was very a male-dominated Victorian society. At that time it was rare for middle-class women to go out alone without a chaperone. Indeed, this would have caused something of a scandal in polite society in Victorian times. The street was seen as a dangerous place for any woman of character to be out on her own. The fear among the middle classes, especially on the part of the husband, was that she might be mistaken for a servant or a prostitute if seen out on her own and then shame would be brought on her family and on him, in particular, as the head of it. But the department store developed in contrast to the street. It was intended as a safe, public space for women and they, as its main consumers, embraced it fully.

But department stores did not just sell people things, they sold them dreams too. The aim was to lure people inside with the seductive promise of luxury – with the signs of what an item might mean as much as its use. The stores were designed as spaces of temptation, as this quotation from the time suggests:

> We are not able to stand against the overwhelming temptations which besiege us at every turn … We go to purchase something we want; but when we get to our shop there are so many more things that we never thought of till they presented their obtrusive fascinations on every side. We look for a ribbon, a flower, a chiffon of some sort or other, and we find ourselves in a Paradise of ribbons, flowers, and chiffons, without which our life becomes impossible and our gown unwearable. There are many shops in London into which one cannot safely trust oneself. … There are two very important changes which have contributed to the temptation of spending money nowadays. One is the gathering together under one roof of all kinds of goods – clothing, millinery, groceries, furniture, in fact all the necessities of life … The other reason for the increased temptation to spend money is the large numbers of women which are now employed … women are so much quicker than men, and they understand so much more readily what other women want.
>
> Lady Jeune, 'The ethics of shopping', *Fortnightly Review*, January 1896 (quoted in Adburgham, 1964, pp. 235–6)

Activity 4

Think about the last time you went shopping for non-essential items. Consider how things were displayed, the use of lighting, music and signs, for example, in the shops you went to. Describe whether you think the shops were trying to engage shoppers into buying things through forms of seduction. What sorts of messages did they present to you as a potential shopper? Did those messages influence you in any way?

Tip: Different shops will try to do this in different ways and with varying degrees of success depending on who their target consumers are (i.e. spending power, gender, age), their size and layout, whether they are a single store or part of a big chain.

Department stores were the first shops with mass appeal; they offered a seductive spectacle of luxury in which the message of a luxurious lifestyle was being sold as much as the goods themselves. These were spaces of fantasy and spectacle that sought to have mass appeal. But it was the image of luxury that was sold to the buying public rather than actual luxury goods (as determined by price). As the cultural historian and sociologist Rosalind Williams (1982, p. 67) put it, 'As environments of mass consumption, department stores were, and still are, places where consumers are an audience to be entertained by commodities, where selling is mingled with amusement, where arousal of free-floating ideas is as important as immediate purchase of particular items.' It was in such places as this, therefore, that modern consumer culture with its emphasis on consuming the social messages associated with commodities in order to create a lifestyle first took shape.

2.2   Shopping, personality and identity

The success of department stores in the latter part of the nineteenth century and into the twentieth century not only brought about a completely different way of shopping to ever widening sections of society and new ideas about luxury and the seductive power of consuming, it was also instrumental in changing how people saw themselves and the role of consumption within their sense of identity. Before the advent of mass consumption – which the department store did much to bring about – shopping was a serious activity undertaken in a way that was in keeping with social conventions about social rank, character and respectability. Afterwards, what began to matter most was believing that consumption could be used as an expression of self-identity and individuality – it came to reflect not so much one's character and rank within society, as it had done previously, but one's personality and individual taste. Character and personality are two more concepts that can be used to help us to explain changes in consumption.

Activity 5

Think about how you would describe yourself as a consumer. Choose one item in your possession, preferably something that you have bought recently rather than been given, that means a good deal to you and think about the following issues. Make some notes for yourself on the following questions.

- Why does this item mean so much to you?
- Did you acquire it just for its usefulness or were there other issues involved? If so, what were they?
- What might the item say about you to someone else (perhaps you might ask someone whom you know this question)?
- Did you acquire it because you wanted to impress anyone or because of any social pressure to fit in?

This argument that consumption could be used to express individuality and personality was first suggested by Warren Susman in the 1970s (Susman, 2003). He developed the argument from a study of descriptions of how to consume which were provided in domestic economy and self-help manuals written during the nineteenth century. These books, aimed principally at the middle-class market, provided advice on how to set up home, what to put in it, how to entertain and host dinner parties, and so on (Mrs Beeton's *Book of Household Management*, published in 1861, is the most famous example in the UK). In effect, they gave advice on what and how to consume. Based on a detailed reading of what they described, Susman suggested that prior to about 1880 these books were mainly concerned with providing advice to people on how best to present their good character, associated with their social position or class, through the consumption of appropriate and tasteful things for their home: through decoration and use of ornaments, management of the family finances, and entertaining. After about 1880 the emphasis in such books shifted away from the concern with displaying character to that of displaying individuality and personality. This suggests that people were becoming less concerned with displaying their rank or class position through the goods in their home and much more concerned with displaying their individual taste and their personality through those things they had acquired. The idea of character was very much tied up with identity issues to do with social rank and class. It asked the question: 'What will people think of us as respectable middle-class people?' Personality is seen as a more individual expression of identity. A concern with expressing oneself through what one has consumed and used to make a home now asked the question: 'What will people think of me as an individual?'

This concern with personality, Susman argues, is one that is still with us now in contemporary society. In consumer society, people are preoccupied, not with class, but with personal taste and individuality. Today, people are less concerned with consuming things so that they aid them in the display of their good character to others than they are with using consumption as a way of expressing individual personalities both for a person's own satisfaction and to say something about themselves to others. People often seek to express this sense of themselves through the material goods they buy; for example, home furnishings, fashionable clothes, or by following certain brands. This shift from character to personality, Susman argues, came about as society changed. Around the time this change first began to become apparent, the 1880s, the importance of leisure and consumption in ordinary people's lives, rather than only for the wealthy, was just beginning to be significant: 'the new personality literature stressed items that could be best developed in leisure time and represented in themselves an emphasis on consumption. The social role demanded in the new culture of personality was that of a performer. Every … [person] was to become a performing self' (Susman, 2003, p. 280). At the centre of this change were the new practices and sites of consumption – most notably associated with the department store and the mail order catalogue. People began to see consumer things in a different way – not just as useful objects that they should own to reflect their social position but as expressions of a particular lifestyle that they might aspire to.

Summary

- Department stores sold the idea of luxury, becoming places of seduction, and helped to shape consumption.
- Consumption is at the centre of a shift in society from a concern with displaying character to a concern with displaying personality and individuality.
- This interest in consuming to reflect our individual personality is still at the centre of our contemporary consumer society in the twenty-first century.

3   The other end of the street

While department stores can still be found in many larger towns and cities, they are no longer at the cutting edge of the retail scene in the way that they once were. In more recent times that role has been taken by newer spaces of consumption such as the shopping mall, retail park and, increasingly in the twenty-first century, by online shopping. If we return to the description of the high street with which this chapter began, but to the other end of that street, away from the city centre and out near the motorway junction that serves it, there is an example of a retail park or shopping mall. All the big-name stores that have edge-of-town branches are there; there is a food court and large car parks that service the shops selling mainly clothing, sports equipment, and household and electrical goods. This place is all about car mobility and shopping. It's a very popular site and is always busy. There is a bus service but the site caters mostly for people, especially families, who come to shop at weekends or in the evening after work. Some come from the town itself but many travel by motorway for an hour or more to make a special visit.

Figure 5   An out-of-town retail park

In many ways, sites like this have come to epitomise consumer society in the early twenty-first century. They are dedicated to shopping and to car mobility as a pursuit of lifestyle and personal expression. Those are now the things that are important to establishing forms of social membership and belonging in society, just as character and class position were in an industrial society. They provide an alternative to town-centre shopping or neighbourhood shopping. Retail parks provide quite a contrast to inner-city streets, just as supermarkets do compared with convenience stores or old-fashioned corner shop grocers.

Recent studies of shopping malls have shown that many customers prefer to use retail parks and shopping malls to traditional street shopping these days. The explanation given is that this is not just because of the range of goods and services available to customers but also because of how people perceive these spaces in comparison with their perceptions of the street. The geographer Peter Jackson carried out a study in north London in the mid 1990s to try to offer an explanation as to why these sites were becoming so popular. He and some of his fellow researchers asked customers about two such sites and the reasons why they liked shopping in these sorts of out-of-town shopping places (Jackson, 1998). They asked people to say whether certain words described their experience of the site. What they found through their study was that most of the people who shopped at these shopping malls did so not just because of the range of goods on offer but also because they had a positive view of them as safe, convenient and modern places for families to shop.

The street, in contrast, was seen as a place of crime, disorder (aggressive begging, for example) and dirt. While both are public spaces the shopping mall was seen by shoppers as regulated, ordered and safe, while the street was seen as unruly, disordered and potentially dangerous. In a way this is a rerun of how department stores were seen in comparison with streets in the nineteenth century. The difference is that department stores were justified in terms of being safe places for women to shop whereas malls are now targeted at a different category of consumer, being seen as safe places for families with cars. Jackson's explanation was that what shoppers valued most about the malls was that they were privatised public spaces – they catered for shoppers as family units who did not have to engage in social interaction with too many strangers, or people who were not like them, when shopping there whereas the street has always been seen as the site of encounters with strangers.

Shopping malls and retail parks are not only full of shops and parking spaces, they are highly regulated places. They are typically privately

See Chapter 2 in *Making Social Lives* to read more about the rise of supermarkets owned, patrolled by security guards and have wide coverage by security cameras – bad news for potential shoplifters and muggers perhaps, but should others be at all worried about this? What worries some about these issues of privatism and surveillance is not that malls should be safe places to shop but that these spaces reflect a broader trend in controlling and regulating public space in ways that are largely outside of democratic control. They are spaces of market freedom rather than civic freedom. They are seen by some social scientists as a potential challenge to the public, democratic character of city spaces of the street as they seek to impose private rules upon it in ways that are not entirely accountable to the public through normal political channels.

The risk seen in this is that such spaces also reinforce forms of social exclusion: some among the old and the poor might find themselves excluded because they find it difficult to shop there as they may not have ready access to a car to get to the site or the money to spend if they can get there. Likewise, the success of these retail parks can mean that there are fewer other sites on the street providing cheap consumer goods because those outlets cannot compete with the large retail parks and are going out of business. You will see in the next chapter that some argue that supermarkets have a similar impact. In such a situation some people might find themselves excluded from the social activities of consuming as a consequence.

As was discussed earlier, Zygmunt Bauman has argued that consumption is creating new divisions that are defining a consumer society. These are no longer based on old social class divisions like middle class and working class, which were determined by the production process and the work that people did, but by access to consumption practices and the ability to use consumption to shape one's identity: the seduced and the repressed. As was discussed, Bauman believes we can call the seduced those who believe in the idea that one can create one's lifestyle and identity through consuming – it is their way of expressing their personality and in doing so gaining access, acceptance, a sense of belonging and status membership within society. If a person has the inclination, the money and is mobile, they can achieve these things in a consumer society. Shopping malls and retail parks, like the department stores before them, cater for these consumers and, as Jackson's study shows, those who use them regularly like them and generally value them and feel at home in them. Membership here is defined largely by the ability to spend, by car ownership and mobility, and by being part of a unit that is likely to find consumer goods and services to meet their wants at such a shopping space. The repressed would be those who are typically excluded because of their social circumstances: the unemployed and the poor, some older members of society with limited means, and the immobile who either might find it difficult to get to such sites or do not have the money to participate in the consumer culture they provide. Being excluded or marginalised within a consumer culture does not just mean that you are restricted in the places where you can shop, it means something more significant for Bauman: that your identity becomes devalued, you might come to be seen as a non-participant in a society where membership and belonging are defined by the ability to consume effectively.

3.1   The seduced, repressed ... and oppositional?

But we have to ask the question as to whether everyone is either seduced or repressed. Bauman's use of these terms to explain how a consumer society works is a simplification. It deals with generalisations and tries to give us a big, sweeping picture of consumer society. While his concepts of the seduced and the repressed might have some uses, they do not offer a particularly subtle picture or one that focuses too much on the detail. Like all social science explanations it is open to question and to scrutiny, perhaps by considering whether there are other variations of approach that people can take to consumption, whether those he calls seduced are able to see through that manipulation, or whether those he calls repressed might be able to create space to consume in ways that they find satisfying and inclusive. While concepts like these are important explanatory tools in social science, they are also open to challenge, adaptation or even rejection if they don't always appear to work. Social scientists don't always agree with each other, they sometimes create competing theories and concepts to explain the same issues.

Bauman's argument could be taken to present a view of the consumer solely as an individual with wants and desires who then goes out to consume. It might be argued that he downplays the importance of shopping for essentials, as a routine activity in which providing for others (family members, for example) is just as important. There are other consumers, too, who might shun the big retail parks and supermarkets as a matter of choice – not because they do not have the money to shop there but because they do not like what such places stand for, for political or environmental reasons. For environmentally conscious people, for example, shopping locally at small outlets, buying organic food, reducing one's carbon footprint, and recycling regularly generate an alternative vision of consumption – one based not on the seductions of fantasy and luxury but more on personal thrift and social responsibility. But theirs is a consumer lifestyle nonetheless, associated not with supermarkets and retail parks but with farmers' markets, organic vegetable boxes being delivered to supplement that which is grown on the allotment, wholefood shops and vegetarian cafes. These consumer outlets tend to appeal to those who are concerned about some of the environmental consequences of shopping – buying locally not only supports local growers rather than large supermarkets, it also means that the goods have not travelled long distances to get to the consumer and therefore have not required much fuel, lessening the carbon footprint. Whether this is an alternative to consuming or something that is just a niche within it for those who can afford to opt out of certain elements of it is a matter open to debate. And debate is a crucial part of social science.

Modern consumer society is challenged by several social movements

Summary

- Shopping malls and retail parks have replaced department stores as the new spaces of consumer seduction.
- Those who are able to consume effectively value malls as safe, privatised spaces for families.
- These spaces can have the effect of excluding some from consuming effectively.
- Some people look for alternative sites and forms of consumption.

How do we know?

Making social science arguments 1: description and explanation

We know from observation, data and description that consuming is an important feature of contemporary British life. As with the street example at the beginning of the chapter, the description of the department store and that of the retail park, we are able to see from such descriptions what consuming involves. Textual description, statistical description and images all aid us in describing consuming.

Social scientists recognise the importance of description but many want to go on to offer explanations of why things are as they are, how change comes about and some of the social problems that might be associated with an aspect of society like consumption.

To offer an explanation they will often use concepts as a kind of shorthand that captures some of the description of social practices in a way that allows it to be analysed. We have encountered a number of concepts in this chapter; for example: consumer society, seduced and repressed and conspicuous consumption.

As a final activity, you should try to put into your own words what you understand these concepts to mean.

While concepts are useful for deriving explanations from description, they do not always give us the full picture. They often simplify things in order to make the explanation clearer and less complex. In reality, society might be messier than that. They are also open to debate, refinement or challenge. When someone reads an explanation, they are not always required to believe it; they can be sceptical or can look for alternative explanations if they do not agree.

This chapter has given one explanation of the significance of consumption to contemporary British society. Whether or not it is convincing depends on whether you believe the description on offer, find the concepts useful as an explanatory tool, or whether you think something might have been missed out. As all students of social science quickly discover, their subjects are often defined by debate, reflection, argument and ongoing development and revision. That is something that is important to any science.

Conclusion

This chapter has introduced the importance that consuming activities have within modern societies. Consuming has been shown to be a social activity as much as an individual one, and one that has a history – practices and trends that developed a long time ago still influence us today. We have looked at some of the issues surrounding consumption that interest social scientists:

- We have looked at a typical city street to see some of the changes going on within the consumer landscape.
- We have considered some of the ways in which people use things to send a set of messages about themselves to others – at different times this has been to do with character and rank and with personality and individual expression.
- We have looked at some of the key sites in which consuming has developed and discussed some of the impacts that they have had on consumer activity.
- We have begun to consider the emergence of concerns about social divisions created by consumption and by some of the consequences of consuming.

While the idea of a consumer society has connotations of self-expression, freedom, leisure and lifestyle, some social scientists have argued that it is just as much characterised by social divisions, inequalities and forms of exclusion as the industrial society that came before it. In thinking about these issues consumption is being considered from a social science perspective. While social scientists are interested in studying the practices of consumption themselves, they are also interested in what consuming can reveal about society as a whole. This chapter has sought to enquire about an everyday aspect of the world people live in and has looked at some different arguments that social scientists put forward to try to explain things. All of these issues are as much the inspiration for further questions about consumption as they are explanations of what it is. To be a social scientist is often to look at an aspect of society like consumption and to try to understand it, formulating concepts which can help us to explain why things are the way they are. But that understanding often prompts new questions and new issues for enquiry. What has been argued here is that in studying consumption it is possible to come to know more about it not only as a set of practices but also as a kind of window onto a whole range of other issues about society. In passing, the chapter has touched on issues of identity, on people's relationship to things, and how some of these practices come under surveillance and social pressure or governance. These are all issues that will be looked at in more detail in later chapters. Above all, the chapter has argued that while the image of a consumer society is premised on ideas of freedom, self-identity and social membership that appeal to many who are seduced by its promises and can enjoy some of its trappings, there are others who are marginalised and excluded because circumstance and social position mean that they are unable fully to participate in society as consumers. Just as earlier industrial society was marked by social division and inequality, so too is a consumer society. The extent to which this consumer society is really about freedom of choice is taken up in the next chapter which asks us to consider the role of big retailers in shaping, even constraining, how people consume and what is consumed.

References

Adburgham, A. (1964) *Shops and Shopping: 1800–1914*, London, George Allen and Unwin.

Bauman, Z. (1988) *Freedom*, Milton Keynes, Open University Press.

Jackson, P. (1998) 'Domesticating the street: the contested spaces of the high street and the mall' in Fyfe, N. (ed.) *Images of the Street: Planning, Identity and Control in Public Space*, London, Routledge.

Office for National Statistics (ONS) (2008) *UK Snapshot: Society: Family Spending* [online], http://www.statistics.gov.uk/cci/nugget.asp?id=284 (Accessed 15 December 2008).

Susman, W. (2003) *Culture as History,* Washington, DC, Smithsonian Books.

Veblen, T. (1899) *The Theory of the Leisure Class: An Economic Study in the Evolution of Institutions*, New York, Macmillan.

Williams, R. (1982) *Dream Worlds*, Berkeley, CA, University of California Press.

Chapter 2

One-stop shopping: the power of supermarkets

John Allen

Contents

Introduction

Now, you may never have given it a moment's thought or, indeed, felt the need to reflect upon it. But, as a consumer, if asked about where you do most of your shopping, or indeed where your friends and family do most of theirs, what answer would you give? From the last chapter we know something about the growing diversity of places to shop along the high street, as well as the increase in shopping malls and the growth of out-of-town retail parks. So where do you think the majority of people in the UK, young as well as old, do the bulk of their shopping? As you have probably guessed, this is not a difficult question to answer, especially if you have local shopping for food and groceries in mind.

For a growing number of people, and you may count yourself among them, shopping amounts to more or less one thing: the regular or weekly shop at the local supermarket. These days you can buy just about anything from them, from the basics of food and groceries to extras like petrol, books, CDs, and even pet insurance in some stores. Open all hours in some places, relatively cheap by most standards, with a range of goods on the shelves inconceivable just ten or twenty years ago, supermarkets have transformed the way that people shop when it comes to life's essentials and a bit more.

One of the striking facts about shopping habits these days, at least those that involve the staples of everyday life, is that most of it is done in so few places. It's worth keeping in mind that, with the arrival of convenience stores such as Tesco Express and Sainsbury's Local on the high street, the big four supermarket chains – Tesco, Sainsbury's, Asda and Morrisons – take nearly three out of every four pounds that are spent on food and groceries in the UK (Bevan, 2006). That is a lot of consumption, and indeed a lot of money, accounted for by just a handful of big retailers.

And, for some, that is precisely what is wrong with the way that people shop today. A major worry is that as the big four chains battle it out for control of the grocery market, consumers in some towns will have no choice over where they shop. Already in places like Bicester, Dundee, Hove and Truro, where one of the big four supermarkets dominates, there are growing concerns that the lifeblood of the community has been drained by such developments. The presence of a big, new Tesco or Asda has often been linked directly to the closure of the old family butcher's or greengrocer's shop further up the high street. The losers in

The big four supermarket chains: Tesco, Asda, Sainsbury's and Morrisons

this battle for domination are, it is claimed, not just the small local shops, but anyone who prefers to buy their meat or fresh produce at the neighbourhood store or nearby street market.

Supermarkets are often seen as convenient places to shop, especially for those who drive, but there are those, and you may well be one of them, who, precisely because of the big four's hold on the market, would prefer not to set foot in them. Or, as is perhaps more common, there are those who would rather not go to supermarkets but end up there anyway because they are more accessible and the car parking is good. Often, it seems that it comes down to a simple matter of choice.

Activity 1

The matter of consumer choice is, in fact, far from simple and the issue is one that divides political opinion on supermarkets. Whether or not you are a regular shopper at one of the big four supermarket chains, what choice do you feel that you have over where you shop in your local area?

Is choice about having a variety of local shops, independent shops and markets in your area? If you can remember them, did the old corner shops provide choice? Or is choice more about price? Is it about the availability of a wide range of goods at affordable prices?

Take five or so minutes to consider why, if indeed you do, you shop at a supermarket and jot down what role choice – in terms of price, the range of goods on offer and the type of shop – plays in your decision. Do you, for example, shop at a supermarket because of its low prices, eye-catching promotions or 'buy one get one free' offers? Or do you choose to go there because it offers a welcome addition to your local stores, giving you a greater choice of fresh and pre-prepared food? If you don't shop at supermarkets, then simply jot down your reasons for not doing so.

Make a short list of the factors which influence your shopping choice and we shall return to it later in the chapter.

If, like me, you are someone who can recall the drab corner stores of yesteryear with their not especially friendly service or prices, then there is still a certain amount of wonder to be had from the sheer range of products and produce on supermarket shelves. You may find yourself enticed, seduced even, by the array of brightly packaged goods on offer. If, however, your experience is one of getting lost in aisles of seemingly endless packets, boxes and tins that pretty much resemble what is on offer at every other supermarket, then your sense of choice is likely to have been dulled. If the only choice available is between chain stores that sell virtually identical goods at almost matching prices, then how 'real' is that choice?

The issue becomes highly charged when the matter of choice turns on the size and power of the supermarkets. Have the big supermarket chains grown so big that they can now dictate our food shopping habits? Do they have an overbearing grip on the nation's shopping basket? The growing dominance of supermarkets up and down the country raises such questions and, in particular, prompts us to ask:

■ Does the power of supermarkets widen or narrow our shopping choices?

This is the broad question that runs through the chapter and one that you should keep in mind as we debate the issues and arguments involved. **Power** is one of the 'big words' in social sciences and is often used to denote influence, control or domination. Who should have it and how much they should have are frequently asked questions, and ones that are endlessly debated. Social scientists draw upon the concept of power to explain all kinds of events, from local political conflicts and ethnic clashes to the manoeuvrings of global corporations and

Power
A complex term used to denote influence, control or domination.

government authorities. Here, we look closely at supermarket power and the clashes that it has provoked in the UK in order to gain an understanding of what 'power' is and how the concept is mobilised politically to explain events around us, in the high street and beyond.

In the previous chapter it was pointed out that even if the UK is now called a consumer society, there are questions raised over the extent to which everyone benefits from such a society. In this chapter, we shall use the concept of power to think in more detail about how the benefits or otherwise of a consumer society are distributed. In the next two sections, I look more closely at the nature of supermarket power and map the lines of disagreement between those against and those in favour of supermarket expansion. Following that, in Section 3, we consider the impact that supermarket power has had over where we shop and the fate of the high street. Then, in Section 4, we explore whether the price of the cheap goods on supermarket shelves is the denial of a living wage to others, both in the UK and in low-cost countries like Bangladesh.

Throughout we shall be looking closely at the forces which shape our choices over where and how we shop, and the critical role of power as a social science concept. We will be looking at different arguments over the effects of supermarkets, and in doing so we shall look at the evidence used by different sides in making their arguments. As with Chapter 1 we'll be interested in drawing upon concepts to help us to explain how society works, but we will also need to think carefully about the concept of power, for it is used differently by different groups.

1   A tale of two superstores

Since their arrival in the 1960s, the growth and spread of supermarket chains has proved controversial, with talk nowadays of some places turning into 'Tesco Towns', where smaller, local shops are said to have all but disappeared and with them the vitality of the local neighbourhood. Popular reaction to such developments has grown, and the rolling out of supermarket power has increasingly been drawn under the spotlight, but things have not always turned out to be as black and white as often anticipated by those who reject outright the expansion of supermarkets along the high street and beyond. You will get a sense of what I mean by that from the following tale of two proposed superstore developments not far from one another in the west of Scotland. What is interesting to note are the quite different responses to Tesco's development plans by the two local neighbourhoods – despite their close proximity – and how supermarket power can provoke mixed reactions.

Figure 1   Tesco's proposed superstore development on the banks of the River Kelvin, Partick. The inset shows the existing brownfield site

If you walk along the bank of the River Kelvin near Beith Street in Partick, Glasgow, it is possible to picture the extent of one of Tesco's proposed developments in the west of Scotland. The retail giant's plans for the area illustrated in Figure 1 include a twenty-four-hour superstore as part of what could potentially be a vast retail and residential development. The proposal on a 10,000 square metre brownfield site has, at various times, included private housing and student accommodation as well as related leisure facilities, but the one constant is the large Tesco superstore. It is this, above all, that members of STOP (Stop Tesco Owning Partick) find objectionable and out of place. The STOP campaign, which was formed by a group of local residents in 2007, opposes the Tesco development on a variety of grounds, but its major concern is that the march of Tesco into this part of Glasgow will wreak havoc among small independent retailers, especially the local butchers, family-owned greengrocers and florists that dot the area. At stake, according to STOP, is the very liveliness of the Partick neighbourhood, which they claim would be eroded by the arrival of a corporate superstore.

They are supported in their efforts by another group drawn from the neighbourhood, All Tomorrow's Particks, who, like STOP, are bent on mobilising local opinion against the proposed store. The All Tomorrow's Particks group have done so largely by staging events that draw attention to alternative uses for the empty site. A recent stunt involved residents 'bombing' the proposed site with seeds in the hope that flowers would bloom like delayed 'explosions'. This soft symbolism has a hard point to it, however, which is that urban regeneration does not have to be supermarket led; the creation of vital green spaces speaks just as much, if not more, to the quality of life in urban areas.

Feelings have run high and the language on all sides has been fairly uncompromising. Both sides, the pro- and anti-development lobbies, have brought pressure to bear on Glasgow City Council and the Scottish Parliament to resolve the conflict in their favour. Concern that the protests have their roots in the wealthier and gentrifying parts of Partick have also been voiced and used to stir up emotions. Not everyone in Partick is resolutely against the development, but the protest element is strong and to the fore, especially when it comes to capturing local newspaper headlines. Whatever the eventual outcome, the political tensions are likely to linger well into the future.

Less than ten miles away, though, in Linwood, a town on the other side of the M8 motorway from Glasgow Airport (see Figure 2), a similar

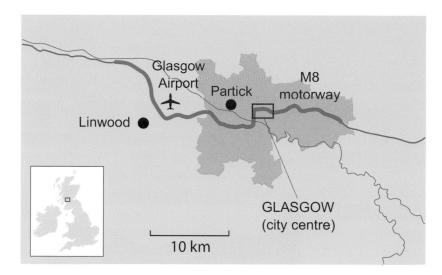

Figure 2   Map showing the location of Linwood and Partick with Glasgow's urban area

proposal for a Tesco superstore has so far failed to ignite any political tension. In striking contrast to Partick, much of Linwood seems eager for the transformation of their local town centre to be led by the retail giant. Previously at the heart of Scotland's car industry, the closure of the Peugeot Citroën car plant in the early 1980s left the town scarred by unemployment and economically run-down (see inset of Figure 3). In that context, the prospect of a redeveloped shopping plaza, as illustrated in Figure 3, with its new supermarket, community centre, library and an upgraded health centre has been enthusiastically received. In partnership with the local community, and strongly supported by the local Member of Scottish Parliament, Tesco's plan is to provide jobs for the local long term unemployed, boost local skills, and more generally to act as a catalyst for the regeneration of the area by attracting new shops, bars and restaurants to the plaza. As in Partick, there is a strength of local feeling, but in this case it seems predominantly in favour rather than opposed to big superstore development.

Nor are the people of Linwood alone in this, for the Linwood plan is precisely the type of 'high-street' scheme that the UK government-supported Underserved Markets project believes can breathe life into once vibrant – but now largely boarded up – neighbourhood shopping centres. Long blamed for their part in sucking the liveliness out of communities by building edge-of-city superstores, the big supermarkets are now increasingly hailed by many public and private bodies as the

Figure 3   Tesco's proposed redevelopment of Linwood's shopping plaza. The inset shows the existing run-down state of the plaza

potential saviours of deprived inner-city areas – although not by everyone, it seems.

For those more sceptical about such a regeneration strategy, this reversal of roles for supermarkets is seen as merely the latest in a series of opportunistic moves by them to get stores built at a time when planners and government frown upon out-of-town developments. In a rather cynical vein, town centre partnership schemes between the likes of Tesco, local councils and community organisations are viewed as little more than masks worn by the big supermarkets to conceal their economic self-interest. The partnerships are regarded as providing a convenient means both to bypass local protest should it arise and to get planners onside.

In fact, such underhand tactics are also thought by some to lie behind the supermarkets' dealings with their food and clothing suppliers, both overseas and closer to home. The supermarkets may act as if they are only interested in using their size and power to bring cheap goods to consumers, but the bottom line is that they are said to be maximising their profits at the expense of both poorly paid garment workers abroad and migrant workers in the UK who pack fresh produce for the big retailers. Or so it is claimed by those who warily eye the growth of supermarket power.

1.1   Two sides to an argument

All this may seem deeply controversial, but supermarket politics and superstore development tend to attract such extremes of opinion, and Partick and Linwood are fairly typical of the accusations that are thrown as the political argument rolls back and forth. What you need to be clear about is that no one is disputing the fact that supermarkets are powerful; rather, the argument revolves around one strand of the broad question outlined above – what supermarkets *do* with that power.

For those opposed to supermarket expansion, the issue, centrally, comes down to one of domination, with the big four chains said to abuse their dominant position at the expense of just about everybody else – consumers, local communities and vulnerable workers here and abroad. In contrast, those who welcome the spread of supermarkets point to the benefits that can spring from supermarket power, as appears evident in the Linwood case. A win–win situation, where everybody gains, is thought possible, as opposed to a scenario in which there can only ever be 'winners' and 'losers'.

Much of this chapter will be taken up with exploring these two lines of argument, and whether those with more power, like the big supermarkets, always get their way over those with less, like small shopkeepers, neighbourhood associations and campaign groups.

Summary

- The fact of supermarket power is not in contention. Rather, there is disagreement over the nature of that power and its consequences, as seen by the mixed reactions to proposed superstore developments at both Partick and Linwood.

2   What makes supermarkets powerful?

If you asked someone from Partick what makes supermarkets powerful, the most likely answer would be their size; not so much store size, but rather the size of their operation and their ability to dominate the marketplace. As supermarkets, most noticeably Tesco, have increased their share of the UK grocery market and moved into other lines such as clothes, books, music and electrical goods, so it is assumed that their power has grown in line with that. In other words, the bigger the supermarket chain, the greater their presumed ability to get their own way in the places like Partick and across the country as a whole. As the big four supermarkets have more than doubled the number of stores under their ownership in the UK since 2000, it seems fair to contend that their economic leverage has grown too. A retailer's size matters in this context because it is said to confer both *market power* and *buyer power*.

Market power

The power to influence market conditions, including price, independently of competitors.

Market power refers to the ability of supermarkets to act in the marketplace in ways that their rivals can do little or nothing about. Market share gives them certain advantages over independent retailers and smaller chains, say for instance over the ability to charge different prices in their stores depending upon whether the local competition is strong or not. In itself, there is nothing wrong with some retailers having a greater share of the market than others. It is only when they abuse their dominant position that their power becomes a matter of concern; for example, when supermarkets use their dominant position to trade unfairly by selling goods below cost or, in the case of a proposed new superstore development like Partick, if they use their size and influence to, say, brush community opinion aside.

Buyer power

The relative bargaining power between firms and their suppliers.

The **buying power** of the big supermarkets is somewhat different, although it too is directly related to the size of their market share. In this case, it is relative size that matters; that is, how big a supermarket is in relation to its suppliers. It comes down to the bargaining power that the supermarkets have in their dealings with food manufacturers, farmers and clothing subcontractors. The larger chains are said to have an advantage over smaller suppliers in so far as they are often able to extract more favourable terms from them, over price for instance where their ability to buy in bulk enables them to demand discounts from a small dairy famer or T-shirt manufacturer. Again, though, it matters most when the big retailers are seen to abuse their dominant position by unfairly squeezing suppliers' margins or colluding among themselves on the price of everyday products such as milk, butter and cheese.

If all this sounds terribly economic, there is a simpler point to hold on to here. Size clearly matters when it comes down to the ability of supermarkets to flex their economic muscle, but the nub of the issue, as mentioned, is how retailers use the resources that they have to hand.

Activity 2

Wal-Mart's headquarters in Bentonville, Arkansas

Think about it for a moment. Are the likes of Asda, with all the resources of its big American parent company, Wal-Mart, behind it, so powerful that they can put others out of business or mould the face of communities to their advantage? Can they impose their will on local neighbourhoods so that those who live there have no choice but to shop at their outlets? Do you feel that your local supermarket is overbearing in that way?

Obviously, nobody can force us to shop at Asda or Tesco, so we are not talking about **coercion** here. But if you think that supermarkets use their economic power to restrict choice and to make it difficult for us not to fall into line with their interests, then the experience you are talking about may well be one of **domination**. Or the experience may

Coercion
To compel by force or its threatened use.

Domination
To impose upon or constrain the free choice of others despite possible resistance.

Seduction
Through enticement and suggestion, to direct our choices along certain lines and not others, closing them down by degree.

See Section 1.4 in Chapter 1 of *Making Social Lives* for a discussion of the concepts of the seduced and the repressed.

be one of **seduction**, where you are pulled towards what is on offer at a particular supermarket simply because the range of goods is more enticing.

Now we know something from the last chapter about the relationship between seduction and shopping, so what would a scenario of 'supermarket domination' amount to?

How you see the big supermarkets using their power is more likely to depend upon whether you think they use their size as a force for good or as a lever to restrict choice so that only they gain. For the situation to resemble anything like domination, the major supermarkets would have to hold a firm grip on the market for groceries, almost to the extent that they had manoeuvred themselves into a commanding position in a number of towns and communities. Before we go too far with this line of thought, however, we need to be clear about the two sides to the debate over supermarket power.

2.1 Checkout controversies

There is something a little contrived in setting up different viewpoints on supermarket power as a stark opposition, given the political variations in between, but it is helpful sometimes to draw the contrast sharply so that the claims and counterclaims are clearly drawn.

Let's start with those who broadly oppose supermarket growth, the *anti-supermarket* campaign groups and organisations. For them:

- The market power of the big supermarket chains has made it increasingly difficult for smaller shops to compete and prosper, with high-street stores closing down in their thousands across the country. This has not only led to a 'hollowing out' of town centres, it has also restricted 'real choice' for consumers in the marketplace.

- The immense buying power of the supermarkets has given them a stranglehold over the food and clothing supply chain. Increasingly, costs and risks are borne by suppliers. While supermarkets may provide a good deal on price for shoppers they do so at the expense of workers both here and abroad – often women, sometimes children – who have to suffer poverty wages.

- The size and financial assets of the big supermarkets enable them to exert real pressure on local planners and politicians. Aggressive lobbying by the big retailers has enabled them to get their own way on superstore development, often, as some in Partick would argue, at the expense of what is best for local people.

On the basis of these claims, those who oppose the spread of supermarkets have done so on the grounds of their dominant position. Too much power is thought to be concentrated in too few hands, leaving the rest of us subject to supermarket domination. In short, there is more at stake here than cheap shopping.

In contrast, the *pro-supermarket* lobby, led quite naturally by the big four supermarkets, see supermarkets as a force for good. They believe that supermarkets use, not abuse, their economic size for the benefit of communities and consumers, suppliers and workers, alike. As they see it:

- The market power of supermarkets has brought about an explosion in diversity and choice for consumers at prices lower than ever before. Rather than posing a threat to local retailers, their high-street stores help ailing shopping parades by drawing specialist or 'boutique' stores to them, enabling small traders to thrive and prosper.

- The buying power of the supermarkets has enabled them to raise standards for their suppliers. In their dealings with factory owners and workers abroad, they have sought to raise wages to a level that, while far from wonderful, has lifted many out of poverty and hardship.

- In run-down areas like Linwood, the economic leverage of the big supermarkets can act as a force for social and economic regeneration. Large superstore development brings tremendous benefits to local communities, in the shape of jobs for the unemployed, improved self-respect and skills development.

The *claims* and *counterclaims* provide different standpoints on what supermarkets do with their power and its consequences: whether our shopping choices are constrained or broadened. As you work through the rest of the chapter you should bear in mind that such claims are the building blocks of an *argument* and they often rest upon *assumptions* about how society, or power in society in this case, is organised more generally. Understanding how an argument is put together, which concepts are mobilised and how evidence is used, is a critical social science skill. As such, you will find it worthwhile to track the different elements involved.

2.2   No gain without pain?

So opinion is divided on the matter of supermarket power and, in practice, it largely turns on whether supermarkets are assumed to wield their power at the expense of others or for the benefit of others. Those opposed to the growing power of the big retail giants believe that the small, independent shops are struggling to survive the onslaught of the big four. As they see it, our shopping choices are now dictated by the big four chains, to the extent that the needs of supermarkets, on the one hand, and shoppers and small high-street stores, on the other, are now mutually exclusive. Or, in language of the sociologist Dennis Wrong (1997), power here is understood as a **zero-sum game**.

One way to grasp this is to think of a game in which there are only winners and losers, so that if one side gains the other side must lose. In a zero-sum game, there is only a fixed amount of resources in play so that the scores of the winner and the loser sum to zero. It is a little like the cutting of a cake where, if one person takes a large slice, there is less cake for everyone else. So, if supermarkets increase their grip on where we shop, dominating the food chain to suit their own ends, there has to be some give in the system. And that give is felt by shoppers in the high street whose choice is denied as local shops are ruined one by one and invariably replaced by lifeless retail parks. The big four's gain, in this case, is experienced by consumers and small shopkeepers as pain.

Needless to say, the pro-supermarket lobby do not see it this way. They argue that the nation's shopping basket, far from being a game whose pay-offs sum to zero, is more akin to what Wrong and other social scientists refer to as a **positive-sum game**, where all parties involved benefit to some extent. Rather than a fixed amount of resources in play, the economic success of the big supermarkets has increased choice for everyone: for example, by meeting the demand for fresh fruit and vegetables from around the world regardless of season. On this view, there is more to the 'cake' than first thought and everyone wins: from the consumer and supermarket shareholder to the supplier, even the migrant worker who washes and packs mixed salad leaves for Tesco. It is all about gain, not pain.

The issue, then, is what are we to make of these competing claims and assumptions about power and supermarket dominance? In social science terms, do the supermarkets operate a zero-sum or a positive-sum game of power on the high street and, more extensively, in the marketplace?

Zero-sum game
A situation in which one party's gain is balanced by another party's loss. If you subtract total losses from total gains, they sum to zero.

Positive-sum game
A situation in which the sum of total gains and losses of all parties involved is positive; that is, they sum to more than zero.

In the next section, we look first at the impact of supermarket power over where we shop and the fate of the high street, before moving on in Section 4 to consider whether the suppliers of goods to supermarkets are better or worse off by working with the big supermarket chains.

Summary

- The growing dominance of supermarkets in the UK rests upon their market power and their buying power. Both forms of power can be used by supermarkets to dominate the food and groceries market.

- Pro- and anti-supermarket campaigners differ markedly over what supermarkets do with the power at their disposal. One side claims that supermarkets restrict our shopping choices, the other side claims that they widen them.

- Both sets of claims rest upon assumptions about how power is distributed and organised in society. A zero-sum game implies that it is impossible for both sides to win, whereas a positive-sum game suggests that both sides may gain to some extent.

3   From monopoly over the high street...

Picking up on your response to the issues raised in Activity 2, around the possibility of the major supermarkets manoeuvring themselves into **monopoly** positions in local neighbourhoods and town centres, I wonder if you felt that the big supermarket chains will always triumph over the small shopkeeper, or that the global retailer will inevitably win out against the local entrepreneur? It is obviously hard to say, but when the language is often in terms of supermarket 'giants' or corporate 'monoliths' the impression of power and reach can sometimes be almost tangible. Wal-Mart, mentioned earlier as the US owner of Asda, the world's largest retailer with just under 2 million workers in over 6000 stores spread across sixteen countries, is a classic case in point.

Monopoly
A position where a firm, or group of firms, has the power to prevent, restrict or distort competition in a particular market.

Wal-Mart and its UK offspring, Asda, are unquestionably big and it is hard not to see them as being able to get their own way despite resistance from others. The UK marketplace for food and groceries is far from a level playing field and that, for some, is simply the end of the story. But for us, it is more of a starting point, where we need to be clear, not only about the nature of supermarket power in the UK, but, equally, as noted before, about what they *do* with that power in terms of shaping our choices over where and how we shop.

So, what is the relevant *evidence* about supermarket power in the UK today?

3.1   Power in store

There is some evidence which appears to be beyond dispute (so much so it is often labelled as 'fact'). One such fact concerns the market power of the big four supermarkets and their ever increasing share of the UK food and groceries market. Tesco became the front runner in 1995 and since then it has steadily increased its market share to around one-third of all grocery shopping in the UK. This is almost as much as the second and third largest supermarkets, Asda and Sainsbury's, combined. Morrison, the fourth member of the supermarket quartet, now has just over 11 per cent of the market, largely as the result of its acquisition of the Safeway supermarket chain in 2004. The Co-op, after buying its rival, Somerfield, in 2008, has just under 8 per cent. Waitrose and Marks & Spencer, as well as the German-owned Aldi and Lidl, and the Danish-owned Netto, make up the rest, all with 4 per cent or less of the market (Competition Commission, 2008; The Co-operative Group, 2008; Financial Times, 2008). (See Table 1 for additional information on UK supermarkets.)

Table 1 Who are the supermarkets?

TESCO	UK-owned	Operates over 3700 stores in 13 countries – of which just over 2000 are in the UK
ASDA	US-owned	Part of the Wal-Mart chain which operates over 6000 stores in 16 countries – of which 300 Asda stores are in the UK
Sainsbury's *Try something new today*	UK-owned	Operates over 800 stores in the UK
M **MORRISONS**	UK-owned	Acquired Safeway in 2004 to gain market share in the south of England. Operates over 800 stores in the UK
ALDI	German-owned	Operates over 7700 stores in 14 countries – of which 430 are in the UK
LIDL	German-owned	Part of the Schwarz Group which operates over 7500 stores in 17 countries – of which over 440 are in the UK
NETTO	Danish-owned	Operates over 1000 stores in Europe – of which over 180 are in the UK
Waitrose	UK-owned	Part of the John Lewis Partnership. It operates over 190 stores in the UK
The **co-operative**	UK-owned	The product of a merger in 2000 between the Co-operative Wholesales Society and Co-operative Retail Services Ltd. Operates over 3000 stores in the UK, mainly at the convenience end of the grocery market
M&S	UK-owned	Operates over 760 stores in 30 countries – of which over 500 are in the UK

Sources: Competition Commission, 2008; SN, 2008; Young, 2004, pp. 1–33

According to the retail commentator Judi Bevan (2006), some 30 million customers pour through the doors of UK supermarkets every week, with Tesco alone, as noted, taking one pound at the tills for every three that we spend on food and groceries. All in all, the big four operate around 3900 stores, a number that has increased of late as the big retailers move back to the high street to gain a share of the 'top-up' market that local stores and small traders previously counted on as their own. Since 2000, Bevan notes that Tesco and Sainsbury's have expanded on the high street by opening in the convenience store format, buying some 1500 stores from independent chains to capture passing trade from local and busy working people. In the recent past, the out-of-town superstores are said to have driven retailing out of the high street, but now with the big multiples returning to the high street as Sainsbury's Local and Tesco Express or Metro, small independents find themselves up against their market power once again, but this time as a direct competitor just along the road.

For food writers like Joanna Blythman (2005), the adoption of the corner-store format by the big chains has sharply accelerated the rate of closure among small independent shops that were just about holding their own. For her, places like Dundee in Scotland are typical of the changes under way. Back in the 1960s, she points out, 'there were ten bakers; now there are two left. There were eight or nine butchers; now there is one. Of the five fishmongers, one has survived. Where there were half a dozen grocers, one remains' (Blythman, 2005, p. 12). Some forty years on, the city of Dundee plays host to four Tescos, one of which is a Metro store, two Asdas, one Morrisons, one Sainsbury's, one Marks & Spencer and a number of low-price outlets. And, in her mind, the demise of the independents and the march of the big supermarkets into Dundee are two sides of the same coin. The big multiples have benefited at the expense of the small independents.

Or, to put it in social science terms: a *zero-sum* game of power appears to be at work here where growing supermarket power is matched by an equivalent decline in the abilities of small local shops to compete. The end result is a high street stripped of diversity and life as the big four limit the possible range and type of shops available. In support of this view, the Federation of Small Businesses points out that, since 2000, some 7000 local grocery stores have been lost, with independents closing at the rate of 2000 a year, whereas, over the same period, Tesco, Sainsbury's, Asda and Morrisons have doubled the number of stores that they operate (Federation of Small Businesses, 2006).

Now, of course, the two trends could simply be a coincidence, rather than one the cause of the other. For anti-supermarket campaigners, however, there is no mistaking the fact that the nationwide market and buying power of the big chains give them an unfair advantage over independents on the high street. It is, they argue, this retail power that enables supermarkets to dominate the marketplace and which gives consumers little choice over where to shop. Or rather, the choice that shoppers have is a choice between an Asda or a Sainsbury's store, or a Tesco or a Morrisons; which in their eyes is tantamount to the big four approaching a monopoly stranglehold on the marketplace.

Activity 3

Supermarkets attract this kind of criticism from consumers too, even though they may end up doing most of their shopping there. The claim that supermarket domination amounts to a monopoly over the high street or local neighbourhood requires looking at more closely, however.

Figures 4 and 5, respectively, provide a snapshot in 2007 of which supermarkets enjoy a dominant position across different parts of the UK and the towns in which Tesco have their highest and lowest market share. Cast your eye down the column in Figure 5, and stop at Dundee. With, as we have seen, its four Tescos and 52 per cent market share of groceries in the city, do you think that that is sufficient to give Tesco a monopoly over the food business in the area? Remember, to exercise a monopoly position Tesco would have to have sufficient power over their rivals to the extent that they cannot effectively compete?

Now go back to what Joanna Blythman had to say in the paragraph above about the changing profile of shops in Dundee and give the matter some thought. Make a note of what other kinds of stores are in evidence in today's retail market in the city. How restricted, in terms of market competition, are Tesco's rivals?

3.2   Tesco Towns?

To be honest, I would have thought it debatable how far one could say that Tesco has a monopoly over food shopping in Dundee, given the presence of the other big supermarkets as well as low-price outlets in the city. But that has not stopped the anti-supermarket lobby from

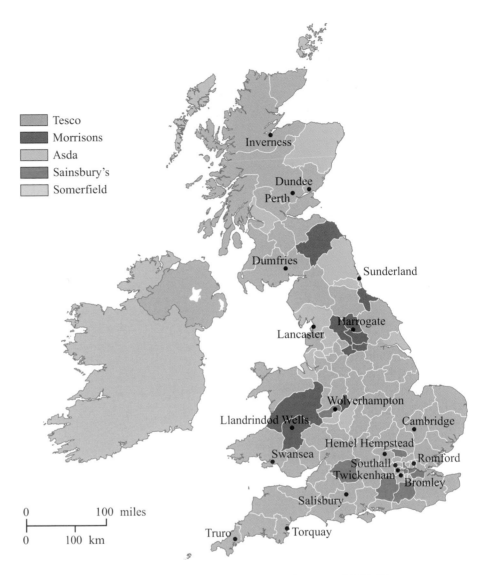

Figure 4   Number one supermarket by postcode area, 2007 (Source: adapted from *The Guardian*, 2007, based on Competition Commission data)

dubbing towns in which Tesco take more than 50 pence in the pound spent on groceries as 'Tesco Towns'. Places like Perth, Salisbury, Swansea and Inverness, because of the number of Tesco stores in the local area, are often cited by the lobby as areas where people have little choice but to shop at Tesco. In Inverness, for example, where three out of the city's four supermarkets are run by Tesco and more than half of all the money spent on food and groceries goes through those three stores, the lobby have been quick to point out the suffocating effects of

Highest Tesco market share

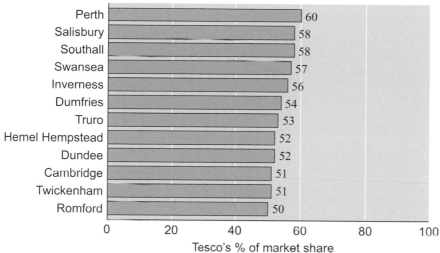

Lowest Tesco market share

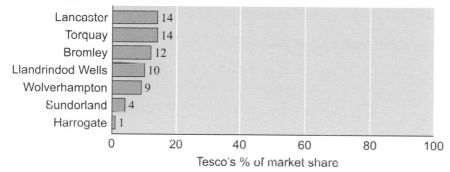

Figure 5   Towns in which Tesco has the highest and lowest market share (Source: adapted from *The Guardian*, 2007, based on Competition Commission data)

the mega-retailers who are able to prosper at the expense of small shops.

At the forefront of the anti-supermarket lobby is the Tescopoly Alliance. Launched in 2005, the Alliance acts as an umbrella grouping for a number of organisations and pressure groups, including Friends of the Earth and the new economics foundation (nef), whose explicit political goal is to curb the market power of the major UK supermarkets. The Alliance draws attention to what it perceives as the negative impacts of supermarket behaviour in the marketplace and acts as a resource for local campaigns who share its aims. A book of the same name, *Tescopoly*, was published in 2007 by one of the leading campaigners in the new economics foundation, Andrew Simms, and while he too directs attention to the excessive power and influence of the big supermarket chains, his prime target is what he sees as Tesco's monopoly power. He points to the fact that, in the UK, the government sets the level at which a monopoly is said to operate at 25 per cent of the market. Above that level, a firm's control of the market is a signal that it not only enjoys a dominant position, but that it effectively has the power to distort competition and prevent others from doing business. Tesco's evident monopoly of the grocery market, he claims, is directly responsible for the ruination of local neighbourhood stores and corner shops, the 'hollowing out' of town centres, and the growth of out-of-town retail parks dominated by identikit chain stores.

The Tescopoly Alliance logo (Source: Tescopoly Alliance, undated)

At times, though, it is hard to know exactly what to make of this sweeping claim, apart that is from the fact that, on the basis of the 25 per cent mark, monopolies may be more common than you or I had supposed. That may well be so, but economists will tell you that it is not as straightforward as it looks to establish whether a firm enjoys a position of monopoly in a given market. For one thing, it is not always immediately obvious what the size and scope of a relevant market is, especially in something like food and groceries. Is the market for the big weekly or fortnightly shop at the edge-of-town superstore different from just nipping out to shop at the small convenience store on the high street? Do shoppers switch between them or is there a clear break in their custom? Do Asda, Morrisons, Sainsbury's and Tesco compete with each other nationally or locally? And, if it is the latter, where do you draw the boundary of the local market? This is just to scratch the surface of what is involved in trying to establish whether or not a firm enjoys a market share that all can agree constitutes a monopoly position. The government's cut-off point that could trigger a monopoly concern, 25 per cent of a market, does after all depend on how the market is defined. It comes down to 25 per cent of what exactly?

3.3   Local or national market?

If, then, you wish to prove that a supermarket enjoys a monopoly position in the market for food and groceries, you would define the market narrowly. If you want to resist that charge, you would opt for the widest market definition possible. The new economics foundation consider that, at the local level, no one supermarket should control more than one-third of the market (nef, 2007), and the percentages in Figure 5 give them plenty of support for their case that at least one supermarket exercises 'monopoly powers'. In response, however, Tesco argues that the relevant geographic market for groceries is *national* with everyone competing against everyone else (Tesco, 2007).

Why national? And why specifically Tesco? This is because, if you look at Figure 4 and the swathes of blue which signify Tesco's dominant position across the country, for them there are no readily identifiable local or regional markets, each with their own profile of competitors, only a national market with national brands, a national pricing structure and a nationwide range of goods. More to the point, if the food and groceries market is national, then shoppers have a wide variety of retailers – the local organic butchers and the farmers' market as much as the countrywide multiple and smaller chains like Spar and Londis – to choose between. Besides, as the big retail chains are not slow to point out, the market in question is strictly speaking not limited to groceries. Life's essentials today include a range of household goods, from clothing to all manner of electrical goods, which are traded by supermarkets and other stores, and this too can be read as an absence of monopoly powers as people shop around for more things in more places.

You read more about how life's shopping essentials have changed in Chapter 1.

There is an important point about supermarket power at stake here. If the market for food and groceries is indeed national, then it is possible for the big supermarkets to claim that they use their not insignificant power for the 'common good', to deliver lower prices and more choice for shoppers over a wider range of products. The rapid growth of supermarkets in the UK over the past forty or so years has, on this view, increased the resources in play, to the benefit of all parties concerned. Compared with the often shabby, overpriced corner shop, consumers now have access to a wide range of affordable goods. High streets too benefit from the new local convenience stores run by the supermarkets, which act as a magnet enticing people to struggling shopping parades and draw in other out-of-the-ordinary stores. On this view, social scientists would argue that a positive-sum game, rather than a zero-sum game, of power is in play with an expanding national market delivering a 'win–win' situation.

So are supermarkets a force for good or do they abuse their dominant market position to suit their own purposes? Before you mull over the opposing claims and the evidence offered, there is a further set of claims to consider: whether the price of those cheap, affordable goods in supermarkets is paid for by others who, in this instance, are part of a wider global picture often far removed from the bustle of the high street.

Summary

- Between them, the big four supermarkets account for around three-quarters of the UK food and groceries market. This gives them significant market power.
- Anti-supermarket campaigners claim that supermarket domination amounts to a monopoly over the groceries market, with Tesco in particular distorting competition and profiting at the expense of small local shops on the high street.
- The establishment of a monopoly, in this case, turns on the definition of the relevant geographic market, whether the market for food and groceries is local or national. If the latter, then a monopoly situation is not proven.

4   ...to the domination of suppliers around the globe

For much of the past decade or so food prices in the UK have been more or less falling in real terms, although in recent times it may not have always felt like it. Much of this can be traced to the efforts of the big supermarkets to increase their market share by buying produce more cheaply and passing on the reduction to the shoppers at the checkout. While this may sound like a good thing, not everybody thinks so. The crux of the matter, as before, is that the benefits passed on to consumers are enjoyed at the expense of the efforts of others – this time, from around the globe. Or so the farmers, subcontractors and manufacturers who rely on the UK supermarkets to get their goods on the shelves claim. What most concerns this group is the imbalance of power between them and the big retailers: the immense buying power that the latter can wield to get their own way on the price that they pay for the chickens, daffodils and shirts that they sell week in, week out.

The relationship between suppliers and supermarkets is often portrayed as a David versus Goliath affair, with the small independents up against the big multiples in much the same way that small shopkeepers on the high street are pitted against the big chain stores. But this is an oversimplification of sorts. Whether it concerns food, clothing, medicines, homeware or electrical goods, the relationship between supplier and supermarket is more complex than that. The likes of Asda, Sainsbury's and the other big UK supermarkets each deal with around 2000 suppliers, some of which are indeed small independents or small farmers who depend almost wholly upon one of the big retailers to get their produce in front of shoppers. But the supermarkets also have to deal with the big, global manufacturers, many of which supply the branded goods that few supermarkets dare to be without. When dealing with conglomerates such as Proctor & Gamble, Nestlé, Unilever or the French group Danone, the balance of power between supplier and supermarket can swing either way, and often does so depending on the economic climate. On such occasions, the bargaining power of the supermarkets is often more than matched by the global muscle of the major suppliers.

As before, corporate size and the superior resources at their disposal matter for both supermarkets and supplier alike, and equate, broadly speaking, to the amount of power held. But also as before, what really matters is whether the big players abuse their dominant position to gain at the expense of others. Small suppliers regularly claim that the big supermarkets squeeze them up to the point that their economic livelihood is in doubt, by coercing them into price cuts. That may well be true at times, but their relationship with supermarkets is particular and complex. What is easier and perhaps more obvious to talk about when it comes to being at the sharp end of supermarket power is the plight of those who work for the suppliers, great or small, without whom none of us would enjoy the benefit of cheap supermarket goods.

4.1   The real cost of low prices

Not so long ago, little was heard about the low-paid, often migrant, workers in the UK countryside who sort, cut and pack the salads and vegetables for the big supermarket chains, or indeed about their fellow low-paid agency workers in the fields picking and gathering them. Like the workforce in overseas factories who sew and stitch the clothes for Asda's George fashion range, for instance, often putting in what some claim are excessive hours for what seems like little return, this labour was until recently both distant and largely hidden. Thanks in part to food journalists like Felicity Lawrence, those who pick the green beans and spring onions for Tesco or who sew the latest Asda garment in Bangladesh are now linked directly through their supply chains to the ability of supermarkets to sell goods at low cost. Without access to such pools of cheap labour, many of the products on supermarket shelves, she points out, would simply be unaffordable or at least expensive enough for us to think twice about buying them.

In her book *Not on the Label* (2004), and in her newspaper investigations, Lawrence has drawn attention to the plight of casualised agency workers employed by 'gangmasters' around the country. Often paid hourly rates below the legal minimum, subjected to illegal deductions from their pay, and bussed from job to job at will, the many nationalities involved – Polish, Romanian, Hungarian, Bulgarian, Latvian and Slovakian workers among them – work in supermarket packhouses and food-processing plants that, for her, largely operate outside the restrictions of the law. More to the point, she claims that much of this abuse of migrant workers goes on with the connivance of supermarkets, who turn a blind eye to the arrangement whilst benefiting from the low wages paid by gangmasters in the farming and food-processing sectors. At arm's length from the actual illegality of employment practices, supermarkets nonetheless gain directly from prices being kept low in the

Migrant workers harvesting cabbages in Lincolnshire

food supply chain. But, she pointedly argues, you will not find any evidence of underpay or illegality on the label of the salad packets or boxes of chicken pieces which grace the big supermarkets' shelves.

For Lawrence, the connection between exploited migrant labour in the more remote parts of the countryside and the cost of what turns up on our plates is an elementary one; namely, that there is a high price to be paid for cheap goods and that cost is borne one sidedly by the weakest and least powerful groups in the supply chain. To her way of thinking, we as consumers benefit directly from low supermarket prices at the expense of those employed by suppliers keen to give us salad and strawberries all year round. Suppliers, she acknowledges, are sometimes themselves caught in the middle of all this, with their financial margins squeezed by supermarkets to the extent that they cannot afford to pay their workers a decent wage. You might like to think of this as another claim about *domination*, where the big multiples, by hiding behind their chain of subcontractors, in this instance give the latter no choice but to pay their workers less as supermarkets drive down prices at the factory and farm gates.

On this view, there is a basic *asymmetry* to the power relationship between supermarkets, on the one hand, and suppliers and their workers, on the other. What this means is that, as with the big multiples and small shopkeepers, those with more power are said to prevail over those with less. On this account, power is used as an instrument of domination and a tally of who gains and who loses falls squarely, as we have seen, into a *zero-sum* game. The high cost of low prices at the checkout falls on both suppliers and their workforce, but disproportionately on the latter.

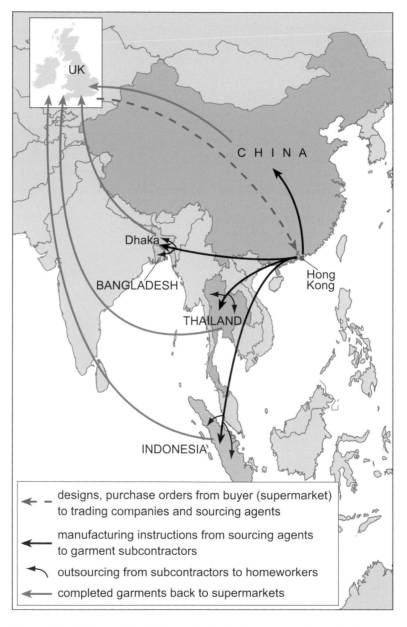

Figure 6   A typical global supply chain for garment production

There is another twist to this argument, however, which is that the more distant the workforce, the greater is the assumed loss, with for instance subcontracted garment factory workers in China, Thailand, Indonesia, Bangladesh and other low-cost locations bearing the brunt of the supermarket's buying power. Subcontracting through a **global supply chain** of the type illustrated in Figure 6 provides options for supermarkets over where to source particular products, as well as giving them control over price, turnaround times and the quality of the finished goods. The chains themselves, I should add, are often disconcertingly complex, with merchandise sometimes passing through the hands of buyers, suppliers, trading companies and sourcing agents before reaching the stores of an Asda or a Tesco in the UK. Even simple operations to do with clothing, say the cutting, trimming and sewing of garments for a supermarket, may involve more than one factory, and some steps may actually be completed by home-based workers. But this tangled and fragmented set of arrangements rarely surfaces when the anti-supermarket lobby seek to press home the political point that supermarkets are directly at fault for the poverty wages experienced by garment workers in faraway factories.

Global supply chain
A chain of suppliers that cuts across national borders, drawing firms and contractors into the process of making and delivering a single product.

4.2   Profiting from poverty wages abroad?

In 2006 and 2007, War on Want, a large non-governmental organisation based in the UK, targeted Asda and Tesco directly, accusing them of boosting profits at the expense of some of the most vulnerable workers in the world: sweatshop garment workers in Bangladesh. Based on a survey of six large factories, each employing between 500 and 1200 workers, in Dhaka, the capital city of Bangladesh, War on Want found evidence that the mainly female workforce had been subjected to forced overtime, overcrowded and unhygienic working conditions, verbal intimidation, and refused access to trade unions. Above all, those factories, all of which were known to be supplying low-cost clothing for Asda and Tesco in the UK market, were found to be paying wages to their workers well below that needed to provide for themselves and their families. The relentless pressure on the factory owners to keep costs down or risk losing the clothing contract was said to leave them no room for manoeuvre. The true cost of the cheap jeans and trousers, as well as the bargain-priced shoes, which line Asda's and Tesco's aisles, War on Want claim, is the absence of a living wage for workers in their supply chains.

If you find it hard to grasp exactly what that experience amounts to, then War on Want can make the connection for you – by way of Lina's story in Activity 4.

Activity 4

Lina is one of many workers named in War on Want's survey of garment workers in Dhaka. It is not her real name, of course, which has been changed to protect her from victimisation. Read the 'How cheap is too cheap?' extract and look carefully at the relative clothing costs in the figure. Then give yourself some time to consider the nature of the appeal.

What is it about Lina's story which also tries to put *you* in it too, not as someone to blame for her predicament, but as someone connected to her? What is the nature of that connection?

How cheap is too cheap?

Lina began working in a garment factory at the age of 13. The oldest of eight children, her parents became unable to pay for her education when her brother became sick. She moved from her village to the Bangladeshi capital Dhaka to get a job and help them make ends meet. Now 22, she works in a factory that supplies Primark, Asda and Tesco. She is one of the lucky ones to have learned how to operate a sewing machine, and so can command a wage of £17 per month. To earn this amount, she must work between 60 and 90 hours each week.

Lina earns far less than even the most conservative estimate of a living wage in Bangladesh, which is £22 per month. Her husband, whom she met in the factory and married three years ago, is now ill and unable to work. She must pay for his treatment as well as for her own living costs in Dhaka, and, despite her best efforts to economise, she is unable to send money to her family, who need it to get by. She says she is happy, though, to have 'done the best she could' for her family.

If you are wearing a piece of clothing bought from Primark, Asda or Tesco, it is quite possible that Lina sewed it. These high street retailers are able to sell their clothes at such an agreeable price because workers like Lina are forced to live on wages well below what they need in order to live a decent life.

Lina is one of 60 workers who were interviewed for this report, across six garment factories in Bangladesh. According to these workers, all six factories are producing 'significant amounts' of garments for Asda; four also produce for Tesco and three for Primark. The workers' testimonies in this report demonstrate the dismal life of a garment worker selling to Britain's bargain retailers.

Poor working conditions like those described in this report are systemic problems that exist across the whole clothing industry. But Asda, Tesco and Primark – like others at the budget end of the market – do raise more concerns than their rivals. The question is quite simply: 'How do they get their clothes so cheap?' The graph below shows just how cheap they are, compared to the rest of the UK high street:

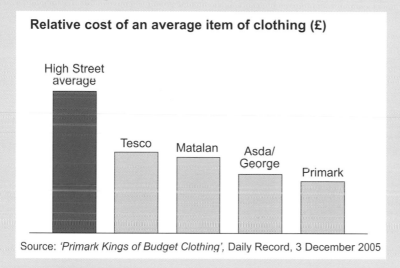

Relative cost of an average item of clothing (£)

High Street average

Tesco   Matalan   Asda/George   Primark

Source: *'Primark Kings of Budget Clothing'*, Daily Record, 3 December 2005

War on Want, 2006, p. 2

What, for me, Lina's story seems to be suggesting is that those who have put on an inexpensive George suit from Asda or bought a pair of cheap jeans from Tesco are somehow caught up in a system that benefits us at the expense of workers like Lina. Because shoppers like a bargain, the pressure that sets up transmits itself directly to the factory floor in Bangladesh and requires others to make the clothes at a cost which fails to deliver a living wage. There is a certain simplicity to the connection, or rather an immediacy, which ties those who wear the suits and jeans to those who stitch and sew them in far-off places. Our role as consumers in the system is merely to go about our normal business of shopping at the supermarket, and enjoying the low prices, but this it seems sets off a chain reaction that deprives others – that is, workers like Lina, in Bangladesh – from earning a living wage.

Garment workers, including children, in textile factories in and around Dhaka, Bangladesh

If you see it like this, and the journalist and political activist Naomi Klein (2000) would want you to be persuaded by the logic, then not only are we caught up in a global system that works to the advantage of the supermarkets and those who shop there, we are also entangled in a system in which there is little give. The benefits are mutually exclusive: either prices rise for consumers and the supermarkets take a cut in profits or workers like Lina suffer pittance wages. There is no happy medium or a trade-off between the different interests; just a straightforward zero-sum game in which shoppers are part of a system of domination which works in their favour. Through no fault of their own, shoppers, the political theorist Iris Marion Young (2003) argues, are tied into a system that produces harm and injustice on the far side of the globe. Bangladeshi wages for garment workers are unacceptably low and consumers, she argues, have a responsibility to see that a living wage is paid regardless of distance.

How much is a living wage in Bangladesh? In the follow-up survey on supply chain wages in 2007, War on Want, together with the campaign group Labour Behind the Label, published a series of figures which alarmed the big supermarkets and put them on the back foot. As you can see from the extract 'How much is a living wage?', the figure for a living wage in Bangladesh is a hotly contested one.

How much is a living wage?

Bangladesh has had more attention paid to it than any other country over the past year, and the result is that more organisations have put a figure on a living wage than anywhere else. A quick comparison of these figures shows how differently the living wage is viewed by some brands and by workers' organisations:

- Sainsbury's says the minimum wage of Tk 1851 (£14) per month should constitute a living wage, and has calculations to back up its case.

- Tesco's work on the ground gives it a figure of Tk 3000 (although this is not implemented).

- During the 2006 minimum wage negotiations, Bangladeshi trade unions called for a minimum wage of Tk 3000, a low-end figure that they thought was politically palatable.

- Next is still calculating, but based on local estimates it says that the figure must be somewhere between Tk 3000 and 4000.

- Jakir Hossain of Bangladeshi think-tank Unnayan Onneshan estimated the figure to be around Tk 4300 in 2006.

- The Bangladesh Institute of Labour Studies has calculated that for food alone, a family of four needs Tk 4800.

Labour Behind the Label/War on Want, 2007, p. 9

Sainsbury's and Tesco differ over the monthly figure for a living wage in Bangladesh, but perhaps what is more surprising is that they engage at all with the issue. If shoppers are not to blame for the harm and injustice done to garment workers in Dhaka, then, on this account, nor are supermarkets in so far as they do not own any factories in Bangladesh and are dependent on their subcontracted suppliers to put their own house in order.

4.3   Bad jobs are better than no jobs

For the pro-supermarket lobby, the low price of goods on supermarket shelves in the UK has less to do with poor working conditions in faraway places like Bangladesh and more to do with the efficiency of their bulk buying practices and their ability to reduce overheads. The working conditions in overseas garment factories may be awful at times, but Bangladeshi factory owners have to follow the discipline of the marketplace and pay their workers the 'going rate' for the job. Any other course of action, the lobby concludes, would simply distort the market and leave open the possibility of retailers shifting their business to another low-cost country. The real losers in that case, they argue, would be the Linas of this world.

More importantly for what concerns us here, what underpins this claim is a *positive-sum view* of the power wielded by the big supermarkets.

Martin Wolf (2004), an economic journalist on the *Financial Times*, has put the more general argument that firms like Asda and Sainsbury's, which seek to source their clothing needs at ever cheaper locations abroad, do indeed exploit the poor by taking advantage of the profitable opportunities that a pool of cheap labour represents. But because incoming firms in places like Bangladesh almost invariably pay more than local companies to attract workers, the garment workers fortunate enough to be employed can be said to 'exploit' the outside firms by extracting higher pay from them. The work and the wages may not look much by UK standards, but in Bangladesh they represent an opportunity that previously was not on offer. Seen in this light, Wolf argues that, as low as wages are in the offshore jeans business, both the big corporates and the workers in the overseas factories stand to gain from the global supply arrangement. Rather than a *mutually exclusive* set-up where one side gains at the expense of another, the kind of global arrangement that Wolf has in mind is all about **mutual exploitation**. Workers in places like Bangladesh benefit from the higher wages available that, while far from wonderful, are a measurable improvement on existing livelihoods, and supermarkets gain through their access to pools of cheap labour. As the pro-supermarket lobby would have it, this is a win–win situation which works to the benefit of all parties.

Since the mid 1990s, the garment industry in Bangladesh has expanded rapidly, with some 2.5 million people working in the thousands of factories that have sprung up. In many respects, such factories represent a path out of poverty and, according to Wolf, the last thing a country like this wants is for the big retailers to stop sourcing their labour from them. That, it is pointed out, would threaten the steadily rising living standards of the garment workers. After all, if the factory jobs are so bad, why do Lina and others actively seek them out? In much the same way that shoppers would go elsewhere if the big supermarkets in the UK failed to deliver choice and affordability, so workers in Dhaka would seek work elsewhere if the jobs on offer in the garment industry failed to pay above the local rate. No matter how bad such jobs are perceived to be by shoppers on the high street in London and Birmingham, despite War on Want's protestations, they are comparably better than most other jobs locally available in and around Bangladeshi's capital city. Or so the pro-supermarket lobby insist.

The pro-supermarket lobby would also claim that the efforts of big retailers to source labour globally is yet another example of the use of supermarket power as a force for good, one that enables such retailers, through their global size and reach, to direct resources and materially affect people's lives in different parts of the world. As successful businesses which bring employment to thousands of people in the UK and overseas, the benefits add up to what we can now recognise as a positive-sum scenario where the amount of resources in play represent a *net gain* for all those involved: supermarkets and consumers at the UK end, and suppliers and their workers at the other, somewhat poorer, end. On this view of power, there are no losers, only winners.

So, the argument over whether supermarkets use their power to bring us unprecedented choice at low prices is far from clear-cut. The two sides, the pro-supermarket lobby and those pitted against them, disagree as to the consequences of supermarket power. In this chapter, we have tried to grasp those consequences by employing the concepts of zero-sum and positive-sum games of power. As I hope is now evident, where and how we shop are not as straightforward as may first appear,

Mutual exploitation
An economic situation which both firms and workers are able to exploit to their advantage without either side losing out.

especially when the issue broadens out to encompass the plight of vulnerable workforces and the future of the high street. The power to shape choices has been critical to both sides of the argument: choices not just about what goes into our shopping basket, but choices too, as in Partick and Linwood, over the make-up of communities and also in relation to where in the world companies should invest.

Summary

- The large market share enjoyed by the big supermarket chains also gives them significant buying power. Suppliers claim that this is used to bargain down prices to a level that is often economically devastating.
- Anti-supermarket campaigners claim that through low prices consumers benefit at the expense of vulnerable workers, both in the UK and in factories abroad.
- In response, big supermarkets and the pro-supermarket lobby point to the mutual exploitation of cheap labour that takes place which benefits overseas workers and retail corporations alike, and which materially changes people's lives around the globe for the better.

Conclusion

Activity 5

At this point, I would like you to revisit your answers to Activity 1, more as a means of pulling together the range of issues discussed in the chapter than anything evaluative.

Run down the list of factors which influenced your shopping choices. If you shop at supermarkets and you jotted down, as I did, the choice of a wide range of goods at low prices, how would you square that with the anti-supermarket campaigner's claim that such a choice comes at a high price? For example, the price could be said to involve the denial of choice to others of a living wage or the narrowing of consumer choice along the high street.

You may find it helpful to think about the variety of claims expressed and the assumptions that they are based upon, as well as the evidence used to support them. To give you a broad idea, I have set out the two sides of the argument and their different components in Table 2.

Table 2   Does the power of supermarkets widen or narrow shopping choices?

Argument	Claims	Assumptions	Evidence
Anti-supermarket lobby	• Supermarkets restrict choice over where we shop • The real cost of low prices is borne by suppliers and their workforces	• A zero-sum game: supermarkets prosper at the expense of local high-street stores • A zero-sum game: cheap shopping is at the expense of vulnerable workers at home and abroad	• Local market statistics and the falling number of independently owned shops • Factory surveys and local case studies to highlight poverty and hardship
Pro-supermarket lobby	• Supermarkets provide a wide choice of cheap goods at convenient locations • Exploiting workers to source cheap goods has led to an improvement in living standards	• A positive-sum game: both consumers and local communities benefit from affordable goods and supermarket-led regeneration • A positive-sum game: the mutual exploitation of cheap labour benefits all parties involved, even sweatshop labour	• National market statistics and local regeneration studies • Factory visits and local wage-level comparisons to highlight improved living standards

How do we know?

Making social science arguments 2: which evidence should we believe?

When faced with opposing arguments like those set out in Table 2, does the supporting evidence used help us to decide between them? The straight answer is – yes and no. Yes, because the evidence presented takes us beyond the mere *assertion* of claims and gives us something to evaluate. No, because political arguments, as well as social science accounts, often choose *different* pieces of evidence to support their claims: local or national statistics, for example, or different case studies which point to divergent conclusions. The nub of the issue, which will be explored in depth later in the course, is that it is necessary to explore *how well* the evidence supports the argument given – how well it fits with the claims, and the level of detail involved.

There is a further reason, however, why the evidence does not 'speak for itself', and that is because even the *same* piece of evidence can be *interpreted* differently. The disagreement over what lies behind the falling number of independently owned shops on the high street is one such example. Where anti-supermarket campaigners use that evidence to support their claim that supermarkets have made it difficult for smaller shops to compete and prosper, the pro-supermarket lobby interprets the same data differently, pointing to other social and economic forces at work and the fact that their presence on the high street often enables small traders to survive and flourish.

For now, you should just be aware that the evidence used to support a particular argument needs to be treated with caution. In the social sciences, you need to adopt a *critical* stance towards the evidence used, as much as you would towards the claims expressed in an argument.

Before you move on, I would like you to stand back and reflect a little on the broader implications of the arguments outlined above. In thinking about the ways in which supermarkets use their power and whether those with more power always prevail over those with less, you have opened a window on what power *is* and how it *works*. In the social sciences, power is one of those concepts that features continually in discussions about how we understand the 'forces' which routinely shape our lives. Power matters to just about everything we do and, in particular, whether we are able to do it or not. When a government official tells us what foods are fit and proper to eat or your boss at work makes a managerial decision which affects your hopes and ambitions, these are both instances of power being used to influence our behaviour and our choices. More often than not, power is something that we find ourselves on the receiving end of, where the experience is one of imposition, of not being able to do quite what we had set out to do.

These kinds of powerful acts are felt as pressures on our lives; often as pressures to conform to certain standards or a certain lifestyle that we ourselves did not propose. Yet when it comes to defining what power is and what it can do, social scientists rarely speak with one voice. Power is essentially a contested concept, one that is sometimes used interchangeably with domination and, on other occasions, is defined positively as a benign force which enables things to get done. In that sense it can refer to the power that we have in ourselves to make a difference in the world. In subsequent chapters, you will meet different accounts of power, when for example you consider the nature of identity and who we are, as well as how UK society is governed and the global authorities that come into play.

From this chapter, you can take forward your understanding of power and influence, as it relates to the big supermarkets, by keeping in mind just what kinds of forces are at work when governments, global firms and campaign lobby groups become involved in our lives. Central to this has been the issue as to whether the big four supermarket chains in the UK abuse their power by constraining our choices in ways that leave us little choice but to go along with their interests and goals. The sense in which supermarkets have 'too much power', so that they are able to gain at the expense of just about everyone else, was key to the assertion made by those opposed to supermarket expansion; namely, that the big supermarkets are guilty of tearing the heart out of our high streets. More than that, they are said to have done so by selling goods cheaply at the expense of vulnerable workers in locations often far from where we shop.

Presented in social science terms, this argument effectively portrays the supermarkets as winners in a *zero-sum* game of power, where the big multiples use their power as a force to boost their profits. The losers, as such, are rendered powerless, or at least left unable to resist the onward march of the big supermarkets. The alternative view, as we have seen, however, points to a different kind of power play: that of a *positive-sum* game in which supermarkets as much as shoppers, suppliers as much as distant workforces, have much to gain from the big retailers exercising their power on the high street and beyond. Gain, not pain, could almost be the mantra of the pro-supermarket lobby, as the likes of Asda and Tesco present themselves as a force for the common good.

It is worth noting, however, that, in the opposition that pits War on Want against Asda, or the new economics foundation against Tesco, each side relies upon quite different assets and resources to press its respective claims and interests. The asset-rich Asda, for instance, with the vast economic resources of its US parent, Wal-Mart, behind it, mobilises its power in a way quite different from that of War on Want, whose aim is to mobilise supermarket shoppers by pointedly illustrating the entanglement of their lifestyles with others less well off half way across the world. More power, in this instance in the shape of economic muscle, does not necessarily prevail over what is perceived as less: the resources of the campaign groups who are able to tap into public concerns to give shoppers on the high street a different set of choices.

But there is a related message that you should also take away from this chapter, which is that the connection between our ability to buy cheap supermarket goods and poorly paid workers abroad, whether seen as victims of the system or as the lucky ones with jobs, draws attention to the fact that the global is already *in* the high street. It is present through the food that we buy and the clothes that many of us wear. In that sense, part of what makes the contemporary UK, part of what shapes the choices about where we shop, depends upon others elsewhere doing their bit for what is sometimes less than a living wage. As you move on to the next chapter, you will see that this global connection holds as much for rubbish and waste as it does for food and clothing. Even the clothes on your back may end up, one day, as part of the global recycling industry.

References

All Tomorrow's Particks (undated) [online], http://www.alltomorrowsparticks.org (Accessed 19 November 2008).

Bevan, J. (2006) *Trolley Wars: The Battle of the Supermarkets*, London, Profile Books.

Blythman, J. (2005) *Shopped: The Shocking Power of British Supermarkets*, London, Harper Perennial.

The Co-operative Group (2008) *Corporate Information* [online], www.co-operative.coop/corporate/ (Accessed 20 January 2009).

Competition Commission (2008) *Groceries Market Investigation: Final Report* [online], www.competition-commission.org.uk (Accessed 20 January 2009).

Federation of Small Businesses (2006) *Submission to the Competition Commissioner Inquiry into the UK Grocery Retailing Market* [online], www.competition-commission.org.uk (Accessed 20 January 2009).

Financial Times (2008) 'Supermarkets sweep for shoppers', *Financial Times*, 28 June.

Klein, N. (2000) *No Logo*, London, Flamingo.

Labour Behind the Label/War on Want (2007) *Let's Clean Up Fashion: 2007 Update*, London, War on Want; also available online at http://www.waronwant.org/Latest20Research20for20Download+8247.twl (Accessed 19 November 2008).

Lawrence, F. (2004) *Not on the Label*, London, Penguin.

new economics foundation (2007) *Detrimental Effects: Defending Consumers from Distorted Markets – A Response to the Competition Commission* [online], www.neweconomics.org (Accessed 12 January 2009).

Simms, A. (2007) *Tescopoly*, London, Constable.

SN (Supermarket News) (2008) *CN's Top 25 Worldwide Food Retailers 2008* [online], www.supermarketnews.com/profiles/top25/food_retailers_worldwide/ (Accessed 12 January 2009).

Stop Tesco Owning Partick (STOP) (undated) [online], http://www.stoptesco.info (Accessed 19 November 2008).

Tesco (2007) *Main Submission to the Competition Commission Inquiry into the UK Grocery Retailing Market* [online], www.competition-commission.org.uk (Accessed 12 January 2009).

Tescopoly Alliance (undated) *Tescopoly: Every Little Hurts* [online], http://www.tescopoly.org (Accessed 19 November 2008).

War on Want (2006) *Fashion Victims: The True Cost of Cheap Clothes at Primark, Asda and Tesco*, London, War on Want; also available online at http://

www.waronwant.org/Latest20Research20for20Download+8247.twl (Accessed 19 November 2008).

Wolf, M. (2004) *Why Globalization Works*, New Haven, CT, Yale University Press.

Wrong, D. (1997) *Power: Its Forms, Bases and Uses*, New Brunswick, NJ, and London, Transaction Publishers.

Young, I.M. (2003) 'From guilt to solidarity: sweatshops and political responsibility', *Dissent*, Spring, pp. 39–44.

Young, W. (2004) *Sold Out: The True Cost of Supermarket Shopping*, London, Vision Paperbacks.

Chapter 3
Rubbish society: affluence, waste and values

Vivienne Brown

Contents

Introduction

Out of sight?

Imagine the scene: there's another ten minutes before the alarm goes off. It's warm under the covers and those extra minutes of retreat from a cold November morning are the most delicious of all… Then, crash!, bang!, the sound of a mechanical pulveriser and the voices of the people working on the refuse lorry remind you that it's rubbish collection day on your street. Normally the refuse lorry has been and gone by the time you wake up, its load whisked off out of the way and out of sight; but this time you are reminded of its existence.

Then you remember that you forgot to put out the rubbish! There was much more this time too: the cardboard packaging for the new TV and computer, and the leftover food as well as the empty bottles and cans from the party you had on Saturday night (not to mention the broken glass and the disposable cutlery, plates and plastic cups). The newspapers and magazines had piled up too and needed to be got rid of. Oh, and the old TV and computer.

Where to put it all now?

Rubbish seems to be the invisible part of consumption. The passage above might suggest that household rubbish needs to be got rid of, and that it ought to be out of the way and out of sight. It can even become offensive if it is not put where it should be – left in the street, for example, instead of stowed away in a rubbish bin before being taken away in a refuse lorry. But rubbish doesn't get there on its own; getting rid of it, or putting it out of sight, requires time, effort and organisation.

Moreover, rubbish doesn't just disappear when it is got rid of by households. The early morning refuse lorry and its contents might be invisible to those still asleep in bed, but collecting household rubbish from the street and disposing of it has to be organised and funded. Disposing of the rubbish involves complicated processes and a chain of activities that might extend around the world. In these respects disposal of rubbish raises similar issues to production and other aspects of consumption which involve the integration of activities across the globe.

In previous chapters you have learned about consumer society, its uneven qualities and how power is exercised by large organisations. In this chapter we'll be studying an aspect of consumption that is easy to overlook – the rubbish that is generated as part of social life. In the process we'll see that issues of rubbish have plenty to tell us about the society we live in. This will include issues of 'value' and 'wastefulness' which are discussed in Sections 1 and 2, and the interconnections between consumer society, rising affluence and environmental unsustainability which are the focus of Section 3. You will also encounter more ideas and approaches that social scientists use in studying the world. In previous chapters you have learned about concepts and the use of evidence. In this chapter we look at the use of theories and models which can aid our understanding of how society is made.

1 Rubbish and values

1.1 Rubbish as disvalued

What is rubbish? One answer is that it is something that has no **value**; it is disvalued. It is what nobody wants, so it is worthless and has zero value. This seems straightforward, but 'value' is a complex term. Items don't simply have value by virtue of their physical properties. Items have value because people value them, or rather values are given or assigned to items by people who value them. Similarly, if rubbish has no value, this is because people disvalue it (not because the item is in and of itself worthless). So looking at rubbish, just as looking at items of high value, can tell us something about the social processes that are involved in valuing, or in this case, devaluing, an item.

To add to the complexity, the notion of 'value' can take on different senses. Sometimes 'value' refers to the usefulness of something. We can think of this as 'use value'. Sometimes 'value' refers to how something is esteemed or viewed as worthwhile for its own sake. We can think of this as 'intrinsic value'. Sometimes 'value' takes on an economic dimension in referring to price. In this sense, something of great value is expensive and something that has no value has a low or zero price. Sometimes, too, 'value' refers to a norm or principle of what is right or wrong. For example, to live according to your values is to live in a way that is consistent with what you think is right or what you think you ought to do. In such cases value takes on a normative sense, in that it provides principles for right action or guides people's decisions about what they ought and ought not to do.

These different senses of 'value' can make it a slippery notion. Sometimes it's used with more than one sense, and it's easy to shift from one sense to another without noticing. I suggested above that rubbish is what has no value. And now I've suggested that the notion of 'value' can take different senses. If this is so, then the notion of 'rubbish' – as something of no value – might also share in these different senses. It has no use. It is worthless. It is not esteemed. It might even be found offensive or may elicit feelings of disgust. It might arouse normative attitudes as to what ought to be done with it. It has a zero price. For example, compare 'Rubbish and empty bottles ought not to be left on your bedroom floor' and 'My computer is rubbish now and isn't worth selling on eBay'.

Value
A complex term that can refer to how useful something is, or the extent to which something is regarded as worthwhile, or the extent to which it can command a price. It can also refer to a 'norm' or principle of what is right and wrong.

Activity 1

Can you find an example in the Introduction to this chapter where rubbish is referred to in a normative way?

The Introduction uses normative language when it says that the opening passage might suggest that household rubbish 'ought to be out of the way and out of sight'. This is in contrast with descriptive language, such as when it says that 'rubbish doesn't just disappear when it is got rid of by households'.

1.2   Rubbish, wastefulness and affluence

In addition to rubbish, there is also 'wasting' as an activity or process. Wasting things is to use them extravagantly or use them up for no good purpose. Similarly 'wastefulness' suggests that objects are not being used as they should. For example, food is 'wasted' if thrown away unnecessarily and electricity is 'wasted' if lights are left on unnecessarily. This suggests that the notion of 'wastefulness' tends to be normative. But this then raises the question of what is 'necessary'. What is considered 'wasteful' is compared against some benchmark or standard of what constitutes appropriate use, proper husbandry of resources, or perhaps conventionally sanctioned standards of comfort and convenience.

We can see this normative notion of wastefulness in a report, *The Food We Waste* (WRAP, 2008a, 2008b). This report presents evidence that as much as one third of the food bought in the UK each year is thrown away – about 6.7 million tonnes of food. This includes fresh fruit and vegetables, bakery items, fish and meat meals. The report calculates that 61 per cent of the amount thrown away – amounting to £420 each year on average for every household in the UK – is wasted unnecessarily in that it could be avoided with better food management. The report is thus working with a standard of good food management, such as not buying more than is going to be used and not cooking more than is likely to be eaten. This standard then provides the benchmark for assessing how much of the food thrown away is being wasted unnecessarily.

Food waste is only one part of household rubbish. It was reported in 2008 that UK households threw away almost 30 million tonnes of rubbish. Can you visualise how much this amounts to? Waste Online recalculates rubbish data as 'wacky waste facts' in a way that they think is easier for people to visualise. They recalculated this figure as the equivalent in weight of 3.5 million double-decker buses, a queue of which would stretch from London to Sydney (Australia) and back (Waste Online, 2008).

A different way of visualising rubbish data

Perhaps the amount of household rubbish is easier to visualise if you think about it in per capita terms (average per person). In 2006/07 the amount of household rubbish for each person in England was 508 kg. This compares with 397 kg in 1983/84 (Defra, 2007). This amounts to an increase of 28 per cent between 1983/84 and 2006/07. Household rubbish per person was thus over a quarter higher in the early years of the twenty-first century than in the 1980s.

This raises two questions. First, an explanatory question: why did household rubbish increase over this period? Second, a normative question: was this increase acceptable or was it too high? I will deal with each question in turn.

Why did household rubbish increase?

The increase in total household rubbish was the result of a number of factors. One of these factors was the growth of mass consumption. As you saw in Chapter 1, shopping and consumption have become more significant in social life. Supermarkets carry a greater range of products than ever before, many of which were unavailable even in the recent past. As you saw in Chapter 2, this introduction of an increasing range and variety of foods at prices that many households could afford is something that the supermarkets claim to their advantage. People in the UK have more clothing and shoes than ever before, eat a wider range of food than even before, and increasingly their homes are fitted with appliances and facilities that would have been undreamed of or classed in the luxury bracket in the past.

Affluence
A high level of prosperity.

Along with this mass consumption there has been rising **affluence**; that is, rising prosperity, in the UK, which makes it possible to afford a higher standard of living. Evidence for this rising affluence can be seen in everyday observation. But can we get an exact measure of something as diffuse as 'rising affluence'? There are different statistics that can provide estimates. No one set of data can give us an exact measure, but taken together they can give an overall estimate.

One approach to measuring rising affluence is to estimate the proportion of total household income that is spent on necessities. With rising affluence this proportion would fall: a smaller proportion of income would be spent on necessities leaving a larger proportion for inessential items and luxuries. This approach makes a lot of sense, although the categories of 'necessities' and 'luxuries' might be open to different definitions. What is a necessity to one person might be a luxury to another, even where they have the same income. Furthermore, what are deemed to be 'necessities' and 'luxuries' arc in turn influenced by the level of affluence. When cars were first invented they were in the luxury category and were owned only by the rich.

Activity 2

Can you think of another example where a good has moved from the luxury category to the necessity category?

There are many possible answers, but when I thought about it, having a black and white television in the 1950s was regarded as a luxury, but now colour television is standard. Advances in TV technology, however, have resulted in a differentiation of the product, for example, with the development of LCD and plasma screens, so that within the category of colour TVs some are still regarded as 'luxury' items.

Keeping these issues in mind, we can examine whether changing proportions of income spent on different kinds of goods and services can tell us something about rising affluence. In Chapter 1, Figure 5 you saw how much, on average, UK households spent on the main categories of goods and services in 2007. How would you expect the proportions spent on different categories of expenditure to compare with fifty years previously?

Activity 3

If people in the UK experienced rising affluence over this fifty-year period, what would you expect to have happened to the proportions spent on different categories of goods and services?

If people experienced rising affluence over the period, then we would expect a smaller proportion to be spent on necessities and a larger proportion to be spent on luxuries. There is some evidence to support this. Table 1 presents data on UK household spending in 1957 and 2006. Constructing data across a fifty-year period cannot be exact as statistical definitions and categories change. In addition, new products come into being and old ones disappear so that the categories used in the data collection change over time. As I noted above, TVs changed hugely over this period. Yet even though an exact comparison can't be made, the data suggest a story that is compatible with rising affluence over the period.

Table 1   UK household expenditure in 1957 and 2006

Commodity or service	1957 Percentage of total expenditure	Commodity or service	2006 Percentage of total expenditure
Housing	9	Housing (net)	19
Fuel, light and power	6	Fuel and power	3
Food	33	Food and non-alcoholic drinks	15
Alcoholic drink	3	Alcoholic drink	3
Tobacco	6	Tobacco	1
Clothing and footwear	10	Clothing and footwear	5
Durable household goods	8	Household goods	8
Other goods	7	Household services	6
Transport and vehicles	8	Motoring, fares and other travel costs	16
Services	9	Personal goods and services	4
		Leisure goods	4
		Leisure services	15
All	100%	All	100%

Source: ONS, 2008a, p. 3

Table 1 shows the percentage of total household spending on various categories of goods and services in 1957 and 2006. The proportion of total expenditure on 'food' in 1957 can be found by reading along the third row of data. This proportion was 33 per cent, which means that 33 per cent of average household expenditure was on food. Reading further along this same row, we can see that in 2006 the proportion spent on 'food and non-alcoholic drinks' was down to 15 per cent. If we take food as a necessity then the proportion spent on this necessity more than halved over the fifty-year period. The proportion spent on clothing and footwear also halved, from 10 per cent to 5 per cent. A category that increased is that of 'services'. Adding together household services, personal goods and services, and leisure services in 2006 comes to 25 per cent. In 1957, only 9 per cent of income was spent on services. Expenditure on services tends to be associated with non-necessities, such as meals out, hairdressing, entertainment and sports activities. Thus the proportion of expenditure on non-necessities increased over the period. As noted above, because of category changes the comparison across the fifty-year period is only approximate. Nonetheless, Table 1 gives some evidence on the rising affluence associated with mass consumption.

In addition to looking at expenditure, we could also look at income and earnings in order to estimate rising affluence. Household disposable (after tax) income increased between 1971 and 2006 by nearly 150 per cent (ONS, 2008b). That is, household incomes per head more than doubled over this period. In case it might be thought that this increase was largely the result of dual household earners, with more women going into paid employment, it's worth noting that earnings per employee also increased. Earnings per employee increased between 1990 and 2007 by 40 per cent (ONS, 2008c, 2008d). The increase in per capita household income over this period was 41 per cent. These increases are 'real' increases in that they take account of rising prices over the period. These data on income and earnings, indicating rising affluence, are shown in Figures 1 and 2.

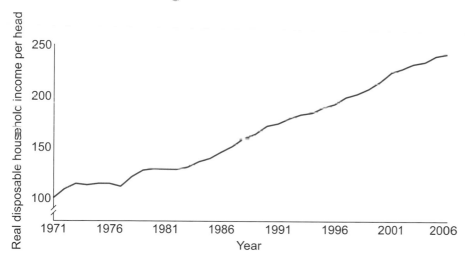

Figure 1   Real disposable household income per head, 1971–2006, UK (Source: ONS, 2008b, p. 62)

(Figure 1 and Figure 2 are based on data calculated as index numbers with base year = 100. This provides a ready way of adjusting for the change in prices over the period. It also makes it easy to work out

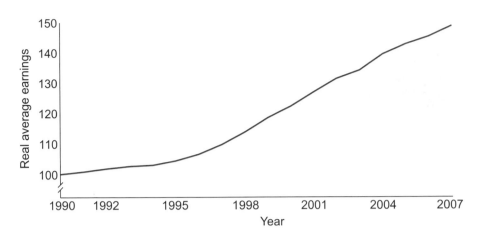

Figure 2   Real average earnings, 1990–2007, UK (Source: ONS, 2008c, 2008d)

percentage changes from the base year, as the difference between any year and the base year gives the percentage change over the intervening period.)

The data in Table 1 and Figures 1 and 2 illustrate how the mass consumption you studied in Chapters 1 and 2 was associated with rising affluence over the period. This also helps to explain the increase in rubbish and the amount of food being wasted. With rising affluence people can afford to buy more products and to replace them more frequently. Most of these products have a faster rate of technological obsolescence than previously, since advances in technology and in electronics-based products have introduced not only new products but also new generations of existing products. Many products also come with elaborate packaging that has to be disposed of. There's also an increased disposability of products, such as disposable nappies and paper products.

In addition to this plethora of mass consumption, rising affluence also affects people's choices between labour-intensive and labour-saving activities. With rising earnings, people's time and labour become more highly valued. This is also the case for women and girls, who had fewer paid employment opportunities previously. The result is a shift towards labour-saving devices. This can be seen in factories where machinery replaces routine manual tasks, but it is also evident around the home where there is a switch towards labour-saving activities. There is less making do, mending, darning and basic cooking (traditionally part of women's domestic work), which are labour-intensive, and a switch

Rubbish – the detritus of consumer society

toward labour-saving appliances, which eventually have to be disposed of, and disposability. Similarly, repair services for household goods and appliances have become more expensive (or even non-existent), so that it becomes cheaper to throw away an item and buy a new one than to get something repaired.

So, explaining the growth in rubbish over recent years involves interrelations between rising affluence, economy-wide shifts between labour-intensive and labour-saving technologies, changing gender roles, and the impact of technological change on consumer products. Explaining the growth in rubbish thus keys into broad issues of social change affecting different areas of people's lives.

This is not to suggest that there is an exact relationship between affluence and rubbish, at an individual level, household level or country level. Individual examples of wastefulness and frugality can be found at different income levels. The overall relation between affluence, consumption, rubbish and wastefulness is affected by many factors, as we shall see in the course of this chapter.

Note that the data on income and earnings cover the period *before* the credit crunch and the onset of recession in 2008. Furthermore, the rising affluence of that period was accompanied by increased indebtedness. By late 2008, average household debt was approximately £9633 (excluding mortgages), suggesting that some of the consumption of the period was financed by increasing indebtedness (Credit Action, 2008). Total UK personal debt, including mortgages, amounted to an unprecedented £1455 billion. This placed UK households in a weaker position to cope with the 'credit crunch' that came with the crisis in the global banking system in 2008. Heavy indebtedness was dramatically shown not to be **sustainable** for many households.

Sustainability
The capacity to endure or continue over the long term.

Is the increase in rubbish acceptable?

We have seen that apparently wasteful practices that save time and effort might seem worth it in an economy where labour is valued highly. For example, disposable nappies might seem worth it to busy parents; and buying additional food at the weekly supermarket trip might seem worth it to a busy household, even if there is some waste involved, if it protects against running out of something midweek. What seems 'wasteful' in terms of goods or food might be the result of careful planning by those who are time-short. Does this make the rubbish more acceptable?

Apparent wastefulness might also have other returns. For example, ostentatious consumption has symbolic significance; it illustrates wealth, taste or perhaps power. (Sometimes it might have negative symbolic significance: too much 'bling' might suggest lack of taste?) It is this symbolic return that is being purchased with what might otherwise seem to be wasteful consumption. So, conspicuous consumption, which you met in Chapter 1, could be regarded as wasteful consumption in some respects, but not in other respects if it has symbolic or social value. And, for many people, expenditure on items such as clothing, hairdressing, home furnishings, leisure activities, and so on, includes an element of symbolic consumption that is geared to perceptions of what is deemed fashionable, cool or chic. Wastefulness might also bring in returns of political power. Vast expenditures on the dignities of office (such as royalty or state presidents), on state ceremony or church ceremony, on armies and weapons that might never be used, might seem 'wasteful' in a literal sense, but there are political returns and so they might be deemed necessary in terms of their political functioning.

In recent years, however, there has been a radically new understanding of the implications of rubbish and wastefulness, and this has to do with their environmental effects. Quite simply put, people in the more affluent countries are consuming (including wasting) at a rate that is **environmentally unsustainable**, thus putting at risk the ability of the planet's ecosystem to continue into the future. There are different approaches to estimating environmental unsustainability. According to one approach, which estimates humanity's annual 'global footprint', in 2008 humankind was annually using up the biological capacity of 1.4 planet Earths (Global Footprint Network, 2008a; nef, 2008). That is equivalent to saying that in 2008 the annual ecological overshoot – the degree to which global resources are used up faster than can be replaced each year, and the degree to which waste (including carbon) is generated faster than can be reabsorbed each year – was 40 per cent greater than the annual resources of the Earth.

According to Global Footprint Network's (GFN) estimate, this degree of unsustainability developed over little more than twenty years. Prior to 1986 humanity was using up less each year than the Earth's annual capacity, although the rate at which the planet's annual resources were being used was increasing rapidly in the years prior to 1986. This is shown in Figure 3 which gives estimates for the period 1961 to 2005, plus 2008.

Figure 3 shows GFN's estimate of the relation between the annual global use of the Earth's resources (upward-sloping line) and planet Earth's annual biocapacity (horizontal line), from 1961 to 2005, plus 2008, where both are expressed in terms of 'number of planets' (the estimated biocapacity of the Earth is always recorded 1). In 1961 the annual global use of resources amounted to 54 per cent (0.54) of the Earth's capacity. By 1986 the annual global use of resources equalled the planet's capacity for the first time (this is where the upward-sloping line, showing global use of resources, crosses the horizontal line, showing the Earth's biocapacity). Since then humankind has increasingly used up more each year than the Earth can replenish. By 2005 the ecological overshoot was estimated at 30 per cent (1.3 Earths were used up). For 2008, as we saw above, it was estimated at 40%. According to these

Environmental unsustainability
The degree to which the Earth's resources and waste absorption capacities are being used up faster than can be replenished.

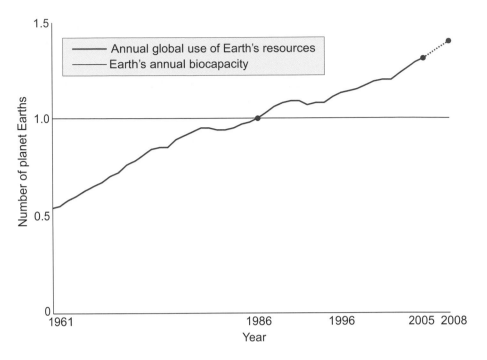

Figure 3   Humanity's ecological footprint, 1961–2008 (Source: GFN, 2008b)

estimates, therefore, environmental unsustainability measured in terms of global footprint grew from 0 per cent to about 40 per cent in little more than twenty years, with the rate of unsustainability apparently increasing more rapidly in the latter part of the period.

Increasing unsustainability has led to fears that the planet may reach an environmental 'tipping point' at which its ecosystems may be damaged beyond repair, with possibly devastating effects for human survival in the future. This is captured by the date each year by which it is estimated that humankind has used up the Earth's annual productive resources, a date known as 'Ecological Debt Day' (or Earth Overshoot Day), also based on the global footprint estimates. In 2008, Ecological Debt Day was estimated to be 23 September, the earliest date ever (nef, 2008; Global Footprint Network, 2008a). Just as excessive financial debt is unsustainable in the long term, so is ecological debt, the environmentalists argue, but with the difference that the ultimate day of environmental reckoning will be that much harder for humankind to adjust to.

In spite of the difficulties and uncertainties involved in estimation, growing awareness of the unsustainability of current consumption has led to a shift in perceptions of rubbish and wastefulness. The slogan 'reduce, reuse and recycle' has become part of a social and policy shift towards reducing rubbish and wastefulness, and recycling what can't be reused. In the report *The Food We Waste* (which I referred to in Section 1.2), it was noted that not only does wasted food cost money – to households (£420 per household each year on average) and to local authorities (about £1 billion each year to send it to landfill) – but the environmental consequences are unacceptable. The report argues that ending the waste of good food in the UK would save 18 million tonnes of carbon dioxide, equivalent to taking one in five cars off the road (WRAP, 2008b, p. 03).

The effects of this shift in attitudes towards rubbish and wastefulness can be seen in the change in the levels of rubbish in the early years of the twenty-first century. As we saw in Section 1.2, per capita household rubbish in England increased by 28 per cent between 1983/84 and 2006/07. But within this period there was a reduction: the amount of per capita household rubbish increased steadily to 2002/03, but then it fell during the period from 2002/03 to 2006/07. This is shown in Table 2.

Table 2 Household rubbish and recycling, per capita, 1983/84 to 2006/07, England (kg per person per year)

	1983/ 84	1991/ 92	1995/ 96	1997/ 98	1999/ 00	2001/ 02	2002/ 03	2003/ 04	2004/ 05	2005/ 06	2006/ 07
Rubbish not recycled	394	417	421	440	453	452	445	420	397	370	351
Rubbish recycled/ composted	3	11	29	39	52	65	75	91	115	135	157
Total rubbish	397	428	451	480	505	516	520	510	512	505	508
Rate of rubbish recycled/ composted as % of total rubbish	1%	3%	6%	8%	10%	13%	14%	18%	22%	27%	31%

Source: Defra, 2007, Table 4

Table 2 shows the total amount of per capita household rubbish (in bold, third row down). It also shows how this total is divided between unrecycled and recycled/composted rubbish (top two rows). The bottom row gives the recycled/composted rubbish as a percentage of total rubbish. The table shows that up until 2002/03 the total amount of rubbish increased every year; in that year it was 520 kg per person. Since 2002/03, however, the total amount of rubbish has fallen, although not consistently year by year, to 508 kg in 2006/07. So although, as we saw earlier, there was a 28 per cent increase between 1983/84 and 2006/07, this was smaller than the increase between 1983/04 and 2002/03, which was 31 per cent. This suggests that, at least over this latter period, the relation between rubbish, waste and affluence was undergoing a shift: people started to reduce their rubbish, even though real incomes continued to rise. Note though that the total amount of rubbish in 2006/07 was still greater than the total amount of rubbish in any year from 1983/84 to 1999/2000.

Activity 4

Describe the data in Table 2 on the rate of rubbish recycled/composted.

There is an increase in the rate of rubbish recycled/composted for every year shown in the table. There was a gradual increase in the recycling/composting rate from 1983/84 to 2002/03, but the rate rose more rapidly after 2002/03. For example, in the three years from 1999/2000 to 2002/03, the recycling/composting rate increased by 4 percentage points, from 10 per cent to 14 per cent. During the next three years, from 2002/03 to 2005/06, it increased by 13 percentage points, from 14 per cent to 27 per cent.

So, UK households were beginning to throw away less than previously *and* a higher proportion of that smaller amount of rubbish was being recycled/composted. This was related to changes introduced by local authorities, but it also suggests that there was a change in people's perception of rubbish. What had previously seemed to be acceptable levels of rubbish, no longer appeared to be so, and this was reflected in people's behaviour. Whether the change is sufficient to affect rates of environmental unsustainability is, of course, another matter.

1.3   The rubbish business

So far I've concentrated on the fact that rubbish has no value. That is, rubbish has no value to the person who throws it away. It may even have 'negative value', in that disposing of it costs time and money. If you have to take your old TV and computer to the council tip for disposal, then they have negative value for you. This is because you have to give up your time and incur transport costs to take the TV and computer to the tip.

But your rubbish may potentially have value for others. This helps to explain why there is 'rubbish business'. There are businesses that make money out of collecting and disposing of rubbish. The old saying 'where there's muck, there's brass' still has some truth. These businesses turn rubbish into something of value. They do this by transforming it into saleable products or by moving it elsewhere for disposal.

With the development of recycling technologies there are more possibilities for recycling. The 'rag-and-bone man' of past times has been replaced by businesses, some of which operate international disposal and recycling operations. We saw in Section 1.2 above that labour-intensive repair work is economically most viable where incomes tend to be low. Just as in the case of global supply chains that you came across in Chapter 2, labour-intensive methods are cheaper in countries where wages are lower (after taking transport costs into account) and where there are fewer safety regulations to protect workers. Labour-intensive disposal processes therefore also tend to be carried out in low-income countries, whereas the more high-tech automated disposal processes tend to be carried out in high-income countries.

There is thus an international disposal and recycling industry just as there is an international consumption goods industry. This is illustrated by the arrival at Felixstowe in November 2006 of the *Emma Maersk*, which was then the largest container ship in the world, able to carry 11,000 containers.

The *Emma Maersk* was arriving at the UK (and other countries in Europe) from China full of consumer goods for Christmas. But having delivered the Christmas goods, the same ship returned to China loaded with products for disposal and recycling. This illustrates both the scale of consumption and disposal, and their joint internationalisation. Here again we can see the connection between labour-intensive low-wage processes in both the production of consumption goods and the disposal of those goods once they become rubbish.

The process of recycling can thus give new value to rubbish and waste by producing outputs that have positive value; that is, positive prices. This often involves transporting rubbish and waste around the world and back again in the form of recycled products for use in production or as new consumer products. For example, there has been a growth of recycling in paper, cardboard, glass and plastic products, which are then

The *Emma Maersk*

sold at a price that covers the cost of the recycling (providing that the price of these materials is high enough to make the recycling process cost effective).

Unwanted household and personal goods aren't always thrown away. Sometimes they get passed on in other ways. Donations to charity shops, passing on to friends and family members, car boot sales, internet auction sites such as eBay, and local second-hand shops, all provide ways in which unwanted goods are channelled to where they are valued more. These activities also give value to rubbish, or revalorise it, since there are others who value the items more than the person who wants to dispose of them.

Next we will use this understanding of the social complexities of rubbish to look in more detail at how values change over time and how social scientists have studied and come to understand these changes.

Summary

In this section we have started to think about the social and environmental aspects of rubbish. In particular you should note:

- Notions of 'value' take on different senses, including use value, intrinsic value, economic value and normative value.

- Evidence of rising affluence in the UK in recent decades is given by data on the composition of expenditure, real per capita household incomes, and average real earning.

- Part of the mass consumption of the early years of the twenty-first century was financed by unsustainable debt.

- Global human consumption, including rubbish, is environmentally unsustainable: it has been estimated that in 2008 global annual consumption amounted to 40 per cent more than the planet's annual resource and reabsorptive capacity.

- Levels of rubbish disposal and what is regarded as wastefulness are influenced by many factors, including mass consumption, rising affluence, changing gender relations, symbolic returns and, most recently, understanding the implications of environmental unsustainability.

2   Revaluation and rubbish

2.1   The category of 'rubbish'

In the previous sections we looked at some of the ways in which rubbish relates to different kinds of value, including normative values and economic values. And we also saw that rubbish and wastefulness are affected by a range of factors, including rising affluence, gender relations and environmental awareness. This suggests that what is regarded as rubbish – as fit only to be thrown away, stored out of sight, recycled, given away, or disposed of by other means – may also be influenced by a range of social factors.

Ideas change as to what constitutes 'rubbish'. Objects may be redefined – first into the category of rubbish, and then out of the category of rubbish.

Activity 5

Can you think of something which you regarded as rubbish but which you then decided or discovered wasn't rubbish?

Michael Thompson, in his book *Rubbish Theory: The Creation and Destruction of Value* (1979), is interested in how objects pass into and out of the category of rubbish. In examining this he argued that there are three different categories of objects:

- *Objects produced for ordinary use:* These Thompson classes as 'transient' because their value tends to fall over time with use. Examples would be clothing and mobile phones.

- *A 'rubbish' category of virtually zero value:* Examples would be worn-out clothing that nobody wants to wear and obsolete or broken mobile phones.

- *A 'durable' category whose value increases over time:* Examples would be works of art, quality jewellery and collectors' items. It also includes museum and heritage pieces.

Thompson argues that objects may be produced for either the transient category (items of mass consumption) or the durable category (items of elite consumption), and he notes the social distinctions this entails. One of the things that interests him is how some items move from the transient category into the durable category. He argues that this transition is made via the category of rubbish. Thus, although invisible and out of sight, rubbish plays an important role in the way that some items are revalued as they move from being transients to durables. In value terms, this implies that when an object moves from the transient to the durable category, its price first falls to zero (or effectively zero).

This is the core of Thompson's 'rubbish theory'. It is a **theory** in that it is a conceptual framework for explaining how something is the way it is or how something comes to be what it is. Thompson's rubbish theory explains how rubbish is both made and then unmade as some things lose and then gain value over time.

Thompson's theory can be illustrated by a graph which shows the change in an object's value as it moves from transient to durable via rubbish. In Figure 4, value (that is, price) is measured on the vertical axis and time on the horizontal axis.

Theory
A conceptual framework for explaining how things are, and/or a coherent body of thinking which can help us to make more sense of the things we study.

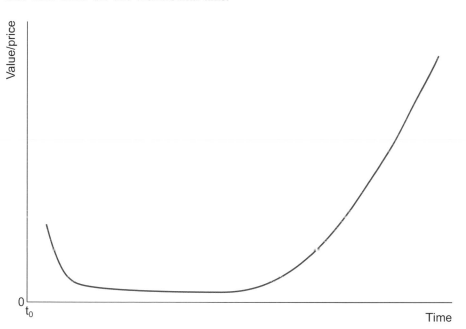

Figure 4   Thompson's 'rubbish theory' (Source: Thompson, 1979)

The line depicting an object's value first falls, then effectively becomes zero, and finally rises. This illustrates an object's move from transient to durable via the category of rubbish. Thompson's notion of 'zero value' is somewhat elastic, however, and includes low price as well as zero price.

An example Thompson provides is that of Stevengraphs. These are silk-woven pictures which were made popular by a Coventry silk weaver Thomas Stevens (1828–88). Stevens used his improved version of the Jacquard loom to weave coloured silk pictures and illustrations for bookmarks and other items such as calendars, fans and sashes. The subjects included portraits of British royalty and other notables (such as aristocrats, politicians, celebrities and sportsmen), royal marriages, English and Scottish castles, London sights, bridges, sporting events, and mythical and historical scenes. These silkworks were modestly priced, many being sold and bought as souvenirs, but from 1879 they provided Stevens with a lucrative business at a time when Coventry was suffering from new international competition arising from the Cobden Treaty, a free-trade treaty of 1860, and changes in fashion away from silk ribbons. Some examples are shown in Figure 5.

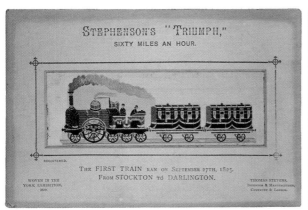 

Figure 5   Two examples of Stevengraphs

On the basis of published price data (Godden, 1971), Thompson noted the trend of prices of Stevengraphs from their production in the latter part of the nineteenth century to the early 1970s. He noted that a Stevengraph depicting 'Dick Turpin's ride to York in 1739' sold for a shilling (that is, 5 pence) in 1879 but had become virtually unsaleable by around the middle of the twentieth century, except for a few individual collectors, particularly in the USA. Then, however, these Stevengraphs picked up in value so that by the 1960s and 1970s they were selling for considerable sums as collectors' pieces. Thus items that were popular in the late nineteenth century came to be seen as 'Victorian kitsch' in the early and middle decades of the twentieth century, but then became transformed into items of value.

The evidence for Thompson's theory is not altogether clear, even for the Stevengraphs. Moreover, as a theory it cannot tell us what happens for all categories of rubbish. But it does help us to think about how rubbish can be a temporary state for some items, when they are moving from being transient to being durable goods. Being rubbish is not necessarily a fixed property, but may be part of a process which involves the creation, destruction and remaking of value.

As we saw in Section 1.1, talk of 'values' tends to slide between different kinds of valuation, for example, economic valuation and normative valuation. Thompson's example of Stevengraphs also suggests that different kinds of revaluation are going on. Two kinds in particular are economic revaluation and aesthetic revaluation; these are considered in more detail in Sections 2.2 and 2.3 respectively.

2.2   Economic revaluation

Thompson offers a description of the social processes involved in the revaluation of Stevengraphs. First, he writes as a sociologist in considering individual buyers and their social backgrounds. He then goes on to consider how such individual transactions could result in considerable price changes:

> Let us postulate that initially one individual suddenly in a blinding flash, as it were, sees an item not as rubbish but as a durable and that his example is followed by another and another and so on, until eventually everyone is agreed that the item is durable. From a logical point of view such a transfer might appear rather unlikely yet in practice it does happen, though not without difficulty, opposition, and confusion. The fact is that individuals are continually making bizarre and eccentric evaluations, the great majority of which do not even trigger off a second such evaluation …

> So, out of this vast range of possible value transformations a tiny fraction actually gain acceptance. When looked at in detail one of these transformations is seen to be effected by a cumulative sequence of eccentric evaluations which, as they accumulate, become progressively less eccentric.

> (Thompson, 1979, pp. 26–7)

Thompson here is tracing what he terms the early 'eccentric' revaluations, particularly in the USA, as being out of line with (what he argued were) the generally zero or very low evaluation of Stevengraphs at that time. These individual eccentric evaluations might not have had any further effect. They were made in isolation of what others thought and they reflected the personal tastes of the few people involved. But as it happened, these eccentric evaluations later began to gain acceptance.

Thompson goes on to remark that these were 'ideal collecting conditions' (1979, p. 29; quoting Goddard, 1971, p. 27). Here Thompson moves into an economic analysis of the early collecting period before a well-defined market emerged in the 1960s. He notes that there was an easy availability or plentiful 'supply' of the Stevengraphs. Also there were only a few people collecting them – 'a general lack of demand' (Thompson, 1979, p. 29; quoting Goddard, 1971, p. 27). The combination of plentiful **supply** and lack of **demand** meant that the early collectors could pick up Stevengraphs cheaply. This analysis is using the language of economics (demand, supply, price, market) rather than the language of sociology in observing behaviours. It is focusing not on the particular evaluations of individual collectors, but on the economic conditions within which such individual collectors were operating. A sociological analysis is combined with an economic one, as the low price of the Stevengraphs during this period is explained in terms of a combination of low demand and plentiful supply.

But then, somehow, according to Thompson, these revaluations caught on and the price of Stevengraphs underwent a tenfold increase in price between 1967 and 1969 when some Stevengraphs were put up for sale at well-known fine art auctioneers. So what changed in economic terms?

The overall effect of the early purchases of these individual collectors was an increase in demand. And this increase in demand resulted in an increase in the price. This increase in price then became a public event that provided a benchmark for other transactions. Whether the price of Stevengraphs would continue to rise would depend on the interaction of demand and supply. With the increased general interest in Stevengraphs and the publicity they were receiving, some new collectors were attracted into the market to start buying them. Some collectors were attracted by the expectation of further price rises in the future, and so bought Stevengraphs as an investment in the hope of a profitable return later on. As Stevengraphs were no longer in production at this time, the total number in existence was fixed. This provided a cap on the extent of supply. On the other hand, there were many Stevengraphs in private

Supply
A measure of the availability of a good or service.

Demand
A measure of consumers' willingness and ability to pay for a good or service.

collections which later became available in response to the increase in price, or for other reasons, so the supply of them onto the market continued to increase.

We have seen that Thompson moves from a sociological to an economic account of the emergence of a developed market in Stevengraphs. Note too how there is a shift towards the notion of **market price** rather than thinking in terms of individual transactions. Market price is a general notion of the going or normal price of a good or service. This notion of market price may be based on an average price across many transactions for a product (for example, the average price of apples). Or it may be based on a benchmark price for a detailed specification of a kind of good (for example, the list price of a particular make and model of car of a particular age). Or it may be based on a representative example of a type of good (for example, the price of a representative semi-detached three-bedroomed house in Scotland). What all these have in common is the idea of a going or normal price of a good, even though in practice the actual price of an example of the good may not be exactly the same as that price.

Market price
The going or normal price of a good or service.

Market price can be analysed in terms of the interaction of demand and supply.

Demand is influenced by the following factors

* *Fashion and taste:* Other things being equal, items that are fashionable will be more sought after by consumers. The increasing appreciation of Stevengraphs was a vital part of the establishment of a market for them.
* *Income:* As real income increases, the more consumers can afford to spend. It's possible that the increasing affluence of the 1960s contributed to a rise in demand for Stevengraphs.
* *Expectations concerning future movements in price:* If people expect the price of a good to rise in the future, this will make it attractive to buy now. Seeing the rising price of Stevengraphs in the 1960s, collectors would have had an incentive to buy them as a financial investment.

Supply is influenced by the following factors

* *Availability and costs of the inputs for producing the good (if it is a reproducible good):* This includes the raw materials for production and labour costs (wages). Stevengraphs were already-produced items.

- *The degree of rarity or exclusivity of the good:* Some goods can be reproduced in large quantities. Others are of limited availability, including rare items such as antiques, special editions, the fixed number of tickets for an event, and exclusive designer items. Stevengraphs are of limited availability; those in a good state with bright colours, or produced in smaller quantity, have a rarity value (Godden, 1971, p. 53).

To understand the reasons for the price change of any particular good at any particular moment in time involves a detailed knowledge of the circumstances. But economists have formulated some general principles for explaining price changes in terms of demand and supply, and these principles can be applied to any situation. Two general principles are fundamental:

1   Price rises when demand increases relative to supply.

2   Price falls when demand falls relative to supply.

Model

A conceptual framework for working out causal explanations.

Market model

A conceptual framework for working out a causal explanation of market price.

These general principles provide us with the beginnings of a basic **market model** for explaining market price. A market model is a conceptual framework for explaining market price in terms of demand and supply. This is a causal model because it explains market price as caused by, or as resulting from, the interaction of demand and supply.

This market model can be applied in very different situations. This means that, for any particular price change that we want to explain, the model provides general guidance on where to look for an explanation. Is it a change in demand? Is it a change in supply? Or are both changing at once? And if so, which is changing more? The generality of the model makes it possible to apply it in different circumstances. It is summarised in Table 3.

Note that I say that these general principles provide us with the *beginnings* of a basic market model. In particular, a full market model would have to include the repercussions of price changes on the actual amounts demanded and supplied. This would then provide a fully interactive model of market price in which demand and supply influence price, *and* price also affects the actual quantities that are demanded and supplied.

Table 3   The basic market model

A rise in market price is the result of an increase in demand relative to supply	A fall in market price is the result of a decrease in demand relative to supply
• if demand increases more than supply	• if demand decreases more than supply
• if demand increases and supply stays the same	• if demand decreases and supply stays the same
• if demand stays the same and supply decreases	• if demand stays the same and supply increases
• if demand decreases less than supply	• if demand increases less than supply

We can see an application of the basic market model in Thompson's account. The initial fall in price is explained by the fall in demand for Stevengraphs. Their low or virtually zero price is explained by the low demand in relation to supply; in such circumstances the supply is relatively plentiful. The later increase in the price of Stevengraphs is explained by the increase in demand relative to supply. In all three instances, price is explained in terms of the interaction of demand and supply.

Activity 6

With the global credit crunch in 2008, the average price of a house fell in the UK from £184,099 in November 2007 to £158,442 in November 2008 (Nationwide, 2008). This was a fall of 13.9 per cent.

Try applying the general principles in Table 3 to explain this fall in house prices.

There was no significant change in the supply of housing over the period, so the explanation must lie in a fall in demand. A result of the global financial crisis and resulting 'credit crunch' was that mortgages were hard to get hold of. This led to a fall in the demand for housing. This in turn led to a fall in house prices. Expectations of further falls in house prices in turn led to further falls in demand.

The UK housing slump in 2008

This provides an example of how value is subject to social factors. Nothing changed in the physical attributes of houses; they still provided the same level of comfort and accommodation. Their price fell because of a fall in demand, itself one of the consequences of the global financial crisis.

2.3   Aesthetic revaluation

Thompson explains the eccentric revaluations of Stevengraphs, before they became durables, in terms of the tastes or aesthetic judgments of the few early individual collectors. Their revaluations were thus based on or accompanied by their aesthetic revaluations of the artistic merits of the silkworks. As we saw in Section 2.2 above, influences on demand include taste as well as fashion, and 'taste' includes aesthetic judgments about what is beautiful and attractive. This gives us a further sense of 'value' – aesthetic value – in addition to those we considered in Section 1.1.

But, as the inclusion of 'fashion' here suggests, aesthetic judgements – of what is beautiful, attractive, elegant, cool, sexy, and so on – are also subject to a range of influences. Thompson calls those early revaluations 'eccentric' because they deviated from the general consensus. Once an item moves into the durable category, however, aesthetic valuation tends to be influenced by the upward market valuation. Thompson (1979, p. 32) makes this into a general point: 'To generalise, we can say that the increasing economic value of objects, once they have entered the durable category, is accompanied by an increasing aesthetic value.' Thus it isn't only that increased aesthetic valuation tends to lead to increased economic valuation. In addition, increases in economic valuation tend to stimulate an increase in aesthetic valuation. By this Thompson does not mean to suggest that the Stevengraphs did not 'really' deserve this enhanced aesthetic appreciation upon entering the durable category. Rather he is arguing that aesthetic and economic valuations are inevitably linked to some degree, and that this tends to hold generally.

This might suggest that there is a clear dividing line between 'rubbish' and what is deemed to have aesthetic value. This itself can be questioned. As we have seen, values are complex and formed as part of social processes. One way of talking about this is to say that they are **socially constructed**. If values are social constructs then they are potentially open to challenge and redefinition.

Social construction
To say something is socially constructed is to say that at least in part the item's features and character are dependent upon the society and social relations within which it is made and used.

Such challenges to aesthetic value are also registered by some 'art' objects. Junk Art challenges the distinction between 'rubbish' and 'art' by using discarded or disposable objects in artworks. Consider the artwork *My Bed* (1998) by Tracey Emin. Along with the unmade bed, this comprises an arrangement of 'rubbish', including, as it says on the Saatchi Gallery website where a photograph of it is displayed, its 'empty booze bottles' and 'fag butts' on the floor (Saatchi Gallery, undated). Here Emin uses the detritus of an untidy bedroom to construct an artwork.

Some Junk Art uses rubbish to make an artistic statement about the social dimensions of rubbish in consumer society. For example, Chris Jordan makes photographic artworks that are computer-assembled from smaller photographs, some of which are shots of the detritus of mass consumption, such as beverage cans, plastic cups, plastic bags, cigarette ends, mobile phones, circuit boards or glass. For example, *Cell Phones* (2007) depicts 426,000 cell phones, equal to the number of cell phones then retired in the USA every day. You have to look closely to appreciate the detail of Jordan's photographs, as from a distance they take on a different patterning from the rubbish that is being represented. This is illustrated in Figure 6 which shows three versions of a photograph depicting a million plastic cups, which, according to Jordan, was the number of cups used every six hours on domestic flights within the USA. The first image shows the entire photograph, and the other two images show different degrees of close-up.

Clearly, there is a broader social point being made by Jordan about the sheer scale and ugliness of the waste generated by mass consumption in an affluent society. Yet, at the same time, in creating that sense of scale, a kind of beauty is produced. Rubbish is transformed into art.

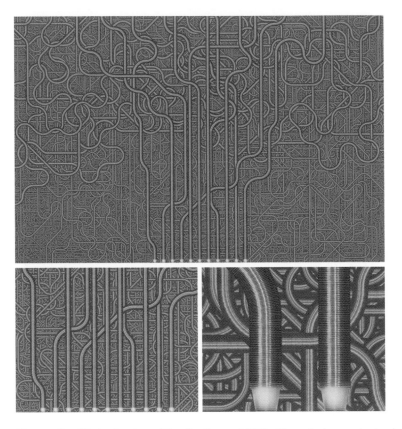

Figure 6   Chris Jordan, *Plastic Cups*, 2008. The photograph depicts one million plastic cups, the number Jordan calculated was being used on airline flights in the USA every six hours. Shown are: complete photograph; partial zoom; close-up zoom

Artworks such as these attempt to challenge the distinction between rubbish and art, although detractors might say that some of this 'art' is itself mere 'rubbish'. Such artworks also challenge the association between economic value and aesthetic value by constructing artworks out of items that individually have little or no value. This in turn is open to inversion, however, if those works become successful as artworks, since they themselves acquire economic value in the process. Such artworks thus illustrate another sense in which 'rubbish' can be given value, by transforming it into an art object that is valued. Jordan's work also makes a critical point about the ugliness of mass consumption and the environmental implications of the scale of rubbish that it produces, although in the process he aspires to produce something of aesthetic value and, hence, of economic value.

In the next section we shall return to the broader social issues that surround rubbish and look at ways in which economists in particular have offered us ways to think about the growing rubbish problem.

Summary

In this section we have looked at the ways in which social scientists have sought to explain the links between rubbish and value.

- Objects are continually open to the social process of revaluation and devaluation, in both economic and aesthetic senses of value.

- This social process of revaluation and devaluation can be analysed in economic terms by using the market model of demand and supply.

- According to Thompson's 'rubbish theory', the category of rubbish may be an intermediary in the transformation of transient items into objects of durable value.

- The blurred dividing line between rubbish and economic/aesthetic evaluation can be seen in Junk Art.

3   Waste, affluence and the environment

3.1   Some economics of environmental effects

Chris Jordan's work emphasises the sheer scale of rubbish produced by the mass consumption of affluent societies. His work complements the arguments of environmentalists that humankind is now over-consuming the resources and absorptive capacities of the planet. So far, I've mostly discussed household rubbish. But far greater is the rubbish from shops, supermarkets, business, manufacture, construction and agriculture. In 2008, household rubbish accounted for only 7 per cent of total rubbish in the UK, which amounted to 434 million tonnes in a year. This was recalculated as the 'wacky waste fact' that the UK rate of rubbish generation would fill the Albert Hall in London in less than two hours (Waste Online, 2008).

A different way of representing the UK rate of rubbish generation

One of the great challenges of the twenty-first century is to come to grips with the ecological implications of mass consumption. And with rising affluence in many parts of the world, the degree of global unsustainability is increasing. The growth in rubbish is part of this wider problem.

Rubbish can be put into landfill sites or incinerated. But UK landfill sites are reaching capacity and, anyway, cause pollution; and incineration directly causes pollution. Putting household rubbish out for collection seems to be a way of 'getting rid of it', but complete disposal is hard to achieve. Disposal often means just moving the rubbish to another place (in the UK or abroad) or creating further pollution. Recycling is therefore more environmentally sustainable, although reducing consumption (including rubbish) in the first place is even better environmentally.

The UK has had a bad reputation on recycling and has been called 'the dustbin of Europe'. For example, in 2007 it was announced that the UK dumped the same amount of rubbish in landfill sites as the combined eighteen European Union (EU) countries with the lowest landfill rates, even though the UK's population was half the size of those countries combined (LGA, 2007). As Councillor Paul Bettison, then Chairman of the UK Local Government Association Environment Board, which produced this research, based on 2005 data, put it:

> Britain is the dustbin of Europe… For decades people have been used to being able to throw their rubbish away without worrying about the consequences. Those days are now over.

> There needs to be an urgent and radical overhaul of the way in which rubbish is thrown away. Local people, businesses and councils all have a vital role to play to protect our countryside before it becomes buried in a mountain of rubbish.

> (LGA, 2007)

There was thus growing pressure in the UK to increase recycling. As we saw in Section 1.2, there was an improvement in recycling rates in England, although they still compared badly with best practice rates in Europe (Austria and the Netherlands) of more than 60 per cent (*The Economist*, 2007, p. 22). Thus other affluent countries achieved better recycling rates than England. Moreover, wide regional variations persisted within England. For example, in 2006/07 the recycling rate in London was 23 per cent and in the East of England it was 38 per cent (Defra, 2007, Table 5).

We have seen that rising affluence is a contributory factor to mass consumption, which itself is a contributory factor to environmental unsustainability. In addition, rising affluence tends to shift consumption towards labour-saving disposability which results in yet more rubbish. In Section 2.2 we also saw how prices change in response to changes in demand and supply. This raises a question why markets don't take care of the environmental effects of mass consumption? If there is a problem about environmental unsustainability, why don't prices change in a way that would provide incentives to make people less wasteful? If the price rise in Stevengraphs registered the new interest people had in collecting them, why don't prices change to provide incentives for people to respond environmentally?

Externalities
The effects on society or the environment of economic activities that are not adequately reflected in the prices of goods and services.

The answer lies in the existence of what economists call **externalities**. Externalities are the effects of activities, such as consuming, making or providing goods and services, that are not registered in the prices at which the goods and services are bought and sold. These effects impact on others, on society and on the environment, but they do not affect economic calculations because they are not registered in the prices of the goods.

Externalities can be positive or negative. There is a *positive externality* when the external effect arising from a good or service is beneficial. Here, for example, the social (or environmental) benefits of consumption extend beyond the benefits to those who consume the good or service. Important examples are health and education. The social benefits of heath and education are greater than the benefits to the individuals directly concerned because society as a whole benefits when any individual has better health or is better educated.

The opposite happens when there is a *negative externality*. Here the external effect arising from the good or service is harmful. This is a cost to society (or the environment) resulting, for example, from individual consumption that is not registered in the price paid by the individual who consumes it. Consider the pollution from car exhausts. This pollution has a harmful effect on health and on the environment; it is a cost to society. Yet this cost isn't fully registered in the price of the car that is paid by individual consumers. Similarly, vapour trails from aeroplanes pollute the upper atmosphere but this environmental cost is not currently covered by the price of airline tickets. These are negative externalities because the price paid by consumers is less than the full cost of their consumption to society and the wider environment.

Activity 7

Can you think of any negative externalities that were discussed in earlier chapters?

Chapter 2 discussed the ways in which the presence of a large supermarket can result in 'hollowing out' a town centre. This hollowing out is an externality that is not captured in the financial calculations of either the supermarkets or their customers.

Can you see the implications of the analysis of externalities for understanding rubbish? Rubbish is an example of a negative externality. Consider all the packaging that is now a part of modern consumerism and supermarket operations. Disposing of this packaging is a cost to society and harms the environment, but these costs are not reflected in the price of the goods that were wrapped in the packaging. Think back to Chris Jordan's photograph of plastic cups. These cups are 'disposable'. But the environmental costs of disposing of them are not registered in the price of the cups.

Externalities have become more significant in recent years because of the systemic nature of environmental externalities. If humankind is over-consuming planet Earth then the entire system of prices is out of line with the realities of the planet's ecosystem. One way of addressing these systemic externalities is to 'revalue' the environment. That would mean not treating it as a free good and not treating it as a 'free sink' for dumping rubbish into. Free goods are those where supply is abundant relative to demand. We saw an instance of this in Section 2.2 where Thompson argues that the price of Stevengraphs fell virtually to zero. In some conditions air and the environment might be free goods, but in general this is no longer the case. Revaluing the environment implies that consumers would have to pay the full cost of all their consumption, including the full environmental cost and the costs of disposal. The structure of prices across goods and services would be very different, with the most polluting goods (e.g. cars with low fuel efficiency, such as sport utility vehicles (SUVs)) and activities (e.g. flying around the world) tending to get the highest price rises and less polluting goods (e.g. bicycles) and activities (e.g. rail travel) smaller price rises.

Activity 8

Why would the most polluting goods tend to get the highest price rises?

The most polluting goods tend to have the greatest negative externality. This cost to the environment would have to be added to the price for it to register the full environmental cost of production and consumption, including disposal.

3.2   Affluence, inequalities and the environment

The analysis of environmental externalities has huge implications for issues of equity – for what is fair or just – across generations and across countries. The analysis of negative externalities and the undervaluation of the environment imply that current generations are not bearing the full costs of their affluent lifestyle. These costs are real, and are being passed on to future generations who look set to inherit a world that is less able to provide them with the resources they need to live.

As we saw in Section 1.2, humankind is increasingly living beyond its means environmentally. Estimates suggest that Ecological Debt Day comes earlier each year and future generations may have to service a growing debt. According to estimates (made in 2008) for 2005, however, if everyone on the planet were to have an average US lifestyle, the resources of 4.5 planet Earths would be required. If everyone were to have an average UK lifestyle, the resources of 2.5 Earths would be required. By contrast, if everyone were to have an average African lifestyle, 0.7 Earths would be required (Global Footprint Network, 2008b, based on 2008 data tables; WWF, LZS, GFN, 2008). But the countries that suffer the most from the environmental effects of unsustainability are poorer countries. For example, less affluent countries are the least able to defend themselves against the effects of global warming, such as rising sea levels, irregular weather patterns and increased natural disasters – all of which threaten homes, harvests and livelihoods.

Within more affluent countries, there are the richer and the poorer: incomes are distributed unequally. Most households get low or middling incomes, and only a few households get high incomes – this is what it means to say that incomes are distributed unequally. In addition, income inequality was increasing in the UK in the last decades of the twentieth century and the early years of the twenty-first century. That is, although real incomes were rising over the period, as we saw in Section 1.2, they were also becoming more unequally distributed. This increase in inequality is illustrated in Table 4, for the period 1979 to 2005/06.

Table 4   Real weekly incomes[1] for three income groups, 1979 to 2005/06, UK/GB[2]

	Poorest 10%	Median	Richest 10%
1979	£130	£231	£408
1988/89	£135	£281	£561
1998/99	£154	£313	£651
2005/06	£181	£362	£734
% increase in real weekly income, 1979–2005/06	39%	57%	80%

1   Real disposable household income, £ per week adjusted to 2005/06 prices.

2   Data for 1998/99 for Great Britain only.

Source: ONS, 2008b, p. 63, Figure 5.3

Table 4 shows real weekly incomes for three income groups – the poorest 10 per cent, the median income level (this is the income in the middle of the range, at 50 per cent), and the richest 10 per cent – over four time periods. To make these incomes comparable across the different time periods, they are all expressed in terms of 2005/06 prices. (This requires adjusting incomes in the three earlier periods when prices were lower.) The bottom row shows the percentage increase in real income over the period 1979 to 2005/06 for each of these three income groups.

Activity 9

What do the data in Table 4 suggest to you about income inequality over the period 1979 to 2005/06?

The richest group gained the most and the poorest group gained the least. The weekly income of the richest 10 per cent increased by 80 per cent on average, whereas the weekly income of the poorest 10 per cent increased by 39 per cent on average. Both the richest 10 per cent and the poorest 10 per cent had an increase in real incomes, but the richest had a proportionate increase that was about twice that of the poorest. In absolute terms, the increase for the rich (£326 per week) was over six times the increase for the poor (£51 per week).

What are the implications of income inequality for the analysis of environmental externalities? One implication is that adjusting prices to reflect externalities is likely to bear hardest on those with the lowest incomes, unless incomes are otherwise adjusted. Similarly, plans to fine or charge households for rubbish disposal may hit hardest those on low incomes. Such 'pay as you throw' schemes charge households for the amount of rubbish to be collected, but such charges are likely to comprise a higher proportion of income for those on low incomes than for those on high incomes.

The interconnections between environmental issues, affluence and inequality are thus complex and difficult to resolve. And some of this complexity is illustrated by questions of rubbish disposal, wastefulness and values.

Summary

- Harmful environmental effects can be analysed in economic terms as negative externalities.
- Rubbish is a form of negative externality.
- Mass consumption and rising affluence have contributed to undervaluing the environment.
- Environmental damage imposes costs on future generations, as well as current generations in poorer countries.
- The UK's experience of increasing affluence was accompanied by an unequal distribution of that increase during the period between 1979 and 2005/06.

How do we know?

Making social science arguments 3: theories and models

In going beyond description to work out explanations, social scientists use theories and models. These are conceptual frameworks that enable explanations to be formulated, and/or coherent bodies of thinking that help us to make more sense of the things we study.

Sometimes the terms 'theory' and 'model' are used interchangeably, but this chapter has differentiated between theories (such as Thompson's sociological 'rubbish theory') and models (such as the market model used by economists). Although both theories and models can be used to provide explanations, theories are used with a broad range of relationships and interconnections, whereas models tend to focus on specifically causal relationships. Thompson's rubbish theory identifies the ways in which rubbish and its revaluation plays a key role in a complex set of changes in which transients become durables. The market model identifies specific causal relationships between demand, supply and price, such that, for example, a rise in price is caused by an increase in demand relative to supply.

The success or usefulness of a theory or model is assessed in terms of how well it explains, or predicts, what happens. This involves evidence, including data. Both Thompson's theory and the market model use data relating to prices.

Different theories and models, using different sets of concepts, are sometimes in competition in explaining what happens. The existence of different theories and models thus helps to underline the existence of disagreements within the social sciences.

Conclusion

In this chapter we have examined some links between rubbish, affluence, waste and values. Rubbish and its disposal are an integral part of the consumption that you have been studying in this strand, and we have seen how mass consumption has been associated with rising affluence. It has also been associated with increasing indebtedness and increased inequality in incomes in the UK, perhaps raising questions about the nature of such a society.

Studying rubbish has enabled us to examine some of the ways in which objects and activities come to be valued, disvalued, undervalued and revalued. Rubbish, we have seen, is disvalued: it has no value to those who want to dispose of it. Yet we have also seen that rubbish can be revalued, or given new value, by recycling it or passing it on to others who have a use for it. Items considered as rubbish can also be revalued by changes in tastes or fashion, which find new uses for, or new delight in, objects previously considered worthless. Environmental concerns also suggest that rubbish should be recycled and revalued, not thrown away as of no value. In fact, disposing of rubbish imposes costs on society, so such rubbish really has negative value for society. We have also seen that the analysis of environmental externalities suggests that the environment has been systematically undervalued. Instead of treating it as something plentiful – as a free good or something that itself has no value – humankind has to learn to revalue it and hence conserve it. Environmental analysis of the overconsumption of planet Earth suggests that this lesson needs to be learnt quickly.

This chapter has thus provided you with some social science 'tools' of analysis for examining a wide range of apparently different situations, by seeing what such situations have in common. The market model gives you a tool or method of analysis that can be applied in many different situations. Here the social process of valuation can be analysed in terms of demand and supply. Thompson's rubbish theory provides you with a means of analysing the ways in which the category of rubbish can function as an intermediary in the transformation of transients into durables of value.

But in all this we have also seen that the notion of 'value' itself can be used in different senses, not only in an economic sense. Questions of value, whether of consumer goods, the environment, or fashion, are thus not only questions concerning economics but involve other social sciences too – as you will learn in later chapters of the course.

References

Credit Action (2008) *Debt Statistics: December 2008* [online], www.creditaction.org.uk/debt-statistics.html (Accessed 11 December 2008).

Department for Environment, Food and Rural Affairs (Defra) (2007) *e-Digest Environment Statistics: Municipal Waste Management Statistics 2006/7* [online], www.defra.gov.uk/environment/statistics/wastats/archive/mwb200607.xls (Accessed 20 November 2008).

Global Footprint Network (2008a) *Earth Overshoot Day 2008* [online], www.footprintnetwork.org/gfn_sub.php?content=overshoot (Accessed 4 January 2009).

Global Footprint Network (2008b) *World Footprint: Do We Fit on the Planet?* [online], www.footprintnetwork.org/en/index.php/GFN/page/world_footprint/ (Accessed 4 January 2009).

Godden, G.A. (1971) *Stevengraphs and Other Victorian Silk Pictures*, Barrie and Jenkins, London.

Local Government Association (LGA) (2007) *Britain Tops Landfill League and Wins 'Dustbin of Europe' Award*, press release, 12 November [online], www.lga.gov.uk/lga/core/page.do?pageId=41558 (Accessed 23 November 2008).

Nationwide (2008) *House Prices,* November press release, 27 November 2008 [online], www.nationwide.co.uk/hpi/historical/Nov_2008.pdf (Accessed 11 December 2008).

new economics foundation (nef) (2008) *Tuesday 23 September: The Day Humanity Starts Eating the Planet* [online], www.neweconomics.org/gen/EcologicalDebtDay23September230908.aspx (Accessed 21 November 2008).

Office for National Statistics (ONS) (2008a) *Family Spending: 2007 Edition*, Basingstoke and NY, Palgrave Macmillan; also available online at www.statistics.gov.uk/downloads/theme_social/Family_Spending_2006/FamilySpending2007_web.pdf (Accessed 20 November 2008).

Office for National Statistics (ONS) (2008b) *Social Trends 38*, Basingstoke and NY, Palgrave Macmillan; also available online at www.statistics.gov.uk/downloads/theme_social/Social_Trends38/Social_Trends_38.pdf (Accessed 21 November 2008).

Office for National Statistics (ONS) (2008c) *Average Earnings Index* [online], www.statistics.gov.uk/StatBase/tsdownload.asp?vlnk=392 (Accessed 12 December 2008).

Office for National Statistics (ONS) (2008d) *Consumer Prices Index* [online], www.statistics.gov.uk/statbase/TSDtimezone.asp (Accessed 15 December 2008).

The Economist (2007) 'The truth about recycling', *Technology Quarterly*, 9 June, pp. 22–6.

The Saatchi Gallery (undated) *Tracey Emin: My Bed* [online], www.saatchi-gallery.co.uk/artists/artpages/tracey_emin_my_bed.htm.en (Accessed 23 November 2008).

Thompson, M. (1979) *Rubbish Theory: The Creation and Destruction of Value*, Oxford University Press.

WWF, LZS, GFN (2008) *Living Planet Report 2008* [online], www.footprintnetwork.org/en/index.php/GFN/page/living_planet_report/ (Accessed 4 January 2009).

Waste Online (2008) *Wacky Waste Facts* [online], www.wasteonline.org.uk/topic.aspx?id=19 (Accessed 20 November 2008).

Waste and Resources Action Programme (WRAP) (2008a) *The Food We Waste* [online], www.wrap.org.uk/downloads/The_Food_We_Waste_v2__2_.8d29769b.5635.pdf (Accessed 20 November 2008).

Waste and Resources Action Programme (WRAP) (2008b) *Executive Summary: The Food We Waste* [online], www.wrap.org.uk/downloads/Summary_v21.cfa2b1d4.5460.pdf (Accessed 11 December 2008).

Conclusion: Material lives

Steve Hinchliffe

Conclusion: Material lives

So what have you learnt about material lives from these three chapters? The broad story being told by the chapters is that an interesting and useful way to study society is to look at *how* people live, their material existence, and how these ways of life have consequences for their own and other people's welfare, for society and for the environment. Shopping and consumption offered us one way to look at how people live material lives. It was a starting point, working out from the street, that allowed us to start to describe and explain how society is made today. People shop for necessities and for the things and services that make their lives and the lives of the people around them exciting, worthwhile, interesting and liveable. In doing so they engage with a world of goods and people that stretches beyond the high street to the sweatshops in Bangladesh, the boardrooms of big institutions and the rubbish heaps on the edges of town and beyond.

In the strand introduction three questions were posed which related to the key questions in the course – who are the winners and losers in a consumer society, what role do material things play in the making of consumer society, and is that society sustainable? You should now be able to think about those questions and answer them by way of descriptions and explanations of a consumer society. So, for example, you should now be able to answer the question: who are the winners and losers in a consumer society? Moreover, beyond describing who the winners and losers are, you should now be able to go a little further by offering some explanations, answering the following question: how do social scientists explain some of the uneven qualities of society?

Winners and losers are clearly related to the wealthy and the less wealthy and the poor, but there are also other categories that become important. Consumer society seems to discriminate in favour of certain age groups, levels of ability and education. These qualities are explained in part through the use of concepts like seduced and repressed, which suggest that people choose to buy into certain lifestyles and that others are actively excluded from those lifestyles. You should also think about the winners and losers described in Chapters 2 and 3 (think about the uneven wages along the global supply chain and the effects that consumption and rubbish have on the environment). You might want to think about how much choice people have, since this is another sign of being a winner or loser.

A similar exercise could be completed for the other two questions. You should now be able to describe the role that things play in making a consumer society (we are, in part, what we consume), and describe the relationship between consumption and environmental concern. Likewise, you have come across social science approaches to explaining these roles and relationships. In Chapter 1, you learnt about the shift from a concern with character to one with personality, a shift that seemed to invite people to demonstrate their personality through the purchase of certain types of goods. (This is an example of the link between consumption and identity, the topic of Chapter 4.) In Chapter 2, you learnt how the choice over where and what to consume might be shaped, influenced and even constrained by some powerful social actors, like supermarkets. Understanding power helps social scientists to explain how consumption is done. In Chapter 3, you learnt about the uneven levels of affluence in the UK, and how this makes it difficult to find ways of consuming in a more sustainable fashion. You also learnt about the causal relationships between supply, demand and price, and how these can be used to explain levels of consumption (and rubbish). These helped us to understand why consumer society can be environmentally unsustainable. So, for example, the atmosphere is a key component of the environment and one that has traditionally been considered to be in plentiful supply, and has a zero price – that is, it is free to use. How can the relationship between price, demand and supply explain why we tend to pump polluted air into the atmosphere rather than find an alternative route for disposing of waste? What's the solution to a polluted atmosphere?

In Chapter 3, you read about a model which can be used to explain consumption practices. According to this model, if something is in plentiful supply and is cheap (or free) then people will want more of it: demand will be high. A solution might be to charge polluters to use the atmosphere for discharging their waste. A price increase would, the model suggests, reduce demand.

As this may have reminded you, in moving from description to explanation you have also come across the use of concepts, which help us to formulate possible explanations in any given setting, and models and theories, which are more or less formal frameworks which attempt to explain society (these are summarised in the 'How do we know?' sections of the chapters). So, in Chapter 1 you used concepts of seduced and repressed, personality and character, to start to explain consumer society. In Chapter 2, you encountered the concept of power which was used, and itself interrogated, as a tool for understanding how consumption is organised and shaped by some quite large and influential actors (the big retailers). In Chapter 3, you learnt to use a causal model which explains the relationship between demand, supply and price. Also, you came across a theory called 'rubbish theory' which brought together a number of ideas and concepts (including value, price, demand and supply) to explain how items moved from being valued as transient to being seen as durable, via being defined as rubbish or worthless. You will learn more about social science explanation and the use of theory in later chapters. For now it is useful for you to be aware that while theory for some social scientists is a formal affair that needs to be tested against the evidence, for other social scientists theory is something that is continuously modified in the light of evidence and argument; that is, theories are used to sensitise us to society and are then modified as society speaks back to theory.

A lot of ground has been covered in the opening chapters, and some of it may seem new and challenging. The remaining chapters in this book may open up equally new areas for you, but they will also be opportunities for revisiting and refining many of things you have learnt so far. As you continue to read you will learn more about how people's lives are connected and ordered, both of which involve and include the material lives that you have already studied. The next strand focuses on connecting lives and directly picks up and extends the issue with which we started: how society is made through people's relationships with other people and with things.

Introduction: Connected lives

Stephanie Taylor

Introduction: Connected lives

Part of the moving picture of society

The street may be busy or quiet, but the movement and activity of society never stops. As people go about their everyday lives, moving from one place to another and taking part in endless small interactions, they are also connected into bigger processes operating around the globe and over time, such as the international communications and trade of goods and labour that bring the world's products to a local supermarket, and the major movements of people over history that have created today's UK population. In the previous strand, 'Material lives', you read about some of the activities associated with the UK consumer society, including shopping, selling and producing, and disposing of all the resulting waste and rubbish. Strand 2, 'Connected lives', continues to explore how people's activities together make up society. Somewhat differently, it also shows how society makes people: how the bigger moving picture shapes their individual lives and their identities, or who they are.

Many social scientists who study identity, especially social psychologists like me, are interested in the two-way processes through which people make society, but society also makes them, so that who they are is determined by their connections to other people, their part in shared activities and how they are seen by the people around them. Of course, this raises the question of how 'who I am' in the street and society more generally is connected, if at all, to 'who I am' personally, in my own idea and experience of myself as a unique person. These issues are discussed throughout Strand 2, more and less directly, beginning with Chapter 4, 'Who do we think we are? Identities in everyday life'.

Identities, at their simplest, are who we are. People of the same age, sex, family or nationality, or who do the same job, can be said to share an identity: they have something in common, in their own view or that of other people, even if only that they are all different from the people with some other identity. Some identities can also be given by people's connections to places, being a southerner or northerner, for example, or describing yourself or others in more local terms, possibly down to the level of a particular neighbourhood or street. In the first chapter of this strand, Chapter 4, I discuss different kinds of identity and how they connect people, and 'disconnect' them too.

Places also have their own identities. In the second chapter of the strand, Chapter 5, 'Connecting people and places' by Steve Hinchliffe, a geographer, the focus shifts from 'who' to 'where'. The chapter traces the changing importance of cities and countryside in UK society in the nineteenth and twentieth centuries. It discusses the life changes that occurred as people moved into the cities, and the new social connections, and divisions, that became established. It looks at the associated images of urban and rural life that still persist, for example, in our ideas about the 'natural' environment. Like people, places have more than one identity. The chapter explores their multiple, social character through the case of an urban garden. The one garden is in fact three: a women's garden, an urban renewal garden and a charity garden, each involving different connections and relations of people and time.

Chapter 6, 'Living together, living apart: the social life of the neighbourhood' by Jovan Byford, another social psychologist, considers people's connections to places in a different way, by looking at the social life of a neighbourhood. This chapter explores how we all live 'with' others in ordinary life, more and less successfully. The focus of the strand has changed again, from 'who' and 'where' to 'who with', although who and where remain important. The chapter argues that, even in unremarkable or mundane everyday interactions between people, there are unwritten rules operating. These affect our lives, although we may not be particularly aware of them. For example, research has shown that disputes between neighbours often occur because some of these long-established rules have been broken, such as those relating to noise. Neighbours will be upset not only by very loud voices or music but also by certain quieter activities which, according to the social rules, should not be heard!

As I have indicated, Strand 2 presents a moving picture of society. The moving picture is not chaotic but (more or less) orderly: you will read more about the important social science concept of order in the third strand of the course, 'Ordered lives'. In Strand 2, Chapters 4 and 6 look at some of the unwritten rules that shape people's activities and maintain and repair this order. However, the order cannot be total, or nothing would ever change. You will also read in this strand about significant changes in the recent history of UK society, including those associated with mass movements of people from countryside to city (in Chapter 5) and from the UK to other countries around the world (in Chapter 4). There are changes, and continuity, in the connections between people, for example in their family and neighbour relationships (discussed in Chapters 4 and 5). In Chapter 6 you will read about situations in which the order appears to break down, and about how, ironically, the rules that usually maintain order can sometimes also contribute to its breakdown.

In Strand 1 you encountered two key questions for the course. These are addressed again in Strand 2.

1 How is society made and repaired?

Throughout the strand there is an emphasis on the processes, relationships, connections and 'disconnections' through which the social world is continuously being made and re-made. Over time, some parts become fixed and established while others unravel, diminish or are actively broken, and are sometimes repaired, but not always. The focus on people's activities was also there in Strand 1, but the additional point is that this strand, 'Connected lives', looks not only at people making society, but also at society making people.

2 How are differences and inequalities produced?

It is often remarked that the people in a busy street are anonymous: no one person stands out because everyone is equally unimportant, or important, as part of the crowd. Society, however, is more complicated and its connections more uneven, as this strand will discuss. Some people know each other well; others are strangers. Some people are closely linked through their activities, for example, in the consumer society through buying or selling, or producing goods and providing services. The connections between others seem more distant. Some people, such as the homeless who have to sleep rough in the street, appear not to be connected at all but excluded or 'disconnected' from society.

In every society, some people are accepted as normal, others marked as odd. Certain people are seen as more important or attractive or good; in other words, their identities are positively valued, while others have more negative identities. It might seem logical that these differences reflect the intrinsic qualities of the people themselves. However, remember the account in Chapter 3 of how the value attached to things (for example, as rubbish or works of art) derives from social processes. The values attached to certain (kinds of) people, or to certain identities, are similarly given by society. These values and the ideas associated with them (for example, about who or what is good or bad, or right or wrong) establish unequal positions for certain people, or maintain unequal connections, often ones that have their origins in history. This inequality makes some people more able to influence, control or dominate; in other words, it gives them more power.

Throughout the strand you will read about how differences and inequalities are produced, and re-produced. In Chapter 4 you will find out more about how exclusion is linked to identity and how inequalities in society are sometimes made part of how people see themselves and others. In Chapter 5 you will read about the difference and inequality associated with the movement of the population from the countryside to the cities in the nineteenth century, during the development of industrial capitalism. And in Chapter 6 you will learn that practices that inform everyday neighbouring activities are culturally specific, resulting from and also reinforcing difference and diversity in society.

Don't worry if these ideas are rather difficult to grasp at this point. They will become clearer as you read the chapters of the strand, keeping in mind the two questions and the moving picture of society.

Chapter 4

Who do we think we are?
Identities in everyday life

Stephanie Taylor

Contents

Introduction

Figure 1   People in UK streets

Activity 1

Look at the photographs in Figure 1. Who are these people? What can you say about who they are from looking at these pictures? Take a few minutes to make some notes. I will ask you to return to these notes at several points throughout the chapter, so it will be useful to answer the questions as fully as you can.

Expressing identity through shopping was discussed in Chapter 1 of *Making Social Lives*.

The answers to these questions are statements about identity, and there are many possible answers because we all have multiple identities. This chapter looks in more detail at some of the different theories and types of identity discussed by social scientists, such as social psychologists. It shows how shared identities connect people to other people and the social worlds they live in, and sometimes can also 'disconnect' or separate them. In Strand 1 you read about some of the interactions and activities of the consumer society, including how people buy things to express their identities, or who they are. This chapter explores a more complex relationship between people and society, showing how those identities are given by social activities and their connections. Section 1 examines what identity is and discusses different types of identity. Section 2 looks at differences between people's identities and at the reasons that some identities are negatively valued. Section 3 is concerned with the links between places and people's identities. Finally, Section 4 focuses on the identities given by family and origins. Studying identity is a way of studying how society makes people who they are, including their similarities and differences.

1 What is identity?

1.1 Social identities

The term 'identity' is widely used but rather difficult to pin down. You probably know what it means to provide proof of identity and, like many people nowadays, you may be worried about identity theft. Yet these references do not cover all the possible answers to questions about who people are. I have said that all of us, like the people in Figure 1, have many different identities. How can we make sense of the multiplicity? This section will begin one task of this chapter: to introduce some different terms and concepts for talking and thinking about identity.

Look back to your answers for Activity 1. You probably noted people's general ages (young, elderly, etc.) and whether they are women or men. This is the kind of information requested in the categories on an official form: age group, sex, occupation, nationality, and so on – there is an example in Activity 2 below. A category refers to a group or collective identity, as if all the people within it (all women, for example, or everyone aged over 65 or under 18) have something in common. Perhaps more importantly, a group or collective identity is also given by difference from other groups: for example, being a woman, *not* a man; one age, *not* another; a child, *not* an adult, and so on.

A group or collective identity is both individual, saying something about a particular person, and social, because it refers to others who are similar or different. Another kind of **social identity** is that given by people's immediate situation – that is, where they are and what they are doing. For example, some of the people in the photographs are shoppers, or passers-by (or they were when the photographs were taken). Situated identities can also refer to people's connections to the street or wider neighbourhood. For example, you might have noted that some of the people in the photographs seem to be local people while others may be visitors or tourists – people with a different connection to the street and general area.

Yet another social identity is given directly by a relationship between people. Examples that you might observe in the street would be seller and buyer, or, in family groups, parent and child, brother and sister, and so on. Some of these relational identities, like the family ones, are fairly fixed (although the child can grow up and become a parent

Social identity
An identity given by connections to other people and social situations (often contrasted with personal identity). Some examples are group and collective identities, situated identities, given by the immediate situation so liable to change, and relational identities, usually given by a two-sided, possibly unequal, relationship.

and therefore have both identities). Others, like buyer and seller, are more flexible; another example would be the identities of 'host' and 'visitor', which can swap about between two people depending on whose home they are in.

Some social scientists focus their research on a particular category of people, such as women or men (gender studies), or one age group, such as young people (youth studies) or the elderly (gerontological studies). This raises a question, which might already have occurred to you, about the extent of the similarity between people who have the same group or collective identity. Activity 2 focuses on this point.

Activity 2

Below is a section of a form. As far as is possible complete the answers for yourself and then look at the questions that follow.

3. Sex

Male / Female

4. Age group

Under 18 / 19-25 / 26-35 / 36-45 / 46-55 / 56-65 / over 65

5. Nationality

UK citizen / Other EU citizen / Other Commonwealth citizen / Other

6. Race or ethnicity

Indian / Bangladeshi / Pakistani / Chinese / White (Scottish / Irish / British /

Caribbean) / White and Asian / Black (African / Caribbean) / Irish Traveller /

Other White background / Other Black background / Other mixed background /

Other Asian background / Any other ethnic group

- If someone else gave the same answer as you have for any *one* of the questions, would you feel you had much in common with them?
- How much would you have in common with someone who gave the same answers for *all* the questions? To what extent do you think you would want similar things and agree about what is important in life?

I asked the last question because group or collective identities are important politically, as a basis for organising or mobilising people to vote or take other action. For example, feminists have worked in different ways to change society to improve the lives of women, including, in the UK, to secure women's right to vote (obtained for all women in 1928) and to receive equal pay (enforced since 1975, although women generally still earn less than men). In the 1970s and 1980s, an important issue for feminists worldwide became whether their collective identity as women was more or less important than differences of race, wealth and nationality. The issue was one of equality and, in particular, the different identities, and associated different experiences and situations, of Western women and women in developing countries, white women and women of colour. In trade unions there was a similar issue of whether a common identity as workers was more important than the different workplace opportunities and experiences of women workers, or black workers, or black women. These examples show how identity becomes a practical political issue precisely because it refers to similarity and difference. Some social scientists argue that, instead of looking at one category alone (such as gender), it is often necessary to consider the combination or intersection of different identities (for example, gender, class and ethnicity) (Phoenix and Pattynama, 2006; Valentine, 2007). You will read more about unequal relationships of identity in Section 2.

Activity 3

Look back to Activity 2 and consider whether any of these identity categories, or others, are important for you politically. Do you think you have shared interests with people of the same category which could, for example, provide a reason for joining a group seeking social change or voting for a particular politician or party?

You may have noted that the different social identities I have discussed can overlap: the definitions are not mutually exclusive. Some collective identities are situated, such as the identity shared by people in an audience who are together for a short time at the same event. A group or collective identity may also refer to people who know each other and therefore have some kind of relationship. For example, I know many of the people in my street by sight and to say hello to; we share a relational identity as neighbours and also a collective identity as local residents, along with many other people who I would not recognise.

I have said that social scientists define many different kinds of identity (including many more than those I have discussed). Why do we need this slightly confusing variety? The answer is that each definition reflects a specific way of understanding identity and also an interest in a social issue or set of problems. As one example, researchers interested in sibling identity have investigated the importance of people's relationships with their brothers and sisters, and how those relationships are themselves influenced by gender, race, religion and culture (Edwards et al., 2006). Researchers interested in group identity have investigated what creates feelings of loyalty to the same group and, potentially, conflict with others. In one study, social psychologists found, rather surprisingly, that simply telling people that they belong to the same group is enough to change their behaviour. Given the opportunity to allocate funds, people will be more generous to others from their so-called group, even if they have never met, don't know why they are in the group or what they supposedly have in common (Tajfel, 1981).

A further question that may have occurred to you is what all these social identities have to do with who you are, as a person.

Activity 4

Look back to the photographs in Figure 1 and your answers to the question 'Who are these people?' (Activity 1). Do you think these people would give the same answers to that question? How would they describe themselves? Who do they *think* they are?

1.2   A personal identity

Personal identity
A person's own idea of who she or he is: 'the real me'.

'Who I think I am' is a **personal identity**. I might refer to it as 'the real me'. This is the kind of identity that a television programme or written biography attempts to present for a famous or unusual person. The account generally begins with the person's childhood and details of their family background. It may sometimes go back several generations, as if identity is partly determined by the past or even by a biological inheritance of personal characteristics, such as talent or optimism or a bad temper. However, many social scientists do not agree with this view of personal identity as 'essential' – that is, as a kind of possession which doesn't change.

One argument against an essential personal identity is that 'who I am' is learned and does change over a lifetime, because of good or bad experiences, or education, or just the passing of time, as most of us would agree. Part of the study of developmental psychology includes the ways that children take on a personal identity as they grow. Some psychologists have suggested that development and change are not limited to childhood but continue throughout our lives (Salmon, 1985).

A somewhat different argument is that personal identities are not completely separate from social identities, including group or collective identities. Most people would agree, for example, that gender identity (being female or male) is both a social identity and an important part of 'who I am'. The same can be argued for other collective identities. Being middle class or working class, white or a person of colour, middle aged, young or elderly are all probably part of who you think you are, as may be your occupation, race, nationality and religion. A similar point can be made about relational identities and even situated identities which, by definition, change with the situation. For example, the shoppers in Figure 1 will no longer be shoppers when they have returned to their homes or workplaces, yet, for some of them, shopping might also feel like part of 'who I am', a way of expressing or living out a personal identity.

- So how is personal identity connected to the multiple social identities we have discussed?

Different theories of identity have been proposed to answer this question. Some begin with the individual person and suggest that she or he is shaped by society through upbringing and education, as part of the process of socialisation. Alternatively, many social psychologists, and other social scientists, suggest that society comes first, and that external categories of identity become internal as part of an extended process of **identification**. In other words, 'the real me' is the product or consequence of my (multiple) social situation(s) and connections: *all* identities are social. This may be a rather surprising idea if you have not encountered it before. The term 'subjectivity' is sometimes used to refer to this complicated personal identity that brings together multiple social identities. Unlike an essential personal identity, subjectivity is not necessarily fixed or stable (Wetherell, 2008).

Identification
An extended process through which one or more social identities become part of someone's complex personal identity, or subjectivity. This is often contrasted with the concept of an essential identity.

The process of socialisation was discussed in Chapter 1 of *Making Social Lives*, and you will look at it again in Chapter 6.

For many people, perhaps most, the idea of an essential personal identity is easier to accept because we do feel that there is a unique 'real me'. Why do we feel this way and how do our multiple social identities become personal? According to theorists of subjectivity, one possibility is that the multiple identities combine, like the pieces of a jigsaw, to make a single unified personal identity. Another is that the unity or 'one-ness' of 'who I am' is an illusion. In other words, our personal identities are themselves multiple and fragmented (the jigsaw pieces remain mostly separate) but we have learnt to think of ourselves in a certain way, as having an identity that remains unchanged through different social contexts and situations.

This discussion of personal identities has taken us away from social worlds, such as the street, and then back again as we considered the connection between social and personal identities. I have been discussing social identities and how they shape or make personal identities. An equally important (or perhaps more important) point for social scientists is that identities are not only an effect or consequence of social life but are also an inseparable part of how it works. This is the topic of the next section.

1.3   Identities in everyday life

The sociologist Erving Goffman (1959) studied people's everyday behaviour. He suggested that in every situation of ordinary life people behave in ways which will tell others who they are, what they're doing and what they expect and want to happen. Social life is an ongoing series of interactions between people. Furthermore, we have learnt the skills of presenting ourselves in these interactions to manage the impressions that we give to others. In Goffman's view, social behaviour is 'dramaturgical', like a theatrical play; we are all actors, trying to give our best possible performance to make our lives work as we want them to.

Goffman's work has been criticised because it seems to assume that there is a 'real me' who is the actor behind the roles; in other words, it returns to the concept of an essential identity. However, his theory is also interesting for the study of social identities, first, because it suggests that to understand the bigger picture of society, social scientists should look at the details of ordinary social life, and, second, because in focusing on what people do and how they interact, it adopts a *moving* picture of society like the one I discussed in the strand introduction.

In such a moving picture, one way to think about identities is in terms of people's practices; that is, their behaviour or actions in social situations. At the simplest level, this is a matter of definitions: a person who gardens is a gardener; the cook is the person who prepares the food; a singer is someone who sings. But this is also the way in which we encounter identity in daily life. People don't usually walk around with labels saying who they are, although in some jobs they do wear uniforms or name badges. However, in most situations, we understand identities in terms of what people *do* rather than what they *are*. Returning to the example of the street, the shoppers are the people who are buying things, or carrying them, or looking in windows and walking around at a certain speed that we associate with shopping. If you go into a big department store, you'll probably recognise the shop assistants even if they are not wearing uniforms and name badges. You will identify them from where they are (perhaps behind the till), or what they are doing, and, more subtly, from the way they look at other people, seeking eye contact for example, or the confidence with which they move around the shop. Other people, the ones who are shopping, will approach the shop assistants to pay for goods or ask for information, setting up the relational identities of shop assistant and customer. All of this will happen smoothly and almost automatically; if there is an interruption, for example, if one customer mistakes another for an assistant, then there will probably be a brief apology.

These ways of practising or performing identity operate in every context of life. People encounter each other and take up identities relationally through what they do: your friend greets you *as* a friend and talks to you in a 'friendly' way; the senior person at work is the one who can ask others to do certain things and expect the request to be taken seriously. Like Goffman, the sociologist Harold Garfinkel (1967) suggested that the best way to study society was to look at the practical activities of people's ordinary lives. People are endlessly engaged in doing things; for example, in the street they are walking, stopping, looking, looking away, passing each other, speaking, not speaking, buying, and so on. Garfinkel suggests that social life is in constant motion, yet it is not chaotic because people have the skills and knowledge to create and maintain **social order** in each situation, as they do in the department store, mostly without thinking about it. If the order is broken, for example if people bump into each other or someone takes the wrong place in a queue, then there are ways to repair it, perhaps through comments and apologies. Social life proceeds rather like an endless slow dance, because as members of society we have the

The development of department stores was described in Chapter 1 of *Making Social Lives.*

Social order
A stable social situation in which connections are maintained without change, or else change occurs in a predictable way (often contrasted with social breakdown or chaos).

You will read more about order in Chapter 6 of *Making Social Lives,* and in Strand 3 of the course, starting in Chapter 7.

commonsense knowledge and skills to keep it going. We do this almost automatically, although we notice immediately if normal behaviour is interrupted (or 'breached', in Garfinkel's terminology), without being repaired.

Summary

- People's multiple identities are given by their similarities and differences, and their connections with others.
- People perform identities and these identities also create the contexts and situations of social life, in a two-way, or reciprocal, relationship.
- Some theories suggest that even my personal identity, or 'who I think I am', is not fixed or essential, but is made up of my multiple social identities, through a process of identification.

2 Identities of difference and negatively valued identities

The previous section mostly considered positive connections between people: the similarities that underpin group or collective identities, the reciprocal relationships that constitute relational identities such as seller and buyer, and the situated identities given by being 'in place'. However, social life is not, of course, always so harmonious. Collective identities refer to difference as well as similarity. Relationships are not necessarily equal or mutually beneficial but can involve an imbalance of power and a lopsided, damaging connection, as with winner and loser or assailant and victim. Identities can be given by being 'out of place'. The orderly dance of ongoing social life sometimes breaks down and it is sometimes maintained through inequalities and exploitation. In this section I look at identities of difference and negatively valued identities. I begin, once again, with an example from the street, this time from the island of Manhattan in New York.

2.1 The Street People

Homeless people on New York streets

In the 1980s, the writer Jonathan Raban visited New York. At that time there were record numbers of homeless people living on the streets of the city and he noticed the negative ways in which other people described them: 'long-term mental patients discharged from hospitals … crack addicts, thieves, alcoholics, hobos, the temporarily jobless, the alimony defaulters, rent-hike victims' (Raban, 1991, p. 78). These separate identities came together into one larger identity: the Street People – Raban suggested it should have capital letters because it was used like a national or tribal identity 'like the Indians in an old Western' (p. 78). This was, of course, a relational identity, although only one identity in the relationship, the Street People, was named; the identity on the other side of the relationship was not. How do you think that other identity could be described? (I will return to this question in the next section.)

Out on the street, Raban experimented with performing each of the two identities. First, he set himself to walk and look ahead, like most of the people on the pavements:

> I straightened my shoulders, focused on an imaginary point in the far distance, and marched, swinging my arms like a marathon walker. Almost immediately, I started to acquire Manhattan tunnel-vision. The Street People moved from the centre to the periphery of the frame; within a minute or two they became virtually invisible – bits of stationary furniture, on a level with the fire hydrants and the trashcans.
>
> (Raban, 1991, p. 79)

An important part of this performance was to keep moving, as he found when he stopped and sat down. He was, of course, still the same person, but for the moving people he was now performing the identity of a Street Person:

> On West 22nd at Broadway I found a vacant fire hydrant, and settled on it, as into an armchair, like the Street People did, to watch the crowd file past. Everyone moved with the same stiff clockwork action; everyone wore the same boiled look on their face. As they approached my fire hydrant, they accelerated slightly from the waist down, locked their eyes into the horizontal position, and swept by, giving me an exaggeratedly wide berth. I tried making eye contact, and managed to catch a few pairs of pupils off-guard; they swerved away in their sockets, as quick as fish.
>
> It was interesting to feel oneself being willed into non-existence by total strangers. I'd never felt the force of such frank contempt – and all because I was sitting on a fire hydrant.
>
> (Raban, 1991, pp. 79–80)

This small 'experiment' of Raban's may remind you of the ideas of Garfinkel. It shows the ways that certain street identities could be performed, at least in the particular situation of Manhattan in the 1980s. It also shows how relational identities are not necessarily chosen but can be imposed or conferred by one person on another. When Raban sat down he took an **identity position** or **subject position**; he positioned himself as one of the Street People. This could be seen as his choice, although of course most of the Street People didn't have a choice about where to live. But the other people also positioned him in a certain way, very negatively, as deserving contempt and hardly more important than a piece of street furniture, like a rubbish bin.

Identity position/ subject position
A temporary identity giving a particular view of the world and the relationship to people in other positions. People can position themselves or be positioned by others.

Activity 5

Look back to your notes from Activity 1. Which of the identities that you listed carry positive values, which are negatively valued and which are neutral? Do the values change if you consider the intersection of identities?

You read about values in Chapter 3 of *Making Social Lives*.

Raban's account reminds us that the distinction between how we are seen by others, and how we experience 'who I am', is a fragile one. Nonetheless, as I discussed in Section 1.2, we probably hold on to the idea that there is a difference between our social and personal identities. For example, we may think of them as external and internal, though some social psychologists would challenge this distinction (Wetherell, 2008).

You may also have noticed how the Street People were seen by others as somehow the same rather than as individuals with different histories. This is part of the nature of group or collective identities. It is interesting that Raban compared them to a nation, another collective whose members are also assumed to have things in common. Think about how we describe nationalities as 'the Italians', 'the Brazilians', and so on. The commonsense assumption that *all* Italians or *all* the people of another nationality are somehow similar is sometimes turned into a political argument, that they *should* be similar and any difference is potentially problematic. In the box in Section 2.3 you will read about some research conducted in the 1930s on an immigrant group whose difference was seen by some people as threatening to the unity of the USA.

2.2   Identities of difference

The poor people who were living on the streets of Manhattan were different from the kind of group who all know each other, like friends or a sports team. First, there were too many of them to be personally acquainted with each other. Many groups in society, perhaps most, are like this. Benedict Anderson (1983) discussed the example of the group of people who read the same newspaper. Each of them imagines many other people reading it at the same time, seeing the same pictures, responding to the same headlines and stories. This sharing with an 'imagined community' is an essential aspect of the news: a newspaper written for one person would not be a newspaper. The same group can also have a social identity: in the UK, politicians are said to think about voters as *Sun* readers, or *Daily Mail* readers, or *Guardian* readers, referring to the views associated with particular newspapers. These are regarded as important identities, even though a group like this never comes together in any situation in which the members can directly encounter each other. To say that a group is 'imagined' therefore does not mean that it doesn't exist at all and is invented and imaginary, like a lie or fictional story. 'Imagined' refers to the importance of our ideas and beliefs about the world. These can have practical consequences. For instance, a political party will prioritise the problems that seem important for the imagined newspaper readers. This point is discussed in more detail in Section 2.3 and you will read more about the importance of imagining in later sections.

A second point to note about the Street People is that their negative collective identity was given by other people, as a label. Psychologists use the term 'label' to refer to a negatively valued identity which, once given, sticks to a person and is difficult to escape. (For example, 'labelling' someone as mentally ill has a negative effect in itself.) Of course, it is possible that their poverty and the experience of living on the streets had made the Street People in New York similar in some ways. At the most practical level, having no fixed address can make life very difficult in contemporary society, and the ways that they were treated may also have helped to constitute the Street People as a group or collective: Raban says he 'felt the force' of other people's negative attitudes and this kind of positioning probably had consequences. Nonetheless, it is unlikely that they initially claimed the identity: 'we are the Street People.' It is an example of a negative identity given to 'them', not 'us'.

Look back to the discussion of the Street People in the first paragraph of Section 2.1: I asked you to describe the identity on the other side of the relationship. Different answers are possible. I suspect that all are more positive than the Street People identity, and also less specific than Raban's description of 'long-term mental patients' etc. This example illustrates a common pattern in the relational identities of groups. On one side of the relationship is a group of 'them' with a detailed negative identity. On the other side are 'us' with a vaguely positive 'normal' identity which is not really described; this is sometimes called the **unmarked identity**. This way of dividing up people can be referred to as **Othering**, with a capital letter.

The Street People identity was special to a particular place and time. Social scientists are also interested in more widely used collective identities, including class identities. The nineteenth-century social theorist Karl Marx famously divided industrial societies into the working class and the capitalists who employed them. However, that neat separation of classes is rather difficult to apply to modern Western societies. Nowadays in the UK the terms 'middle class' and 'working class' combine references to money, education, family background, confidence and accent in a very complex way, along with related terms such as 'professional', 'white collar', 'blue collar', 'upper class', 'lower class', 'posh' or 'common' (you can probably think of more). Their precise meanings and values are often difficult to pin down because of the Othering around class identities. Social scientists have suggested that a recent example of this Othering occurs in the reality television programmes in which an expert guides people in matters of lifestyle and taste. The sociologists Beverley Skeggs and Stephanie Lawler argue that these programmes are about contemporary class identities (Lawler, 2005). The expert's identity is unmarked but middle class. The people in the programmes who apparently don't know how to eat or dress properly, or how to decorate their homes or bring up their children, are being positioned as working class. The programmes invite viewers to position themselves with the expert, against 'them', the working class.

'Othering' can also explain some of the ways we understand global divisions. The expressions 'the Orient' and 'the mysterious East' are rather old-fashioned now, but advertisements and films still play with stories of hot foreign countries in which a visitor encounters exotic people who are dangerously attractive. The relational and contrasted identities are Western (that is, the rich countries of Europe and North

Unmarked identity
Part of a pair of unequal relational identities in which the unmarked identity is taken for granted as normal, but the marked identity never goes unnoticed and usually carries a negative value.

Othering
The social process through which the difference of other people is marked and their negatively valued identity becomes established.

You will read about Karl Marx's class divisions in Chapter 5 of *Making Social Lives*.

America) and Eastern (the rest of the world, but especially poorer countries that were formerly colonies of the West). The Western is the unmarked identity. The cultural theorist Edward Said (1978) suggests that this 'Orientalism' arose in a process of Othering: people in the rich and powerful West liked to think of their own societies as normal by contrasting them with poorer countries in which they imagined that life was immoral and disorganised, and therefore also rather exciting in contrast to the West. This might sound like a silly but harmless way of thinking. However, as Said argues, it can have serious consequences because it positions the West as superior to other countries. For example, a Western government's intervention in another country's politics and economy might seem justified if the poorer country's authorities are believed to be incompetent and corrupt.

The final example of Othering and identities of difference I will discuss is that of race and ethnicity.

2.3   Racial and ethnic identities

Activity 6

Look back to Activity 1 and your answers to the question 'Who are these people?' Did you refer to race and ethnicity? If so, did you notice the **racial and ethnic identities** that are different from your own?

Racial and ethnic identities
Marked identities that have a historical basis and refer to (imagined) differences of colour, origin, religion, etc.

Race and ethnicity are widely referred to, including on official forms (you saw an example in Activity 2). The terms are used in many different ways, and often interchangeably. One possible distinction is that race refers to features of the physical body, especially skin colour, and ethnicity refers to language, nationality and culture, including religion (Lewis and Phoenix, 2000). This does not always work in practice. For example, by this definition my own racial identity is white and I am ethnically an English-speaking New Zealander. However, my racial identity in New Zealand is also 'pakeha' (a Maori term for non-Maori people) or 'European', since for historical reasons 'European' is an alternative term for white skin colour there (rather like 'Anglo' in the USA). A more important point is that I would very seldom describe myself, or be described by other people, in these ways because in both New Zealand and the UK my identity is generally unmarked. (The exception is my accent, which causes comment in both countries: people in the UK describe it as 'New Zealand' but New Zealanders call it 'British'.) There has been a considerable amount of social science research on race and ethnicity, most of it focused on marked identities: the box entitled 'Researching identities 1' presents a famous early example. More recently, social scientists have begun to research whiteness as a taken-for-granted, unmarked ethnic identity.

■ In the terms I have presented in this chapter, what kinds of identities are racial and ethnic identities?

Racial and ethnic identities are collective identities which have become widely used categories, along with gender, age, class, sexuality (e.g. lesbian, gay, bisexual, transsexual, heterosexual), and others. As with present-day class identities, there are not one or two fairly neat categories of race and ethnicity but an almost infinite range of possible distinctions and terms. The form in Activity 2 attempts to present a fairly full list for the UK today, but it is certainly not complete. This variety occurs because both racial and ethnic identity categories are situated, having a reference and value which depend on the social and historical context.

It might seem logical that, if race refers to the body rather than culture, racial identities will be more fixed than ethnic ones. However, different societies have always identified different racial categories (in nineteenth-century England, the Irish were often described as black). Racial categorisation is generally linked to exaggerated stereotypes, a point which psychologists have studied in detail. There have been political attempts to divide societies according to race (for example, in South Africa under apartheid), but there have invariably been many people whose category was unclear or disputed. Clearly people's bodies vary, but the differences do not separate them neatly into this category or that: there is as much biological variation *within* so-called races as *between* them. Some social scientists put the terms 'race' and 'ethnicity' in inverted commas to emphasise the situated and relational nature of the identities they refer to.

In the terms of this chapter, racial and ethnic identities are also marked identities that are usually negatively valued. The categories are difficult to separate. They are in a certain sense identities of place and generally refer to some historical movement of people, even though the movement may have occurred generations before. A common aspect of racial and ethnic identities in the UK is that they often position people as recent immigrants to the country in which they were born and grew up. However, in some other parts of the world, such as South Africa, Australia and New Zealand, the marked identity is that of the indigenous people; the white identity is still unmarked, even though it derives from the movements of 'settler' immigrants. This apparent inconsistency is explained if we realise that most racial and ethnic identities in the UK today also refer to former colonial relationships. The British Empire established unequal identities for both people and places; indeed, differences of identity were essential to the power relationships through which a large part of the world was ruled from Britain as the imperial centre. In both the UK and the other countries I have referred to, the unmarked identity is that of the former colonisers. As in the example of Orientalism, the relational identities of colonisers and colonised peoples were linked to an imagined history involving conquest, cultural superiority, civilisation, economic development and the achievement of prosperity and order. You may wonder if this history is still relevant. It persists in the continuing associations of racial and ethnic identities with somewhere *else* (at its most extreme, a common demand in **racist rhetoric** is that people should 'go home'). Yet, paradoxically, the imagined histories of contemporary British society often 'forget' centuries of connection with India and Africa, not to mention Ireland.

Racist rhetoric
Speaking or writing, especially for a public audience, which talks about society as divided into completely separate, closed and unequal groups that can supposedly be distinguished by the physical appearance and origins of the people in the inferior group(s).

Researching identities 1: men on the streets

In 1936–40 the sociologist and anthropologist William Foote Whyte conducted a research project in an 'Italian slum' area of the US city of Boston (see Figure 2). At that time, Italian immigrants were considered a problem group who were likely to become involved in crime ('racketeering') and who probably supported Italian fascism rather than US democracy. Whyte refers to them as a 'race'. He wanted to investigate the social structure of the North End slum district which he called Cornerville. He focused on the 'gangs' of young men who spent most of their time together on street corners and he became close to one gang, the Nortons, and especially their leader, Doc. Whyte socialised with them and also talked to them individually about their lives and problems; as a participant-observer he almost became part of the gang. This was a qualitative study for which the data were Whyte's observations and conversations. The analysis was interpretive and Whyte does not say much about how it was done. His book about the research, *Street Corner Society* (Whyte, 1993), is rather like a novel in which Doc is the main character.

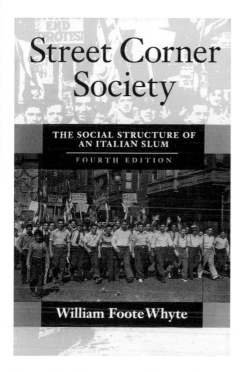

Figure 2   The cover of *Street Corner Society* showing a demonstration of Italian-American men in Boston, 1939

Whyte found that each street corner gang had a very stable, hierarchical structure. A man's personal identity and self-esteem, and his standing in Cornerville society, were closely linked to his status position in the gang. Whyte concluded that the slum society was not chaotic, as outsiders might imagine, but, on the contrary, too rigidly structured. He suggested that the immigrants would not fit well into US society because they were accustomed to living within these hierarchical structures of support and obligation, rather than as free individuals. His argument was that their identities as members of the gang and this immigrant society would conflict with a US national identity.

Summary

- Section 2 has explored social identities related to difference and non-connection.
- Marked and unmarked identities are a particular kind of unequal relational identity.
- Collective or group identities, like those represented by the categories on an official form, can be imagined, which is not the same as being imaginary.
- Identities of place, class, race and ethnicity vary with context. They are not easily separated but tend to refer to each other.

3   Identities of residence

3.1   The values attached to place

In Jonathan Raban's account in Section 2.1, why was the Street People identity so negative? The details of their individual life histories, such as the experience of becoming homeless after losing a job and going bankrupt, or suffering from mental illness (or even being a successful writer who wanted to try a brief experiment for a new book) would not necessarily explain why other people viewed the Street People so negatively. I want to suggest that the Street People identity comes partly from a bigger set of ideas linked to city streets in general and to the city in contrast to the country, and partly from another common assumption: that identity is somehow connected to the place where we live. The following activity will make this clearer. Try to do it quite quickly, without thinking about it too hard.

Activity 7

Which of the following would you associate with urban life (in the city) and which with rural life (in the countryside)?

Pollution, litter, excitement, freedom, crime, tradition, danger, nature, work, pleasure, fashion, health, money, noise, quiet, late nights, early mornings, immorality, morality, convention, new lifestyles.

Different answers are possible but I would guess that you associated the city with pollution, crime, noise, danger, late nights, immorality (for example, 'red-light' districts) and probably also with excitement, freedom, money and new lifestyles. These ideas aren't necessarily linked to fact. However, most people would recognise the association of the city with pollution, crime and noise; the ideas have a 'logical' connection that we might attribute to general knowledge or common sense, and which almost certainly derives from a major period of social change in the nineteenth century.

This period when cities were new and strange gave rise to the set of ideas about them (as exciting, dangerous, unhealthy, unconventional, and so on), sometimes called a **discourse**. It created certain identity positions for the kinds of people who live in the city or the country

Chapter 5 of *Making Social Lives* looks in more detail at the growth of the UK's cities since the nineteenth century, and at the dramatic changes in people's lifestyles as they left the countryside.

Discourse
A set of ideas that is shared by (some) members of a society, creates identity positions and gives a certain view of how the society functions and which people and practices are positively or negatively valued.

and, of course, the kinds of people who live on the street. Going back to our list above, we might see, or position, country people as calmer, healthier, more tuned to nature and perhaps more traditional or even old-fashioned, and city people as busier, more up-to-date and more stressed. This could lead us to position people differently according to where they live. These associations are reinforced through advertising and fictional characters (think of films and television programmes that depict country or city people). The identification of people and place can also be two-way, with the place taking a certain character from the people who live there, as in the Chinatown area in a big city.

3.2   Identity work and residence

The associations of a particular place can also become part of the way we talk and think about ourselves, and present ourselves to others. Look at this extract from an interview conducted for a research project in which people were asked 'What do you value most about where you live now?'

> Although we're living in London, here in particular we're very close to the river, we've got lots of parks. It is built up but there's quite a bit of space around. We're very fortunate to have lots of royal parks and we're very close to the river as well. It's close to central London so that should we want to use museums and the theatres etcetera we can do that.

You may notice that this is slightly repetitive. This is a normal feature of talk. The extract has been tidied to remove some other features, like hesitations and false starts, and make it more like written language. The use of talk as evidence in research is discussed at the end of this chapter.

Identity work
The performance of identity in (the details of) talk, including how the speaker positions her- or himself.

The woman who said this had grown up in the north of England and then moved to London with her husband. Her description is factual but it also helps present an identity for her: she does **identity work**, performing an identity and also positioning herself through the details of her talk. She describes the positive features of the place where she now lives, perhaps boasting a little or just presenting herself positively (remember Goffman's theory about impression management). First, she mentions those features of her home which are similar to the countryside, even though she lives in London: proximity to parks, space and the river. Second, there are the things that are (mostly) special to the city and offer opportunities for a certain kind of city life: museums and theatres, *central* London, *royal* parks. She is using two different 'big' sets of ideas or discourses here, which we could call 'nature' and 'culture', and she is positioning herself as a certain kind of person: as someone who appreciates nature *and* culture. She enjoys parks and the river, and she also values being able to go to museums and theatres. Think about the different positions that would result from different references, such as clubs, markets, sports centres or discount shops. You have probably received quite a strong impression of a certain kind of person of a certain age, lifestyle and class.

There is a lot of identity work in this short piece of talk, although the speaker is probably not fully aware of it. Goffman suggested that social scientists should study the ways that people present themselves in everyday situations. Some psychologists focus on the fine details of what people say, in interviews or just in ordinary talk. These *discursive psychologists* do not assume that people always present themselves in a calculated way (although that may sometimes be what is happening). They suggest that whenever we describe ourselves, or where we live, or anything else, we are always making small choices about wording that give one meaning rather than another. Talk is therefore a way of performing identity and also a kind of practice which does identity work, in a similar way to the movements of the shoppers and shop assistants around the store discussed in Section 1.3.

See also Chapter 6 of *Making Social Lives* for more on talk as research evidence.

Discursive psychologists are interested in the details of talk because they suggest that, just as a collective can be constructed partly through naming or labelling, each of us constructs a personal identity through references in talk to 'I', 'myself', and so on, and also through the personal life stories we tell. This 'theory of the linguistic self', proposed by Rom Harré and others, is one answer to the question I raised in Section 1.2, of how a personal identity is made (Harré and Gillett, 1994).

Another answer to the problem of 'who I am' is proposed by Anthony Giddens and other sociologists (e.g. Giddens, 1991). They suggest that each of us needs a personal identity and in contemporary society we have to make it for ourselves. This is because so many traditions have been lost that the collective identities that used to be given to us by birth and family background, such as those associated with an occupation (e.g. farming, fishing or mining) or a certain level of wealth or poverty, have now become less important. This 'theory of the identity project' emphasises personal rather than social identity,

The discussion of identity in Chapter 1 of *Making Social Lives* broadly follows this theory of the identity project.

although, as I have noted, many social scientists argue that the two are not easily separated. The theory proposes that instead of following a life course that is mostly dictated from birth (so that, for example, we live in the same place as our parents, reach a similar level of education, follow on in the family business or trade, and reach the same milestones at about the same age), each of us plans and shapes a life for ourselves, and each of us constructs 'who I am' as an individual project. We do this through the ways that we live, dress and present ourselves, including how we talk about ourselves and our personal histories and plans for the future. Talking about where we live could be another way that we do this. The box 'Researching identities 2' presents a research project that looked more generally at the importance for people's identities of the physical environment of the streets and houses where they live.

Researching identities 2: changing streets

The original Arkwright Town

In 1992–98, the social psychologist Gerda Speller conducted a research project with residents of a 100-year-old mining village who were being relocated for safety reasons (Speller, 2000; Speller et al., 2002). Arkwright Town had five rows of terraced housing with no front gardens; the front doors opened directly onto the streets. In Arkwright New Town, a short distance away, there were detached and semi-detached houses with front and back gardens, laid out in winding streets and cul-de-sacs. Speller was interested in the importance of the change in the spatial environment for people's individual and group identities.

Arkwright New Town

There were 160 households in the old town. Speller went door to door to invite residents to participate in her research. She based her findings on the twenty-two people who she was able to interview five times over six years, before, during and after the move. Her data were the interviews, which she analysed as qualitative data. She found that people's responses to the new housing in Arkwright New Town depended partly on the values they placed on collective and individual identities. In the old town, people had been more closely connected, through their memories of the past, including the mining history of the town (the mine was closed in 1988), and through their physical proximity; the terraced houses were not soundproof and it was easy to see people's comings and goings. In the new town, physical contact and connections were reduced and the collective identity of the previously close-knit community was weaker. Some people associated the change with social isolation and loss of security, others with greater freedom to live their own lives in their own ways.

Speller concluded that the change in the physical environment did not produce change in itself; it was part of a changing social context, but the new environment favoured or facilitated a more individual, less group-focused way of living.

Summary

- The many meanings attached to certain places, like the city or the country, streets or suburbs, can provide identities for the people who live there.
- The theory of the linguistic self suggests that people position themselves and construct personal identities for themselves in their talk.
- The theory of the identity project suggests that, in contemporary society, social identities have become less important and each of us makes our own identity.

4   Origins and family

4.1   A family photograph

In the previous section we saw how identity can be connected to a place of residence. The negative identity of the Street People came partly from images of streets as dirty and dangerous, while the attractive features of the woman interviewee's home seemed to extend to her as a person. Where we live seems to say something about who we are, and we often assume people who live in the same place have some collective identity; for example as 'Scousers', 'Brummies', 'Weegies', 'northerners', 'southerners' or just 'locals'. We also assume that most people have a link to some particular, original place, which has further implications for their identity. We may ask new acquaintances where they grew up or came from, as if that tells us something more about them than where they live now. (Did you notice that the woman interviewee had moved to London from the north of England?) Identities of race and ethnicity often involve an imagined link to some (other) place of origin. This emphasis on origins is not really logical because we all have connections to a number of places. We may have moved several times within our own lifetimes, and in most UK family histories there was at least one big move during the nineteenth and twentieth centuries, from the countryside to the city or from one country to another in search of better opportunities or simply a safe place to live. Nevertheless, people researching their family history look back to find their 'roots', as if every family had some single original home. This section will look at the discourse of the family to see how it provides identities and also life courses that carry certain values. It will show how some of our taken-for-granted ideas about what is normal are reinforced through everyday life practices.

It might seem obvious that a family is a known rather than an imagined group, but in the idea of origins we can see how the distinction is not clear-cut. For example, the geographer Catherine Nash has researched North Americans, Australians and New Zealanders exploring links to Ireland in their family histories. She suggests that they seek an 'imaginative repossession' of 'a land of rolling green fields and cottages' (Nash, 2003, p. 189) and they may also want to make contact with the Irish relatives they have traced. This can create tensions if they visit people in Ireland who perhaps have less interest in ancestral connections and a different, more limited imagined family.

Figure 3   The Taylor family in Auckland in 1932

Figure 3 is a photograph from part of my own family history. It was taken in 1932 and it shows three generations. A family carries certain relational family identities within it, such as parent and child, wife and husband, brother and sister. You can probably work out quite easily which people in this family are the grandparents, or first generation; which are the second generation of adult children, with husbands and wives; and which are the grandchildren who are the third generation. The newest grandchild, and first child of his parents' marriage, is being held by his father. The grandparents, the newest grandchild and his proud father are posed in the centre, showing the continuity of the family line. The baby's mother is the woman sitting on the ground in the central position. The family identities are also relational identities of gender (father/mother, brother/sister, etc.) and age or seniority (parent/ child, grandparent/grandchild).

The photographer, a neighbour, has arranged his subjects according to the conventions of the time. Nevertheless, a posed photograph of this kind can be seen as a kind of performance of identity. It represents the family but also helps to construct it; for example by including the new baby, and his parents in their new identities as mother and father, in the family led by the grandparents. The people in the photograph are dressed up in 'good' clothes and I suspect that the occasion was the christening of the baby, so it was one of the milestones in a family history and probably the first time the baby had been included in a family group. The photograph makes a statement of identity ('*we* are the Taylors'), while reinforcing established ideas of what a family should be and established values or statuses for different identities. Copies of the photograph were probably framed and displayed in various homes; this was an everyday practice and functioned as a further statement of family identity.

The arrangement of people in the photograph indicates the values attached to certain identities. Seniority is important, as are the heterosexual couple relationships through which children are to be raised to carry on the family. The women sitting on the ground on either side of the baby's mother were both unmarried. In a photograph that celebrates a certain version of the family, in which heterosexual couples become parents, it is clear that these unmarried women have a marginal position. They are less important than their parents and married siblings, standing above them; less important than their sister-in-law, in the centre, who has recently become a mother. The photographer has posed them in almost the same position as the two children, as if they, too, have not yet grown up. As a child from the next generation of this family, I was aware of the different status of these unmarried sisters. They led very different lives but both remained 'Miss Taylor' throughout their lives, and when I was a child the title seemed to me rather sad (although they were not unhappy).

Because I grew up within a family, the succession of generations in which children become parents seemed to me the normal course of life. Now I can see this photograph as a selective presentation of this normality, reinforcing the idea that there is one kind of family and also a certain life course in which children grow up to marry and have their own children. This is a celebration of heterosexual behaviour and a lifestyle centred on heterosexual couples. It reinforces 'heteronormative' values because gay identities are excluded and there is no clear forward narrative for a life that is not based on coupledom and parenting. There is also no place in the photograph for childlessness, adoption or divorce, although these too were of course part of the experience of the family.

4.2   Reinforcing normality

A display of family photographs

Photography is now much cheaper and easier than in 1932 and families have greater numbers of photographs, most less formally posed. However, when the geographer Gillian Rose (2003) studied the practices around family photographs at the beginning of the twenty-first century, she found some similar kinds of identity work taking place. Photographs were taken to commemorate important events and milestones in family life, including many of the 'first' occasions in a child's experience such as the 'first bath, first visitors, first outing, first smile, first solid food, first tooth, first shoes, first swim, first plane flight, first wedding and first birthday party' (Rose, 2003, p. 14). Some of these milestones were probably different from those celebrated in 1932 but a similar version of the normal family was constructed in the displays of photographs which Rose found in people's homes and in careful arrangements in their family albums. This kind of display reinforced similar norms and values to the 1932 photograph, bringing together successive generations of relatives, even if they had not all met in person, and sometimes covering over gaps created by emigration, divorce and death.

The psychologist Jerome Bruner (1991) suggests that we understand our lives and all the different things that happen to us by organising them into fairly conventional narratives, such as stories, histories, explanations, and so on. (An example is usually the sequence that is followed in the biographies of famous people, as I noted earlier.)

This, again, reinforces ideas of what is normal in a society, and it also 'repairs' breaks or breaches. Some of the people Gillian Rose studied arranged their photograph displays to repair the gaps in their families. The sociologist Janet Finch (2007) suggests that this kind of display may be particularly important for contemporary families which are different or have changed their relationships; for example through some members of the family moving to live elsewhere. The Taylor family photograph presents examples of this kind of repair, in this case to create new connections over time and distance. The grandparents and their children had emigrated to New Zealand from England about twenty years before the photograph was taken. The three children in the photograph, the boy and girl and the baby, were the first generation to be born in a new country, the first to be New Zealanders rather than English. The photograph is taken in the garden of the family house in Auckland (visible on the right of the photograph; the neighbour's house is behind them). The house was then fairly newly built; it is now in one of the oldest suburbs in the city. Although they were the first people to live in this house, it acquired the kind of status as the centre of family life and the site for special celebrations that traditionally belongs to a much older building, as if other generations of the family had lived there before.

The photograph therefore constructs a connected family history that extends halfway around the world. The arrangement of the photograph can be seen to construct a history backwards from this day, a narrative of family and origins that repairs the break created by emigration. It is also a photograph of hope, constructing a future for the family with a new generation to take it forward. This may have had a special importance since one of the two adult sons (the baby's father) had survived serious illness as a child and the other had been to war and returned safely.

In the same way that it constructs a certain family history, the photograph can also be seen as a part of the construction of a particular colonial and racialised national history and identity. This family were part of a migration from the British Isles that changed the meaning of 'New Zealander'. In the nineteenth century, that identity belonged to the indigenous Maori. After 1859, the majority of the people living in New Zealand were white (Belich, 1996, p. 228). By presenting this family as belonging here, in this house and garden, this photograph reinforces a version of the national history in which New Zealand begins with colonisation and the settlement of immigrants from the UK. In this history, the normal identity for a New Zealander is white and English-speaking, not brown and Maori-speaking. In the twenty-first century, after further immigration, the New Zealand identity is changing again. The white identity is being challenged, both by Maori and by recent immigrants from other parts of the world, including south-east Asia, although it still remains the majority and unmarked identity in many situations.

Summary

- Families and places of origin are another source of social and personal identities.
- Everyday practices, such as posing for photographs and displaying them in homes, can establish and reinforce as normal certain identities and lives, including family and national identities, and the lives associated with heterosexual families.

You will read more about experiments in Chapter 6 of *Making Social Lives*.

How do we know?

Collecting and analysing data 1

This chapter has discussed different kinds of identity and it has also shown some of the different ways in which social scientists theorise and research identity, including the different kinds of data they collect and analyse. Harold Garfinkel suggested that people are continuously doing things, using the skills and knowledge they have acquired as members of a society. Their activities combine to create a social world; for example, a department store functions because people know how to behave and interact as customers, shop assistants, and so on. Using the knowledge and skills they have learnt as members of the society, they maintain and repair order in society.

Garfinkel's theory of how society works is partly invented and partly based on evidence he obtained through his observation of the world. He also conducted 'breaching' experiments to test the theory and obtain further evidence. These were not formal laboratory experiments but were conducted in the 'field' or the social world. Garfinkel recruited his students to behave and interact in ways, in the streets and in their homes, that did not follow everyday practices. One experiment was for the students to behave in their homes as if they were guests rather than members of the family!

Unsurprisingly, this interrupted the order of ordinary life and created confusion and anger among the other people whose expectations of how life would proceed were breached by the students' behaviour (Garfinkel, 1967, pp. 47–8).

Jonathan Raban's discussion of the Street People was based on observation, and Raban also made himself part of the situation he was observing, as a participant. Although he is not a social scientist, he used the important research method of participant observation, in which the researcher becomes part of the situation she or he is studying, collecting observations and experiences as data. The box in Section 2.3 entitled 'Researching identities 1' describes a famous example by William Foote Whyte.

Observation and participant observation (sometimes called 'ethnography') are different ways of collecting data; that is, pieces of evidence that can be used to support or test an explanation. Another very common form of data collection in social research is an interview. Survey interviews collect 'yes' or 'no' answers that can be counted to produce **quantitative** data (for example, '45 per cent of the interviewees supported the Prime Minister'). In Section 3.2, I discussed a short extract from an interview as **qualitative** data. This was closer to the kind of interview conducted on television or radio. Social scientists often use interviews in research, in different ways. Sometimes they are just interested in the information or opinions given by the interviewees, but sometimes they look at the talk much more closely, for example to sift out the kind of half-hidden assumptions and meanings which are referred to in Section 3.1 and also in the discussion of the photograph in Section 4. In this kind of discourse analysis, the aim is to understand the commonsense or everyday knowledge of a society. Researchers might study history books, newspapers, advertisements, television programmes, photographs, talk, or any other media in which people express and receive ideas. This is also the way in which they might analysis data collected in participant observation. You read in Section 2.2 about research analysing reality television programmes. Depending on the theory the researcher is using and the question she or he is trying to answer ('Who are the people living on the streets of New York?'), any of these might provide evidence.

Gillian Rose also interviewed women for her research on family photographs. In addition, her study involved some participant observation when she went into participants' homes and was shown photographs and albums. Social science research often combines different methods of data collection, and different kinds of data

Quantitative research
Quantitative research uses evidence which can be counted and turned into percentages or other numerical data (e.g. population numbers; the percentages of people who gave certain answers in a survey).

Qualitative research
Qualitative research uses evidence which is not in numerical form (i.e. not counted). There are many different qualitative approaches; for example, using words, pictures or the researcher's observations as evidence.

Some research produces data which can be analysed either quantitatively or qualitatively. For example, a researcher could count the answers to interview questions, as in a survey (quantitative analysis) or look closely at what was said in the interview, including the words used (qualitative analysis).

(observations, pictures, interview transcripts) in this way. The box in Section 3.2 entitled 'Researching identities 2' presents another piece of research about streets and place of residence conducted by a social psychologist, Gerda Speller. Her research was also qualitative, but it is part of a social psychological tradition of work that often employs quantitative studies with results which can be counted and turned into percentages or other numerical results.

Because of the changing, constructed nature of much of the social world, most social research produces situated knowledge. For this reason, social science researchers often attempt to be part of the situation they are studying, for example as participants in participant observation or as interviewers in an interview study, and to use their own 'insider' knowledge as members of society. In Garfinkel's experiments, the researchers needed to know what counted as ordinary behaviour in order to breach it. A social scientist studying discourse would find it difficult to analyse material such as advertisements, photographs or conversation without knowing about the everyday life which these are part of. This is also the reason that social scientists may refer to themselves in the writing and in the evidence they use, and use a more informal writing style (for example, using contractions like 'don't' instead of 'do not'), as I have done in this chapter, in order to acknowledge their own presence in the research.

Activity 8

Go back to your notes from the first activity in this chapter, when you looked at photographs of people and answered the question: 'Who are these people?' Can you give any further answers, referring to the different kinds of identity and theories that this chapter has presented? Which of your answers are neutral and factual (in other words, it is unlikely anyone would disagree with them) and which involve some interpretation on your part?

Conclusion

This first chapter of the 'Connected lives' strand began with the question 'What is identity?' In Section 1, I discussed social identities, including those that are group or collective, situated and relational. The theories of Goffman and Garfinkel support a moving picture of social life in which identities and social situations are mutually constituted through people's practices. I argued against the notion of an essential personal identity, proposing instead that our subjectivity is given by our multiple social identities; in other words, all identities are social.

In Section 2, I discussed identities of difference and negatively valued identities. I began with the example of the Street People in New York and discussed Othering and unmarked and marked identities. I suggested that racial and ethnic identities are marked collective identities. They are linked to imagined communities, histories and places and continue to be shaped by the valuing and power relationships of colonial histories.

In Section 3, I discussed the identities given by where people live. These are sometimes chosen or constructed by the people themselves; for example when they use established sets of ideas, or discourses, to position themselves in certain ways, through their behaviour and in their talk. However, people are also positioned by others in ways that they cannot control; some identities may be conferred by others and are difficult to escape because of circumstances such as poverty.

In Section 4, I considered the family identities that connect people to a place of origin. Discussing a family photograph as data, I suggested that people's everyday practices, such as posing for family photographs and displaying them in their houses, may reinforce and fix ideas about normal identities and lives. My own family photograph connects personal identities to collective family and national identities, and to claims to national places. A display of photographs can also present, and repair, personal family identities.

Throughout the chapter you read about research on identities, including Whyte's famous study of street corner society, from the USA in the 1930s, and Speller's 1990s study of Arkwright Town. The final box in the chapter reviewed the different research approaches, introducing the 'How do we know?' theme for this strand – collecting and analysing data. In the next two chapters of the 'Connected lives' strand you will read more about place (Chapter 5) and about the connections and disconnections in people's relationships with their social environments and each other (Chapter 6).

References

Anderson, B. (1983) *Imagined Communities: Reflections on the Origin and Spread of Nationalism*, London, Verso.

Belich, J. (1996) *Making Peoples: A History of the New Zealanders*, Auckland, Allen Lane.

Bruner, J. (1991) 'The narrative construction of reality', *Critical Inquiry*, vol. 18, pp. 1–21.

Edwards, R., Hadfield, L., Lucey, H. and Mauthner, M. (2006) *Sibling Identity and Relationships: Sisters and Brothers*, Abingdon, Routledge.

Finch, J. (2007) 'Displaying families', *Sociology*, vol. 41, no. 1, pp. 65–81.

Garfinkel, H. (1967) *Studies in Ethnomethodology*, Englewood Cliffs, NJ, Prentice Hall.

Giddens, A. (1991) *Modernity and Self-Identity: Self and Society in the Late Modern Age*, Cambridge, Polity.

Goffman, E. (1959) *The Presentation of Self in Everyday Life*, Harmondsworth, Penguin.

Harré, R. and Gillett, G. (1994) *The Discursive Mind*, London, Sage.

Lawler, S. (2005) 'Disgusted subjects: the making of middle-class identities', *Sociological Review*, vol. 53, no. 3, pp. 429–46.

Lewis, G. and Phoenix, A. (2000) '"Race", "ethnicity" and identity' in Woodward, K. (ed.) *Questioning Identity: Gender, Class, Ethnicity*, London, Routledge/Milton Keynes, The Open University.

Nash, C. (2003) 'They're family!': cultural geographies of relatedness in popular genealogy' in Ahmed, S., Castaneda, C., Fortier, A.-M. and Sheller, M. (eds) *Uprootings/Regroundings: Questions of Home and Migration*, Oxford, Berg.

Phoenix, A. and Pattynama, P. (2006) 'Intersectionality', *European Journal of Women's Studies*, vol. 13, no. 3, pp. 187–92.

Raban, J. (1991) *Hunting Mister Heartbreak*, London, Pan.

Rose, G. (2003) 'Family photographs and domestic spacings: a case study', *Transactions of the Institute of British Geographers*, vol. 28, pp. 5–18.

Said, E.W. (1978) *Orientalism*, Harmondsworth, Penguin.

Salmon, P. (1985) *Living in Time: A New Look at Personal Development*, London, J.M. Dent.

Speller, G.M. (2000) 'A community in transition: a longitudinal study of place attachment and identity processes in the context of an enforced relocation' [online], PhD thesis, University of Surrey, http://epubs.surrey.ac.uk/cgi/viewcontent.cgi?article=1000&context=theses (Accessed 28 January 2009).

Speller, G.M., Lyons, E. and Twigger-Ross, C. (2002) 'A community in transition: the relationship between spatial change and identity processes', *Social Psychological Review*, vol. 4, no. 2, pp. 39–58.

Tajfel, H. (1981) *Human Groups and Social Categories*, Cambridge, Cambridge University Press.

Valentine, G. (2007) 'Theorizing and researching intersectionality: a challenge for feminist geography', *Professional Geographer*, vol. 59, no. 1, pp. 10–21.

Wetherell, M. (2008) 'Subjectivity or psycho-discursive practices? Investigating complex intersectional identities', *Subjectivity*, vol. 22, pp. 73–81.

Whyte, W.F. (1993) *Street Corner Society: The Social Structure of an Italian Slum*, Chicago, Chicago University Press.

Chapter 5
Connecting people and places

Steve Hinchliffe

Contents

Introduction

Figure 1   Harvest day in the Concrete to Coriander garden

Close to Birmingham's city centre, just off Small Heath High Street, there's a garden with around thirty raised beds where the gardeners, all of whom are women, are growing tomatoes, squashes, rhubarb, carrots, potatoes, beans and more (Figure 1). Like some of the other gardens that these and other women have taken on, this was formerly a derelict and unused area. This particular plot had been partly covered in concrete and was once used to store old machinery. The garden came about as a result of a social project initiated and run by a non-governmental organisation, or NGO (a name used to refer to organisations that are neither profit-making companies nor part of a government department). The NGO is called 'CSV (Community Service Volunteers) Environment' and it managed the project with the help of national lottery funding. The people at CSV Environment called the project 'Concrete to Coriander', and with it aimed to help the women, many of whom had recently migrated to Birmingham from rural areas of Pakistan, Kashmir and Bangladesh, to socialise and learn new skills. Before the project, the women had few opportunities to meet people beyond their immediate families. They felt less able than others to enjoy the outdoors. The gardening project therefore aimed to reduce isolation and 'disconnection', and to improve the women's health. It also aimed to make this part of Birmingham a little greener, or more environmentally friendly. The garden is organic, using no pesticides or artificial fertilisers. The NGO people were keen to lead projects that managed not only to get urban dwellers onto the land, but also to help those people enjoy healthy food grown locally without lots of chemicals, and without having to transport the food over long distances (adding to what many refer to as food miles – or the distance from farm to fork). In short, the project aimed to make Birmingham a better place by making some connections (between the women, between the women and the city, between urban dwellers and their environment) while replacing others (shifting food provision and consumption towards fruit and vegetables and away from food production systems that require a lot of artificial inputs and transport). It was a project that hoped to reconnect people to one another and Small Heath to its environment, and in doing so to turn Small Heath into a healthier and better place.

We'll return to the garden later on in the chapter, but for now I want to use this sketch to pose a question – why are projects like this necessary?

Activity 1

Try to jot down some answers to this question. Why do you think projects like this are necessary? Why garden projects?

You may have suggested that garden projects like this are necessary to help people who have recently moved to an area to connect to the city, to the land, to their food and to each other. The implication is that people here, in Small Heath, in Birmingham, perhaps in the UK as a whole, or certainly in its cities, find it hard to connect to each other, to their environments and to their food. For people who have recently moved to the city, making these connections may be especially difficult, but it's a general theme of the NGO's work. For CSV Environment and for other environmental NGOs, people in general need connecting to place and environment. Why should this be the case? What has happened to make some people feel that such environmental projects are necessary? A broader social science question might be to ask why some people think that modern societies are so disconnected from their place and environment.

In order to be able to generate informed discussion of this question, we'll do three things. First, in Section 1, we look at some of the ways in which British society in particular has changed in the last two centuries, as more and more people started to live in large towns and cities. What changes did this involve? Second, in Section 2, we look at the relationship between the growing cities and what became known as the countryside. Were people more connected to their environment when they lived in rural locations? Finally, in Section 3, we return to the case of the urban garden to look in more detail at its successes and problems in order to assess whether such projects can work to connect people and environments in more sustainable ways.

As you read the chapter, it is important to keep in mind that a main issue being addressed is the relationship between who people are and where and how they live. You have already learned that identities are made partly through relations with and connections to others. If where people live has an effect on the connections they make to people and to the material world, then where and how people live are important in understanding identities. In this chapter you will read about the effect that an increasingly urbanised life has on how people live and how their identities are shaped by, and can go on to shape, such experiences.

You learned about making identities through connections in Chapter 4 of *Making Social Lives*.

1   Urban experiences

1.1   Urbanisation

In 1800, four-fifths of the British population lived in small villages, in what we would now call the countryside. By 1830, half the population lived in towns. In this time of rapid change, many people in Britain, or coming to live in Britain, moved to the rapidly growing towns and cities. The reasons for these migrations were undoubtedly complex but, briefly and crudely, changes in farming (particularly the loss of common access land through changes to landholding practices), and the growing importance of manufacturing and trade to the British imperial economy, meant that a living wage was more likely to be made in a city than in the countryside.

In order to give a sense of the scale of these changes, it is useful to look at the available data on where people lived and how this changed over the course of the nineteenth century. This is not as straightforward as it sounds. Where people lived was often difficult to determine exactly. The numbers involved and the difficulty in defining the boundaries of rapidly growing towns meant that counting and classifying people as rural or urban were difficult operations. The population census, which started in 1801, had to deal with these and other difficulties. One of the first attempts to collect together the uneven census data on urban populations, and in turn give shape to modern urban studies, was Adna Weber's *The Growth of Cities in the Nineteenth Century: A Study in Statistics*, first published in 1899.

You will read more about the census in Chapter 9 of *Making Social Lives*.

Activity 2

Look at Table 1, which uses Weber's quantitative data on urban growth. Describe in words how the total population of England and Wales changed between 1801 and 1891. In comparison, how did the population of large towns (of over 20,000 people) change in the same period? What about the smallest settlements (of under 5000 people)?

Table 1   Estimates of the populations of different-sized settlements for
England and Wales, 1801–1891

Classification of settlement by population size	1801 population	1851 population	1891 population
Over 20 000	1 506 176	6 265 011	15 563 834
10 000–20 000	389 624	800 000	2 362 376
5000–10 000	418 715	963 000	1 837 054
Under 5000	6 578 021	9 899 598	9 239 261
Total population	8 892 536	17 927 609	29 002 525

Source: Weber, 1899, p. 4

There are various ways of summarising quantitative data in a table like
this, but it is important not simply to repeat what is in the table.
Instead, try to offer a descriptive overview, looking for patterns or
trends in the data. So, for example, a good way of describing the total
population change is to say that, in the first half of the nineteenth
century, the population of England and Wales doubled from nearly
9 million to almost 18 million people. By the end of the century it had
nearly doubled again to just short of 30 million. Meanwhile, the
population living in large towns increased over ten-fold in the same
period (from 1.5 million to over 15 million). It went from being a
relatively small proportion of the population (1.5 of 9 million is
17 per cent of the population) to being over half the population by
1891 (54 per cent of the total population living in the largest settlement
category). Finally, the number of people living in the smallest
settlements increased relatively slowly in the first half of the century
and then actually decreased by the end of the century.

Looking at some of the detail of the census data for individual towns, it
is possible to find some particularly intense periods of change. Between
1821 and 1841 the populations of towns and cities grew at
unprecedented rates. Populations in Glasgow, Cardiff, Belfast, Sheffield,
Birmingham and Leeds grew by over 40 per cent in this twenty-year
period. In some cities, growth was even more spectacular: Manchester's
population grew by 71 per cent between 1831 and 1841 alone. Most of
this population growth was in the centre of cities, with many people
housed in appalling conditions. But cities also spread out, with farmland
and country estates giving way to suburban housing for the growing
middle classes. So towns and cities grew in terms of the number of
people living there (their population), the density at which people lived

(the number of people per square mile/kilometre), and their built-up area or spatial extent.

These changes of *where* people lived were accompanied by changes in *how* they lived – how, for example, they made a living, the kinds of acquaintances they made, the sorts of building they lived and worked in, the kinds of environment that they contributed towards making. Indeed, **urbanisation** involved more than a physical change in the population and where it lived, it also referred to the subtle and sometimes momentous changes in the ways in which people lived their lives. The social changes and new experiences that accompanied this incredible period of growth and movement prompted one historian to describe Manchester in the 1830s as the 'shock city' of its time (Briggs, 1990).

Urbanisation
The growth of cities, including the increase in the number of people living in cities, the changes in how they live, and the experiences of living in an urbanised society.

■   Why do you think the word 'shock' is used to describe a city?

When historians and social scientists talk of shock cities they are suggesting, first, that the speed of change was rapid, not only occurring within people's lifetime but within a few years. Imagine living in a city that nearly doubled in size within ten years. Second, the word shock suggests a significant, almost traumatic, change in people's experience of the town and in their daily lives.

Some of these changes included the tendency to live closer together and at greater densities than had been the case in the countryside. People may have had to deal for the first time with living and moving among crowds and strangers. Suddenly, there were new religions to encounter, different dialects and languages to be heard. Some of the new urban dwellers may have found that established ways of doing things were now being brought into question. People, it is often said, knew their place in the countryside, whereas the possibility existed in rapidly growing towns and cities for changing some of the make-up of society. Another change was that for many people (though by no means all) the place of work became separate from their place of dwelling. There were also significant changes to how people made their living. People were less likely to be employed on the land, growing food. Instead they were more likely to be employed in manufacturing and services. Factory employment involved long hours, all year round. Wrested from the land, people might pay less attention to the details of their physical environments – gone was any direct dependence on or contact with the soil, the weather, the seasons. People's sense of time might have altered too – as more and more dwellings and streets started to be illuminated, so the relationship of day and night to people's work and leisure

Recall from Chapters 1 and 4 of *Making Social Lives* how this change could be both exhilarating and alienating (Chapter 6 will discuss some of the problems of neighbours living close together in the city or its suburbs).

patterns started to alter. Factory clocks, and clocking in and out of work, would have regulated the working day in ways that were unfamiliar to agricultural workers. To an extent, the seasons became less and less significant while the working week gained in importance (although religious and other festivals, often tied to seasonal rituals, maintained at least some memory of the importance of autumn harvests, spring and summer festivals).

Some seasonal rituals, like Whit walks, survived and thrived in cities

One way of talking about the experience of urbanisation is as a loss of place. Indeed, all of this upheaval, the 'shock' of becoming urban, prompts some social scientists to argue that urbanisation is one in a long line of social changes (including industrialisation, modernisation, globalisation) wherein people's place in the world starts to become less and less certain.

However, these observations are rather casual and general, and we need to look in some more detail to see whether or not they are justified, or hold for different cities and apply equally within those cities. Social scientists tend to develop particular approaches in order to avoid making general arguments that are unsupported by evidence. We have already come across one way of doing this, typified by Weber's use of data. Looking at data over a period of time allowed us to say some general things about changes to how and where people lived in the nineteenth century (though only in England and Wales). Another approach is to make case studies. A **case study** involves social scientists focusing their attention on a particular issue, place or event, and looking at it in detail. It may involve tracing something over a period of time. It may involve looking at how one issue, person, place or event is connected to other issues, people, places and events.

Case study
The study of a particular issue, place or event.

1.2   Urbanisation in Manchester

In order to acquire more detail on the experience of urbanisation in the nineteenth century, so that we can think more about its effects on how people live today (in particular, their possible disconnection from each other and from their immediate environments), we can look at accounts from the period. We can start with Alexis de Tocqueville, a French aristocrat who visited England in 1835. Tocqueville had previously been in the USA and was quite taken with the new nation and its politics. He saw England in the light of his experience in America. After visiting London, Tocqueville travelled to Birmingham, a city he described as being made up of independent shopkeepers and artisans. It reminded him of America, the inhabitants of the city being full of 'enterprise, self reliance and moral uplift' (quoted in Platt, 2005, p. 4). He wrote of the city's inhabitants: 'They are generally very intelligent people but intelligent in the American way' (quoted in Platt, 2005, p. 4). Whatever you make of this 'compliment', it seems he recognised in Birmingham at the time a pioneering spirit. Then, after a visit to Liverpool, he went to Manchester. Things there were quite different. Tocqueville wrote of a city already boasting 300,000 people as 'the new Hades' (hellish religious imagery was common in accounts of industrialising cities, and industrialisation was often compared to a fall from grace or to being cast out of paradise or Eden). The city, which Benjamin Disraeli claimed in his novel *Coningsby* was 'as great a human exploit as Athens', was to Tocqueville more like an alien world. Tocqueville described a world of astonishing social polarisation, a city of hovels and palaces, with remarkable wealth being produced at one and the same time as incredible poverty. He also described a world stripped of nature, detached from its place, where the soil had been taken away to be replaced by a labyrinth of streets and where the rivers had been stained orange and red with factory effluent. Even the people looked less than human to him. Stripped of individual identity, they moved as a mass, thronging the streets as crowds. Here is his description of the sights and sounds of Manchester's streets in the 1830s:

> A thousand noises disturb this damp, dark labyrinth, but they are not at all the ordinary sounds one hears in great cities. The footsteps of a busy crowd, the crunching wheels of machinery, the shriek of steam from boilers, the regular beat of the looms, the heavy rumble of carts, those are the noises from which you can never escape in the sombre half-light of these streets. You will never hear the clatter of hooves as the rich man drives back home. … Never the gay shouts of people amusing themselves, or music heralding a holiday. … Crowds are ever hurrying this way and that in the Manchester streets, but their footsteps are brisk, their looks preoccupied, and their appearance sombre and harsh. Day and night the city echoes with street noises.
>
> (quoted in Platt, 2005, p. 5)

Manchester had a lasting effect on Tocqueville. He left with a sense that he had witnessed the dark underside of progress.

Another account of nineteenth-century Manchester paints a similar story of a polarised or divided city. Friedrich Engels, who worked as a clerk in Manchester in the early 1840s, and who would go on to co-author the *Communist Manifesto* with Karl Marx, wrote in detail about Manchester's uneven social geography. In *The Condition of the Working Class in England* (in which he wrote about Manchester and also, in spite of the title, about cities and towns in Ireland and Scotland), Engels was primarily concerned to analyse the workings of a form of economic activity, **industrial capitalism**, which produced and entrenched class distinctions in industrialising nations. One of the ways in which Engels investigated capitalism was to focus on two kinds of street. The first kind was the street where many of the workers and urban poor lived. These were the people who were often employed in the new factories, were paid a pittance, and were easily laid off when economic conditions made production less profitable. In these streets there were

> usually one or two-storied cottages in long rows, perhaps with cellars used as dwellings, almost always irregularly built. These houses of three or four rooms and a kitchen form, throughout England, some parts of London excepted, the general dwellings of the working class. The streets are generally unpaved, rough, dirty,

Industrial capitalism
This form of capitalism is associated with a large investment of private money in machinery and plant, the ensuing changes in the speed and scale of production of goods, and the ways in which workers tended to become specialised within one part of the product line. It also involves a division between workers and the owners of factories, or capitalists.

filled with vegetable and animal refuse, without sewers or gutters, but supplied with foul, stagnant pools instead. Moreover, ventilation is impeded by the bad, confused method of building of the whole quarter, and since many human beings here live crowded into a small space, the atmosphere that prevails in these working-men's quarters may readily be imagined. Further, the streets serve as drying grounds in fine weather; lines are stretched across from house to house, and hung with wet clothing.

(Engels, 2005 [1845], p. 71)

Relatively new terraces, being built in an area that was known at the time as Manchester's new town (also known as Irish Town), were often no better (Figure 2). Engels noted how, in these recently built slums, the terraced houses were characteristically arranged in three rows – see

Figure 2   Densely packed urban housing built in mid-nineteenth-century Manchester

Figure 3. The houses in the first row each had a back door and a yard, and commanded the highest rent. Behind these lay a narrow alley and then two rows of back-to-back houses (having their rear walls in common). The third row faced a street, while the middle-row houses opened only onto the alley. The middle-row houses commanded the lowest of the three rents. Here ventilation and sanitation were at their worst and the risk of cholera and other infectious diseases was considered to be greatest.

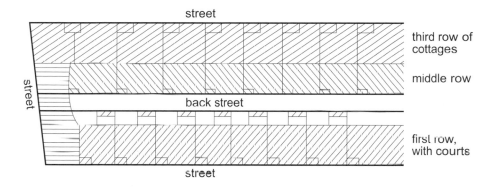

Figure 3 Engels's sketch of working-class row housing (Source: Engels, 2005 [1845], p. 95)

The second kind of street that Engels focused on was the thoroughfare, which brought middle-class commuters into the town centre. Famously, Engels remarked on just how effective these streets were at bypassing, or failing to reveal, the urban squalor that lay around them (see Figure 4).

You read about class in Chapter 1 and also in Chapter 4 of *Making Social Lives.*

> Outside, beyond this girdle [of unmixed working people's quarters], lives the upper and middle bourgeoisie, the middle bourgeoisie in regularly laid out streets in the vicinity of the working quarters ...; the upper bourgeoisie in remoter villas with gardens ... in free, wholesome country air, in fine, comfortable homes, passed once every half or quarter hour by omnibuses going into the city. And the finest part of the arrangements is this, that the members of this money aristocracy can take the shortest road through the middle of all the labouring districts to their places of business without ever seeing that they are in the midst of the grimy misery that lurks to the right and the left.

(Engels 2005 [1845], p. 86)

Shop fronts, walls and raised sections afforded a physical and mental barrier that, according to Engels, allowed the beneficiaries of urbanisation to remain untroubled by the sights, smells and sounds of the poor and unemployed. Engels saw these conditions, both the poverty and the ability of some to shield it from view, as symptomatic of a greater predicament that lay in the very ways in which society was organised.

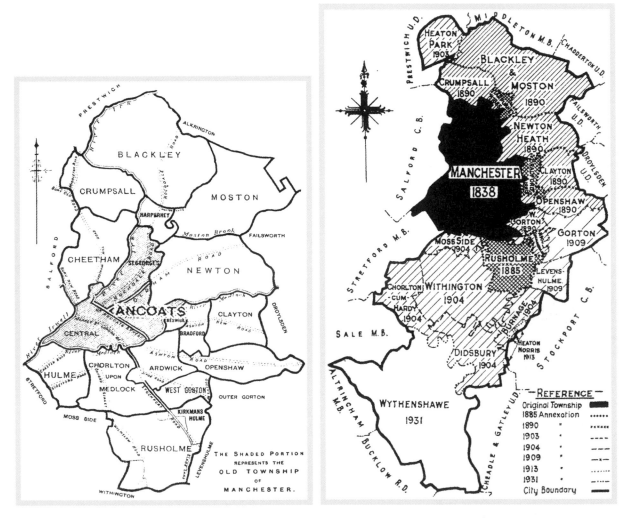

Figure 4   Maps of Manchester showing area townships in 1893 and subsequent growth of the city. The main routes in to the city are marked on the left-hand map. The original township contained most of the lower-class housing (Source: Platt, 2005, pp. 50, 315)

Activity 3

Do you think society is still divided like this, with the relatively well-off able to ignore the plight of the poor? Think about your experiences of cities that you know or have visited.

Your answer will depend on the cities with which you are most familiar, and you may want to ask others what they think. My sense is that it is still fairly easy for the relatively well-off to move around a city without being confronted by poverty and urban deprivation. The roads and train lines into Manchester and into other cities run along the same routes now as they did in Engels's day, so the same areas are bypassed and may still be shielded from view. A visitor to central Paris may be oblivious to the conditions that exist in some of the *banlieues*, or the suburbs, on the periphery of the city. The same could be said for Edinburgh and Glasgow, for Cardiff and Swansea, Newcastle and Sheffield, where the remodelling, historical restorations and general tidying of city centres is seldom matched by investment in outer suburbs. The rise of spectacularly sanitised shopping spaces, like the large malls that sometimes recreate clean and poverty-free versions of urban streets, possibly takes this process one stage further.

The Trafford Centre in Manchester, with its themed and 'sanitised' streets

You read about similar divisions between producers and consumers of goods in Chapters 1 and 2 of *Making Social Lives*.

Another aspect of this ability 'not to see' social polarisation is perhaps more developed today than in Engels's time. For a lot of the wealth that is enjoyed in places like Manchester is not simply produced by an underclass in the city's poorer areas; it is, and always has been, a wealth that is made possible by the activities of people elsewhere. So, while Manchester's factories are now mostly silent, and the streets sound very different from the day when Tocqueville made his observations, the goods that people buy in Manchester's busy high streets are being manufactured in places where poor working conditions and poverty are as rife as they were in nineteenth-century Manchester. Just as 'Cottonopolis' (as Manchester was known in the nineteenth century, owing to its wealth being derived from the finishing of textile goods) could be implicated in the production of poverty in India through the operations of the British empire and its colonial relations with cotton plantations, so can the cultural and consumer excitement of 'Madchester' (a name given to Manchester during its revival in the 1990s and later as something of a hedonistic party city) be linked to poverty and environmental problems elsewhere. The brightly illuminated high-street shops full of goods from all over the world and the designer drugs sold on the streets tell us nothing of the conditions of the working people who made those goods possible. The poverty felt in southern China or Columbia, for example, is arguably even more shielded from view than was the case in Engels's analysis (despite a much expanded mass media today).

Twenty-first century slums in Mumbai

In other modern cities the creation of poverty and wealth side by side is more apparent, but even here the wealthy tend to keep poverty 'out of sight' for most of the time. The geographer Mike Davis's (1990) depiction of Los Angeles as a city where the wealthy inhabitants of large parts of west LA can, riots notwithstanding, easily ignore the poverty of east and southern LA through bypassing them on raised freeways and interstates is one of the clearest examples. However his later work entitled *Planet of Slums* suggests that the rapid growth of poverty in many cities of the world, and the emergence of slum cities, will soon become something that politicians can no longer sweep under the carpet (Davis, 2007).

In this section we have looked at urbanisation, in a nineteenth-century British industrial city, using some historical evidence and accounts to describe and start to analyse the changes that occurred in where and how people lived in nineteenth-century Britain. For some observers, such as Tocqueville, Manchester's urbanisation was **alienating** and disruptive, reducing people to stern faces in a crowd and places to dark landscapes with little sign of nature. Both he and Engels recognised that urbanisation, and the economic changes that allowed it to occur, also produced great inequalities. The leafy suburbs and the thoroughfares that Engels described capture some of the uneven geography of the growing cities. Cities may have been shocking, but the shock was not necessarily experienced equally or evenly.

Alienation
The detachment or disconnection of people from the world or from a place. The term is sometimes used to imply a loss of identity.

Summary

- Urbanisation describes the growth of cities, the changes in where and how people live, and the experiences of living in an urbanised society.

- Urbanisation is sometimes understood to involve a disruption to people's lives, and to their relationships with each other and the environment.

- Urbanisation may differ between cities, and within the same city at different times, as its effects are unevenly felt.

2   The good life? The rural as more than local

If life in nineteenth-century cities was hard, divided and possibly alienating, what about the life in the countryside that so many left behind? Was that any easier? Or even if it had its hardships, was it somehow more authentic, connected to the rhythms of the seasons and the productivity of the soil? Is this where real identities existed?

When city life is compared with traditional rural life, the latter is often portrayed as authentic while the former is considered somehow artificial and therefore inauthentic. In this section we will look at this tendency to celebrate aspects of rural life. My aim is to show how understanding rural life as somehow more authentic than city life is both a recent idea and one that is based on a questionable view of place. In being critical of such a view, we will start to develop a sense of place as being 'more than local'.

2.1   The rural idyll

Images of rural Britain and Ireland today often seem to suggest that it is the countryside where 'real' life is to be found, where the 'real' nation and culture are located. Sometimes this imagery can be highly exclusionary, even racist, and can certainly act to engender feelings of alienation in those who, by virtue of their skin colour, dress, body shape or ability, tend not to be included in these kinds of depiction. But even where care is taken not to reproduce such limited senses of who inhabits rural Britain or Ireland, there remains a sense that the rural way of life, its embodied connections to the land, its links to the seasons and exposure to the elements, is something that reveals the true make-up of the nation. In such images, fields, farmhouses and footpaths replace streets as the locus of true national identities. Landscapes are used, in tourist brochures for example, to reflect and amplify national identities. Scotland and Wales are often depicted as rugged, a little wild maybe. Ireland is pitched as green and hospitable, with England as a land of gentle fields and landed gentry. Is this the real life that was threatened by urbanisation? In this subsection we will look at the country and the city, how the growth of cities that you have read about in Section 1 created certain feelings towards, and perhaps nostalgia for, a different life: a life connected to the fields and rhythms of Old England and ancient Celtic nations.

Images of rural UK used by the tourist industry and some 'lifestyle' publications

Comparing the images of rural life on the front of tourist brochures and countryside magazines with accounts of city life such as those supplied by Tocqueville and Engels, it would be hard not to agree that while one looks beautiful, healthy, peaceful and balanced, the other can look grim, diseased, violent and fractured. The sense that countryside and city are opposites is commonly reproduced by tourist offices, estate agents and some political commentators. Indeed, it is quite easy to construct a table like Table 2 out of these divergent views of country and city life.

Table 2   The city and the countryside as opposites

City	Countryside
Violent	Peaceful
Diseased	Healthy
Individualistic	Cooperative and communitarian
Amoral	Moral
Ugly	Beautiful
Polluted	Pure

You came across a similar set of ideas about countryside and city in Chapter 4 of *Making Social Lives*.

Yet, even while many people may be partly seduced by the imagery of a rural life, the myth of the rural idyll can usually be exploded without too much effort.

Activity 4

Reverse the headings on Table 2 so that the countryside becomes associated with violence, disease, etc. Does the table still make sense? Can you think of contemporary aspects of rural life that could be described as violent, diseased, and so on?

When I thought about it, the table still made sense – I can think of lots of instances where the countryside is violent (hunting, barbed-wire fences, poor working conditions for migrant labourers, high incidences of suicide), diseased (foot-and-mouth), individualistic (the highly competitive farming business), amoral (factory farming), polluted (forty years of nitrate fertilisers, pesticides, carbon emissions arising from the need to drive everywhere). There are clearly beautiful elements to cities (from impressive views to iconic buildings), and more and more areas of many British cities can be green and healthy. Urban rivers still have problems but can support many species of fish. Parks and open spaces are accessible and often rich in species. Cities are often highly cooperative in terms of financing public services but also sometimes in terms of collective actions (protests) and community spirit.

A famous work that helps us understand how we have come to see town and country as opposites is Raymond Williams's (1993) *The Country and the City*. In it he questions just how 'ideal' the countryside really was. He uses literary sources to provide different accounts of rural life. For example, using the parliamentarian and critical writer William Cobbett's (2001 [1830]) *Rural Rides*, written in the 1820s, Williams emphasises the abject quality of life that existed in the countryside:

> (Near Cricklade) ... The labourers seem miserably poor. Their dwellings are little better than pig-beds, and their looks indicate that their food is not nearly equal to that of a pig. Their wretched hovels are stuck upon little bits of ground *on the road side*, where the space has been wider than the road demanded. In many places they have not two rods to a hovel. It seems as if they had been swept off the fields by a hurricane, and had found shelter under the banks of the road side! Yesterday morning was a sharp frost; and this had set the poor creatures to digging up their little plots of potatoes. ... And this is '*prosperity*', is it?
>
> (William Cobbett, quoted in Williams, 1993, pp. 108–9)

Cobbett was clearly appalled by the living conditions and somewhat sympathetic to the plight of the rural poor near Cricklade, which is in Wiltshire. Importantly for us, accounts like this emphasise that poverty and misery weren't confined to the cities. As we noted earlier, one of the reasons for urbanisation was the new opportunities offered to rural people who had always lived a precarious and hard life. The people Cobbett encountered were clearly struggling to make a living. They had taken to dwelling on roadsides, presumably having lost any right to live on common land, as more and more of it became enclosed as private property.

Activity 5

Earlier it was noted how urbanisation has often been described as people losing something, especially their connection to the environment, to place, and perhaps becoming out of touch with natural rhythms (for example by working against rather than in harmony with the seasons and the soil). Reread Cobbett's account of the people in Cricklade: would you say they were in harmony with their environment, connected to or disconnected from their location? Do they have a more authentic identity than the crowds that Tocqueville lamented? Are you reminded of any other people living in rural areas today?

When I read it, I had no impression of people living in harmony with nature and environment; I understood this to be a life of hard frosts and possibly other unpredictable events, resulting in a scramble to save a small and precious (because life depended on it) crop. Life was a struggle against nature rather than a beautifully harmonious relationship with it. People were also connected to the land in the most precarious ways. Cobbett's description of people metaphorically being swept off the fields by a hurricane suggests that the dynamics of rural life were just as turbulent and hard to live with as those that affected the rapidly growing cities. Finally, the 'creatures' he refers to resemble Tocqueville's alienated crowd – these rural folk were just as much the subject of and alienated by economic and other forces as their urban contemporaries.

You read about present-day supply chains in Chapter 2 of *Making Social Lives*.

When I tried to relate Cobbett's descriptions of the landless poor to rural inhabitants today I thought of migrant workers on British farms, living on precarious wages and often in poor conditions. I also thought of the impoverished conditions that exist in many countries, and especially in the countries of what is called the global South, where worldwide changes in food prices, unfair trade relations and shifts in agricultural technologies, which result in restrictions on, for example, seed use, can have devastating effects on rural economies and rural people. Many geographers have written about the ways in which rural landscapes are deeply affected by changes elsewhere. Indeed, just as we expect prosperity in the City of London to rise and fall as share prices and global markets shift, so we can expect a farm in Cheshire, Antrim or rural Argentina to find its fortunes linked to changes elsewhere. And, given the sometime precarious nature of agriculture and the reliance on a limited number of income sources, the character and prosperity of rural locations may be even more dependent on events elsewhere than their urban counterparts.

Reading these kinds of account suggests that people who moved from the country to the city didn't necessarily leave behind real identities and real places to enter an urban world of alienation and disconnection. There was already plenty of turmoil in the countryside. A nostalgic sense of rural people being in tune with nature, and those same people being 'of' a place by being deeply connected to it, doesn't capture these realities of rural living. Struggling against the elements and living with changes that may occur on the other side of the planet is perhaps a more accurate account of rural life.

If life in the countryside was or is rarely so golden, where did this kind of view originate? Another argument we can take from Williams is that city and countryside are intimately *related*. Rather like the idea that somebody's identity is given by their relationships with others, so too were the identities of city and countryside dependent on one another. The relationship, in this case, was largely one of 'opposites'. So, if the city seemed chaotic to a newcomer, the countryside was remembered fondly as orderly. Likewise, the more the nostalgic view of countryside celebrated social cohesion, the more the towns and cities seemed to be alienating. As urban problems grew, so countryside was re-imagined as a fix for society's ills. Indeed, one common response to the urban deprivation that occurred in British and Irish cities in the nineteenth and twentieth centuries was to argue that people needed either to leave or to find some other way of escaping this artificial world of streets and factories, in order to reconnect to the *real* country – the countryside. A lot of different reasons were articulated as to why living in densely populated and industrialised towns and cities with thick winter smogs (from coal burning) and with limited access to places for physical exercise, for growing plants, for leisure, was bad for public health and social order. A critical moment may have arrived in the 1880s, when economic growth in Britain faltered and attention turned to the plight of cities, which were becoming increasingly polluted and full of political and social uncertainty and unrest (much as Engels had predicted). Urban populations were subject to disease epidemics and the health of the nation was causing concern especially as Britain embarked on a new round of wars in the far reaches of its empire and needed a healthy fighting force. Partly as a result, ideas about the countryside being some kind of panacea, a cure-all for society's ills, started to take root in the popular imagination (and really came to a head during the First World War, 1914–18, as the 'country' and the countryside became places to defend). Indeed, the countryside was increasingly linked to a golden age – becoming a lost paradise, an Eden, an Arcadia – and represented all that the city was not. There was a nostalgia for a seemingly lost place. As the trials of rural life became largely forgotten by the urbanised majority, the countryside became a romantic dream – a place to return to in order to re-create or mend the society, the nation and oneself. In many ways, this is the root of the term 'recreation', a means to mend oneself, very often in a different setting, after the toils of an

You read in Chapter 4 of *Making Social Lives* about how identity can be given by people's relationships with one another.

urbanised life. Before the city, there was no countryside. In sum, the city made the countryside, and the countryside, so made, helped to colour negative impressions of the city.

2.2   Place and identity

We have now unsettled views of the countryside as timeless, harmonious and the product of seamless relationships between inhabitants and landscapes. Rather than being closed off and self-contained, places, perhaps most particularly rural places, are open to influences from near and far. They are not simply the product of local activities. The image of a rural landscape being gently tilled by generations of farming families for years on end neglects the powerful ways in which a place is also shaped by, and possibly contributes to, things going on elsewhere. There are two ways in which this mutual shaping goes on. First of all, there are the material relationships that link places to other locations (the movements of people, money, commodities and technologies, as well as the movements of animals, air masses, plants, rivers – for this is a more than human sense of place). Second, there are the **semiotic** relationships, which here refer to ways in which meanings of places are built through their relationships with other places (for example, how countryside became defined in relation to the city). Taking these together we can say that rather than being internally coherent, bounded, and only local, places are mixed, open and **more than local**.

Semiotics
The study of how meanings are built through symbols, signs and representations.

More than local
Places are not just made by the activities and things that exist within their boundaries, but are also made by connections with and to other locations. Places in this sense are made of meetings between local and non-local activities.

To be sure, places, like people, still have their identity – just because they are affected by similar kinds of processes doesn't mean that Manchester and Cricklade become difficult to separate. Rather, what made Manchester different was its particular mix of climate, cotton weavers, canal and rail links, and many other things besides. It is the particular mix of activities and influences that give a place its character, its identity.

This view of place as a specific confluence and mix presents opportunities and challenges. As the geographer Doreen Massey has put it:

> what is special about place is not some romance of a pre-given collective identity or of the eternity of the hills. Rather, what is special about place is precisely that throwntogetherness, the unavoidable challenge of negotiating a here-and-now.
>
> ...

There can be no assumption of pre-given coherence, or of community or collective identity. Rather the throwntogetherness of place demands negotiation. In sharp contrast to the view of place as settled and pre-given, with a coherence only to be disturbed by 'external' forces, places as presented here in a sense necessitate invention; they pose a challenge.

(Massey, 2005, pp. 140–1)

So, it is not only the kinds of people and things that meet but also *how* they meet that make a place interesting and different and give it its charm, contradictions, difficulties, problems and/or possibilities. This has consequences for how social scientists and others can intervene in the politics and policies that aim to make better places. Improving a place is not an exercise in closing borders or stopping outside influences; it is rather about improving the relationships within and without. So, as an example, while it may be legitimate and right to complain that high streets from Inverness to Plymouth have lost some of their place identity as they all share the same suite of fast-food, coffee and store premises, the argument should not be based on the idea that there once existed a high street that was somehow home-grown, coherent and disconnected from the world outside. Rather, if we were to lament the loss of a sense of place on these streets, then our argument would have to be that it is not that high streets have become more and more connected to the outside world, and therefore somehow weakened as unique places, but that the quality of the connections has changed. The challenge would be to seek to build better connections and so make better places.

Activity 6

Think about a high street you know. Is there any attempt to give it a sense of place of its own? How would you improve things? (Try to think about this without reverting to a 'local is best' argument.)

This is a really tricky problem and one that no doubt exercises councils all over the country, keen as they are to generate rent from high-street premises at the same time as marketing the high street as different from every other high street. Some councils go for a mix of stores, farmers' markets and special events, and make sure the built environment is well planned – with trees, benches, squares, and so on. They are often trying, in other words, not to stem outside investment but to manage the components into a place-specific mix. But the end result can be that everyone does the same. Making a place can be difficult and is not always something that can be planned.

In this section we have done two things. First, we have demonstrated how urban *and* rural places are the product of their internal and external relations. These relationships are thought of as both material and semiotic. Second, it has been argued that places are more than local, and that their identity and character is dependent on how various people, things and activities are thrown together and relate to one another. Making better places requires attending to the complex mixing of people, things and activities. In the next section, we return to the urban garden in order to think about how to make better places.

Summary

- The rural–urban divide is often overstated. Divisions within are often greater than divisions between these categories.
- Modern views of countryside are contested.
- Places are made from their internal and external relationships. They are more than local.

3   Making better places and environments

In this final section, we return to the gardening project with which we started. Remember that the project was an attempt to make Small Heath a better place. Urban regeneration and renewal, and making cities better places in which to live, are currently highly salient issues for social science practice. The stakes are particularly high given that the majority of the world's population now lives in cities (the global figure was 49 per cent urban in 2005, and was estimated to have reached 50 per cent a year later – UN, 2008). And the environmental stresses and strains of such large and concentrated populations are of pressing significance.

Activity 7

Revisit your notes for Activity 1, when you jotted down some of the things that the gardening project was trying to achieve. Do you think now that the project was simply about connecting people to a rural past?

In the light of Sections 1 and 2, we might now add that, rather than simply trying to reconnect people to their rural past, this project was attempting to make a better place, and a better future for Small Heath and its residents.

In this section, we look at the project in more detail and record its successes and difficulties. Our aim is to think about some of the issues faced when trying to make better places.

3.1   The multiple practices that make a garden project grow

Like many things social scientists study, the gardening project is quite complex – it is produced or made by a variety of people, lots of different practices and an array of different objects, tools and other non-human elements (from worms to sunlight, from application forms to money). For example, the gardens are not only shaped by the women gardeners with their spades and hoes, they are also partly shaped by the arrangements and practices that secure funding for the project.

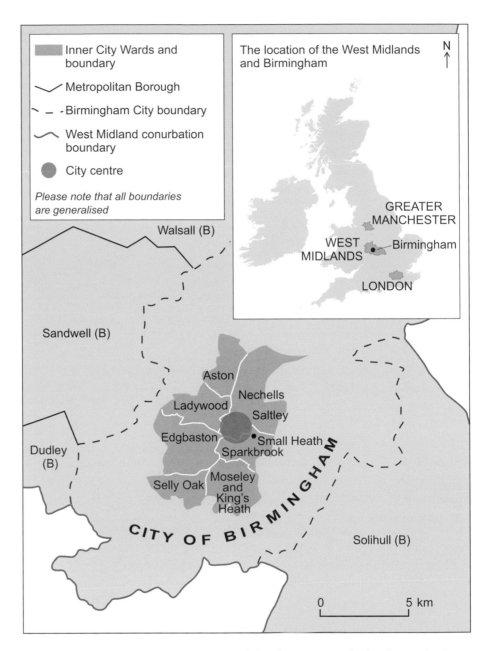

Map of Birmingham and the location of the Concrete to Coriander project

Regarding the latter, the project has to be made manageable and accountable to the people who supply the funding. They want a measurable return for the money that they offer. So, a lot of attention is given to making sure that the project manages to attract and retain a target number of gardeners, that a certain number of training courses are offered and taken up, and that a significant number of gardens are cultivated in and around Small Heath. Numbers like these are useful in justifying, governing and ordering the project. They circulate easily on pieces of paper and in offices, so that those who are funding the project (and this is a wide body of people from lottery ticket buyers to decision panels and fund managers) do not have to visit the project itself in order to feel satisfied that the money is being well spent. The project is therefore made manageable at a distance, but in being so there is some effect on how the gardening project is shaped (from the training that the women must do to how the garden is planted, and how many garden plots are taken on and therefore what degree of effort is expected from the women and the NGO team). Crucially, the funding has another large effect on the gardens. It only lasts for three years and throughout the life of the project the NGO and the women must try to imagine and then realise ways in which the gardens can continue after the money runs out.

In order to emphasise these different practices that make a garden project, and eventually to think about their relative importance and their effects on one another, it is useful to separate them out and look at how each contributes to the project. So, I will introduce the garden three times, in each case emphasising one set of practices that help to make it a reality.

Garden 1: The women's garden

A plot of land on the edge of Small Heath Park now contains raised beds in which onions, carrots, rhubarb, potatoes and lettuce are growing. There is a small greenhouse where seedlings are thinned in the spring and tomatoes are ripened in late summer. The women are busy watering, weeding, hoeing, preparing beds, checking soil fertility, staking out plants and chatting. They are growing more organic vegetables than they can eat. From time to time they cook for open days and festivals. Before they started the gardening, the women had relatively few contacts outside their families, and few places to go where they could safely enjoy being outdoors. Their health has improved, they say, and they have developed new, or rediscovered old, skills.

Garden 2: The urban renewal garden

Small Heath is a residential and former industrial area, just east of Birmingham's city centre. According to the indicators, this is a poor area. In terms of deprivation, it is in the bottom 2.5 per cent nationally. Health problems and social exclusion are particularly prominent. It is a majority minority area, with 50 per cent of residents described as British Muslim. There is a relative lack of open space. It is an action area in terms of both national regeneration budgets and open space initiatives. The garden is part of a sustainable future for the area – it helps to green the city, provides healthy activity and good food for residents, and reduces social exclusion.

Garden 3: The charity garden

At the offices of National Lottery Charities, the garden sits on various pieces of paper. There are the application forms on which garden targets are specified (how many gardens will be made over the three-year life of the project, how many women will be involved, how visual improvements will be 'dramatic' and how these will be recorded). There is a schedule of payments. There are reports written by the director of the NGO that runs the project on the gardening activities, confirming that various targets have been met and justifying others being dropped or respecified. There are written statements on the purpose of the gardening project. For example, the completed and successful project application form contains handwritten entries that speak a language of social, and personal, development: *'The project develops new skills and knowledge which foster personal development, confidence, capacity to affect change, language skills and accessing training.'* Texts like these and the pieces of paper on which they are written help the funding agencies to justify their expenditure on gardens to their trustees, to purchasers of lottery tickets and to government ministers.

The women's garden

The urban renewal garden

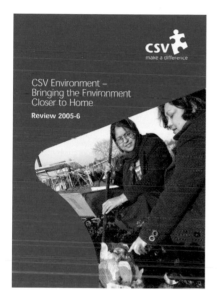

The charity garden

The three gardens overlap, of course, but they also speak of three different sets of actors (the people, and sometimes things or institutions, that have a major role in shaping affairs), different tools, different practices, different goals and different notions of time. The women's garden is shaped by hands, seasons, soil fertility and plants. It aims to produce a crop and provide a safe space for socialising. It involves 'timely' events, such as planting, thinning, pinching out shoots and harvesting. The urban renewal garden is shaped by attempts to provide a greener city, and involves future visions of redevelopment. The charity garden is shaped by spreadsheets, numbers and returns that add up over the three-year period for which funding has been granted. The garden we see on the ground, so to speak, is the result of all these practices and different kinds of time (seasons, future plans and financial returns) – see Table 3.

Table 3   What is shaping the garden?

Garden	Shaped by	Most important version of time
Women's	Bodies, weather, worms, plants, soils …	Seasons, timely events (sowing, thinning, harvesting). Rotations, maturing and skills development
Urban renewal	Plans, future visions …	Long-term change, sustainability
Charity	Spreadsheets, numbers, targets, returns …	Annual financial reports, three-year finite period for funding

The garden in Small Heath is partly a result of the 'throwntogetherness' of these three gardens. The women's enjoyment and hard work combine with the city council's backing of a greener city and the charity funding to make the garden a possibility. These gardens combine to make a garden multiple. But like any 'thing' that is made from multiple practices, there are sometimes tensions, disagreements or conflicts that can make the garden multiple start to unravel. The final column of Table 3 starts to suggest a possible tension – the garden has a number of different times associated with it, from its maturing over the years, to the future plans for a green city to the finite time of the funding. Herein lies a major tension. How can a lasting garden be produced when the funded or charity garden will soon end?

The question is an important one, for it is very difficult for projects like this to continue to secure endless financial support. Funding, as we have seen, is made manageable and orderly by having fixed time periods and set returns. Meanwhile, funders tend to sponsor new rather than existing projects, and there is a widely held assumption that funding is to help projects get off the ground rather than to keep projects running. Funders assume that, after the initial funding runs out, projects should be able to fend for themselves. Like many projects in areas where resources are scarce, this is a real problem for the women and for the NGO. While the women have learned new skills and are less isolated, without the tools, transport and guidance of the project officer who is employed by the NGO with project money, things might soon grind to a halt. Some of the women are relatively elderly, and most require help getting to and from the garden. Others in the group have paid employment and family commitments and can't take on organising the gardening. Some are reliant on social welfare payments and can't risk taking on more of a role in the garden if it means being unavailable for paid employment. Likewise, any attempts to raise money for the garden by selling produce or becoming more of a business would significantly increase the amount of time needed (and risk penalties on welfare payments). The women's future is unlikely, therefore, to be as a group of entrepreneurs, setting up and running a new business.

So what will happen when the money runs out? Will anything be left to mark the success of the project? One approach to this kind of problem and to the general issue of improving living places has involved a contested concept in social science called 'social capital'. We will look at this in the next subsection before returning to the garden to see whether or not this concept helps us to engage with making better places.

3.2   Social capital

One thing that often characterises better places is the degree to which people feel able to form friendships and acquaintanceships, to be able to meet others for social activities (such as gardening or bowling, or chatting in a pub), or to gather support in times of need. In short, it is the connections or bonds between people living in an area that are sometimes used to say whether or not it is a good place to live. Not that these bonds have to be too tight – people tend to like to be both private and public; they don't want to feel suffocated. Rather, they are ties that can be used when necessary or when desired. A term that was developed in the social sciences to capture some of this sociability is **social capital**. The term has a long history and has been used to refer to different ideas, but relevant here is the way it was reworked and popularised by the American sociologist Robert Putnam (1993, 2000), particularly in a book about American cities where life, he argued, had often become alienating and placeless. The book's title, *Bowling Alone*, communicates some of the pathos of its subjects. In these cities, the amount of social capital had decreased to almost nothing.

The concept soon took on a new life when a rough but positive correlation between the amount of social capital and the degree of affluence in an area was suggested. A correlation *describes* a relationship between two measures, or variable attributes. A positive correlation is suggested when the two measures increase or decrease together (so when social capital goes up, the area is economically better off, when it

Chapter 6 of *Making Social Lives* discusses how people manage to live close together, and how public and private are constructed through everyday activities and unwritten rules.

Social capital
The value, in terms of happiness and potential economic prosperity, of social connections and networks. The term is also used in a number of other ways in the social sciences.

goes down, people are less well off economically). A negative correlation, in contrast, is where one variable rises as the other declines. Note that correlation is only ever a description of what is observed, it does not demonstrate that one variable causes the other to change. To suggest that the relationship between the two measures is somehow causative, that one affects the other, we need to find a logical argument that links the two together. This is a form of explanation.

However, as a result of this correlation, social capital soon became a favourite tool for governments, policymakers and funding agencies. Working to raise social capital would, it was argued, raise economic well-being. The correlation was assumed in this instance to imply a causal relationship. Social capital was therefore thought of as a resource for mutual benefit and economic development. Leaving aside the fact that some very wealthy areas have little or no signs of social capital, and there are areas where reciprocities are high and economic prosperity is low, increases in social capital soon came to be the simplistic diagnosis for economically deprived areas. Cynics would say that, rather than seeking ways to improve wages or to increase employment possibilities, social capital is a rather fuzzy concept and measure of improvement, and it tends to place the responsibility for social and economic development on those people who are sometimes most disadvantaged. There is an echo of the Victorian doctrine of 'self-help' in all of this.

Returning to the garden, one of the ways in which funders justify their spending, and their withdrawal of funding for the project after the allotted time has elapsed, is to use the term social capital as a loose measure of the success of a project. If a project has worked, it will have increased social capital, which itself should help the people involved to continue making a better place. So the success of a project like this, for the funders, would not so much be whether or not the garden was beautiful, productive and enjoyable, or even that it would continue long into the future, but that there had been a growth in social capital.

Activity 8

Think about this use of social capital in terms of the other two gardens in our garden multiple (the women's garden and the urban renewal garden). Do you think an increase in social capital is a satisfactory outcome for these 'gardens'?

If the project aims to increase the social capital of the women, then the fate of the garden after the funding period has no bearing on the success or otherwise of the project. The garden becomes *immaterial* to the project. If social capital is the only criterion on which to judge the garden, then at the end of the three years the women's garden might close (for there is nothing about social capital that is particular to the gardening activity), and the women, who have worked hard to become gardeners, might find it difficult to carry on gardening. In a similar vein, those interested in greening the city would be left with little if the urban renewal garden closed. Indeed, you could say that social capital not only fails to view places as about more than people, it also fails to see them as more than local. For one of the aims of the garden was to reduce food miles, and so change the connections between Small Heath and other parts of the world. So, if the garden is only understood as a *means* to raise social capital, and is not an *end* in itself, then both the women's garden and the urban renewal garden have short and not very satisfactory lives. There is then a conflict between the different gardens. The throwntogetherness of the garden, its being made of more than one practice, requires some careful negotiation if all parties are to be satisfied with the outcomes.

There is a broader social science point here. Social capital tends to focus on a very narrow part of social life: the relationships between people. In doing so, it erases or neglects to include the importance of materials, environments and things like gardens and plants, in social life. Social life is about more than people. Social science has been complicit here in studying and eventually contributing a rather anaemic version of 'social' to the policy world. In this sense, and in the case of the gardens in Birmingham, the theory of social capital can be criticised for deflecting attention away from issues of environmental concern. We need, therefore, better measures of success than social capital, and better definitions of 'social' that allow for the fact that social life and places are about more than people. A more environmental social science might attempt to use something like moving towards **sustainability** as an indicator of building better places. The gardens, with their contribution to reducing food miles, to greening the city, to improving people's health, might constitute a small but important contribution to moving towards sustainability.

Interestingly, and as a postscript, the garden actually carried on beyond the funding deadline – it had momentum. The women had not only produced a garden, they had become gardeners (a good example of how

As you saw in Chapters 1–3 of *Making Social Lives*, social life is about more than people.

Sustainability
Defined by the World Commission on Environment and Development (1987, p. 43) as 'meeting the needs of the present generation without compromising the ability of future generations to meet their own needs'.

identities are formed from relationships with more than people!) and they, and most particularly the workers at the NGO, continued to find ways of keeping things going.

In this section, we have used a case study to reflect on efforts to make better places. We have looked at a particular project and reviewed the various practices that helped to shape its outcomes. It was useful to consider one of the project gardens as being made up of multiple practices, involving different people, artefacts and goals. Looking at 'the' garden in this way allowed us to see the work that went into making the project a reality, but also some of the tensions that existed within the project. We looked at the concept of social capital as a means to understand how some policymakers judge projects. We noted a number of concerns with the concept as it is currently used in policy work, most notably the tendency to treat everyone as potential social entrepreneurs and a tendency to underestimate the importance of environmental relations. The 'How do we know?' box reflects on this and other case studies discussed in the chapter in order to develop an enhanced understanding of their role in studying society.

Summary

- Making better places is hard work and involves the juggling of many issues and demands.
- The concept of the multiple allows us to think through the various ways in which projects and places get pushed and pulled as they develop.
- Better places are not only more than local, they are also more than human.

How do we know?

Collecting and analysing data 2: case studies

You read about several approaches to collecting and analysing data in Chapter 4 of *Making Social Lives*.

This chapter has included a variety of data, including quantitative data (Table 1). The urban garden study provides an example of one particular research approach to data collection and analysis: case studies. A case study involves social scientists focusing their attention and looking in detail at a particular issue, place or event. It may involve tracing something over a period of time; it may involve looking at how an issue, place or event is connected to other

---

issues, places and events. We can talk generally about two kinds of case study.

First, some social scientists use case studies in order to trace *broader processes*. So, for example, Engels looked at the detail of Manchester's urbanisation in order to say something about urbanisation more generally, and to produce a more general argument on how and why nineteenth-century urbanisation happens, and what its common characteristics or effects are. In this way, he pioneered a form of social science that uses a case study to develop arguments about broader, historical, processes.

In the terms of the sociologist John Law (2004), this is a form of *looking up* from the case study to bigger forces or structures and to bigger consequences, which can explain our smaller case or place it in a wider context. An apple falls (small) because there is gravity (big). A city grows in a particular way (small) because there are new relationships between business owners and working classes called industrial capitalism (big). These social scientists look for the 'macro' which organises and/or emerges from the 'micro'.

Second, case studies can be used to draw attention to the irregularities rather than the general themes of social life. They focus on social complexity, the unfinished qualities of social life. They suggest that social life is made of things that don't quite fit together. They are less happy with the notion that there are bigger forces that can be used to explain a case. Using Law's terms, this is a form of *looking down* – an attention to detail not as illustration or example of bigger and broader pictures, but as a means to understand complexity and things not quite fitting. Urbanisation in Manchester, in this view, involves much more than changing relationships between employers and employees. For Engels, the working-class populations of towns and cities were something of a mass. Engels had little to say about religious divisions, seemed to accede to a derogatory view of Irish immigrants, and had nothing to say about gender. Later, feminist and postcolonial social scientists would go on to focus on the inconsistencies within the broad category of class. Likewise, in the urban garden, the details in the case were used to challenge a restricted view of what makes good social change. Social capital, as a general tool for policymakers, was, it was argued, insufficient to capture the complexities of the issues that were faced in Small Heath.

You might see advantages in both of these approaches – looking up can give us satisfying explanations, pointing us towards the processes that we would need to alter if we wanted to change things for the better. It may, however, reduce our ability to see detail and consign some people and things to the periphery of social study. It may also make everything look almost inevitable, so that there can seem little point in trying to change things. Looking down can help us to be alert and to be affected by the details and the lack of coherence of social life, and therefore allows us to have a feeling for the complexity of making society. It can help us to see instances where people and things don't quite fit the expected pattern, and it possibly helps us to see in these details alternative ways of making and repairing social life and relationships. On the other hand, we can become so seduced by the intricacies of the case that it is easy, critics would argue, to lose the ability to make claims that can work outside the confines of our study.

While the emphases certainly vary, in practice most social scientists do both of these things – they look up and they look down and they look for multiple connections. They look for patterns in their data but are aware that things may not fit, so they need to be alert to what they might miss if they become too general or too focused.

Conclusion

This chapter has focused on where and how people live and how these can make a difference to who they are. We started by looking at the process of *urbanisation*. By looking at nineteenth-century cities I highlighted, first of all, that urbanisation has its detractors – people who felt that something human was lost as more and more people started to live in cities. But, second, we also noted that urbanisation was uneven. There were differences within cities. In the following section we looked at this sense of loss in a little more detail, noting how the notion of a rural idyll was certainly not representative of many people's experience of agricultural life. This prompted us to think some more about place and to develop an argument that all places were 'more than local'. Places are made, it was argued, through a 'throwntogetherness' of practices, people, materials and connections to other places. Making better places involves handling this kind of complexity. In the final section, we returned to a gardening project that was introduced at the start of the chapter as an example of an attempt to make a better place, not by reconnecting it to a rural past but by handling its current suite of connections. We investigated the ways in which a garden project can be thought as a multiple, made up of numerous practices, people, tools, artefacts and so on. Doing this threw up some tensions in the project and highlighted the use of a limited sense of social capital as a problem for such projects. Places and identities are not only more than local, they are also about more than people. To make better places involves attending to the connections to other places, and also to the connections between people and their environments.

References

Briggs, A. (1990) *Victorian Cities*, London, Penguin.

Cobbett, W. (2001 [1830]) *Rural Rides*, London, Penguin.

Davis, M. (1990) *City of Quartz: Excavating the Future in Los Angeles,* London, Verso.

Davis, M. (2007) *Planet of Slums,* London, Verso.

Engels, F. (2005 [1845]) *The Condition of the Working Class in England*, London, Penguin.

Law, J. (2004) 'And if the global were small and noncoherent? Method, complexity, and the baroque,' *Environment and Planning D: Society and Space*, vol. 22, no. 1, pp. 13–26.

Massey, D. (2005) *For Space*, London, Sage.

Mol, A.M. (2002) *The Body Multiple: Ontology in Multiple Practice*, Durham, NC, Duke University Press.

Platt, H.L. (2005) *Shock Cities: The Environmental Transformation and Reform of Manchester and Chicago,* Chicago, IL, University of Chicago Press.

Putnam, R. (1993) *Making Democracy Work: Civic Traditions in Modern Italy,* Princeton, NJ, Princeton University Press.

Putnam, R. (2000) *Bowling Alone: The Collapse and Revival of American Community,* New York, Simon and Schuster.

United Nations (UN) (2008) *Urban Population, Development and the Environment, 2007*, New York, United Nations.

Weber, A.F. (1899) *The Growth of Cities in the Nineteenth Century: A Study in Statistics*, New York, Cornell University Press.

Williams, R. (1993) *The Country and the City*, London, Hogarth Press.

World Commission on Environment and Development (1987) *Our Common Future*, Oxford, Oxford University Press.

Chapter 6

Living together, living apart: the social life of the neighbourhood

Jovan Byford

Contents

Introduction

The photographs of residential streets in Figure 1 have been taken at different locations in the UK. You cannot see any people in the photographs, but the houses look as if they are being lived in. We can therefore assume that they are inhabited by people who, to each other, are neighbours.

However, the still images reveal virtually nothing about how residents of these neighbourhoods and local communities get on with one another. We cannot tell whether they know or visit each other, where and how often they interact, whether they like each other or, indeed, whether they even care who else lives in their street. The photographs tell us nothing about the levels of community cohesion or neighbourhood satisfaction, about whether these streets are home to a harmonious tight-knit community in which people 'look out for one another', or whether every household lives in isolation from the rest of the neighbourhood. For all we know, these streets might be what the media and the government sometimes refer to as a 'problem neighbourhood', in which some semblance of order can be maintained only with the help of anti-social behaviour orders, court injunctions and regular patrols by police community support officers.

In this chapter we consider in more detail aspects of life in the street that are invisible in the photographs: namely, how people live together. The terms 'street' and 'neighbourhood' denote more than a geographical space inhabited by people. They also signify a set of social relations and interactions among residents that cannot be captured in a still image but need to be understood as part of a moving picture of society.

Because most people have neighbours somewhere nearby, the everyday practice of being a neighbour is often taken for granted. After all, human beings are believed to be intrinsically 'social animals' to whom living with and relating to others comes naturally. You have already read about the concept of social order – the idea that social life, while being unpredictable, fluid and ever-changing, is most of the time not disordered. Order exists because people have shared knowledge about how everyday life and social interaction should proceed, and they use it to create and maintain order. For instance, we know how to behave in a supermarket, in the street, in a cinema or in a library. We act differently in the company of our boss, friend, neighbour or child, because each of the relational identities that we take up in those interactions ('employee',

Figure 1   Some residential streets in the UK

'friend', 'neighbour', 'parent') has associated with it a distinct set of rules, habits and conventions. Life in the neighbourhood is similarly ordered and structured. It has its own norms, rules and customs; we might call these the 'grammar' of neighbouring.

And yet, as this chapter shows, living together with neighbours is not at all straightforward or easy. Take another look at the photographs in Figure 1. Part of any street's infrastructure are timber fences, hedges, walls, gates, doors, locks, curtains and other structural artefacts that are designed to keep residents *apart* rather than bring them together. The expression 'good fences make good neighbours', which you may have heard, captures the essence of a paradox that permeates life in every neighbourhood. On the one hand, neighbourhoods are, or at least are expected to be, communities of people living together, while, on the other hand, they are a collection of distinct homes inhabited by individuals, families and households whose privacy is guarded from intrusion by outsiders, including neighbours.

I became acutely aware of this paradox of contemporary neighbouring when my partner and I were buying our first home not long ago. As we viewed dozens of properties on the market, we noticed that sellers and estate agents, in making their sales pitch, often mentioned how great 'the neighbourhood' was. What they were selling was not just a roof over our heads, the bricks and mortar of our first home, but also a relationship with people living in the same street. What was interesting, however, was that, more often than not, the description of our prospective 'neighbourhood' contained within it a fundamental contradiction. On the one hand we were told that 'the next-door neighbours are really nice and quiet ... most of the time you wouldn't know that they are there', while at the same time we were being assured that 'in this street there is a real sense of community'. Thus, neighbours were said to provide the sought-after sense of solidarity, security and proximity associated with the word 'community', but they were apparently able to do so while being virtually invisible!

Much of the social life of a neighbourhood – that is, what people do *as* neighbours and what they expect *of* neighbours – can be said to reflect this paradox. As the subsequent sections show, different aspects of neighbouring – from everyday mundane interactions (Section 1), through neighbourhood complaints (Section 2), to responses to dramatic instances of violent crime in the street (Section 3) – all revolve around the need to manage and negotiate living *together* and living *apart*. Neighbours, in enacting the relational identity of 'a neighbour', are

You were introduced to social order and to relational identities in Chapter 4 of *Making Social Lives*.

continuously engaged in the process of constructing, modifying, breaching and repairing boundaries, both physical and symbolic, between the 'home' and the 'street', and between 'public' and 'private' space. In this chapter we explore how this is achieved, and how some semblance of social order and communal life in the street emerges from continuous negotiation and adjustment.

1   Everybody needs good neighbours?

Activity 1

Spend approximately five minutes thinking about a neighbourhood you live in (or one you have experienced in the past). What role do your neighbours play in your life? Do you get on with them? What do you think makes a 'good neighbour'? How many of the residents of your street or apartment block do you think you would be able to recognise? How many of your neighbours do you know by name? How often (if ever) do you talk to your neighbours? Where and when do you talk to them and what do you talk about? Have any of your neighbours ever been inside your home? Have you been in theirs?

In recent decades, sociologists, geographers, anthropologists and environmental psychologists have all been involved with the study of neighbourhoods. They have been interested in exploring neighbouring networks and practices and assessing their meaning and significance in contemporary society. The questions in Activity 1 reflect some of the issues that have attracted interest from social scientists conducting research in this area.

Every individual's relationship with neighbours depends on a variety of factors, including age, cultural background, socio-economic status, length of residence at a particular address, personality characteristics and individual preferences. However, one thing that social scientists try to do is to extrapolate from the massive amount of individual data about neighbouring relations to identify some trends and patterns that appear to be fairly constant across the UK population. These findings cannot, of course, be generalised to every person, household or street, but they nonetheless enable us to talk, in broad terms, about the state of neighbouring in contemporary UK society.

A consistent finding in social science research on neighbouring in the UK relates to the question 'what makes a good neighbour?' Studies conducted over the years in a variety of different settings found widespread agreement with regard to what residents in a neighbourhood want from those living around them. Neighbours are expected to have a 'general disposition towards friendliness' while, at the same time, respecting others' 'need for privacy and reserve' (Willmott, 1986, p. 55).

A neighbour is supposed to be 'available in times of trouble', 'friendly' and 'a bit of a giver', but they should also 'mind their own business' and not be 'intrusive' (Crow et al., 2002, p. 136). A range of studies conducted in the 1980s found that the principal neighbourly characteristics highlighted by the British public were, on the one hand, friendliness and helpfulness and, on the other hand, distance (Abrams and Brown, 1984). This finding is not unique to the UK: virtually identical conclusions were reached by researchers in the USA. In New York in the 1970s, neighbours were expected to be 'friendly', but without 'intruding on one's privacy' (McGahan, 1972, p. 402).

One conclusion that emerges from these findings is that the definition of a good neighbour revolves around the division between private and public domains. Being friendly without being intrusive, and distant without becoming a stranger, requires neighbours constantly to negotiate the fine line between, on the one hand, their own and others' demands for privacy and, on the other hand, the need to live together and foster a sense of 'community'. You may remember that social life has been compared to an endless 'slow dance', which keeps going thanks to the fact that people have the relevant *shared* knowledge, skills and understanding about the required steps and direction of movement. Pursuing the dancing analogy, I suggest that the smooth progress of social life in a neighbourhood demands that the dancers (i.e. the neighbours) maintain proximity to their partners, but without getting too close!

Social life was compared to an endless 'slow dance' in Chapter 4 of Making Social Lives.

Activity 2

How do you think that neighbours can achieve this balance between being a 'busybody' and a 'nobody' in the street (Crowe et al., 2002)? Think back to your answers to Activity 1. Do they suggest any unwritten rules that operate in neighbouring practices?

Rules governing appropriate conduct in the neighbourhood are not contained in any special 'code of conduct' or manual that gets placed on the doorstep when a person moves into a new home. Instead, what people have is culturally specific knowledge about how to interact with those living around them. They acquire and develop this knowledge through socialisation – through the practice of being a neighbour. Most

You read about socialisation, or the process of learning through experience, in Chapter 1 of Making Social Lives.

people have been neighbours and have had neighbours since birth, so they have had plenty of opportunities to pick up the necessary skills and become versed in 'being neighbourly'. Thus, when people move to a new home, even though they may not know their neighbours, they will nevertheless have some idea about how to meet, greet and interact with them as well as about what might be expected from them, as neighbours.

1.1 The geography of neighbouring: between public and private space

The unwritten rules of neighbouring – including the requirement to be friendly but without undermining the privacy of others – operate in the mundane practices of everyday life in the street, which are, for the most part, performed automatically, without conscious thought. They determine, for instance, when, where and how neighbours interact. In Activity 1 you were asked to consider where and when you talk with your neighbours. Did you mention, as I did, things like 'in front of the house', 'in the drive', 'over the garden fence', 'in the street' or 'in the local shop'? These answers indicate that my interaction with neighbours is confined mainly to public spaces (the street or a shop) or is across a physical structure (a fence or a wall) that delineates the boundary between our private spaces: namely, our homes. A 2004 study of neighbouring relations in Manchester suggests that this is quite a widespread practice. Residents reported that they communicated with neighbours primarily outside the home. They told researchers things like 'If I go out of the house and I see them I'll chat with them. But we don't go in each other's houses' or 'We don't neighbour in each others' houses' (Harris and Gale, 2004, p. 33). Even those interviewees who reported visiting or being visited by their neighbours displayed an awareness of the danger of 'over-neighbouring'. The frequency and length of neighbourly visits were mediated by the need to be seen to respect the host's right to privacy.

Social anthropologist Kate Fox's (2004) light-hearted book *Watching the English: The Hidden Rules of English Behaviour* offers an interesting example of what we might call the geography of everyday neighbourly interaction. Despite Fox's title, much of what she says – including the extract that follows – can be said to apply beyond England to other parts of the UK. Among the different spaces where neighbouring takes place, Fox identifies the 'front garden' as a typical venue for social interaction among residents of a street:

> A person busy in his or her front garden is regarded as socially 'available', and neighbours who would never dream of knocking on your front door may stop for a chat (almost invariably beginning with a comment on the weather or a polite remark about your garden). In fact, I know of many streets in which people who have an important matter to discuss with a neighbour (such as an application for a planning permission) or a message to convey, will wait patiently – sometimes for days or weeks – until they spot the neighbour in question working in his front garden, rather than committing the 'intrusion' of actually ringing the door bell.
>
> (Fox, 2004, p. 126)

Fox's somewhat caricatured account of neighbouring contains an important observation. The front of the house (even where there is no front garden as such) constitutes the interface between the public space of the street and the private domain of the home. In the UK it is not all that common to see people sitting and relaxing in front of their house in the way that they would inside their home or in the more private back garden. This is because the front of the house – being visible from the street – is for the most part thought to be too public for what are perceived to be private activities, such as sunbathing, taking a nap or having a meal. At the same time, the front garden is not a public space in the true sense of the word. In most cases, it is closed off from the street by a boundary marker in the form of a fence or a hedge. Kate Fox's reference to the front garden as a habitual space for social interaction reflects its status as something of a 'grey area' in terms of public/private, home/street division. It is a venue where neighbours can safely interact with each other without having to worry that intrusion or invasion of privacy will occur. While 'neighbouring in each other's houses' opens the possibility of 'over-neighbouring', doing so in front of the houses is evidently much less problematic.

1.2   The timing of neighbouring interaction: neighbouring as an occasioned activity

A recent ethnographic study conducted in a British suburb described neighbouring as above all an 'occasioned activity' (Laurier et al., 2002). Neighbours tend to exchange pleasantries with each other when they happen to meet in a public place (or the front garden, the drive, or a corridor in an apartment block), but ringing the neighbour's doorbell is usually associated with a specific reason, including misdirected post, a missing pet, an unexpected shortage of milk or sugar, or some kind of emergency.

Activity 3

Think back to an occasion when you knocked on a neighbour's door or they knocked on yours. Can you remember what was said when the door was answered? What reason did you or the neighbour give?

A neighbour recently came to my front door after a courier delivered a parcel to the wrong address and my neighbour found herself in possession of items that I ordered from an internet bookseller. Here is how our conversation over the doorstep went:

Neighbour:	Hi, Mr Byford?
Me:	Yeees …
Neighbour:	I'm sorry to bother you. I live over there in Cherry Avenue.
Me:	Oh … hello.
Neighbour:	I just came over to bring you this. They accidentally delivered it to 15 Cherry Avenue, rather than Cherry Grove.
Me:	Oh! Thank you very much! That's very kind of you! These things happen, I suppose, when they don't read the label properly.
Neighbour:	Yes, that's right.
Me:	Thanks for bringing it around.
Neighbour:	No problem. Bye now.
Me:	Bye … Thank you.

Let us look more closely at this brief interaction. To do this we will use a discursive psychological approach, which involves examining ordinary talk and everyday social interaction to see how identity work and

You read about discursive psychological approaches in Chapter 4 of *Making Social Lives*.

self-presentation are accomplished. As people enact particular identities, they also maintain and repair order in society because they reproduce and enforce patterns of behaviour and expectations associated with that identity. Every knock on a neighbour's door and the ensuing, often brief, interaction is an enactment and a display of the relational identity of 'neighbour', inevitably reflecting the implicit 'code of conduct' of good neighbouring.

Look back to what my neighbour said. After ensuring that she is talking to the right person ('Hi, Mr Byford?'), the next thing she says is 'I'm sorry to bother you'. This is a fairly routine greeting in such encounters, even among neighbours who know each other fairly well. The regularity with which it occurs reflects its underlying social function. It constitutes a subtle way of acknowledging that the unexpected arrival of a neighbour on the doorstep might be seen as an 'intrusion', an invasion of private space, both in a physical and a symbolic sense. My neighbour's apologetic and polite greeting implicitly acknowledges my right to privacy, and recognises that a knock on the door might be interpreted as an infringement of that right.

The next sentence is similarly revealing: 'I live over there in Cherry Avenue.' This establishes the caller's identity as a neighbour. The category 'neighbour' carries with it certain entitlements. In contrast to a representative of the gas company eager for me to change supplier, or a door-to-door salesperson offering cleaning products, a neighbour, when they knock on someone's door, can expect to be listened to courteously. After all, the norm that neighbours should be friendly and helpful to each other is one of the principal rules of neighbouring. By identifying herself as a neighbour, the caller invokes my response of 'Oh … hello' rather than the much less courteous 'Thanks, but no thanks!' with which I usually greet door-to-door salespeople. This sentence is therefore not just a piece of factual information about where the caller lives; it is a way of invoking a particular relational identity and initiating a mode of conduct associated with 'friendliness', or at least civility.

My neighbour's third utterance in our brief conversation reveals the actual reason why she knocked on my door; saying 'I just came over to bring you this' effectively pre-empts a possible question such as 'how can I help you?' or 'what can I do for you?' In other words, both of us, as skilled neighbours, were aware that knocking on someone's door is usually an 'occasioned activity' for which there ought to be a logical reason, usually a minor favour. I was expecting a reason, and the neighbour provided one without me having to prompt her. Our neighbourly 'dance' was progressing very smoothly!

So, in a few fairly routine sentences, probably uttered automatically, without careful consideration, the basic principles of neighbouring were played out – my right to privacy was acknowledged, the assumption that neighbours are to be treated in a friendly and helpful manner was invoked, and the expectation that interaction between neighbours is purposeful and occasioned was met. Note that I did not invite the neighbour to come inside the house. I am quite sure that she did not expect to be invited in either. The place of our interaction, over the doorstep and across the boundary between the outside and inside of my home, reinforced the required standards for friendliness and distance that are enshrined in neighbouring relations and which govern even such mundane, routine interactions.

1.3   'Culture clash' in the neighbourhood

Rules governing how people live together and interact in a neighbourhood are not universal. Different cultures and societies have different rules and customs regarding social interaction, both in the neighbourhood and more generally. In the Manchester neighbourliness study, one participant – identified in the report as an asylum seeker – reported being puzzled that British people whom they invited to drop by and visit their home never took up the offer. Evidently, this person – a recent arrival into the country – was not yet aware that 'just dropping by' is not a widespread neighbouring custom in the UK, although there are many countries in which it is.

Cultural differences in neighbouring 'styles' can be quite profound. In the 1970s, the anthropologist Stanley Brandes travelled to Spain to study the effect that the processes of modernisation and urbanisation (which were taking place in that country at the time) had on the life of small rural communities. In particular, Brandes was interested in the way in which traditional community life was being affected by increased economic migration of the rural workforce to large cities. To conduct his research, Brandes moved to the village of Becedas, in the mountains of Castile, in western Spain, where he observed everyday habits and customs of the residents. Compare the style of neighbouring that he

This migration in 1970s' Spain was similar to the nineteenth-century movements of people from the countryside to cities in the UK, which you read about in Chapter 5 of *Making Social Lives*.

experienced on arrival in Becedas with that which takes place in your street today:

> Neighbors entered our house without hesitation, helped us unpack and get our things in order, and offered advice on how to make our stay in the village more comfortable. Typically, they introduced themselves by saying, 'Hello, I am your neighbor, Fulano. I live just over there. If you need anything you know where [your neighbor's] house is' … Neighbors took us under their wings to such an extent that we felt as if we had been initiated into a large family.
>
> (Brandes, 1975, p. 145)

Note the comparison that Brandes makes between neighbouring in Becedas and 'family'. To the author – an American – the proximity and intimacy among neighbours in the village seemed more akin to relations within a typical American family than among residents of a neighbourhood. Brandes goes on to describe how in Becedas the distinction between the 'inside' and the 'outside' of the house was constantly blurred: residents kept the front door ajar throughout the day, neighbours went in and out of each other's homes without seeking permission; they sometimes even placed a television set on the windowsill and watched the programme from the street together with casual passers-by.

It appears, therefore, that, in Becedas, doors and windows did not delineate private and public space in the way that they do in some other societies, including the UK. Brandes goes as far as to suggest that villagers not only did not seem to care about privacy, but that they exhibited a 'pathological fear' of it (p. 154). Anyone demanding or expecting privacy was subjected to criticism and censure from other members of the community. In Becedas, 'not being intrusive' and 'reserve' were not seen as characteristics of a 'good neighbour', but of someone who is rude and impolite!

The Becedas example can be seen as an illustration of a different style of neighbouring – one that might seem exotic to an audience used to more 'distance' from neighbours. But, as Stanley Brandes discovered soon after moving to the village, there was more to neighbouring relations than was revealed by the first impression. Communal life that appeared to be defined by very close interpersonal relations in fact concealed a more complex reality.

Because Becedas was a very poor village, its residents relied on one another for work, social and practical support, household chores, etc. Villagers were heavily dependent on manual labour and old-fashioned farming techniques, which meant that neighbours needed each other to survive. And yet, this proximity and dependence on each other coexisted in everyday life with a chronic feeling of distrust among neighbours:

> It is simply assumed that if a person can get away with it, he will engage in almost any activity to further his own well-being regardless of how his actions affect others. People are viewed as compulsively unlawful, driven to lying, cheating, or stealing whenever they are given the opportunity. The saints are admired for their selflessness, but, in the real world, the trusting person is at best naive, at worst a fool, particularly vulnerable to the underhanded methods of schemers who will inevitably surround and drain him. The only bastion of reliability is the nuclear family, a protective shell that insulates its members against incursions and hostile attacks by the world outside.
>
> (Brandes, 1975, pp. 149–50)

Thus, contrary to Brandes's first impression, life in the village was actually not at all like 'a large family'. The constant visibility of neighbours, the transparency of everyone's actions and the 'pathological fear' of privacy, did not reflect trust and confidence comparable to those associated with the family. Quite the contrary, 'closeness' developed as a form of surveillance and control to ensure nobody was hiding anything or scheming against other villagers behind their backs. So, the complex network of practices and customs that appeared at first sight to signify family-like harmony and cohesiveness in fact provided the community of Becedas with a way of living together amid a broader climate of mistrust and suspicion.

Brandes's findings are interesting for two reasons. First, they suggest that, even in outwardly close-knit communities, there is a struggle going on behind the scenes to regulate (often in very subtle and non-obvious ways) the boundaries between outsiders and insiders, and between family and community. Second, Brandes's conclusions about life in Becedas were the outcome of detailed and systematic observation. His work demonstrates how social scientific research can shed light on the meaning of cultural practices, provide novel interpretations of what goes on in society and uncover things about everyday life that are not always immediately obvious.

Summary

- Life in the neighbourhood is ordered and structured. There are rules, habits and conventions – the 'grammar' of neighbouring – which regulate how people live together and interact in the street.

- Social order in the neighbourhood is reproduced even in the most mundane neighbouring practices; it determines where and how neighbours meet and talk to each other.

- Underpinning life in the neighbourhood is the need to manage the boundary between private and public space, and between home and the neighbourhood.

- Neighbouring rules are culturally specific. Rules differ across cultures, although in all of them their role is to regulate how people live both together and apart.

2   When neighbouring goes wrong: repairing social order in the neighbourhood

As I noted in the previous section, the rules that guide life in the neighbourhood are not set in stone. The boundaries between helpfulness and distance, friendliness and intrusiveness, are often fuzzy and subject to interpretation. When neighbours cannot agree on a particular interpretation of neighbouring rules, disputes arise. Because disputes between neighbours are invariably about an alleged violation of some rule of neighbouring etiquette, they provide a useful insight into the way in which social order in the neighbourhood is made and repaired. In this section we will look at a discursive psychological study that examined mediation sessions aimed at resolving neighbourhood disputes.

An official UK Government website on neighbouring (Directgov, 2009) recommends 'talking to whoever is responsible' as the first step in settling any disputes or misunderstandings. Although this is indeed how most disagreements are resolved, communication between neighbours occasionally breaks down. This is when a formal complaint is filed and the state becomes involved. A trained mediator, usually from the local council, will try to resolve the dispute to prevent it from going to court, which can be both expensive and time-consuming for all the parties involved. It is important to bear in mind, however, that the mediator is not in possession of a special rulebook containing clear guidelines regarding conduct in the neighbourhood. The mediator's role is to facilitate communication and ensure that neighbours *themselves* reconcile their differences, by talking to each other. This is what makes mediation valuable to social scientists interested in neighbouring. In discussing their problems and misunderstandings with the mediator, neighbours argue over, interpret and renegotiate the informal rules that regulate how people live together in the street.

2.1   Dealing with 'noisy neighbours': studying neighbourhood complaints

■   What do you think are the main causes of disputes between neighbours?

According to the Citizens Advice service, the most common sources of breakdown in neighbouring relations in the UK are disputes over space (boundaries, high hedges, parking space, etc.) and 'noise'. News reports and TV shows often show 'neighbours from hell' who listen to loud heavy metal music, or own dogs that bark in the night. However, the noisy neighbour problem is more complex than that because noise is not a value-neutral phenomenon definable solely through measurement of volume. It is sometimes about *what* neighbours can hear.

Social psychologist Elizabeth Stokoe (2006) examined neighbourhood complaints about a very specific noise: namely, the sounds of sexual intercourse emanating from 'next door'. What makes this type of noise the subject of neighbourhood complaint is often not the volume, but the fact that the sound itself – because of its normatively private nature – seems to violate the neighbours' private space. The widely held expectation that neighbours should maintain distance includes keeping private activities *private*.

You have also encountered transcripts in Section 3.2 of Chapter 4 of *Making Social Lives*.

In her study, Stokoe looked at transcripts from recordings of mediation sessions involving complaints about intimate noises. (A transcript is a written record of talk, of the kind discussed in Section 1.2 of this chapter.) She found that making a complaint of this nature is rarely straightforward. Taking up the government advice and simply talking about the problem can be difficult. This is at least partly because the complaint itself could be interpreted as infringing the neighbour's right to privacy, like a meddling attempt to interfere in someone's freedom to behave as they wish in their own home. What is more, any display of knowledge about what goes on in next door's bedroom leaves the person making the complaint open to accusations that they acquired that knowledge through excessive curiosity and nosiness.

Stokoe examined how neighbours in dispute managed and negotiated the various problems and difficulties associated with making and responding to complaints about intimate noises. Consider the following extract from a mediation session in which a neighbour is discussing with two mediators the conduct of a couple next door that gave rise to their complaint:

> We still talk to next door don't get us wrong, we're not uh, you know, we're not sort of walking by or whatever else, but that was basically the final straw wasn't it, but we put up with very bad language hadn't we, effing and blinding and on three occasions we've had to come in from the garden because, how

shall we – well in a delicate way of saying the young lady's love-making next door with all the windows open, you know, you wouldn't have known more of what was going on if you'd have been actually in the room.

(Stokoe, 2006, Paragraph 1.1)

The extract is interesting for several reasons. First, before describing the behaviour about which he complained, the speaker presents himself and his cohabitants as good, reasonable and tolerant neighbours. They are doing everything that neighbours are expected to do: they 'talk to next door', they are not 'walking by', they even tolerate 'bad language'. The speaker emphasises the issue of tolerance by stating that he did not complain straight away: his family retreated ('had to come in from the garden') *three* times before finally going to the authorities. Thus, in giving an account of the activities of the inconsiderate 'young lady' and her partner, the speaker also describes his actions as those of the good neighbour.

Second, note that, in making the complaint, the emphasis is placed not so much on the activity itself (lovemaking) but on the neighbours' failure to take the necessary steps to minimise the intrusion on others. The focus of the complaint is making love with 'all the windows open'. By suggesting that 'you wouldn't have known more of what was going on if you'd have been actually in the room', the neighbour making the complaint implies that he and his family were not being 'nosy neighbours', eavesdropping on the young couple. Rather, they could not help hearing what they heard. The complaint is that *their* privacy had been invaded and *their* routine (sitting in the garden) disturbed by the insensitive and inconsiderate neighbours.

What this extract shows is that the very act of making a complaint about neighbours involves a negotiation of what constitutes appropriate conduct. There is a description of what neighbouring *should* be like: that neighbours should speak to each other on the street, that they should be friendly and courteous, that they should be tolerant and put up with occasional transgression, but also that neighbours should be *considerate* to others and take every step to ensure that their private activities do not encroach on others. Therefore, underpinning the dispute about a specific case of a 'young lady's love-making' was a wider debate about what constitutes '*normal, innocuous and reasonable* versus *abnormal, provocative and unreasonable* behaviour' in the neighbourhood (Stokoe, 2006, Paragraph 3.30). In that sense, complaints, disputes and neighbourhood mediation are all essentially about creating, reproducing and reinforcing the neighbourhood's social order.

2.2   'Distancing mechanisms': dealing with neighbourhood noise without complaining

As you might imagine, neighbourhood noise is not a new problem. In her book on the history of working-class cultures in Britain, Joanna Bourke (1994) notes that, in the late 1940s and early 1950s, in working-class estates that suffered from overcrowding and where inadequate housing resulted in poor sound insulation between adjoining homes, residents regularly heard more than they wanted from 'next door':

> Neighbours complained about knowing too much about each other's intimate lives: 'you can even hear them use the [bedside] pot', blushed one woman … Others deplored hearing neighbours talk in bed: 'You sometimes hear them say rather private things, as, for example, a man telling his wife that her feet are cold. It makes you feel that *you* must say private things in a whisper.'
>
> (Bourke, 1994, p. 142)

There is little evidence to suggest that the residents of the estates mentioned by Bourke complained to the authorities about their noisy neighbours. They certainly did not have at their disposal a sophisticated, government-sponsored mediation process. In fact, you can see in the above quotation that residents were as concerned about the potential embarrassment of being overheard as they were about hearing what their neighbours were up to. So, in order to cope with the chronic lack of privacy, neighbours developed various 'distancing mechanisms' (Bourke, 1994, p. 142). They made minor adjustments to daily life in order to minimise intrusion. It was not uncommon, for instance, for conjugal beds to be 'turned away from the party-wall, so that "embarrassing noises" would not be heard' (p. 143). By physically moving their beds, neighbours endeavoured to create the optimal levels of 'distance' needed for good neighbourly relations to be maintained.

The various distancing mechanisms (which developed spontaneously and over time) reflect the very same neighbouring rules alluded to in the more recent disputes examined by Elizabeth Stokoe. In both instances, there is an underlying assumption that neighbours have the freedom to do what they like in their homes, provided that they take the necessary steps to minimise intrusion on those who live nearby. Furniture arrangement in the 1950s and the more formal neighbourhood complaints and mediation today are underpinned by the same underlying social function: to manage living, at the same time, both together and apart.

Summary

- Social order, which regulates everyday social interaction between neighbours, often consists of contradictory obligations and norms, which have to be negotiated in the course of everyday social life in the street.

- One way of studying social order in the neighbourhood, and how it is reproduced, is to look at what happens when it breaks down; that is, when disputes arise between neighbours, for instance about noise.

- Complaints, just like mundane interactions between neighbours, are about negotiating what being a 'good neighbour' is, and how a balance can be struck between the demands for 'privacy' and for 'community'.

3   Neighbours: between bystanders and intruders

The social order of the neighbourhood is not just negotiated spontaneously in everyday social interaction, or more formally through neighbourhood mediation. Neighbourhoods are a popular topic of wider public discussion and a favourite target for policymakers. There is currently a government department in charge of 'communities and local government' whose remit includes creating 'strong, attractive and thriving communities and neighbourhoods' (Department of Communities and Local Government, 2009). Also, the UK media write and broadcast about 'problem neighbourhoods', helping to perpetuate the culturally available assumptions about how neighbours should conduct themselves. Neighbourhoods are typically presented as places that ought to offer a sense of belonging, solidarity, proximity (psychological as well as physical), equality and security, but also tolerance, acceptance and a respect for autonomy, privacy and independence. Soap operas too – typically located in a 'street' or a 'square' – offer their own, somewhat exaggerated, perspective on what a local community or neighbourhood should be like (see the box below).

From Ramsay Street to your street: soaps and 'real-life' neighbouring

What would you say is the best-known neighbourhood, street or local community in the UK? Most afternoons and evenings, millions of people in the UK gather in front of their TV sets to watch soap operas such as *Coronation Street*, *EastEnders* or *Neighbours*. One of the distinguishing features of the British and Australian soap opera, as a television genre, is that at the centre of the narrative is a 'local community' (Geraghty, 1991). The action in these dramas takes place in imaginary neighbourhoods, in London ('Albert Square' in *EastEnders*), Manchester ('Coronation Street' in the soap opera of the same name) or Melbourne ('Ramsay Street' in *Neighbours*). The neighbourhood is, in fact, the principal character in these programmes. As Suzi Hush, a former producer of *Coronation Street* explains, soaps are about an exemplary local network defined by the presence of 'gossip, curiosity and belonging' (quoted in Geraghty, 1991, p. 85).

The UK's best-known street?

Although viewers generally recognise soaps to be works of fiction, 'idealised neighbourhoods', which most of the time caricature real life, such programmes have an important social function. The influence of soaps in society extends beyond mere entertainment lasting for the duration of the broadcast. At home and at work, in classrooms, pubs and cafes, viewers discuss what happened in 'the street' or 'the square' and jointly interpret and debate fictional events portrayed in these long-running programmes:

> Talking about soap operas forms part of the everyday work culture of both men and women. It is fitted in around their working time or in lunch breaks. The process takes the form of storytelling, commenting on the stories, relating the incidents and assessing them for realism, and moving from the drama to

discussing incidents which are happening in the 'real world', as reported in the media.

(Hobson, 1989, p. 150)

In the course of these discussions, referred to as 'soap talk', fiction emerges as a model, or prototype, of a neighbourhood and community life against which real-life experiences of the audience can be measured and assessed. In talking about soaps, people reiterate, reinforce and renegotiate expectations about what 'real-life' neighbourhoods should be like.

The sociologist Marie Gillespie (1994) examined 'soap talk' about the Australian drama *Neighbours* among young members of a Punjabi community in London. In spite of the important cultural differences between the predominately white, middle-class, suburban community presented in the Australian soap and the everyday life of London's Punjabi youth, Gillespie (1994, p. 145) found that *Neighbours* provided an important 'collective resource' that is used by the young Punjabis to 'compare and contrast, judge and evaluate the events and characters in the soap and those in "real life"'. The young people she spoke to used characters, plots and storylines of the soap – especially those dealing with issues of family, gender, sexuality, neighbourliness and kinship – to make sense of relations in their own families, neighbourhoods and community.

For instance, within the Punjabi community, nosy neighbours prone to rumour-mongering are often seen as threatening, especially to young women whose standing within the community is linked to the culturally specific notions of 'family honour' (or *izzat*) and the value attached to chastity. By discussing the central role that gossip, intrigue and nosiness play in the Australian soap's narrative, the young people interviewed by Gillespie were in effect commenting on acceptable and unacceptable neighbourly behaviour in their own daily lives. *Neighbours* – as a fictional neighbourhood – provided the means for making sense of everyday life and for negotiating where the boundaries between 'privacy' and 'community' should be placed.

One of the most basic assumptions about the function of the neighbourhood is that it should offer a sense of *security* to its residents. A 2001 government survey found that 84 per cent of respondents defined the 'neighbourhood' as a place where people 'look out for each other' (Attwood et al., 2003, p. 58). Authors of the Manchester neighbourliness study (who published their findings under the title *Looking Out for Each Other*) also found that respondents spoke of their neighbourhood as a 'safety zone' and as providing a 'sense of protection' (Harris and Gale, 2004, p. 16). All this suggests that, within the culturally available assumptions about neighbouring, *looking out* for one another is regarded as an intrinsic part of what it means to live together.

Because of the importance of security in popular understandings of neighbourliness, instances where specific neighbourhoods apparently fail to fulfil the prescribed protective role attract considerable attention and controversy. This is the case, for instance, when the inattention of neighbours seems to have allowed violent crimes to be committed. In this section we examine two specific examples, one from the USA and one from the UK, and explore what they can tell us about how people live together in contemporary society.

3.1   Victims of dysfunctional neighbourhoods? Catherine Genovese and James Bulger

One of the most widely reported cases of a 'neighbourhood crime' is the murder in New York, in 1964, of a young woman called Catherine 'Kitty' Genovese. She was attacked in the street where she lived late one night as she was returning home from work. During the attack, which lasted for more than half an hour, she was stabbed several times before she died, virtually on her doorstep. During the subsequent police inquiry, it emerged that the assault had been noticed by thirty-eight residents of her street. Witnesses heard Catherine Genovese scream for help and some even observed the attack from their windows. And yet, apart from a single person who yelled at the attacker to 'leave the girl alone', none intervened to help the young woman. Eventually, one of the neighbours called the police, but by then Genovese was already dead. The coroner later stated that she would have survived had the ambulance arrived only minutes earlier (Rosenthal, 2008 [1964]).

In the 1960s, murders in New York's suburbs were so common that they were not widely reported, but the Catherine Genovese story made the front page of *The New York Times*. As well as receiving huge press attention, her tragic death was later turned into a play, a feature film and a book. Many saw in the event not just a tragic end to a young life, but also the failure of a modern neighbourhood and local community to

The scene of Catherine Genovese's murder

fulfil the duty of care expected of neighbours. Commentators, journalists and professionals blamed the actions of 'indifferent' bystanders on a broader social problem, a 'Cold Society' populated by a new breed of selfish city-dweller, alienated from the community and oblivious to responsibilities towards fellow citizens (see Rosenthal, 2008 [1964]).

Periodic anxiety about the failure of the neighbourhood is not unique to the American press. Almost thirty years after the Genovese case, similar debates occurred in the British media following the abduction and murder of the 3-year-old James Bulger. In February 1993, he was taken from the Strand shopping mall in Merseyside by two 10-year-olds, Jon Thompson and Robert Venables. After leaving the shopping centre, the two boys walked with James through the suburbs of Bootle and Walton for over two hours, before taking him to an isolated section of railway track where they killed him.

The murder of James Bulger and the subsequent trial of the killers attracted unprecedented media attention both in the UK and abroad. Much of the astonishment and public outrage associated with the case was provoked by its most unusual and shocking feature: namely, the fact that the killers were only 10 years old. However, this was not the only aspect of the case that attracted press attention. During the trial of Venables and Thompson in November 1993, thirty-eight members of the public appeared in court and testified that they saw the three boys as they walked through the streets of Merseyside. (It is a curious

CCTV footage of James Bulger being taken away by his abductors from the Strand shopping centre

coincidence that the same number of bystanders — thirty-eight — were present in both the Bulger and the Genovese cases.) Most of the eye-witnesses reported that they were aware that James Bulger was in distress. Some stated that they were concerned at the time that the older boys were too young to be left in charge of a toddler without adult supervision. Others remembered observing inappropriate behaviour towards James: the older boys were said to have been 'rough', the 3-year-old was seen being 'dragged' and even 'kicked' by one of the accused. And yet only a couple of witnesses reported challenging Venables and Thompson, urging them to take the injured child to his mother. None of the thirty-eight 'bystanders' intervened in a manner that might have prevented the tragic outcome of the abduction.

The apparent indifference of the thirty-eight witnesses was instantly pounced on by the media. The newspapers branded the witnesses the 'Liverpool 38': 'the ones who saw but didn't act' (Morrison, 1996, p. 68), who 'passed by on the other side and who allowed it to pass' (Horan, 1993, p. 25). An editorial in *The Guardian* ('Lessons of an avoidable tragedy', 1993, p. 25) wondered 'Does no one "have a go" any more?', implying that the thirty-eight bystanders should have intervened to protect the young child from harm. Although the witnesses were not James Bulger's immediate neighbours, their failure to intervene was interpreted as the violation of the norm that all of us, as good neighbours, responsible citizens and members of the community, sharing a common space, walking the same streets and living together, ought to look out for each other and especially for the most vulnerable members of society: children. Just as in the Genovese case, the conduct of the 'Liverpool 38' was interpreted as a breach of a social norm governing life in and on the street.

Activity 4

Why do you think bystanders did not intervene to help Catherine Genovese or James Bulger? Do you think the same reasons applied in each case?

The murders of James Bulger and Catherine Genovese both prompted social psychological research on 'bystander intervention' to investigate the factors that determine whether onlookers (including neighbours) will or will not assist someone in an emergency situation. In the rest of this section we will explore two specific psychological studies: one from the 1960s, which followed the murder of Catherine Genovese, and the other from the 1990s, which deals directly with the James Bulger case. We will look at the insight they provide into bystander responses to real-life crimes and at two possible explanations for the 'malfunction' of neighbourhood norms that the murders were said to have exposed. The two studies used very different methods to investigate the topic of bystander behaviour, so you will be introduced to two different approaches to social psychological research.

3.2   Experimenting with emergencies: from the neighbourhood to the laboratory and back

In the aftermath of the murder of Catherine Genovese, two American psychologists, Bibb Latané and John Darley, sought to explain the failure of the thirty-eight bystanders to intervene and stop the attack. They argued against the dominant media accounts, which focused on the alleged 'apathy' of the neighbours (Latané and Darley, 1970). Latané and Darley pointed out that Genovese's neighbours were, in fact, not at all 'apathetic' or 'indifferent'. Contrary to what was reported in the media, they were disturbed by what they witnessed, and at the time of the attack they were sincerely concerned for the welfare of the young woman. The problem was that none of them *did* anything about it, at least not until it was too late. Therefore, the whole issue was not about what the bystanders *thought* or *felt* at the time of the murder (i.e. whether they were 'indifferent' or 'apathetic') but about their *failure to act* (i.e. their 'unresponsiveness'). Furthermore, Latané and Darley proposed that what happened in Catherine Genovese's street had nothing to do with the supposedly alienated, self-centred and 'un-neighbourly' residents of New York's suburbs. In their view, this was a manifestation of a broader phenomenon: namely, how people respond to an emergency situation. As Latané and Darley put it: regardless of whether we are talking about a neighbourhood crime, a car accident, a fire or an instance of drowning or attempted suicide, the reality is that, when faced with an emergency, 'people sometimes help and sometimes don't'. What they were interested in was 'What determines when help will be given?' (Latané and Darley, 1970, p. 4).

One specific issue about the Genovese case that Latané and Darley explored in their research was the widespread assumption that the sheer number of bystanders (thirty-eight) makes their inaction more surprising and worthy of scorn, as if *one* passive bystander would have been excusable, but *thirty-eight* could not be forgiven for their unresponsiveness. Latané and Darley decided to test whether and in what way the presence of other bystanders in an emergency situation affects the likelihood of intervention. Are people more likely to intervene in an emergency if they are the only witness, or if there is at least one other person present?

'Lady in distress'

Latané's and Darley's research consisted of a series of cleverly designed and carefully controlled **experiments**. Each experiment consisted of a simulated 'emergency situation' (such as an epileptic seizure, an accident at work or a fire) staged in a laboratory. The pretend 'emergencies' were witnessed by people who are known in psychology as 'participants' (or 'subjects', as they were called in the 1960s). These were members of the public (mainly psychology undergraduates) who agreed to take part in the study but who did not know what the experiment was about or that the event in question was staged. In each study, Latané and Darley systematically varied or 'manipulated' the experimental situation, including the number of other bystanders present.

Let us look in more detail at one of the experiments, which Latané, Darley and their colleague Judith Rodin called 'lady in distress'. In this study, participants were invited, either individually or in pairs, to take part in a study, which they were led to believe was about 'market research'. This was just a cover story, a minor deception used to entice prospective participants into the laboratory without having to tell them what the study was actually about. At the start of the experiment, each participant was greeted by a female 'market research representative'. The woman was a 'confederate' of the experimenters – that is, someone who

Experiment
A research method used to investigate the effect of one variable on another. It examines whether two variables (events, properties, characteristics or behaviours) are causally related.

275

acted with them in order to create the deception. She gave the participants a bogus 'market research questionnaire' to fill out, and then left the room. Shortly afterwards the following happened:

> While they worked on their questionnaires, subjects heard the representative moving around in the next office, shuffling papers, and opening and closing drawers. After about four minutes, if they were listening carefully, they heard her climb up on a chair to get a book from the top shelf. Even if they were not listening carefully, they heard a loud crash and a woman scream as the chair fell over. 'Oh my God, my foot …' cried the representative. 'I … I … can't move … it. Oh, my ankle. I … can't … can't … get this thing off … me'. She moaned and cried for about a minute longer, getting gradually more subdued and controlled. Finally, she muttered something about getting outside, knocked the chair around as she pulled herself up, and limped out, closing the door behind her.
>
> (Latané and Darley, 1970, p. 58)

The sounds from 'next door', the moans and the cries, were in fact pre-recorded and played from a tape. This ensured that each of the hundred or so participants who took part in the study had an identical experience of the 'emergency'.

The procedure was repeated over a hundred times, once for each participant, with only a very slight variation. As part of the study, the researchers varied the conditions in which those taking part heard the sounds of distress. In the original study there were four different variations, or conditions, but for the purposes of this chapter, we will look at three of them. In the first variation, twenty-six participants were alone in the room when they heard the 'emergency' next door. The researchers called this the 'Alone condition'. A further fourteen participants were in the room with one other person, another confederate of the experimenter who was pretending to be a participant, but who was instructed to ignore the sound from next door and do nothing. This was labelled the 'Passive confederate condition'. In the third variation, participants took part in the experiment in pairs. This means that two participants who did not know each other and were both oblivious to the deception, were in the room together, filling out the bogus questionnaire when they heard the 'screams' from next door. Forty participants took part in this condition, divided into twenty pairs. The experimenters called this the 'Two strangers condition'.

During the experiment, researchers recorded the number of participants in each of the conditions who abandoned the 'market research questionnaire' and went out to assist the 'lady in distress' within the predetermined time limit of two minutes. Results from the three conditions were then compared in order to see whether there was a difference in responses. Latané, Darley and Rodin wanted to determine whether the experimental manipulation (presence of others) affected the readiness of 'bystanders' to help.

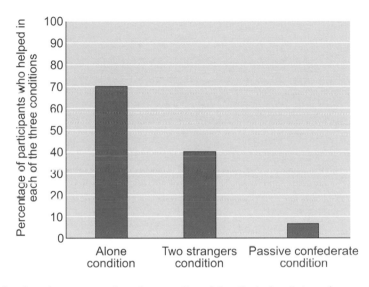

Figure 2   Graph representing the results of the 'lady in distress' experiment (Source: based on Latané and Darley, 1970)

Activity 5

Can you, just by looking at the graph in Figure 2, work out the findings of the 'Lady in distress' study? Along the horizontal axis (the *x*-axis) are three bars, each representing one of the conditions ('Alone', 'Two strangers' and 'Passive confederate') designed by Latané, Darley and Rodin. The vertical axis (the *y*-axis), which determines the size of the bars, indicates the percentage of participants (on a scale from 0 to 100) who responded in the emergency. Which condition yielded the highest rate of response? Which yielded the lowest? Try to express these findings as a sentence (or two), rather than as a graph. This activity should take you no more than five minutes to complete.

How did you get on? You probably spotted that the tallest bar represents the results from the 'Alone condition'. Indeed, in this condition, where participants witnessed the emergency on their own, as many as 70 per cent (18 out of the 26 participants) intervened to help the 'victim' within two minutes of hearing the emergency. In the 'Two strangers condition', where two participants who did not know each other were together in the room, one of them intervened in only 40 per cent of the cases (8 out of 20 pairs). This is quite a dramatic finding. According to the results, being in the presence of just one other unknown 'bystander' during an emergency reduces the chances of intervention almost by half (70 per cent compared with 40 per cent). The contrast with the 'Passive confederate condition' was even more striking: in this group only one out of the 14 participants (7 per cent) helped the 'lady in distress'. Thus, seeing another bystander do nothing is enough to reduce the chances of a person intervening in a clear emergency from 70 per cent to just 7 per cent! Put differently, a person witnessing an emergency alone is ten times more likely to intervene than someone who witnesses the same event in a company of another 'unresponsive bystander'.

Bystander effect
The finding that an individual is less likely to intervene in an emergency situation when other people are present.

The finding that the mere presence of another bystander reduces the likelihood of intervention has come to be known as the **bystander effect**. Latané, Darley and their colleagues obtained similar results in numerous other experiments involving different types of 'emergencies' which were staged both in a laboratory and outside it. In one study they found that even theology students going to a seminar on the Good Samaritan (the story from the Christian Bible about a person who helps a stranger in need) were susceptible to the 'bystander effect' (Darley and Batson, 1973). They were less likely to help a person in distress, if there was another bystander nearby. What these finding suggests is that helping behaviour in an emergency does not depend so much on what 'sort of person' someone is, or what values they subscribe to, but rather on a variety of situational factors, most notably whether someone else is present. Going back to the Catherine Genovese case, it appears that the fact that thirty-eight bystanders witnessed the attack actually reduced the chances of any individual neighbour intervening to help.

Explaining the bystander effect

How did Latané and Darley interpret these findings? Why does the presence of others inhibit intervention? First and foremost, they argued that in most cases of emergency, the appropriateness of intervention is not obvious. Most of the time, norms that regulate social life, what

Latané and Darley (1970, p. 21) call our 'mental rule book' are contradictory. For example, I have already noted the contradiction that good neighbours should be actively helpful and also distant. As Latané and Darley put it, 'the injunction to help other people' is always qualified by the requirement 'not to meddle in other people's business' (p. 20). When people witness an emergency, they therefore have to make a quick decision about which of the two conflicting norms to follow.

Bystander intervention studies have found that, when *alone*, people are more likely than not to act in an altruistic way, in other people's interest, and offer to help the person in need. Recall that in the 'lady in distress' experiment 70 per cent of participants in the 'Alone condition' responded to the emergency. However, in situations when other bystanders are present, the dynamic is different. The presence of others means that the obligation to help, implicit in the 'mental rule book', is spread among several individuals: each bystander observing an emergency can assume that one of the others will intervene. This reduces the likelihood that any of them will do so. This is the 'diffusion of responsibility' effect: each individual bystander feels less obliged to help because the responsibility seems to be divided between all the people who are present. The effect is compounded by the fact that – in deciding about whether intervention is appropriate – people tend to look to others for clues about what course of action to take. If a bystander, faced with uncertainty, sees that others are not taking action (as was the case in the 'Passive confederate condition' in the 'lady in distress' experiment) he or she is likely to reassess the situation and conclude that intervention might in fact be inappropriate.

This diffusion of responsibility partly explains the conduct of Catherine Genovese's neighbours. During the investigation, many of the witnesses told the police that they realised that the young woman was in distress, but that they still decided not to 'get involved'. This decision was made easier by the fact that the whole neighbourhood could hear the screams. Many of the witnesses probably thought 'Well, someone has probably called the police by now... maybe I could just stay out of it'. Also, as nobody seemed to be doing anything, bystanders interpreted this as an indication that what they were witnessing might not be all that serious. Otherwise someone would have phoned the police already. Hence, the fact that no one acted strengthened everyone's conviction that 'doing nothing' was probably the right course of action to take.

The bystander effect?

Much of the media frenzy at the time of the Genovese murder interpreted the passivity of the bystanders as a breakdown of neighbourhood and community life. And yet, it could be argued that the thirty-eight witnesses did not, in fact, breach any fundamental rule of 'good neighbouring'. Faced with a dramatic event in their street, they tried to work out whether they should 'look out for others' or 'mind their own business'. Latané and Darley's research on the bystander effect is valuable because it reveals a possible reason *why*, in this specific case, the neighbours ended up making the decision that they did. Latané and Darley's explanation suggests that many of Genovese's neighbours, had they been alone, would have acted in an altruistic way and called the police straight away. However, with so many other bystanders present, the responsibility for their neighbour's welfare became diffused: non-intervention seemed to be the most appropriate reaction.

3.3   The boundary between 'family' and 'community': a social psychological perspective on the abduction of James Bulger

Although Latané and Darley proposed the 'bystander effect' as a general principle that determines how people respond to emergencies, their findings cannot be said to be applicable to every real-life instance involving bystanders and an emergency. For instance, social psychologist Mark Levine has argued that the 'bystander effect', as postulated by Latané and Darley, cannot adequately account for the specific facts of the abduction and murder of James Bulger. In this case, there was considerable variation in the experiences of the thirty-eight witnesses. Some were alone when they encountered James Bulger and his abductors, while others saw them in a busy street where other passers-by were present. The bystander effect would predict a difference in reaction depending on the number of people present, yet none of the 'Liverpool 38' intervened. This led Levine to conclude that something else, above and beyond the bystander effect made the witnesses 'unresponsive'.

To explore what the decisive factor could be, Levine (1999) examined the testimonies which the thirty-eight witnesses gave in the 1993 trial of Venables and Thompson. He analysed in detail the reasons which they offered for not confronting the three boys in the street. Note the difference between the methodology used by Levine and that used by Latané and Darley. Levine did not design an experiment involving a staged emergency. Because he was interested in the details of a particular, real life case, which took place in a specific social and historical context, like Elizabeth Stokoe in her work on neighbourhood mediation, Levine analysed transcripts of interactions, accounts and explanations which occurred in a real-life context.

In his study, Levine found that the explanation for non-intervention given by bystanders in the Bulger case lay in the perceived relationship between Bulger, Venables and Thompson. Almost without exception, witnesses reported that they believed that at least one of the older boys was the toddler's brother. To the bystanders, the interaction between James Bulger and his abductors looked – at the time – like a situation involving a young child who had been left in the care of an older sibling. Although witnesses observed inappropriate behaviour by the older boys, they attributed it to poor or neglectful family care. None of them felt that what they saw constituted a matter of *public* concern or sufficient grounds for intervention by a mere passer-by.

The implication of this finding is that the inaction by the 'Liverpool 38' was not determined by some general situational factor, such as the number of bystanders present. Instead it was about the way in which witnesses, in this specific historical and social context, categorised and interpreted what they saw. They failed to act because they believed that 'strangers' do not in fact have the responsibility (or the right) to interfere in *family* affairs.

The assumption that meddling in family matters is unjustified is often taken for granted in contemporary society. During the trial itself, the witnesses did not feel compelled to explain or justify either to the court or to the general public *why* it would have been inappropriate for them as 'outsiders' to approach a group of boys whom they assumed were 'siblings'. This was accepted as part of the natural order of things. As the barrister for the prosecution noted at the time of the trial, when dealing with what is perceived as a private, *family* matter, non-intervention by outsiders is simply 'reasonable' (quoted in Young, 1996, p. 130). More disturbingly, this was something that the abductors, Jon Venables and Robert Thompson, were aware of. Two eyewitnesses who challenged them in the street and asked them about the injured toddler in their company backed away as soon as one of the boys misinformed them that James was his 'brother'. Thus, although just 10 years old, Venables and Thompson were conscious of the fact that invoking a sibling relationship would deflect suspicion and establish a symbolic boundary that curtails the curiosity of 'outsiders' and makes intervention less likely.

■   Do you think that Levine's findings satisfactorily explain why the bystanders in the Bulger case did not intervene?

With hindsight, of course, the individual judgment of each of the thirty-eight witnesses could be brought into question. It would have been better if at least one of them had called the police, or approached Venables and Thompson and questioned them with more determination about their actions. The bystanders themselves recognised this after learning of James Bulger's tragic fate. However, it is also apparent that the inaction of the bystanders reflected (rather than contravened) the norms that govern life in the street. As I have pointed out throughout this chapter, life in the neighbourhood is a maze of competing obligations, constraints and prohibitions. The requirement to exercise duty of care ('watchfulness') is always restricted by the boundaries which delineate 'insiders' and 'outsiders', the 'family' and the 'community', 'home' and the 'street'. The conduct of the bystanders in the Bulger case dramatically illustrates that, in contemporary society, the normal social rule is that people should not intervene in the family matters of others. As Levine (1999) points out, even though most instances of child abuse take place within the family, it is 'strangers' who are perceived as the greatest threat to children's well-being. This assumption about 'stranger danger' is so widespread that adults exhibit reluctance to approach children in the street, for fear that – as strangers – they might be viewed with suspicion. Thus, the conduct of the bystanders in this case was informed by broader cultural assumptions about what the appropriate conduct in the street is, and where the boundaries between 'privacy' and 'community' lie.

The murders of Catherine Genovese and James Bulger are more than just poignant examples of life in the neighbourhood that illustrate, in a dramatic way, an aspect of contemporary society. Because of the publicity they attracted, these cases also *influenced* how people interpret living together. In the aftermath of the murders, the conduct of bystanders became a topic of media scrutiny and of widespread public discussion. Mediated by the press and the electronic media, the deaths of Genovese and Bulger became embedded in popular imagination. They prompted debates, questions and re-evaluations of the norms governing conduct in the street. Like the more mundane fictional events portrayed in television soap operas, the crimes became a 'cultural resource', used by the public to make sense of the world and to challenge existing assumptions about people's rights and responsibilities towards each other and the community. Even today, the conduct of Genovese's neighbours and the inaction of the 'Liverpool 38' are occasionally summoned, in both private and public debates about what it means to be a responsible neighbour or passer-by. They have become part of the contemporary discourse of neighbouring, and as such continue to exert influence on how people perceive the world around them and how they negotiate their reaction to it.

Summary

- Social psychologists use a variety of methods to gain insight into bystander behaviour in emergencies, including experiments and detailed exploration of actual real-life instances of bystander (non-) intervention.

- Representations of neighbourhoods in the media constitute an important tool through which people make sense of their rights and obligations as neighbours and members of the community.
- Social life in the street is dynamic. The rules that govern it evolve and are transformed in the face of experience, including dramatic instances of crime reported in the media.

How do we know?

Collecting and analysing data 3

In this third chapter of Strand 2, you were introduced to experiments, a research method commonly used in psychological research to study different aspects of human behaviour. Experiments are not the only method used by psychologists, nor are they as dominant as they once were. Nevertheless, experiments occupy an important place in the history of psychology as a discipline and have provided many important insights into human behaviour.

The main feature of the experiment, as a research method, is that it involves the creation of carefully controlled experimental conditions in which the researcher is able to *isolate*, *manipulate*, and *measure* specific aspects of human behaviour. This makes it possible, in certain circumstances, to establish the causal relationship between variables. For instance, in the case of Latané and Darley's work which we looked at, by examining, in a controlled environment, how the *number of bystanders* (the variable that was manipulated in the experiment) affects the *likelihood of intervention in an emergency* (a variable that was measured in the course of the experiment), researchers were able to determine that there is a causal relationship between the presence of bystanders and non-intervention. The 'bystander effect' is, in actual fact, a description of the relationship between these two variables.

Experiments are believed to uncover general principles about human behaviour, which are independent of the broader historical and social context, and which can therefore be extrapolated to any real-life event where the relevant variables (in this case an emergency and one or more bystanders) are present. For example, although Latané and Darley discovered the 'bystander effect' in the laboratory, using psychology students as participants, they treated it as a phenomenon that accounts for behaviour in any real-life emergency situation, including the murder of Catherine Genovese, in a street in New York.

The main problem with experimental research is that the society in which people live their lives is not at all like a laboratory where experiments are conducted. In fact, the main advantage of the laboratory is that is *not* like everyday life. By design, experiments involve greatly simplified, controlled simulations which hardly mirror the complexity of everyday life and social interaction. Thus, no matter how sophisticated, cleverly designed or well thought through an experiment might be, it is inevitably artificial, and lacking what is known as **ecological validity**. This is why we should not assume that findings yielded by experimental research always shed light on real-life situations.

This was clearly revealed in Levine's study which found that the *bystander effect* is too simple to explain the conduct of witnesses in the James Bulger case. In that instance, the responses of bystanders were mediated by an additional 'variable', namely the fact that the emergency was seen as being located *within* the family. Witnesses' assumptions about the perceived rights and responsibilities of the family were not a situational factor (like the number of bystanders) but a culturally specific, evolving, historically situated influence, which could not be manipulated and measured in a controlled laboratory setting.

Ecological validity
The extent to which a study reflects naturally occurring or everyday situations. Ecological validity is often low in laboratory experiments because of the artificial nature of the controlled environment created for the purpose of the study.

Conclusion

This chapter has looked at how people live together in the neighbourhood. Section 1 examined mundane, everyday social interaction in the street – the 'where', the 'when' and the 'why' of neighbouring interaction. Section 2 looked at neighbourhood disputes and the different ways in which people go about resolving them, thus maintaining orderliness in the street. Section 3 looked at what dramatic instances of violent crime can tell us about how people live together, and how, by being discussed and debated in the media, they affect broader perceptions of community life and an individual's role in society.

This chapter also explored a number of social scientific methods which have been used to study neighbouring, including analysis of recorded and transcribed data, ethnographic studies and experiments.

The various aspects of life in the street which we looked at in this chapter all point to the fact that living together encompasses a complex set of social practices. The relational identity of 'neighbour' is not so much about *who* we are as *what we do*. Being a neighbour is a way of talking over the doorstep, knowing where and when it is appropriate to start a conversation, ring a doorbell, move a bed, close a window, make a complaint, or in some instances interfere in affairs of the family or call the police. It is about knowing, following, adapting, contesting and reproducing the culturally available (but also culturally specific and continuously changing) set of informal social rules through which order in society is maintained. This is why, as I mentioned in the introduction to this chapter, living as a member of the community is not easy. It requires the continuous negotiation of the boundaries separating 'private' and 'public' space, the 'home' and the 'community', as we coordinate and live our *connected lives*.

References

Abrams, P. and Brown, R. (1984) *UK Society: Work, Urbanism and Inequality*, London, Weidenfeld and Nicolson.

Attwood, C., Singh G., Prime, D., Creasey, R. et al. (2003) *2001 Home Office Citizenship Survey: People, Families and Communities*, London, Home Office; also available online at www.homeoffice.gov.uk/rds/pdfs2/hors270.pdf (Accessed 13 August 2008).

Bourke, J. (1994) *Working-Class Cultures in Britain 1890–1960: Gender, Class and Ethnicity*, London, Routledge.

Brandes, S.H. (1975) *Migration, Kinship, and Community: Tradition and Transition in a Spanish Village*, New York, Academic Press.

Crow, G., Allan, G. and Summers, M. (2002) 'Neither busybodies nor nobodies: managing proximity and distance in neighbourly relations', *Sociology*, vol. 36, no. 1, pp. 127–45.

Darley, J.M. and Batson, C.D. (1973) 'From Jerusalem to Jericho: a study of situational and dispositional variables in helping behavior', *Journal of Personality and Social Psychology*, vol. 27, no. 1, pp. 100–8.

Department of Communities and Local Government (2009) 'About communities and neighbourhoods' [online], www.communities.gov.uk/communities/about/ (Accessed 13 August 2008).

Directgov (2009) 'Noise nuisance and neighbour disputes' [online], www.direct.gov.uk/en/HomeAndCommunity/WhereYouLive/NoiseNuisanceAndLitter/DG_10029682 (Accessed 28 January 2009).

Fox, K. (2004) *Watching the English: The Hidden Rules of English Behaviour*, London, Hodder and Stoughton.

Geraghty, C. (1991) *Women and Soap Opera: A Study of Prime Time Soaps*, Oxford, Polity.

Gillespie, M. (1994) *Television, Ethnicity and Cultural Change*, London, Routledge.

Harris, K. and Gale, T. (2004) *Looking Out for Each Other: Manchester Neighbourliness Review* [online], Community Development Foundation, www.cdf.org.uk/site/upload/document/ManchesterNeighbourlinessReview.pdf (Accessed 13 August 2008).

Hobson, D. (1989) 'Soap operas at work' in Seiter, E., Borchers, H., Kreutzner, G. and Warth, E.-M. (eds) *Remote Control: Television, Audiences and Cultural Power*, London, Routledge.

Horan, M.D. (1993) 'We are all guilty in the Bulger tragedy', Letter to the Editor, *The Guardian,* 26 November, p. 25.

Latané, B. and Darley, J. (1970) *The Unresponsive Bystander: Why Doesn't He Help?* Englewood Cliffs, NJ, Prentice Hall.

Laurier, E., Whyte, A. and Buckner, K. (2002) 'Neighbouring as an occasioned activity: "Finding a lost cat"', *Space and Culture*, vol. 5, no. 4, pp. 346–67.

The Guardian, 'Lessons of an avoidable tragedy' (1993) 25 November, p. 25.

Levine, R.M. (1999) 'Rethinking bystander non-intervention: social categorisation and the evidence of witnesses at the James Bulger murder trial', *Human Relations*, vol. 52, no. 9, pp. 1133–55.

McGahan, P. (1972) 'The neighbour role and neighbouring in a highly urban neighbourhood', *Sociological Quarterly*, vol. 13, no. 2, pp. 397–408.

Morrison, B. (1996) *As If*, London, Granta.

Rosenthal, A.M. (2008 [1964]) *Thirty-Eight Witnesses: The Kitty Genovese Case*, New York, Melville House.

Stokoe, E. (2006) 'Public intimacy in neighbour relationships and complaints', *Sociological Research Online*, vol. 11, no. 3 [online], www.socresonline.org.uk/11/3/stokoe.html (Accessed 13 August 2008).

Willmott, P. (1986) *Social Networks, Informal Care and Public Policy*, London, Policy Studies Institute.

Young, A. (1996) *Imagining Crime: Textual Outlaws and Criminal Conversations*, London, Sage.

Conclusion: Connected lives

Stephanie Taylor

Conclusion: Connected lives

At the beginning of Strand 2, I set out the course questions for you to keep in mind while you read Chapters 4, 5 and 6.

To answer the first of these, 'How is society made and repaired?', the strand has presented a moving picture of society, discussing the different interactions and activities through which people's connections to each other, and to places, are made, re-made and repaired. These activities include people's movements, in the street and through the city, and, on a larger scale, as part of historic migrations from the countryside to the city or from one country to another. The moving picture also includes the small activities of everyday life, such as walking about a department store, sitting in the garden of a suburban house, talking to people, and posing for family photographs and displaying them. These are all shaped by society and, in turn, contribute to the making of society, even though most are carried out automatically, without much conscious thought. You also read about a project to establish a garden in an inner-city area, and a mediation service that attempted to resolve disputes between neighbours. The garden was intended to improve the urban environment, the lives of local women and even the local economy. The mediation service aimed to repair problems between neighbours before they escalated to become expensive court cases. One was funded by the National Lotteries Charity Board, run by an NGO (non-governmental organisation), and the other by local and national government. Both could be seen as more formal attempts to repair and improve society, and to establish and reinforce a certain order. You will read more about social order and the ways in which it is produced and maintained in 'Ordered lives', the third strand of the course.

The second course question I asked you to consider was 'How are differences and inequalities produced?' An important concept here was identity. You read how people's identities are social. Who they (and we) are is given or made by society, and in turn it contributes to the making or re-making of society, in a two-way process. The issue then becomes less a matter of how differences and inequalities were originally produced than how, once established, they are re-produced and reinforced through everyday activities, or, alternatively, how they are challenged or contested. Even the ways that people walk about in a street or department store are part of these processes. Jonathan Raban saw how the 'normal' passers-by of New York re-produced their difference from the Street People, by ignoring them or looking down on them. You read about how the roads and layout of cities function in a similar way, on a larger scale, in both nineteenth-century Manchester and present-day Los Angeles, enabling the wealthy to bypass poverty and slums. Throughout the strand you read about the importance of history for understanding society today, including how the colonial relationships of the British empire of the eighteenth and nineteenth centuries continue to shape racial and ethnic identities.

The third question of the course 'How do we know?' was addressed at the end of each chapter and also in the examples of research discussed throughout the strand. The moving picture of society can be difficult to study because there is so much detail to take in. Social scientists sometimes freeze the moving picture in order to look at one part of it more closely; they might focus on one street or neighbourhood, as in the two research projects, by William Foote Whyte and Gerda Speller, discussed in Chapter 4, or on a community project, such as the urban garden in Chapter 5, or on a well-publicised event that seemed to mark a special problem or breakdown of society, such as the cases of Catherine Genovese and James Bulger discussed in Chapter 6.

Social science research involves the collection and analysis of different kinds of data: both quantitative data, presented as numbers (such as the statistics on population in Chapter 5), and qualitative data. Some examples of the qualitative data you read about in this strand were pictures, official documents, and talk and transcripts, including talk from interviews (the extract in Chapter 4 of a woman talking about where she lives), from witnesses in a murder trial (in the study by Mark Levine), and from mediation sessions (in the study by Elizabeth Stokoe). You also read in Chapter 6 about various questionnaire- and interview-based research projects that collected both quantitative and qualitative data to investigate what people value in their neighbours, or where, when and how often they interact with them (e.g. the Manchester neighbourliness review).

The most important method used by social scientists to collect research data is probably observation. This usually produces qualitative data, although observations can sometimes be counted. In Chapter 4, you read about William Foot Whyte's participant observation of Cornerville society, Gillian Rose's observation of her research participants' homes, and also Jonathan Raban's more informal observation of the Street People in New York. In Chapter 5, you read about the observations of several nineteenth-century writers: Alexis de Tocqueville, Friedrich

Engels and William Cobbett. You might also have noticed that Steve Hinchliffe's study of the urban garden was based partly on his own observations. In Chapter 6, you read about another ethnographic or participant observation study in which the researcher, Stanley Brandes, moved into a neighbourhood in order to experience, first hand, its rules and practices. In this chapter, Jovan Byford also introduced the important psychology method of experiments and looked in detail at the carefully designed and executed laboratory experiments used by the social psychologists Bibb Latané and John Darley to study the behaviour of bystanders.

The moving picture of society becomes more complex

In Strand 2, 'Connected lives', you have read about people's connections to each other and to places, including streets, neighbourhoods, cities and countryside, and places of origin. As in the previous strand, 'Material lives', you have seen how the different levels or scales of small and large, personal and social life, 'micro' and 'macro', are not easily separated but connect and disconnect in complex and interesting ways. As you continue your reading, you will see further examples and you will be able to make your own connections across different chapters and strands of the course. The moving picture becomes more complex and even more interesting. The next strand explores the order within that complexity.

Introduction: Ordered lives

Simon Bromley and John Clarke

Introduction: Ordered lives

In this third strand of the course, you will be building on what you have learnt so far about studying social lives. Here the focus changes again to bring questions of social order and the ordering of social lives to the foreground. This does not mean that questions about material lives or forms of social connection disappear from view, only that more attention is focused on issues of order. The next three chapters explore some of the ways in which social life is governed and ordered. They pick up on ideas that you have met earlier in the course – for example, you have encountered issues about the ordering of lives in earlier chapters, even though their authors have not specifically drawn your attention to them. But the ways in which people live together and interact, concerns about people behaving badly, and even questions about power are closely linked to processes of ordering, or making social order.

In the following chapters, you will encounter different aspects of social order – and different social science approaches to thinking about the processes of ordering social life. But why is social order such a significant issue? We can start by thinking about the most banal or everyday examples – how do people know how to conduct themselves when they go shopping, eat a meal or study an Open University course? Such aspects of lives are ordered in the sense of being governed by rules and expectations that are more or less explicit. People (usually) become competent in living with these rules and expectations. Social order, in this sense, is a way of describing the rules and expectations that make up the ways in which we live together. By itself, this sense of social order would be enough to fascinate social scientists: how do people make up and maintain these rules and expectations, especially if they are largely unspoken or implicit? It is important that only some of these rules of behaviour or social conduct become codified – that is, written down in authoritative statements such as laws. As members of societies, people learn to read signs – both the literal authoritative signs (like 'Keep off the Grass' or 'Stop: Children'), and also the more subtle clues about how to behave, how to speak to different types of people, how to manage the process of shopping. When people are away from their own society – on holiday, for work or as a refugee, for example – they find it harder to negotiate social life and social interactions because they lack the signs and cues that allow them to make sense of everyday social order.

KEEP OFF THE GRASS
请勿践踏草坪
PEIDIWCH Â CHERDDED AR Y LAWNT
ПО ГАЗОНАМ НЕ ХОДИТЬ!
¡No pisar el césped!
A füre lépni tilos
धास पर चलना मना है

Authoritative signs?

Social scientists are interested in both the explicit and the implicit sets of rules and expectations that organise social lives and enable people to live together. They are also interested in questions about why some rules (rather than others) or some expectations (rather than others) organise social order in particular places. So, in the following chapters you will see questions about:

- how social order is made and maintained
- how social order may be disrupted or damaged
- how social order is enforced or restored in the face of threats
- how authoritative knowledge about social lives is collected and used to order or govern societies.

1 How are differences and inequalities produced?

Rules provide a mundane sense of order in which people usually know how they are expected to conduct themselves – and usually know how they expect others to behave. So, in Chapter 7, Elizabeth Silva explores how such rules (what social scientists often call norms) are shaped – and how they shape people's expectations and behaviour. Sometimes, such rules are mundane. Sometimes, they become matters of public concern and debate about how social life should be reordered – to meet new demands, challenges or possibilities. In Chapter 7, you will see examples of how the interrelationship of people and motor traffic has been ordered and reordered at different times. This points to one of the issues that you might keep in mind as you read these chapters: the idea that there are *different social orders*.

Here we can see some of the other questions that engage social scientists: how does social order differ from place to place, and from one time to another? It might be obvious that all societies have social order, and we might indeed ask: could they be societies if they did not? However, they do not have the same social order. Rather, each society has its own specific order: whether this concerns how traffic is ordered, how people go about shopping, or how different positions or roles in society are interrelated (for example, how lords behave to peasants; how parents treat children). Social orders also change over time – societies are not static things. Many aspects of social relationships and social behaviour change, sometimes, as Chapter 7 indicates, as a consequence of intentional action. So, social scientists are fascinated by these questions about difference (different social orders in different places); change (and how it comes about); and attempts to organise, direct or change aspects of social order. In short, we can rephrase the course question about how differences and inequalities are produced for this strand as: *how do social orders differ and change and with what consequences for people's lives?*

Order/disorder or different social orders? Askham, UK and Christiania, Denmark

2 How is society made and repaired?

In everyday life, people often become conscious of social order (and its rules) at moments where those rules appear to be threatened or broken – where disorderly conduct or behaviour happens. We can rephrase the course question about how society is made and repaired for this strand as follows: *how are social order and disorder connected in social life?* Disorder may range from tiny social failures (e.g. addressing someone in an impolite way) to much larger moments of social and political disorder (e.g. the breakdown of order following disasters or invasions). Between these extremes are concerns about the social disorders of disruptions to everyday life, uncivil behaviour, crime, violence, disturbances of the peace, and so on. Here members of the public, the mass media, governments and the social sciences tend to share an interest in disorderly behaviour and disorderly people. Since the end of the twentieth century, there has been anxiety about 'anti-social' behaviour in the UK. Chapter 8, by Bob Kelly and Jason Toynbee, looks at such concerns about disorderly behaviour, including these recent ideas of 'anti-social' behaviour. The chapter explores the relationship between our ideas of social order and disorder, and looks particularly at the contributions of social scientists to explaining and understanding disorderly behaviour of various kinds.

Chapters 7 and 8 both point to relationships between governments and social order – as public authorities try to plan, shape our environment and intervene in how we behave. Chapter 9, by Evelyn Ruppert and Engin Isin, builds on these concerns to explore how governments know who we are. The UK population – like the populations of other countries – needs to be known by governments so that governments can do the business of governing. Systematic knowledge about populations is a relatively recent development – but censuses and surveys are now well-established techniques of government. Such knowledge is collected to enable policies and decisions to be taken on an 'informed basis'. But what sorts of information are produced by censuses? Who decides how the population is to be categorised and subdivided? Chapter 9 opens up the techniques and practices of census making to a revealing enquiry about how knowledge about us is produced and used.

And don't forget … we know where you live!

Together, these three chapters introduce central social science concerns with the ordering of social lives. At the end of the 'Ordered lives' strand we will return to the question of why social scientists are interested in social order and ordering. Studying how social order is made and remade implies an interest in the processes (how do ordering processes shape or govern social life?) and practices (what actions, activities and actors are involved in the processes of ordering?). Of course, these three chapters will not tell you everything about ordering social lives – they are starting points for thinking about these issues.

Chapter 7
Making social order

Elizabeth B. Silva

Contents

Introduction

I drove down Harehills Avenue, stopped at the traffic lights and turned right into Harehills Lane, towards Chapel Allerton. About 400 metres uphill the car concerned (a Vauxhall) emerged at speed out of Avenue Hill on my left driving immediately in front of my car. I braked but the Vauxhall braked and continued across Harehills Lane turning into Sycamore Avenue, which is nearly immediately opposite Avenue Hill on Harehills Lane. No right turn sign was given. To avoid hitting the side of the Vauxhall I swerved to the right, also into Sycamore Avenue. Because the Vauxhall was driven onto the right lane, instead of the left, my car hit its back right panel. When the collision occurred I was almost stopping (1–2 km/h).

All the roads are on a two-way system and I had to do some careful and skilful driving to prevent a major accident. The woman driving the Vauxhall had a young, tall and strong male companion who came over to me in a threatening manner asking me to settle the matter without insurance involvement. I said 'No, we'd better exchange details. This is clearly not my fault.' (I provided paper and pencil and wrote the details – names, contact details, number plates, the location of the accident, insurance companies – for me and her.)

What might a social scientist draw out from the account above in relation to questions of social order? The extract, written for the purpose of an insurance claim, tells how a car accident occurred and what ensued immediately afterwards. We can see that an accident of this sort, which started with a momentary disorder (a driver not giving way to a car on a main road and not giving a signal), is in breach of the rules that govern motor traffic in the UK. Is this a breakdown of a social order? The car driver making the claim is following all the required **norms** about driving along an urban street: speed limit, traffic lights, side of the road to drive on. She is met by the other driver who is not following the norms: she is speeding, not keeping the required distance from another car, nor signalling a right turn. Trying to avoid a major accident, the first driver also breaks the norms, swerving into a road on her right-hand side. A companion of the second driver, identified as tall, strong, young and male, appears to threaten the first driver with a suggestion that she feels to be entirely *out of order*.

Norms
Shared sets of values or expectations about how people will or should behave.

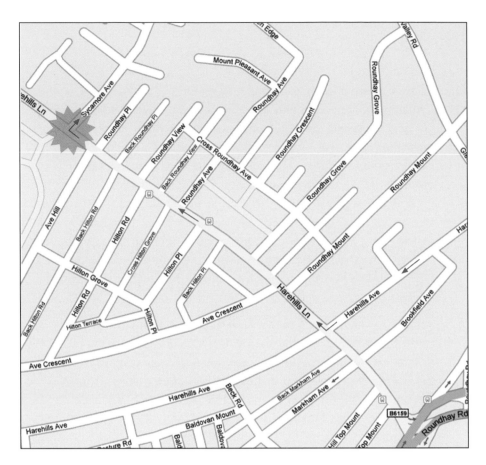

The scene of the car accident

These interactions build on the breaches of the rules of the road. They do not comply with the rules governing traffic accidents (especially reporting to insurance companies). But the first driver also feels that the companion's behaviour breaches rules of social conduct: she sees him as acting in a threatening manner. She nevertheless insists on following the rules of exchanging details, as prescribed for these sorts of events.

Where do rules and norms such as these come from? Driving rules are created to manage some of the dangers and risks of motor traffic. Insurance procedures serve to guide conduct by individuals offering prescriptions about what to do to make claims for damages. How people behave towards one another is also governed by rules, although often in ways that are very imperceptible or not explicitly stated. How do people know when someone is being threatening, rather than assertive or insistent? A social order involves a sense of how individuals all fit together in shared spaces. The car accident is an example of how we make sense of, and make use of, shared norms. First of all, there needs to be a clear understanding, sophisticated enough to include reading signals and signs and behaving appropriately. This is a basic ingredient of interaction in common social practices. The knowledge about what is shared in human conduct, which is often not articulated, implies a grasp of physical and social spaces, like in a map where people and things are located in particular places, and in relation to each other, where routes and behaviours are indicated, making it possible to understand how the relationships work.

The collision results from disorderly behaviour breaking these rules of conduct. Looking at this event we can see the complexity of the ordering of the social. We can see several different sorts of rules or norms for managing disorder in this illustration. There are understandings or expectations of how driving should proceed, of how people involved in an accident should speak to each other (breached by the companion's behaviour), and of the procedures that are to be followed. Here, social order contains and manages disruption because a sort of code of behaviour is in place to deal with what happened. The extract, written for an insurance company, is in itself an instrument for this management. It is written for a particular context and purpose, in a style different from, for example, telling a friend what happened.

In this chapter I will discuss social order as a central issue in social life and for the social sciences. In Section 1, I start by looking at how everyday life is ordered in many imperceptible ways, to set the context for presenting, in Section 2, two important and contrasting accounts of social order in the social sciences. One, by sociologist Erving Goffman, focuses on the social patterns of everyday life interactions. The other, by social philosopher Michel Foucault, centres on more abstract conceptions about the power of knowledge and discourse in ordering social life. I chose these two approaches because, while the first focuses on **micro**-social phenomena, the latter explores larger scale or **macro** dimensions of social life. In Section 3, I explore these two approaches to social order through an extended investigation of traffic regulation. My interest is not in transport or transport policy itself but in how this topic can be a valuable illustration for making visible important issues of social order. I present two case studies offering contrasting concerns about the ways in which roads, experts, drivers and other users are related in traffic **governance**. That is, I explore the principles, rules, knowledge and sorts of authority that the two approaches to traffic governance put to work in producing an ordering of motor traffic in

Micro and macro
Social scientists often distinguish between different levels of social life: *micro* – the smallest scale, often meaning particular interactions between people; *meso* – an intermediate level referring to social organisations or institutions, or patterns of behaviour; and *macro* – the large-scale patterns, systems or structures of social life.

Governance
Governance concerns the action or manner of governing, the exercising of authority, or of being governed.

social life. One case study is the Buchanan Report; the other is Monderman's thesis. Drawing the case studies together I consider the significance of different conceptions about social life and the role of certain material objects in the social orders envisaged by each case. The concluding section compares and contrasts the views of the social scientists discussed in Section 2 with those of the social practitioners presented in Section 3, drawing some lessons for the study of social sciences.

1 Everyday life and social order

In everyday life we have a sense of how things usually 'go' and of what does 'not go'. When living together people generate understandings which make it possible for them to make sense of the practices of the society they live in. The philosopher Charles Taylor (2004, p. 58) has argued that 'the human capacity to imagine order is at the foundation of society itself'. Order is part of the way people both imagine and practise their social existence. Order is about how individuals fit together with others and with things in the world. It is about people's expectations and the deeper notions underpinning these expectations. Ordering is something intrinsic to social life and it is continuously practised.

The making of social order involves many things like imagination, practices, the fitting together of people and things, and ideas about the past and the future. How, then, can the making of social order in everyday life be studied? This question is explored throughout the chapter but I introduce it in this section so you can progressively follow the complexity of this theme.

To understand the making of social order it is important to retain the idea that human behaviour, like the material components of the world, has not always been as it is now, nor will it carry on being the same. Paradoxically, social change is intrinsic to the process of making social order: social order is constantly having to be remade, even as it provides the rules, norms and expectations that enable people to go about their daily life.

When a social scientist draws material from ordinary life experiences, it is particularly relevant to distinguish a short account of any interesting or amusing incident from evidence or proof that can be corroborated by other sources, based on factual description or archival material which can be verified. To make clear the point about the role of different sorts of evidence in knowing about social issues it is useful to look at an example. The coordination of driving practices, and some of the explanations for differences across countries and times, offers an illustration.

It is very much taken for granted that in the UK people drive on the left side of the road, drivers sit on the right side of the vehicle and change gear with their left hand. Traffic signs are positioned to catch the eye of a driver driving in this position, road markings direct the left-hand flow of traffic, rules of priorities and exits on roundabouts are marked from the left to the right, and the whole system adequately falls into place. This is normal in the UK: that is to say, it is the accepted convention that governs people's conduct. As a result, people in the UK tend not to think of this system as peculiar or deviant, despite the fact that it exists only in about a quarter of the countries in the world, nearly all former British colonies. Yet, if one goes to continental Europe, or to most other countries, the position of the driver in the car, the rules of driving and traffic are all geared by the principle of driving on the right-hand side of the road. Different social orders concerning traffic exist in different places. These affect the movements of pedestrians on the streets, as well as the manufacture of vehicles, the devising of highway codes, and so on.

Despite the peculiarity of the left-hand driving of the British, however, a lot of other issues are common to the UK and other car-using cultures. Drivers are involved in a complex system of coordination of social order in public space. Regulation of these movements is enforced through a system of penalties for violation to increase the safety of humans. As the dangers of road use increased over time, with the growing numbers of vehicles capable of speeding, a dynamic process of devising controls emerged: some aspects of this are described in the box 'Why the UK drives on the left – some anecdotal evidence'.

Why the UK drives on the left – some anecdotal evidence

Up to the late 1700s, everybody travelled on the left side of the road because this was the way feudal, violent societies of mostly right-handed people found most safe and sensible. Jousting knights with their lances under their right arm naturally passed on each other's right, and if you (presumably a male) passed a stranger on the road you walked on the left to ensure that your protective sword arm was between yourself and him.

Revolutionary France, however, overturned this practice in the second half of the eighteenth century as part of its sweeping social rethink. This was triggered by Napoleon, who was left-handed and thus made his armies march on the right so he could keep his sword arm between him and any opponent. The change was carried out all over continental Europe.

Left-driving countries
Right-driving countries

0   3 000
km

Right-driving and left-driving countries

Public traffic in parts of the world which were at some time part of the British Empire remained left-hand while in areas colonised by the French a right-hand norm was imposed.

Early car design in the United States was right-hand drive. Ford changed to left-hand-drive vehicles in the 1908 model year. A Ford catalogue from 1908 explains the benefits of placing the controls on the left side of the car: *The control is located on the left side, the logical place, for the following reasons: travelling along the right side of the road [with] the steering wheel on the right side of the car made it necessary to get out on the street side and walk around the car. This is awkward and especially inconvenient if there is a lady to be considered. The control on the left allows you to step out of the car on to the curbing without having had to turn the car around. In the matter of steering with the control on the right, the driver is farthest away from the vehicle he is passing, going in opposite direction; with it on the left side he is able to see even the wheels of the other car and easily avoids danger.*

Technical reasons apart, the country was also anxious to cast off links with its British colonial past. Once the US moved to drive on the right, left-side driving became a minority in the world. Many countries which bought American cars or had American subsidiaries producing cars on their soil changed out of necessity. Today, the European Union would like Britain to fall into line with the rest of Europe, but it would cost billions of pounds to change everything round. The last European country to convert to driving on the right was Sweden in 1967. Almost always, in countries where one drives on the right-hand side of the road, the cars are built so that the driver sits on the left-hand side of the car. Conversely, driving on the left-hand side of the road usually implies that the driver's seat is on the right-hand side of the car.

Based on material from users.telenet.be, undated, and 2pass.co.uk, 2009

Activity 1

Reflect on the chapter so far, or reread it if you need to, and identify the different sorts of evidence that have been used in discussing social order. What differences can you see between these types of evidence?

The opening paragraph of the chapter offers an account of a car accident, produced for the purposes of an insurance claim. It presents itself as an objective or *factual* description of the events surrounding the accident: distance, speed, road ground covered, behaviour of participants. It both sets the scene in a rational and objective manner and includes an account of intimidating behaviour. This evidence would need to stand scrutiny of a legal kind, including challenges from other accounts of the event.

The box on 'Why the UK drives on the left' offers *anecdotal evidence* about why in some countries driving is on the left and in some it is on the right. It assembles material from different websites and their reliability cannot be corroborated. Can you trust the historical information provided here? The description of medieval knights' body movements is plausible. Perhaps Napoleon was left-handed, but whether or not it was a motive for changing the side of marching of his armies requires more historical proof. Amid this anecdotal evidence some *archival evidence* is also invoked. The source of the italicised text in the last paragraph is apparently an advertisement by Ford from 1908. This could potentially be found in archives to validate the claims made.

I will be returning to these issues during the chapter, because the different types of evidence – and the uses that are made of them – are vital matters in the social sciences.

Summary

- Social order is woven into our ordinary everyday actions.
- The ordering of social life derives from a process of coordination of various entities, including human and material ones.
- Social order varies from place to place, and across time, often quite sharply.

2   The social sciences and social order

The explanation of social order is a central concern in the social sciences. In the Introduction I said that Section 2 of the chapter concentrates on two important and contrasting ways of thinking about social order. Focusing on these two views means a large simplification of substantial debates at the centre of the social sciences, where there are many other explanations of social order, particularly in the sociological literature. I also want to note that my presentation of the work of Goffman and Foucault, as exemplars of two contrasting ways of addressing social order, does not represent the full richness of their thought. This is an introduction to some of their work. I have selected them because, while they are both very influential in social sciences thinking about the ordering of social life, the aspects of social life they are concerned with, and their understanding of the ways that social order works, are particularly distinct. In what follows, I look at what they think society is, what main components of social life they include in their views, and what sort of social order emerges in their thinking.

2.1   Goffman's interactional order

Goffman developed a number of studies concerned with the functions of rituals and order in everyday life, showing the ways in which societies are ordered through a multiplicity of performances in specific contexts. He attended to the minutiae of interactions in the everyday, attempting to show the bridge between these and the broader concerns of social life. What do people do when they are in the presence of others? Where does the orderliness of momentary and chance encounters between strangers come from? How do people play roles and manage the impressions they make on others in different settings?

Goffman's work is part of an approach to studying social life predicated on the idea that there are many different ways in which people come together. Sometimes they come together cooperatively, other times competitively or in conflict. In this way of thinking, society is nothing other than people living their lives. Society is not a separate entity with needs of its own: instead, it is a construction produced by the actions and interactions of many individuals. So how does the large-scale pattern, or 'society', come about? If society is a vast network of individuals, social order emerges from the concerted lines of action put together by its individual members. Regularity is produced and implemented through actions and repetitive practices. But these are not repeated in exactly the same way on every occasion. Social change happens as actions are always built and rebuilt, worked and reworked.

Goffman (1959, 1971 and 1972) undertook detailed studies working within this framework. For him, patterns of interaction – the interactional order – create social order. Working in establishments like restaurants, hotels and hospitals, Goffman drew on the metaphor of the theatre, designating the front stage as the setting for the demands of the interaction order and the back stage as the place where individuals could let go of their performance. For example, in a restaurant waiters are courteous, constrained and respectful. They mount a performance to project themselves as capable and committed deliverers of the service. They withhold negative emotions and deport themselves physically using postures of stillness or agility depending on demands. Entry into the kitchen would transform their restrained mode emotionally and physically; there they would then relax, let off steam, loosen their clothing, reverse the relationship of servility, and sometimes would even manifest contempt for those they were serving.

See also Chapter 4 of this book for a discussion of Goffman's views.

Goffman examines the rituals of trust and tact in everyday lives, which provide the parameters of daily social interactions, through control of bodily gesture, the face and the gaze, and the use of language. For instance, a person encountering another on the street shows with a controlled sort of glance that the other person is worthy of respect and, by adjusting the gaze, that he or she is not a threat to the other, while the other person does the same. These 'strangers' meeting on the street exchange a number of codes of 'civil indifference' as an implicit contract by which they acknowledge each other and the rules which protect their encounter. This contract is drawn up by individuals participating in a public setting of modern social life, like a street. Yet street interaction is often of an unfocused kind because individuals, although in one another's visual and aural range, go about their respective businesses *unconnected* in their attention, despite sharing one same contract. Think of yourself walking in a busy city centre. Going about on a street, you meet other people but you do not wear the expressions you are expected to wear when purposefully meeting someone else. In these public situations you are often not conscious of being a social participant in an interaction. Yet, not only do you participate in a social context but most often you are bound by a set of rules of conduct. These are part of the invisible social order. Still on a street, or perhaps in other social contexts, gazes may be misinterpreted, exchanged in different ways, or not exchanged at all. To gaze may be forbidden, or it may provoke fear. The readings of particular encounters between strangers in public spaces differ greatly, and yet social groups have consensual codes of behaviour to understand and adjust behaviour. Punishment may follow when codes are misinterpreted or violated.

The situation of the car accident that I explored earlier involved a number of rules of conduct, some formalised, some derived from unwritten rules of socialised behaviour. The use of vehicles on the roads requires social coordination that configures a particular way of ordering social behaviour and interaction, but one that people are often not aware of. In other areas of everyday life, there are many more issues and situations that are implicated in the making of social order, often in quite invisible ways. For instance, first impressions are clearly important in everyday life. Individuals frequently try to manage the impressions they give to others. A popular view exists that one 'puts on a show'. In the account at the start of this chapter, the young man coming towards the first driver in a threatening manner could be seen as putting on a show to intimidate her in order to avoid his companion being found liable through an insurance claim. All three people were performing their parts and no doubt 'giving off' and 'taking' first impressions. This process is one of ordering, or classifying, things and people into categories that allow us to 'read' the situation and to define how best to act to get the desired response: some of Goffman's key ideas are summarised in the box 'Goffman's propositions'.

Goffman's propositions

- Understanding society means understanding the way individual action and joint action (or interaction) are organised.
- Individuals construct and communicate a sense of self in the course of interaction with other people. This presentation of the individual self is a collective affair.
- Individuals display, and perform, selves according to the requirements of the situation concerned and their roles in it.
- The pattern of behaviour demanding the presentation of the self pervades the whole social organisation. Everyday activities are explored to provide clues about the workings of institutions and power beyond immediate individual interactions.

> • Social change occurs through the process of building and rebuilding social interactions, which lead to innovations in the ordering of social life.

Goffman sees social order as being built up from social interactions and is relatively unconcerned with the historical processes that embed these social orderings and the ways in which various orders of interaction are authorised. In contrast, Michel Foucault's work is more explicitly directed to these issues.

2.2   Foucault's order of things

Foucault's work examines how social order is shaped and organised by authoritative knowledge, particularly forms of knowledge that are put to work in social and political institutions. But, like Charles Taylor quoted at the start of Section 1 above, Foucault begins from a concern with the powerful ways in which social order is imagined, talked about and written about – the ways in which knowledge about order comes to circulate in society. He uses the idea of discourse to explore how knowledge and power are connected in the processes of shaping what can be known, what can be thought and what can be said about social life.

For Foucault, social institutions, such as family, school, workplace, the neighbourhood, welfare systems, and so on, have different means and powers of intervention into the regulation or governing of human conduct. Power is an instrument for ordering the social that operates through invisible processes or through purposeful and explicit pressures. The interventions aimed at regulating conduct discipline human performances and produce ordered or orderly behaviour.

Foucault shows that the authority to intervene in social life is allocated to certain individuals, such as parents, doctors, teachers, priests and policemen, and this authority is exercised through practices of law, punishment, management, parenthood, education, and the like. Foucault is concerned about identifying who can claim authority over conduct and in whose interest this authority is claimed. Who has the power to rule how others should behave?

In Chapter 2 of *Making Social Lives* you saw that power is one of the forces which routinely shape social life.

According to Foucault, power works in subtle ways through discourse – what can be talked about – to shape popular attitudes. These discourses

Chapter 4 of this book also talked about 'discourses' in relation to questions of identity. Here the focus is the connections between discourse and power.

can be used, and are used, as a powerful tool to normalise behaviour. Discourses provide the frameworks that shape what can be thought about and talked about. In relation to social order, discourses make it possible for people to know that if they behave in a certain way they are normal. Thus, forms of knowledge serve as a force of control. Whereas for Goffman the centre of his analysis is the individual performance, the sum of which constitutes the social, the idea of discourse is at the centre of Foucault's thinking. He shifts the individual from the centre of social analysis, seeing the individual as being made up by social practices: as socially constituted.

Foucault's ideas are often regarded as obscure and it is difficult to make his theory accessible. Yet he has been very influential since the 1970s in studies of social life and its orderings. In his vision of social order, people are both shaped and constrained on all sides by social determinations. People live their lives through the **socially constructed meanings** that are available to them. Discourses provide the assumptions and prescriptions that mould everyday practices and relationships. These discourses are social phenomena. What does this mean? It means that individuals do not create either the meanings of the discourses that construct them, or the practices that inform the meanings of these discourses.

The ideas that circulate, and prevail, in particular social contexts become a dominant discourse, when they are seen as common social assumptions (Foucault 1972, 1977, 1978). This means that such ideas have gone beyond the institutional confines that originated them. One example is the development of the modern discourse of sex. Originating from a concern to ensure the thriving of bloodlines of the bourgeoisie, ensuring hereditary and racial purity, these ideas about sex were later adjusted and exported to the subordinate classes as a means of suppressing sexuality and controlling fertility. For both the higher and the lower classes, notes Foucault, these developments placed a moral obligation on people to subject their sexual conduct to surveillance to ensure that their behaviour would not detract from the strength of the physical inheritance for the wealthy, and to ensure that sexual habits were controlled and disciplined by individuals themselves. Who had the power to rule about this? Who benefited from these assumptions and resulting behaviours? Foucault suggests that sometimes we cannot pin down the origins or causes of such discursive assumptions. But it is, he argues, important to see how social control is internalised and becomes self-control, rather than being external surveillance or direction. In these

Socially constructed meanings
The meanings that people use to navigate social life are constructed in social processes. As a result, they are socially and historically specific, rather than either natural or universal.

circumstances, people come to see themselves as engaged in 'normal' ways of thinking and behaving through socialisation processes in the family, schools, workplace or public space. In turn, they can contrast themselves with the 'deviant' or 'abnormal' people who lack self-control or self-discipline (and therefore behave badly).

I said that in Foucault's work the individual is removed from centre stage. He strongly contests the idea, held by some other social thinkers, that the individual is a coherent being, self-aware and in control of herself. He sees individuals as having little control over their own destinies, and he regards historical processes as shaping both individual subjectivities and the practices and power relations that define the social locations in which people live their everyday lives. In Foucault's framework, the power to discipline human conduct has been exercised by many different organisations. In Foucault's studies it is possible to trace (very crudely) three different types of power (associated with different types of organisation) involved in the making of social order. There is what he calls sovereign power, where society's ruling authorities (a monarchy, a state, a single political authority) exercise power through the capacity to punish wrongdoers or the wrong sort of people – visibly and publicly. Public executions, torture, the public brutalisation of targeted groups – such forms of punishment dramatised the power and authority of the rulers. Foucault suggests that in many European states this power gave way to other techniques based on certain sorts of expert knowledge and institutional arrangements (from schools to prisons). Surveillance – the keeping of information about people in order to control their behaviour – is an ever-present element of this second form of power. For example, prisons and schoolrooms were designed so that individuals could be seen (and would know that they could be seen) by those in charge. Experts, and the institutions in which they work, produce discipline – they install 'good habits' of thinking and behaving among those in their charge (prisoners, schoolchildren, workers, students, and so on).

Clearly, in the present mass-mediated and highly informatised society, systems of surveillance have increased enormously. By understanding that you are constantly under surveillance, you begin to oversee yourself and to regulate your conduct in the light of its assumed visibility to others. Power thus comes to operate *within people* through internalised disciplines. Individuals seek to make their identities, routines and practices 'normal' because this is what they desire to be, since they are disciplined beings. For Foucault, this points to the third form of power in which individuals come to see themselves as self-directing, active and choosing agents. This is what he identifies as liberalism – a social order in which people see themselves as unique individuals as a result of having internalised social disciplines, social orderings and the discourse of individualism.

Despite a concern with everyday practices and procedures of power, Foucault's focus is on the historical conditions and dynamics of discourses (what he calls their *genealogy*) that discipline people and create power. This leads him away from a concern with face-to-face encounters that constitute a large portion of everyday life. These face-to-face encounters are a strong concern of Goffman, as I described earlier, but Goffman doesn't have a historical preoccupation with explaining links between the individual and the social.

Disciplinary society
Practices of/in a social location where corrective action is used to obtain and enforce obedience and order.

In Foucault's analysis, individuals appear as passive, even docile, subjects who cooperate in their own subordination. To repeat an important point: for him, modern society effectively instils disciplined *self-control* combined with an increasingly encompassing surveillance system. Power is thus everywhere and does not emanate from any specific source. The patterns of discipline, and the knowledge that serves them, are formed independently of anyone's purposes. Foucault's **disciplinary society** is dominated by rationalist discourses used by professionals, based on professionalised knowledge and power connections. Society is characterised by coherence and order: some of Foucault's key propositions are presented in the box 'Foucault's propositions'.

See Chapter 9 of *Making Social Lives* for an example of how people become objects of knowledge in relation to states and their knowledge of populations.

Foucault's propositions

- In any given historical period, ways of thinking and talking are organised in systems of discourses. This means that thinkers come up with ideas guided by these frameworks. Only certain kinds of thoughts are thinkable at different historical times.

- Thinking is something done through language. Things that can be talked about are things that can be thought about. These are discourses. Without discourses things cannot be talked about.

- Patterns of social change show two connected phenomena:

  (a) Within modern discourse people are identified as an object of knowledge. People are something that can be talked about.

  (b) Knowledge and power are linked. This means that discourses are shaped by both authority relations and

changes in dominant ways of thinking. For example,
bodies of professional and administrative functionaries
equipped with 'scientific' knowledge have the power to
reorganise social activities along supposedly more
rational and efficient lines. (See the case studies of
traffic governance in the next section.)

The work of these two social scientists show different ways of capturing
the social and that there are diverse components of social life which
they include in their views. Goffman involved himself as a participant
observer in different social situations to explore the nature of face-to-
face interaction. He employed social science tools like ethnography and
participant observation. By these processes of investigation Goffman
started off with current familiar issues to make sense of the invisible
social order, to understand how this could be captured, how it is
manifested and the ways in which the social is ordered. Foucault did the
opposite. He dug into the past, investigating historical documents to
question what is familiar in the present. The present order of things was
thus made visible by accessing it from the past, by viewing how it has
been made through processes of social development. He did this
through the reading of texts and documents to find the traces of the
present. In doing so he found a method of exploring his concerns
about social life from a philosophical and political point of view.

Neither Goffman nor Foucault presents a general theory of society. For
both, social life is made out of an integration of fragments ordered in
different ways. For Goffman the fragments are individuals in social
interaction. For Foucault the fragments are the discourses that organise
particular fields of knowledge and power.

The choice between these different approaches is significant for doing
social sciences. I shall return to some of these points as I develop the
case studies of Buchanan and Monderman to show the operations of
links between individuals interacting in social environments and
connections between knowledge and power in specific historical
configurations.

Summary

- Goffman and Foucault provide two ways of viewing social order in the social sciences which focus on different components of social life and different views of what society is.

- The work of Goffman places human interaction at the centre of analysis. He uses the metaphor of the theatre, conceiving social action as performances collectively adjusted by invisible contracts which govern the social order. Social change emerges from the process of reworking interactions.

- In Foucault the central focus is on discourses, which are sets of ideas allowing for certain kinds of thoughts to be thinkable, talked about, and made into effective tools for normalising conduct, at different historical times. Social change emerges when a new discourse achieves greater power, replacing the old one.

3   Ordering social life: the case of road traffic

In this section I explore the ways in which the ordering of social life is informed by knowledge about, and interventions in, the social world. This ordering presupposes ideals about social interaction. I look at the authority of governmental and scientific knowledge in configuring and transforming social life. To do this I focus on road traffic and the design of streets. I emphasise that my concern is not with traffic or traffic policy but that I use this as a teaching device: a case study to help us understand how social order is being constructed in different historical moments.

The original layout of most old towns in the UK corresponded to movements of people on foot or by horse and, later on, by horse carriage. When regulation of road layout began, the main concern was with the spread of fire. Before that there was the issue of ensuring the passage of air between buildings in densely built-up areas and of guaranteeing that sunshine would get to each house. It was not until after the Second World War, and particularly with a dramatic increase in car ownership and car use in the UK from the 1960s onwards, that considerations of traffic movement were to affect the design and regulation of roads and streets, in the ways we see nowadays. Increasingly, movements on foot and by motor vehicles were allocated to different spaces. Decks, bridges, subways, and roads with different functions were created. A number of government initiatives at national and local levels have sought to plan, design and implement road systems following different philosophies about the benefits of segregation of pedestrians and motor vehicles. I want to explore here two different strategies for managing the relations between humans and vehicles in streets. The first relates to a very influential report commissioned by the UK Government, the Buchanan Report, published in 1963, predicated on the segregation of pedestrians and cars. The second, based on the idea of 'shared space', derives from the work of Hans Monderman, a Dutch engineer, who in the 1980s devised the principle of the 'naked street', which has become influential in street design and planning in the early twenty-first century.

3.1   The Buchanan Report

The road network in the UK was of great political importance in the late 1940s and the 1950s. A national programme of road building was set in motion, gathering speed throughout these decades. A government report in the early 1960s predicted a time when cars would rule the UK transport system (Ministry of Transport, 1963). Table 1 shows some of the social changes in traffic growth that both the Buchanan Report and the more recent developments inspired by Monderman have aimed to tackle. This table offers *statistical evidence* produced by a reputable source. Social scientists produce and often use this sort of evidence to understand social phenomena. The table measures density of traffic in terms of the number of vehicles multiplied by the number of kilometres driven (vehicle-kilometres) in selected years from 1949 to 2006. The traffic for each year relates to the public road network in place in that year. Thus, growth over time is the product of any change in the use of the network (kilometres) and the change in traffic flow (vehicles).

Table 1   Road traffic by type of vehicle: UK, 1949–2006 (billion vehicle-kilometres)

Year	Cars and taxis	Larger buses and coaches	Light vans	Goods vehicles	All motor vehicles*
1949	20.3	4.1	6.5	12.5	46.5
1959	62.2	4.0	13.7	14.6	104.2
1969	147.9	3.8	19.3	17.4	192.5
1979	201.5	3.3	25.1	19.6	255.9
1989	331.3	4.5	39.7	25.5	406.9
1999	377.4	5.3	51.6	28.1	467.0
2006	402.4	5.4	64.3	29.1	506.4

* includes motor cycles and the like.

Source: Department for Transport, 2007a, p. 124, Table 7.1

In 1949 there were 46.5 billion vehicle-kilometres on the road network of the UK. By the time Buchanan was commissioned to work on traffic problems, this volume had more than doubled. Between the Second World War and 1969 the number quadrupled. Most of this growth was accounted for by cars as there were seven times more car-kilometres on the roads in 1969 than in 1949. When the Buchanan Report was commissioned it was assumed not only that more roads needed to be built but also that a new way for towns to live with cars needed to be implemented. Table 1 provides evidence of the continuing preference of the population for the individualised and flexible form of transportation afforded by cars. In the nearly sixty-year period presented in the table, 'all motor vehicles' on the UK roads, as measured in vehicle-kilometres, grew by more than ten times, with the number of 'cars and taxis' growing by nearly twenty times. In 1949, 'cars and taxis' accounted for 44 per cent of 'all motor vehicles' while in 2006 this proportion had increased to 79 per cent. I now explore how the growth in number of vehicle-kilometres on British roads has been related to processes of creating social order by focusing on the Buchanan Report and the Monderman thesis.

■   What other changes in road traffic shown in Table 1 do you find interesting?

Proportions of 'larger buses and coaches' expanded minimally during the period explored in the table. This suggests that public transport has not increased much in this half century. 'Goods vehicles' are only 2.3 times higher in 2006 compared with 1949, showing perhaps that there are other ways of transporting goods that competed with this or that each vehicle got bigger and carried more goods. 'Light vans', used by trades people and for transporting smaller batches of goods, grew by about ten times showing a preference for more flexible transportation of smaller amounts of goods, compared with the increase in 'goods vehicles'. All of these changes, together with the dramatic growth in the numbers of car-kilometres on UK roads, show a preference for a way of life that privileges privatised choices and flexible arrangements in the ordering of social life.

In this context of large growth of motor vehicle usage and road expansion, with major stretches of motorway opening, Colin Buchanan, an engineer, was commissioned by the UK Government in 1961 to start work on the report *Traffic in Towns* for the Ministry of Transport (1963). The topic was an extremely contentious political issue at the time. A future of choking road congestion was feared unless the rapid rise in demand for car travel was matched by an increased supply of roads. But more than roads were tackled. The *Traffic in Towns* report aimed to produce a new design for urban space in order to engineer the efficient distribution and access of large numbers of vehicles to a large number of buildings while achieving a satisfactory standard of environment for life in towns. It was all about the need of humans to live with motor vehicles.

Rush hour in London in the 1960s

The key principle was to isolate 'rooms' for working, shopping and leisure from the 'corridors' where the traffic would move. Buchanan called these isolated areas 'environmental units' (I keep in inverted commas the main terms used in the report). In the overall context of growing ownership and use of cars, if a 'civilised environment' was to be retained or created, either the use of cars would have to be radically restricted or towns would have to be radically reconstructed to hold many more vehicles. The choice of the latter would demand a great deal of money and a willingness to accept comprehensive redevelopment, with the invasion of private property rights on a scale never contemplated before in the UK. The restriction of car use in towns became the chosen vision for ordering space.

The approach in the report was one of **scientific rationality**.
Buchanan claimed that:

> The whole subject of traffic in towns … is capable of being put
> on a rational and quantitative basis. Guesswork and intuition can
> be largely eliminated; given the necessary information, many
> aspects are precisely calculable; and there is scope for techniques
> which will greatly ease the burden of decision between alternative
> courses of action.

(Ministry of Transport, 1963, paragraph 443)

After the mid 1960s, towns for the motor age were built on the explicit
principle of segregation, sometimes with strict separation of vehicles
and people. Cars were afforded their own generously proportioned
network and pedestrians were safely tucked away in residential blocks
often terminating in quiet cul-de-sacs. Children might walk to school in
the areas segregated from traffic. But generally, driving and walking
were seen as incompatible: you either walked in the segregated areas or
drove – or were driven – in the traffic corridors. Templates for town
planning began to follow these segregation principles, encompassing
cases from Brasilia, the capital city of Brazil, built in the late 1950s,
when the segregation ideas emerged, to Milton Keynes, joining together
a number of small villages through a grid system of horizontal and
vertical fast roads in the early 1960s. The 'environmental units', free
from extraneous traffic, and outside the city centres, led to the creation
of housing layouts in which some dwellings could be reached only by
indirect and at times tortuous and inconvenient routes. Some new
housing schemes in older towns were physically isolated, like Hulme in
Manchester and Castle Vale in Birmingham.

Activity 2

On the basis of what you have read about the Buchanan Report, what
role do you see traffic playing as an agent of social order and social
change?

Traffic is viewed in the report as an agent because it has an active role
in shaping the ways people live, how space is designed, and how people
interact with each other and with their environment. Traffic is presented

Scientific rationality
The understanding of
science, or knowledge,
as bound by standards
of reason presumed to
be universally
acceptable.

Milton Keynes and Brasilia

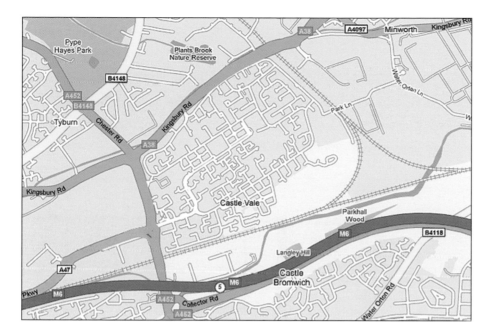

The isolation of housing estates in Castle Vale, Birmingham

as an agent that is dangerous, and in order to contain its dangers it has to be segregated, isolated and bounded by rules imposed through visible displays in space.

There was considerable public debate about the prescriptions of the Buchanan Report. The expansion of mass communication in the early 1960s contributed to this. Some of the ideas appeared controversial, but their appeal to planners at national and local levels, in need of solutions to managing growing traffic, was strong. As government commissioned work, sanctioned by the media, the report acquired great authority and its thinking about road planning has influenced nearly half a century of road design in the UK. Traffic-led thinking became a dominant influence on the design and use of public spaces. Road hierarchies privileged the movement of vehicles, marginalising pedestrians and cyclists. The principle that roads were for motor traffic filtered down into the design of streets of all sorts (Marshall, 2004).

Activity 3

Reflect on two questions:

- Are people prisoners of their cars?

- Does the car represent personal freedom and should roads be built everywhere to allow for this freedom?

Issues you might think about in relation to these questions include:

- how ideas about 'should be' are part of an imagined social order
- how public governance is able to act to implement this vision
- how visions can change over time.

Segregated space

As traffic congestion continues to grow – Table 1 clearly shows the continuing trend – some competing rethinking has emerged. This favours creating areas with 'a sense of place', with people living in places without needing to go far to find what they want. This is part of a different imagination of communal life, a new proposal for ordering the social, with repercussions for both material dimensions and the governance of individuals and public spaces.

3.2   Monderman's thesis

The years of segregation of pedestrians and vehicles, since the early 1960s, generated an increasing array of traffic lights, kerbs, railings, road markings, and so on, and an ever-expanding assortment of 'traffic calming' measures, like warning signs, speed humps and others. More recently a new approach has challenged the principle of segregation and the use of these 'calming' measures. The 'shared space' philosophy builds on different approaches to, on one hand, public spaces and, on the other, highways. It confines the segregation prescribed in Buchanan to highways. While it is recognised that shared space designs are not appropriate everywhere, like major urban centres, and highways for fast traffic remain in corridors, the neighbourhood is subject to major rethinking in the ways vehicles, cyclists and pedestrians move: 'The trouble with traffic engineers is that when there's a problem with a road, they always try to add something. To my mind, it's much better to remove things' (Monderman, quoted in McNichol, 2004).

Monderman's thesis is that the best way to improve road safety is to abolish roadside markings and warnings. This is called 'psychological traffic calming'. Measures include removing centre white lines, eliminating the kerb to blur the boundary between pavement and road and changing the colour of the tarmac. The aim is to create the need for motorists and pedestrians to negotiate with each other the use of the road. It is thought to be more effective to encourage motorists to take responsibility for their actions rather than to tell them what to do. Monderman pioneered the concept of the 'naked street' within his 'shared space' model. The model builds on the idea that a natural interaction between the driver and the pedestrian would create a more civilised environment than that achieved by segregating cars and pedestrians. The segregation is criticised as an imposition by the state, unsuited to communal life.

Monderman's model gained momentum in the early years of the twenty-first century. He started his experiments in the Netherlands in 1982 after being appointed a traffic safety officer for the region of Friesland, where he stripped the village of Oudeshaske of highway signs and barriers, creating a plain and even surface. Drivers, more aware of their surroundings, cut their speed by 40 per cent when driving through the village. The 'shared space scheme' was replicated in other places, increasingly combining engineering with psychology and demonstrating an appreciation of a place as a contextual situation, and of how people would read it.

Being a practitioner, Monderman's philosophy and work is mostly not found in written texts but in the projects he developed, as well as in interviews he gave to newspapers and magazines – from the *New York Times* and *International Herald Tribune* to *Wired* magazine – and to politicians. Writings by the British expert in shared space, Ben Hamilton-Baillie, together with many interviews, helped bring Monderman's work to wider attention. The application of Monderman's ideas in the town of Drachten in the Netherlands is discussed in the box 'The Drachten experiment'.

The Drachten experiment

Drachten is a town of 43,000 people in the flat Friesland pastures in the Netherlands. Journalist Max Gaskin gave the following account of an application there of Monderman's shared space approach.

Innovation: the end of the white line

Driving through, it initially looks like any other quiet northern European town … until you notice that something is wrong, that something vital is missing.

In 1989 the councillors of this post-war town voted to begin the removal of every single traffic light […] They also decided to abolish white road lines and all warning and give-way signs.

'The lights were causing problems,' says Koop Kerkstra, the head of traffic policy, in Drachten's modern town hall. 'People were forever waiting to get across junctions. We also had more than 140 casualties a year. It was difficult to know what to do, and we certainly didn't want to ban cars. We love cars in Drachten […] Fortunately, I met a traffic engineer who had an unconventional solution.'

The engineer was Hans Monderman and the solution was to get rid of the lights and erase the white lines. 'If you treat drivers like zombies, they'll behave like zombies,' explains Monderman. In other words, if motorists are taught to blindly follow instructions, they stop thinking for themselves, and accidents follow.

[…]

[Kerkstra] wanted to test [Monderman's] idea on one junction east of Drachten's town centre that was causing problems during peak hours. Jams built up at the lights of such lengths that other junctions froze and gridlock loomed every working day.

[…] the lights were ripped out and the road surface was raised to the same height as the adjacent pavements and cycle paths. Most of the road markings were erased and the stop signs taken to the municipal dump. Today what is left is a curious zone where four roads meet and the space in the middle is owned by everyone – motorists, cyclists, pedestrians and even skateboarders. It's not a place where anybody wants to hang around and nobody there has the right of way over anyone else, but all traffic must negotiate its way through.

Driving over this junction was a curious and slightly frightening experience for me [...] but there is no doubt that my concentration levels were higher than if I were simply obeying a green or red traffic light. And after attempting the same junction several times I found that I instinctively looked at the other drivers to judge where they were intending to go, and the crossing became – while not exactly easy – certainly less perilous.

[...]

So eye contact is what makes the Drachten junctions work. Motorists look at each other and look out for cyclists and pedestrians. In each glance, lasting a fraction of a second, they signal what they are planning to do.

But surely not every decision can be left to drivers; there must be some instruction on the road? Not so, argues [UK's shared space consultant] Hamilton-Baillie. 'If you are driving down a street full of shops and there is a sign that reads, "Beware Pedestrians", what it really tells you is that you're stupid, because only an idiot wouldn't recognise the need to beware of pedestrians,' he says. 'So you stop thinking for yourself and simply obey the signs, and as a result motorists stop following their instincts and driving gets dangerous.'

[...]

Of course, Monderman's solutions are only appropriate in the areas where cars are [but one] part of the social scene. Traffic lights, lane markings and signs are vital on highways that are used only by vehicles. But where drivers are just one element in the ever-changing, multi-purpose zones of town and village streets the end of the line could well be nigh.

Glaskin, 2004

In residential communities, Monderman began narrowing the roads and putting in design features like trees and flowers, red brick paving stones and even fountains to discourage people from speeding, psychologically calming traffic. These design features, also referred to as street furniture, are landmarks or landscapes that become integral to the public space and are apparently irrelevant to the traffic world. While something of a libertarian, Monderman conceded that road design can do only so much. For instance, he says it does not change the behaviour of the 15 per cent of drivers who will behave badly no matter what the rules are.

Shared space

In a publication on shared space (Shared Space, 2005) it is noted that, while the improvement of traffic flows and traffic safety has traditionally determined the ways in which public spaces are designed and used, the new approach strives to combine rather than separate the various functions of public spaces, such as traffic and residence, facilitating people's activities. Traffic should become an equal, not a dominant, partner. The conduct of individuals on a street is specific to that space. Highway behaviour is largely guided by legal traffic systems and signals, with little eye contact. The choice about the type of behaviour dominant in a particular space is related not only to what goes on in the space but also to what is to happen in it. The choice is political and it conveys an ideal of social order.

Activity 4

Read your reply to Activity 3 and compare it with the ideas presented in the 'shared space' approach. Was your reply closer to the Buchanan Report's philosophy or to that of Monderman? What were the issues you had not thought about at that stage which you find present in the vision of 'shared space'?

The vision of the person in the 'shared space' approach is of a civilised, disciplined individual, who, in the way they behave, takes account both of others and of where they are. While a driver in a public realm is 'a guest' and behaves accordingly, their behaviour is different in a traffic area designed for rapid movement to destinations (Shared Space, 2005, p. 10). Contextual signals are of utmost importance in the shared space approach. It is thought that the visible presence of a school or children playing has more effect on the behaviour of drivers and speed than a sign warning about children crossing the road. So this is about making what is going on in public space visible.

How has the work on shared space been received? European experiments have been devised for implementation in various countries including Germany, Denmark, the Netherlands, the UK and Belgium. In the UK the shared space ideas have informed the work of the Commission for Architecture and the Built Environment in its advisory role on urban design and public space (CABE, 2007). With its remit being to encourage policymakers to create places that are safe, beautiful and efficient to run, Monderman's philosophy provides a source of inspiration and practical support. The Department for Transport guidance document *Manual for Streets* (2007b, p. 6) states that 'streets are not just there to get people from A to B', and stresses that, in common with the ideas of 'shared space', they have a role in the life of a community and bring opportunities for social interaction. The break with the approach of *Traffic in Towns*, centred on traffic 'movement' and the segregation of vehicles from pedestrians, is significant. Instead, the place-function of the street in communal life is accorded great importance, disclosing a way of ordering social life where vehicles and humans share space and reminding individuals that a vehicle always has a person driving it. Whether this will become a dominant vision of organising traffic has been an object of controversy, and I discuss below the different visions of social order these two approaches to ordering road traffic carry.

3.3   Machines and humans in visions of social order

With the advent of the motor vehicle, traffic experts emerged and the institutions concerned with managing traffic evolved. A rising number of problems, including congestion, pollution and fatal road accidents, required political action. Tools and plans to combat unsafe traffic conditions for human life and the environment were developed. The design of public spaces became increasingly determined by traffic concerns. Individual lives and group behaviour in public spaces came to be determined by traffic controls. Must choices favour motorised transport and, in particular, the car?

Between the middle of the twentieth and the early twenty-first century, motor vehicles have been at the centre of the dominant vision of ordering social life in urban areas. If the vision were to change towards public space for the people, a different way of planning and a different governmental role would be required. The governance required would not be of a state as the solver of all problems, but as an enabler and facilitator of interactive negotiations. The role attributed to the state in the 'shared space' approach is the enabling one. The responsibility for solving problems about how to live together is to be placed in the hands of citizens, companies, social groups and institutions. Power and knowledge are relocated from the rules and signs and placed with individuals to enable them to negotiate rights of way in the changing landscape of their local areas.

A core vision in *Traffic in Towns* was that public powers ought to assure individual mobility, allowing for an expansion of car ownership. Buchanan coined the phrase a 'car-owning democracy' to warn how, as individual mobility increased through car ownership, there would be inevitable conflict between those demanding more freedom of movement and those opposed to the road-building programmes that would be needed as a result. When Prime Minister Margaret Thatcher asserted in 1986 that 'a man who, beyond the age of 26, finds himself on a bus can count himself as a failure' (House of Commons, 2003), she was making explicit that her government's accelerated road-building programme was an exercise in both civil and social engineering (Monbiot, 2005). A different democratic quality is intrinsic to the shared space project, stressing involvement, cooperation, commitment and responsibility of 'stakeholders' (Shared Space, 2005, p. 33). Two visions of social order compete here: one stresses the value of a social environment in delivering the conditions for individual mobility and (car) acquisition as a valued mark of success; the other stresses a social order where involvement and cooperation emerges from an individual capable of negotiating with others a shared use of public space.

The **modernist approach** prevailing at the time of the Buchanan Report prescribed the development of standardised uniform spaces commanding uniform behaviour, leaving no room for individual interpretation, explaining everything with signs and texts. The government and public authorities (sometimes known as the state) look after the citizens. In the **flexible approach** of the shared space philosophy, tailor-made layouts are required for a more individualised style to emerge: every site is unique and it has its own story which gives information about how the space is used. Authorities do not set general rules for citizens' behaviour.

Modernist approach
An approach emphasising standardisation and rationalisation.

Flexible approach
An approach emphasising fluidity, adjustment, lack of prescribed rules.

In shared space prescriptions the layout makes the story explicit and readable, interpretable. Spatial elements are used to achieve the required behaviour. As Monderman remarked, roads talk back to people: a wide road with a lot of signs is saying 'go ahead, don't worry, go as fast as you want, there's no need to pay attention to your surroundings. And that's a very dangerous message' (quoted in McNichol, 2004). 'The road user must be able to tell from the space, i.e. the road and its surroundings, which behaviour is appropriate and required' (Shared Space, 2005, p. 37). Traffic measures, such as speed bumps, chicanes and central islands, encourage legal traffic behaviour, bound by written rules, as opposed to social ones, negotiated in social interaction, binding people to their environment. In this vision, the importance of a place is relative to its position in the network. Street, junction, section of a street, traffic volume, mode of traffic (bus, bicycle), are all different parts of a whole, requiring different designs according to their role in the network.

In the modernist approach the space is split by rules, prohibitions and orders requiring individuals to adapt to the system. The chief way of enforcing behaviour is the road sign. The shared space movement claims to reverse these roles, making human behaviour central. In shared space thinking, the street is not the tarmacked space between pavements, but part of a place. Streets are embedded in the complexities of public life, including the promotion of civility. In the shared space approach, individuals are called upon to regulate themselves, moving the emphasis from traffic rules to social rules. The new prescription is for social behaviour to be encouraged, using less regulation in the form of signs and markings. But this regulation is limited to eye contact which can only happen when speed is below 30 kph, which is the limit of speed for humans running. It is assumed that in this condition, without explicit regulation, drivers will automatically reduce speed. The approach is not about eliminating risks but about using the perception of risk to increase safety, building on the paradox of making roads that seem dangerous so they will be safer.

Activity 5

In Activity 4 you compared the ideas of the Buchanan Report and Monderman's thesis. Can you outline two aspects of their implicit visions of social order?

The individual moving on the street in a private car unaware of their surroundings, or the pedestrian segregated into compartmentalised areas or funnelled into corners to 'safely' cross busy streets, is a very different type of person from that portrayed in the vision of shared space. Interestingly, in the latter the gaze occupies centre stage, and one might see links to Goffman's view of interaction as the foundation of social order. Shared space requires people to look at one another and interact to produce order (rather than relying on externally imposed rules and directions). But the centrality of the gaze has led disabled people's groups to criticise the shared space approach's disregard for the visually impaired. Such criticisms have been taken on board. Recent documents emphasise catering for fluidity and diversity of humans and materials, through measures ranging from wider choice of paving materials, changes in surface friction standards and lane width requirements, introduction of tactile paving, changes in levels of functional areas, improvement in orientation and navigation for the young, older and disabled people, and provision for people with visual disabilities (CABE, 2007, pp. 7–9). Concerns still remain about the safety of those who might be unable to look after themselves, like the drunk at night-time.

Summary

In this section the connections between knowledge and the authorising of social order were discussed by considering the case of governance of road traffic. This shows that:

- The Buchanan Report was a critical historical actor in the establishment of social policies for traffic flows in towns.

- The explicit social order privileging segregation of humans and motor vehicles created an array of measures in urban design and the regulation of the conduct of both drivers and pedestrians.

- A contrasting vision of social order appears in the approach of shared space, put forward by Monderman, in which people are not segregated from traffic.

- Each approach to traffic governance rests on a different set of problem identifications and produces different requirements for social organisation.

- The Buchanan model assumes an individual who is individualistic and conforms to rules, and a state that solves problems and looks after individual behaviour (setting the rules).

- Monderman's shared space approach assumes a person who is cooperative and can afford to be exposed to unpredicted situations, and a state that does not set general rules but enables and facilitates interactions and negotiations between individuals. It involves the redistribution of expertise (ordinary people become experts at negotiating shared space) and the creation of social order as an ongoing process.

How do we know?

Evidence, theories and case studies

A central question pursued throughout this chapter is how the making of social order in everyday life can be studied. Three of the instruments for dealing with this question in the chapter are evidence, social theories and case studies.

Evidence can be of varied kinds. The chapter has used anecdotal, factual, archival and statistical evidence, and has pointed to the importance of establishing that the evidence being used can be corroborated and verified.

Social theories cover a wide range of perspectives which bear on the sorts of social worlds emerging from them. To compare theories it is important to consider the basis of the arguments, their coherence and their relevance in terms of the concerns each one addresses. Theories convey a vision of the social world.

Case studies are used to illustrate and also to develop an argument, to discover how a theory works, to perfect and enlarge a theory, to establish evidence and generally to probe the reach of certain ways of conceiving the social.

Conclusion

This chapter shows the centrality of social order to social life. In many ways social order is an invisible issue which various social scientists have grappled with and attempted to unravel. I presented two contrasting academic views – those of Goffman and Foucault. Their views differ in that Goffman emphasises human interaction in familiar settings to disclose invisible patterns of ordering, while Foucault looks at historical genealogies to make visible from the past how the ordering of the familiar present has come about. In Goffman's approach, individuals occupy front stage although their individuality is not his concern. In Foucault's view, individuals matter only as they are shaped by and involved in the systems of power and knowledge that organise the order of things.

As a way of exploring social science ideas about the making of social order I discussed two approaches to configuring public space, linked to particular visions of social life, as epitomised by the Buchanan Report and Monderman's thesis. I found Foucault more useful for my exploration of the experiences of these two experts of creating social orders. Why? Individuals are required to play their part in the game of civility, as emphasised by Goffman. Indeed, Goffman's view of the centrality of interaction is certainly visible in Monderman's approach to negotiating 'shared space', as I noted towards the end of the previous section. But, as Foucault shows, social order tends to be specified by experts within particular historical discursive frameworks. Although both Buchanan and Monderman were important in their own right, their ideas were developed and taken up within particular contexts that 'authorised' their development (made their ideas seems appropriate and fitting to the needs of the time). Foucault claims that expert discourses, established by those with power and authority, are often disputed by competing expert discourses. Buchanan's ideas have dominated for a long period. Monderman's are perhaps gathering force and challenging those of centralised planning and direction.

But while leaning towards Foucault here, I am critical of some of his ideas. I indicated in Section 2.2 that in Foucault's work individuals are constrained to make choices according to the dominant views at the time. As a result, there is a danger in Foucault of dissolving individuals into social processes, erasing human creativity and the autonomy of human agency. He seems to neglect the fact that individuals' personalities can have different effects or impacts on social order.

However, Foucault's view of how the authority to order social life is bound up with scientific knowledge is demonstrated in the discourses and practices of both Buchanan and Monderman.

Colin Buchanan and Hans Monderman

I drew on these cases as a means to reveal how knowledge and authority have worked in the field of traffic and space planning, using this as an illustration of ways of ordering social life. Professional authority functions as a bridge between scientific knowledge and policy implementation. The technical voices of these two experts were employed as tools or devices for governing in administrative matters. The expert knowledge they offered was supported by 'common sense' and other forms of evidence: quantifiable, objective and rational. Experts are often called to the task of articulating a vision of everyday social life and establishing how it works in practice.

Foucault discusses how authority is produced in certain individuals, but his main concern is with how the schemes of regulation of human conduct induce the capacity of individuals to exercise authority over themselves. How do professional practices come to appear authoritative, objective and rational, with certain expert agents authorised to speak in the name of the many? The authority of experts derives from their location in a 'field', or a network, where individuals, who control different resources, occupy particular positions. From these positions they can articulate the vision of the social circulating among agents similar to themselves. Expertise is granted on the basis of the individual's education, accreditation and experience in the field. But social position, marked by social class, gender, ethnicity and age, also has a strong effect in the granting and recognition of expertise. Experts tend to be male, white, middle-aged and occupants of high positions within their professional hierarchies (Bourdieu, 1992; Ruppert, 2006).

Buchanan and Monderman fit these criteria. Not only do their profiles as individuals fit the frame, but also the generally invisible principles of social division of which they are a part are articulated within their visions of the social. This process tends to link the persistence of social inequalities with the replication of social order.

There are things in common between Buchanan and Monderman. One of them is the argument for an improvement of social life through changed design of urban space, a sort of natural social control achieved through the application of materials, aimed to enforce conduct. Another is a persistent rationality: that designing spaces creates and enhances forms of natural surveillance increasing security (Buchanan) or of social cohesion increasing security (Monderman). A third commonality is that technologies of zoning (different areas for action) persisted in both approaches, as well as some flexibility of adaptation to fit particular local circumstances. A fourth common issue is that not only did these two experts appear to be invested with authority but they also produced their own authority through ways of talking and writing that made their claims appear factual, objective and truthful, as a kind of specialised knowledge. They and their supporters used maps, statistics, photos, reports, interviews and debates as types of inscriptions, conveying through these an imagined order of how life in urban space should be lived.

Their visions differ in accordance to the field and times to which their expert knowledge is linked. The designs of cities like Milton Keynes and Brasilia in the 1960s were connected to a particular phase, while roads in Ipswich today, where some shared approach design has been implemented, are connected to another historical time. Yet, in both these times, utopian images promise to resolve all the problems of the street. A brief summary of differences between the ideas of Buchanan and Monderman is given in Table 2.

Table 2   Buchanan and Monderman compared

Ideas in common
Improving social life through design of space – applying material to enforce human conduct
Embracing a rational approach: quantifiable and objective, to achieve the goal of increasing security for individuals
Devising technologies of zoning, and specific street furniture, to fit diverse behaviour
Appearing as authority and producing their own authority in the process of authorising a social order.

Different ideas	
Buchanan	*Monderman*
Modernist approach:	Flexible approach:
• humans and vehicles are segregated	• humans and vehicles share space
• social state delivers through central control	• enabling state delivers in partnership
• individuals are individualistic, acquisitive and looked after by the authorities	• individuals are cooperative and equipped to be exposed to unpredictable situations, looking after themselves

Differences between Buchanan and Monderman relate strongly to governance projects of the times when their ideas prevailed. The 'social state' that delivers through central control, typical of the Buchanan period, becomes the 'enabling state', typical of the Monderman period, that delivers in partnership with individuals, parents, schools, firms, and so on, making all sorts of partners responsible. Both cases offer scenarios for imagining social existence – our 'social imaginary': how we fit together as individuals and with things that exist in our environment and that we want to possess or use.

In the next chapter in this strand, Chapter 8, you will see how social order relates to disorderly behaviour, and in the final chapter in the strand, Chapter 9, you will look at the ways in which population comes to be talked about in the processes of governing a social order.

References

Bourdieu, P. (1992) *The Logic of Practice*, Cambridge, Polity.

Commission for Architecture and the Built Environment (CABE) (2007) *This Way to Better Streets: 10 Case Studies on Improving Street Design*, London, CABE; also available online at http://www.cabe.org.uk/default.aspx?contentitemid=1978 (Accessed 12 February 2009).

Department for Transport (2007a) *Transport Statistics Great Britain 2007*, London, TSO; also available online at http://www.dft.gov.uk/pgr/statistics/datatablespublications/tsgb/edition20071.pdf (Accessed 12 February 2009).

Department for Transport (2007b) *Manual for Streets*, London, Thomas Telford Publishing; also available online at http://www.dft.gov.uk/pgr/sustainable/manforstreets/ (Accessed 12 February 2009).

Foucault, M. (1972) *The Archaeology of Knowledge*, New York, Vintage Books.

Foucault, M. (1977) *Discipline and Punish: The Birth of the Prison*, Harmondsworth, Penguin.

Foucault, M. (1978) *The History of Sexuality, Vol. 1: An Introduction*, New York, Vintage Books.

Glaskin, M. (2004) 'Innovation: the end of the white line', *Sunday Times*, 22 August [online], http://www.timesonline.co.uk/tol/driving/article472085.ece (Accessed 12 February 2009).

Goffman, E. (1959) *The Presentation of Self in Everyday Life*, New York, Anchor Books.

Goffman, E. (1971) *Relations in Public*, London, Allen Lane.

Goffman, E. (1972) *Interaction Ritual*, London, Allen Lane.

House of Commons (2003) *Hansard*, 2 July, Column 407 [online], http://www.parliament.the stationery office.co.uk/pa/cm200203/cmhansrd/vo030702/debtext/30702-10.htm (Accessed 13 February 2009).

McNichol, T. (2004) 'Roads gone wild', *Wired*, no. 12.12, December [online], http://www.wired.com/wired/archive/12.12/traffic.html (Accessed 13 February 2009).

Marshall, S. (2004) *Building on Buchanan: Evolving Road Hierarchy for Today's Streets-oriented Design Agenda* [online], University College London and University of Westminster, http://home.wmin.ac.uk/transport/download/Marshall_on_Buchanan_ETC_2004.pdf (Accessed 6 March 2008).

Ministry of Transport (1963) *Traffic in Towns*, London, HMSO.

Monbiot, G. (2005) 'They call themselves libertarians; I think they're antisocial bastards', *The Guardian*, 20 December, p. 25; also available online at http://www.monbiot.com/archives/2005/12/20/the-anti-social-bastards-in-our-midst/ (Accessed 13 February 2009).

Shared Space (2005) *Shared Space: Room for Everyone*, Leeuwarden, Shared Space; also available online at http://www.shared-space.org/files/18445/SharedSpace_Eng.pdf (Accessed 21 February 2009).

Ruppert, E.S. (2006) *The Moral Economy of Cities: Shaping Good Citizens*, Toronto, University of Toronto Press.

Taylor, C. (2004) *Modern Social Imaginaries*, Durham, NC, Duke University Press.

2pass.co.uk (2009) *Why in Britain Do We Drive on the Left?* [online], http://www.2pass.co.uk/goodluck.htm (Accessed 10 February 2009).

users.telenet.be (undated) *Why Do Some Countries Drive on the Right and Others on the Left?* [online], http://users.telenet.be/worldstandards/driving%20on%20the%20left.htm (Accessed 10 February 2009).

Chapter 8
Making disorder on the street

Bob Kelly and Jason Toynbee

Contents

Introduction

'The group, mainly consisting of men, is striding purposefully along the street and the pace is gathering momentum. Shouting and snatched conversations are being replaced with loud singing. Individuals and small groups on the pavements look on with mixed expressions of interest, annoyance and perhaps fear. Occasional mutterings which could be of support or dissent can be heard.'

Disorderly behaviour?

The first chapter in this strand looked at social order and how it is created and maintained. The situation described above is certainly relevant to the social in that it involves individuals coming together and apparently acting with common purpose. The group seems to be behaving in agreed ways, with the shouting and singing being accepted and expected by its members. The mixed reactions of onlookers may, however, indicate that not everyone present in the street is in agreement with, or approves of, what is happening.

In order to interpret the situation, further questions would need to be asked:

- Who are the people 'striding purposefully', and how do they relate to the onlookers?
- What is their purpose?

- Is it spontaneous or organised?
- When and in what circumstances is it taking place?

The brief description could refer to a whole array of different situations:

- a group of football supporters on their way to a football match
- a march by an environmentalist group against plans for a nuclear dump or reactor or by the British National Party to protest against the presence of asylum seekers in the local district
- a group of late-night drinkers moving from one hostelry to another
- the annual march of one particular community in Northern Ireland, passing through a mixed or hostile area.

This is far from an exhaustive list of possible explanations of what is happening, but it does show the complexity involved when we study social behaviour. To the participants, whatever the motivation, this is a social activity – there is apparent agreement on what they are doing. To some onlookers this may be behaviour that threatens to disrupt their stability or their sense of social order. They may feel themselves, their property, their interests or their very presence on the street threatened by the marchers.

In Chapter 7 of this book the issue of social order was examined, looking at how social scientists see social order being made or managed.

This chapter will look at questions about social *disorder*, especially 'disorderly behaviour', asking how it is defined, why it is of interest to social scientists, what forms it may take, how it may be controlled or punished, and how it might be studied. Section 1 explores the question of what is meant by 'disorderly' behaviour, while Section 2 looks at historical and contemporary ways in which societies have defined and responded to such behaviour. Section 3 turns to look at the roles of mass media in shaping disorderly behaviour and in shaping how societies respond to it. Finally, Section 4 considers some of the ways in which social scientists have studied these questions, with a particular interest in the uses and limits of official statistics on crime. Overall, the chapter suggests that, rather than assuming that social disorder is just the absence of order, exploring disorderly behaviour can provide insights into how social order is made and maintained.

1 Defining and dealing with 'disorderly behaviour'

In society as a whole, expectations of behaviour sometimes take the form of laws with penalties against those that break them. In modern democratic states such as the UK, these may be the product of long-standing traditions or Acts of Parliament which have been passed according to accepted procedures.

This may sound straightforward, but it is important to ask: what factors influence both the creation and resilience of social rules in general and laws in particular? Tradition and established practices have a role to play, but what may influence the government or parliament to pass a new law? Some of the factors we would identify are:

- recent events
- campaigns by particular interest groups
- pressure from the press and other media
- the influence of powerful individuals or groups
- the particular beliefs or interests of the government or prominent members of it.

One example of a new law relating to disorder was the Dangerous Dogs Act of 1991(Lodge and Hood, 2002). This was passed after several incidents of serious injuries inflicted by aggressive dogs, particularly on children. The tabloid press headlined these incidents, leading to widespread public concern. Politicians took up the issue and government ministers rapidly stepped in to have a law drafted which placed major restrictions on the ownership of four breeds of dog, the most prominent being the pit bull terrier. The result has been some confusion as individuals have fought to prevent what they claimed were their 'harmless' pets from being neutered or 'put down', by producing arguments such as that they are of 'mixed breed' and therefore not covered by the law.

Activity 1

Think about the example of the Dangerous Dogs Act and the potentially influential factors listed above, and note down which factors seem to have been relevant in this case.

The Act certainly followed what had been recent events highlighted in newspaper articles. There was little evidence of interest groups or powerful individuals being behind the campaign for a change of law, although groups representing dog owners expressed concern at the implications of it. The particular beliefs of government members are not known, but in political terms it may have seemed a more attractive option to protect children rather than dogs.

The issue of 'power' was discussed in Chapter 2 of this book in relation to supermarkets, with their market and buyer power.

Here we can see power being exerted by the press, with the government acting in response to the press campaign which portrayed the ownership of 'dangerous' dogs as being 'anti-social'. The question of the power of the press and other elements of the media will be returned to in Section 3 of this chapter.

So far we have been arguing that we need to consider specific social factors which influence what becomes law and what is defined as 'disorderly'. However, this approach stands in contrast to a commonly held belief that law and order derive from clear-cut, sensible or even 'natural' rules which ought to shape everyday behaviour. Any glimpse of newspaper headlines would confirm that there are indeed strongly held views about social order, but – significantly – also a sense that this order is under threat. Figure 1 shows a selection of newspaper headlines from 2007.

From these headlines it is clear that not everybody is following what are regarded as the rules of society, and they certainly indicate that some people, at least on occasions, have disrespect for them. It may be, however, that in some cases it goes beyond this, with some groups actually having different sets of values. Within any society there are numerous interests which may be in competition. For instance, within the UK there are divisions based on nationality, region of the country, rural/urban differences, religion, income and wealth, gender, age, and so on. Members of each 'group' may well have their own expectations of behaviour which may conflict with what general societal expectations may be. For example, many young people object to, or ignore, existing laws on alcohol or cannabis; some religious groups wish to change or

Yobette generation is plaguing our streets
The Daily Express, 7 May 2007

Girl of 16 banned from town centre she had terrorised
Daily Mail, 14 April 2007

The Big Issue: Ban Alco-Yobs
The Mirror, 9 July 2007

Respect will not get thugs off the streets
Daily Telegraph, 23 January 2007

7 Girls Drunk
The Daily Record, 26 April 2007

Violent Britain: where do you stand?
The Sun, 24 July 2007

Figure 1   Newspaper headlines on disorderly behaviour

extend the enforcement of laws on blasphemy; and 'animal rights' activists oppose practices of animal experimentation that are currently legal.

It may also be the case that almost everyone breaks the law or commits disorderly acts at particular times.

Activity 2

Look at the following list of questions and decide in each case (there is no need to write down your answers), whether you have committed this action and how frequently (never, once, several times, frequently).

- Have you been involved in a loud argument or scuffle in public after an evening's drinking?
- Have you dropped litter, stamped out a cigarette butt, or spat out a piece of chewing gum in the street?
- Have you driven a car over the speed limit or blown a car horn late at night in a built-up area?
- Have you bought or used illegal drugs in a public place?
- Have you ever pushed a large pram or trolley along a narrow pavement to the possible inconvenience of other pedestrians?
- Have you, in the company of a group, sung loudly, shouted abuse at other people, or used threatening behaviour?
- Have you failed to clear up the mess after a dog you have been walking has defecated on the pavement?

The list of questions could go on, but we hope that this has made you aware that disorderly behaviour is not necessarily what 'others' do. We (the chapter authors) individually admit to some but not all of the actions listed and we have no intention of stating which ones. There are also questions of frequency and whether specific behaviours were associated with particular times in our lives or groups with whom we mixed. Some social scientists have suggested that people may 'drift' occasionally into disorderly or delinquent behaviour (Matza, 1964). If they are not caught or charged with an offence and if they mix with other groups of people, then the behaviour loses long-term significance. If, on the other hand, they are caught and 'labelled' as being 'disorderly', or continue to mix with the same people in the same circumstances, then the label can turn into what the US sociologist Howard Becker (1963) termed a **master-status**. By this he meant that if a person has been singled out as differing from 'normal' people, then a common reaction is for that label to take on much greater significance in their lives. So instead of being a person who has been convicted for theft, they become 'a thief'. In other words, the complexities of personality and individuality are ignored and people are identified by a single aspect of themselves, which may distinguish or even isolate them from what is seen as 'mainstream' society. This can obviously shape the lives of those directly involved and significantly affect those of others. The treatment of offenders, or, more generally, what Becker (1963) called 'deviants', therefore becomes very significant to society at large and of particular interest to social scientists.

Master-status
The social position that is the main identifying characteristic of an individual, overshadowing all other features.

You may think back to the discussion of 'street people' in Chapter 4 of *Making Social Lives* as isolated from mainstream society.

These points indicate that the definition of disorderly or 'anti-social' behaviour is not something generally agreed or universal, but is actually constructed in specific societies and therefore differs across time and between places. Indeed, the very term 'anti-social' is of relatively recent origin. It was used in the 1980s by critics of Margaret Thatcher's governments (accusing them of creating 'anti-social policies'; see Squires, 1990) It was used in a different way following the election victory of 'New Labour' in 1997, with Lord Williams in the House of Lords stating that 'Anti-social behaviour is a menace on our streets; it is a threat to our communities' (quoted in Burney, 2005, p. 1). So, use of the term 'anti-social' can be seen as a recent way of talking about forms of disorderly behaviour.

Returning to our focus on the street, as you have seen in earlier chapters, streets can vary incredibly in terms of both time and place. Many of us live in them, use them as thoroughfares, work in them, shop in them or play in them. But if streets work *for us* in this way, helping to form identities and providing us with material things, then they may also be sites of *breakdown*, of conflict or danger – as our earlier glimpse of newspaper headlines so vividly suggests. An obvious example would be a city centre street late in the evening, with CCTV pictures of drunken and loutish behaviour; people arguing, fighting, smashing windows, vomiting in the gutter, and so on. Concern about 'yobs', 'louts' and 'anti-social behaviour' was not limited to city streets – there has also been a great deal of media attention devoted to similar scenes in small towns and villages.

Crimes and related behaviour such as prostitution and kerb crawling, drug-dealing and consumption form one dimension of disorderly behaviour. Beyond crime, however, there are other kinds of behaviour that may create disruption, personal hardship and social damage, yet are rarely classed as disorderly or anti-social. Examples here might be the closing down of the local post office, or the polluting or health-damaging effects of the factory at the end of the street. We might also include the driving of large, fuel-guzzling, four-wheel drive cars which has been criticised by the more environmentally conscious in the community. Some writers suggest that it is the rich and powerful in society who determine what is disorderly or criminal, and that they are able to prevent their own actions being viewed or defined in such terms (e.g. Taylor et al., 1973, 1975; Whyte, 2008).

Crimes
Acts punishable by law.

Given these problems of definition and interpretation, it seems reasonable to ask: what actually constitutes disorderly or 'anti-social' behaviour? The UK Government, which is responsible for shaping state policy, and Parliament, which passes laws, certainly have significant roles in this. The government's website states that anti-social behaviour refers to 'selfish and unacceptable activity that can blight the quality of community life' (Respect, 2008), and goes on to list examples such as 'nuisance neighbours', 'yobbish behaviour' and the 'reckless driving of mini-motorbikes'. It also gives a legal definition that is found in the Crime and Disorder Act 1998, which describes anti-social behaviour as acting in 'a manner that caused or was likely to cause harassment, alarm or distress to one or more persons not of the same household' as the perpetrator. It is important to note that:

- Like all things social, any description or definition of disorderly/anti-social behaviour has a history. There is no universal and essential definition of certain things being 'right' and others 'wrong'.

- Such an attempt at definition raises the key questions of who or what embodies the disorderly/anti-social (which people are identified as anti-social or disorderly) and for whom (such definitions are potentially an issue of conflict and power).

- This leads to the issue of the value-laden nature of defining disorderly/anti-social behaviours and people via law, social policy and media.

- A definition of disorderly/anti-social behaviour is also a concept invoked by communities, an imagined 'we' who judge some activities and people as disorderly/anti-social in the separated, yet overlapping, social space of the street.

The criminologist Elizabeth Burney points out that this emphasis on 'anti-social behaviour' in the UK replaced the terminology in the USA of the 1970s and 1980s that spoke about 'incivilities' and 'disorder'. She argues that this is significant because it moved the emphasis away from collective behaviour onto that of morally deficient individuals who require discipline and punishment, as it is seen as an outcome of personal choice with individuals portrayed as the authors of their own predicament (Burney, 2005). This reveals the significance of the selection and use of particular terms or phrases, with their use in everyday speech incorporating particular interpretations of behaviour or institutions.

Summary

• Expectations of orderly behaviour and the identification of disorderly or 'anti-social' actions are partly based on law, but are always influenced by the way particular societies are organised, and may therefore vary across time and between places.

• Some individuals and groups may be identified with disorderly behaviour, but it may be that almost everyone commits such actions at particular times of their lives.

• To some extent 'the eyes of the beholder' are important in deciding whether an action is to be so defined.

2   Concern with disorder

From what we have looked at already, we can see that what is regarded as 'disorderly behaviour' varies from place to place. Also, some of the examples suggest that there is a time element to it – clearly, the reckless use of mini-motorbikes can only have been a recent phenomenon. When we look into history we can find interesting examples that illustrate continuity across time but also some changes that give us an insight into how definitions of disorderly and 'anti-social' behaviour are made and by whom.

2.1   Disorderly people in the past

In ancient Athens, Aristotle identified the problem of unruly youth that finds distinct echoes of today. He is reported to have stated that 'the young people of today ... have bad manners, they scoff at authority and lack respect for their elders. Children nowadays are real tyrants ... they contradict their parents ... and tyrannise their teachers' (Brake, 1980, p. 1). This would suggest that older people had a key role in definitions of the anti-social as long ago as around 350 BCE.

The historian Heather Shore has argued that while reports of juvenile and petty crime can be located in the sixteenth century, 'the late eighteenth and nineteenth century was a pivotal period' in our recording and treatment of such offences (Shore, 2000, p. 21), with fears of skilled pickpockets progressing to become burglars. The phenomenon was associated with the growth of cities and the concentration of poor people in certain parts of cities. In 1898 a Brighton magistrate giving evidence to the Howard Association on Penal Reform argued that 'the child of today is coarser, more vulgar, less refined than his parents were', and it was in that year the word **hooligan** entered the English language 'in the wake of a rowdy August bank holiday celebration in London when hundreds of people appeared before the courts on charges of assault and drunkenness' (Pearson, 2006).

Hooligan
A person who engages in unruly and disruptive behaviour.

The origin of the use of 'hooligan' as a term to describe anti-social behaviour is contested. Some suggest that the term was named after a particular family in Southwark led by Patrick Hooligan who indulged in drunken and rowdy behaviour (Quinion, 1998), others that it simply derives from the Irish word *houlie* which refers to a wild party (Wikipedia, 2009). Whichever version is true, it has become a term in common use today to characterise such behaviour.

These examples would suggest that the growth of towns and cities in the late eighteenth and nineteenth centuries and the consequent increase in population density and social complexity have played a role in the growth and perception of disorderly behaviour. By 'social complexity' we mean the development of new social groups and classes with varying access to income and wealth, as well as people from different geographical and cultural backgrounds now living closely together.

In his book *Hooligan*, the sociologist of deviance Geoffrey Pearson noted that in nineteenth-century England there were perceived problems at various times with gangs of girls terrifying people on the streets with their unruly and violent behaviour. This has some echoes for us in recently identified complaints about the drunken and unruly behaviour of 'ladettes', and a judge in 1977 being terrified by the advent of 'the female mugger' (Pearson, 1983, p. 225). It indicates that what are sometimes highlighted as 'shocking' contemporary events may simply be echoes of the past.

Pearson also points out that in every generation there is a tendency to look back at the past as an era of morality and decency, and to draw the contrast with the social problems and degeneracy of the present. As Pearson (1983, p. 7) puts it, society is dominated by the view that 'the past … was a golden age of order and security. Nowadays we need the iron fist of policing in order that we may sleep soundly in our beds'. A contemporary version of this view stresses the breakdown of family life, a general lack of respect for others, and rampant alcohol and drug abuse. This view is often taken up and amplified by the media and politicians, leading to demands for stronger laws and law enforcement. The sociologist Stanley Cohen (1973, p. 9) termed this sort of process a **moral panic**, pointing to the periodic identification of groups of people that are seen to threaten 'our whole way of life' and from whom society 'must be protected'. The idea of the moral panic is examined in more detail in Section 3 of this chapter.

Moral panic
When a pattern of behaviour, group of people or a condition becomes defined as a threat to society, its values and its interests.

Perhaps the main point to take away from this discussion of disorderly conduct in the past is that while what is classified as 'anti-social' has changed historically, there seems to be a tendency in all periods to idealise the past and contrast it with a dangerous present. This would seem to be true, in recent decades, about 'football hooligans', 'lager louts', 'muggers', 'hoodies' and 'paedophiles'. In the case of the street, we can see the growth of 'Anti-social Behaviour Orders (ASBOs)' as a recent reaction to a moral panic. The 1998 Crime and Disorder Act introduced the concept of the ASBO to deal with behaviour which constituted a criminal offence but which was likely to become bogged down in court processes and result only in very minor penalties. We examine this topic in the next section.

2.2   Disorderly conduct in the recent past: inventing the ASBO

Disorderly behaviour may be identified in different behaviour patterns by different people, but it nonetheless can cause distress and disruption to other people's lives. It can be argued that in present-day societies people have less direct contact with and knowledge of neighbours, so increasingly they look to governments or public authorities to exercise control. Powers are therefore given to the police and courts to deal with offenders and to restore social order by taking preventative measures and by meting out punishment. In terms of preventative measures, there have been attempts to predict which groups or individuals might be most prone to disorderly behaviour and to provide greater supervision and facilities to deter it from happening. It has even been suggested that it is possible to identify 5-year-old children as likely future offenders, and that their details should be recorded on a DNA database (Townsend and Asthana, 2008). In terms of the meting out of punishment, locking people up in prisons and young offenders institutions has been a frequent response, leading to high costs, prison overcrowding and new prison-building programmes. One recent initiative involved the use of Anti-social Behaviour Orders (ASBOs).

ASBOs were court orders which banned named individuals from committing particular acts. Various bodies, such as local authorities and the police, could apply to courts to ban offenders from continuing with their disorderly behaviour, from spending time in the company of particular friends or from visiting certain areas. The orders were issued for a minimum of two years. The ASBO itself was not a criminal penalty and it did not appear on the individual's criminal record. However, a breach of the ASBO was a criminal offence, punishable by a fine or even a prison sentence.

The aim behind the ASBO was to encourage local communities to become more involved in reporting and dealing with petty crime, thereby building feelings of community loyalty and control. Members of the public were encouraged to report incidents to Anti-social Behaviour Teams at the local council or police station, and they were not themselves required to appear in court.

ASBOs were part of a raft of measures designed to tackle such behaviour. At an earlier stage an Acceptable Behaviour Contract (ABC) could be drawn up, listing acts such as drawing graffiti or harassment, and the signatures of offenders added, committing them not to continue with such behaviour. If the contract were broken, then the ASBO was likely to follow. The police and community support officers also had powers to break up and ban for up to twenty-four hours groups who were, or potentially might be, harassing others. If they refused to disperse they could be given a fixed penalty notice involving a fine. The police and local authority could also designate 'no-go zones' for particular people or specific behaviours (e.g. drinking alcohol), and the police could take home unsupervised children found in such areas after 9 p.m.

Similarly, parents could be held to account by 'parenting contracts' and 'parenting orders' requiring them to attend parenting courses and holding them responsible for school attendance; failure to comply could result in a large fine.

Scotland has a very different legal system from that of England and Wales. However, a similar approach influenced legal developments there. In Scotland the Antisocial Behaviour Act was passed in June 2004, granting powers to local authorities to:

* disperse groups of more than two people in designated trouble spots
* introduce parenting orders
* extend electronic tagging to children under 16
* ban selling spray paint to people under 16
* set fixed penalty notices for offences involving such behaviour as leaving litter, drunkenness or consuming alcohol in a public place
* set more powers for councils to deal with private landlords who turn a blind eye to anti social tenants
* give police more powers to close 'crack houses'
* extend ASBOs to 12–15-year-olds (BBC Action Network, 2007).

The logic of ASBOs and these related measures was that there had been a genuine upsurge in disorderly behaviour that required serious action. Moreover, there was the belief that court procedures had been slow and inadequate in their treatment of offenders. Finally, there was the implication that the community itself had failed to deal with the problem and required state support; families and neighbourhoods had failed to control their potentially unruly elements.

An informal teenage gathering, or the potential for disorder?

It is important to note that just as definitions of disorderly behaviour are socially constructed and contested, so too were ASBOs. For many critics of government policies, ASBOs were seen as part of the growing authority over and intrusion into people's lives in recent years. They were being taken out against people whose behaviour fell short of what courts might have readily accepted as being proven criminal behaviour, and therefore the rights to justice of the accused were being removed (Kennedy, 2005).

The development of the ASBO reflected a particular view of the causes of criminal behaviour and of how it should be treated. It emphasised the culpability of the individual and tended to ignore the structural pressures of living in areas of high unemployment and social deprivation. It stressed the role of punishment and control rather than help and support, with critics suggesting that the outcome was greater exclusion from society rather than the reform of the individual or the reduction of incidents of such behaviour (Squires and Stephen, 2005).

A present-day hooligan?

This links with a view that has international significance – that there has been a growing threat to social order from the bad behaviour of young people and serious action needs to be taken about it. At a popular level, in both the UK and the USA, there have been television series such as *Brat Camp* and *Bad Lads Army* which have depicted 'lazy' and 'loutish' young people whose behaviour and attitudes could be challenged by programmes of discipline or therapeutic treatment. One growing strand of this anxiety about young people has been to combine educational policies with those on public order by focusing on preventative measures to identify vulnerable children at an early age and provide support systems to ensure a suitable environment for healthy development. Two versions of this were the UK Government's Sure

Start programme and the National Action Plan in Germany. Sure Start focused on the role of adults who work with children, to ensure the child was aided in the processes of learning, communicating and growing healthily. A 'framework of effective practice' was laid down to provide 'support, information, guidance and challenge for all those with responsibility for the care and education of babies and children from birth to three years' (SureStart, 2005, p. 4). In Germany, a National Action Plan was launched in 2005 which focused on identifying children at risk and on the need to boost parenting skills so that these children would not become the victims of violence, would not become delinquent, would have greater educational opportunities, would receive better health care in a less polluted environment and would benefit from more exercise and a balanced diet (Federal Foreign Office, 2007).

Summary

- Fear of disorderly behaviour can be traced throughout history, with particular emphasis on the activities of 'young people'.
- There is a common fear that can also be traced over time that order is breaking down and life in the past was more disciplined and secure.
- A recent illustration of this has been the use of Anti-social Behaviour Orders (ASBOs).
- Such policies reflect a view that disorderly behaviour is the product of poor parenting and community failure rather than being rooted in social inequality.
- Public attitudes and government policies in the UK have been similar to those in other countries.

3   Mediating 'disorderly' conduct

Sections 1 and 2 showed how disorderly conduct is *defined*, how these definitions are *constructed* by society, and the ways in which these definitions have been *shaped historically*. Bearing these factors in mind, people might be forgiven for thinking that the advent of the ASBO marked an important shift in the way the disorderly was being treated in the UK. After all, the ASBO created a new category of 'near crime', and as a result became a bitterly contested issue. Yet, as has also been noted, anxiety about violence and disorder, or the bad behaviour of young people, has a long history. So, how can this continuous yet changing history of the disorderly be explained? This section examines debates on social disorder which give the media a key role, and introduces the term **mediation**.

Mediation means the way things (here, the issue of disorderly conduct) are represented to us through language or customary ways of thinking about the world. In an important sense those processes of definition, construction and historical shaping examined in the previous sections all depend on mediation; that is, they involve some form of constructing disorderly conduct through language. This is why in the section heading above we put the term 'disorderly' in quotation marks – to emphasise that it is a word with powerful connotations, a word which *does* things. Indeed, it should be clear by now that disorderly behaviour cannot be considered on its own, without reflecting on the way this word and ideas about it help to shape and define, include or exclude, those physical actions – and those people – which we treat as disorderly.

Reflecting on mediation helps us to think about radio, television, newspapers and the internet – the mass media themselves. They have an immensely powerful role to play in mediation, but not an exclusive one, and frequently they do not initiate ways of thinking about disorderly conduct. Rather, they tend to mediate ideas which come from elsewhere, such as government, powerful social groups or historically embedded, 'common-sense' ways of thinking about the world.

Mediation
The way things are represented to us through language or customary ways of thinking.

Activity 3

Cast your mind back to Section 1 of this chapter and those British newspaper headlines from 2007 about disorderly behaviour (Figure 1). Look at them again and consider their effect on readers in an everyday context – how they might react to them. The headlines provide information certainly – they tell us about things in the world. But perhaps more significantly they give cues about how we should understand anti-social behaviour, what our attitude towards it ought to be. Try to identify these cues as well as the possible feelings they might generate among readers.

You may have come up with the following, or something similar:

- fear

- indignation

- a feeling that we live in a dangerous society

- the sense that girls and the homeless are now responsible for a great deal of violence

- that some kinds of people – the 'yobette', 'alco-yobs', 'thugs' – are distinct from the rest of us, are naturally violent and must be dealt with accordingly.

Folk devils
People who are portrayed as deviant and are blamed for crimes and other social problems.

Now one important approach in social science has suggested that this sort of media depiction of anti-social behaviour helps to construct **folk devils** (Cohen, 1973). They are the 'yobettes', 'alco-yobs' and 'thugs' of the headlines or, in the case study where Stanley Cohen originally developed the idea, the 'mods' and 'rockers' who fought in seaside towns in the UK in the mid 1960s. Cohen argued that the portrayal of folk devils in the media creates a moral panic in society at large whereby people are both terrified and outraged. A key point about moral panic is that it is irrational, and that the fears generated are out of all proportion to the scale of the actual behaviour which is the subject of the panic. Much of this has to do with the way that folk devils are represented – that is, as distinct evil beings rather than as human beings who live in the real social world and do things for reasons.

For Cohen, then, the media play a major role in fostering irrational fears about anti-social behaviour. However, beyond suggesting that the media reflect deep-seated cultural anxieties, Cohen offers few reasons why the press or television should create folk devils and so start off new moral panics. The cultural studies scholar Stuart Hall and his co-authors argue in *Policing the Crisis* (1978) that media coverage of crime in the UK in the early 1970s contributed to a widespread belief that there was a crisis in society, in particular to do with the sudden rise of the

Street violence or playful behaviour?

'mugger' or street robber. Just like Cohen, then, Hall et al. emphasise the mediation of violent disorder, but also suggest that this media construction has its roots in social conflict.

By the early 1970s, they argue, a period of stabilised consent (widespread agreement or acceptance) as to what the role of the government should be in relation to British society was coming to an end, in the face of diverse forms of social and political dissent. This dissent ranged from strikes and industrial unrest, intense political and military conflict in Northern Ireland, to the emergence of new social movements trying to promote or provoke social change. In this context, the British state (seen by Hall et al. to be representing the most powerful groups and interests in society) 'cracked down' on crime and violence, particularly among young black men. In doing so the state became a 'primary definer' of disorder. The media then took their cue from government, police and judges – for instance, in the use of the term 'mugging' – and extended the primary definitions further, giving them a popular ring. In this view, the deep-seated causes of social conflict, chiefly inequality, were obscured and the issue was turned into a moral and legal struggle against what was defined as 'mindless violence'. For Hall and his colleagues, this was the creation of a 'Law and Order society'.

Cohen and Hall et al. accept that street violence actually existed, but are much more concerned with how it became defined and amplified through media representation, how public perceptions changed as a result, and how this then enabled governments to justify more vigorous policing and sentencing – rather than tackling the causes of social unrest, which, in their view, lay in ever-deepening social inequality and social conflict. Arguably, this approach to disorder is as valid now as it was in the mid 1970s, as shown by the newspaper headlines presented earlier and in government responses towards prison building and punishment.

However, another social science perspective has a much simpler account. In this view, the media directly cause disorderly behaviour. Here the argument is that disorderly behaviour is a direct effect of how the media portray violence.

The key issue for social scientists who take up this 'media effects' approach is whether it can be shown that watching violence actually makes people act violently, or, in the terms we have been using in this section: what evidence is there for a link *from* exposure to media violence *to* actual disorderly behaviour? Governments have become interested in this question, in part, perhaps, because if it can be demonstrated that there is such a link then the policy solution is relatively simple. The media can be told off, codes of conduct drafted for schools and parents, or even outright censorship of the media imposed. As a consequence, there has been a succession of officially commissioned reports into media effects. In 2007, for example, the British Prime Minister Gordon Brown announced one in his speech to the Labour Party conference. As he put it:

> Today amongst the biggest influences on children are the Internet, TV, commercial advertising. And like many parents I feel I'm struggling to set the boundaries so that children can be safe – and that's why we have asked Dr Tanya Byron [a clinical psychologist and a resident expert on TV parenting programmes in 2004–06] to look at how families can make the most of the opportunities new technology gives while doing our duty to protect children from harmful material.

> (BBC News, 2007)

The focus on children is typical of the media effects debate. Children are presumed to be particularly vulnerable to the representation of sex, violence, and so on, liable to copy it in real life or 'learn' anti-social behaviour. Yet, although common sense might tell us this is likely, proving it is more difficult. In fact, there is now a deep division in the social sciences between those who argue that the evidence clearly shows media-violence effects, and those who are sceptical about such claims.

A look at one quite recent study reveals some of the problems involved. The research team claim that they are the first to show long-term effects, of watching violent television content during childhood on actual violence in adulthood (Huesmann et al., 2003). Their method is the **longitudinal study**. This involves going back to a group of people (the 'research subjects') who have previously been studied, in order to find out whether there have been changes in their behaviour in the intervening period. In this case, the first study took place in 1977 when 557 children were interviewed and tested, including collecting information on their patterns of television viewing. The follow-up research began in 1991. After four years the team managed to track down and interview 398 people from the original study to establish whether the aggressive behaviour of some of these adults might be correlated with their watching television violence as children. The authors claim that there was indeed such a correlation – in other words, a relationship where a change in one factor leads to a change in another.

Longitudinal study
A study of the activities or attitudes of individuals or groups of people over long periods of time.

However, the team cannot demonstrate conclusively in which direction influence is being exerted. It might have been the case that the aggressive adults in the study were already aggressive as children, and as a result watched more violent television. Indeed, on this point the authors can only say that 'it is more plausible that exposure to TV violence increases aggression than that aggression increases TV-violence viewing' (Huesmann et al., 2003, p. 216). Now to argue the plausibility or likelihood of an explanation is perfectly valid in the social sciences, as evidence is rarely conclusive. The problem in this case, however, is that opinion about media effects is strongly divided among researchers. It is therefore hard to know on what this appeal to plausibility might be based, except 'common sense'. As the next section shows, a major aim of social science research is to go beyond everyday common sense by gathering and using evidence in a logical and consistent way.

A further problem with media effects research is that, even if a correlation between watching violence and behaving violently can be shown, there may still be another factor at work which is driving *both* these factors. In other words, a cause (or set of causes) might lie 'behind' cases where people act aggressively and also watch violence on television.

Activity 4

Can you think of what such a 'third factor' might be? Consider the possible factors people can come up with to explain why others act in disorderly ways and appear to like violence.

Here are some ideas we came up with:

- low intelligence (less intelligent people like violence)
- evil (some people are inherently violent and anti-social)
- weakness or susceptibility (certain individuals are more likely to copy anti-social behaviour, whether it is in the media or in real life)
- inequality (poverty – including unemployment, poor educational opportunities, a degraded environment – can itself be viewed as a form of violence which harms people so that sometimes they express their pain in disorderly ways).

The first three are all what might be called 'naturalistic' explanations. They suggest that certain people are born with an anti-social nature. The fourth is a social explanation. It attributes the things people do, in part at least, to social organisation – in this case, systematic inequality which is reproduced generation after generation, and which confines large numbers of people to a difficult and troubled life. A social explanation of this sort may imply that power is at work, whereby some people are poor while others are better off.

It is possible to combine naturalistic and social explanations. For instance, it might be that social factors have a greater effect in the case of individuals who are more susceptible to behaving aggressively. Or, in an extreme version: poverty and disorderly behaviour are two sides of the same coin, and the poor are born less intelligent and more violent. However, here the social starts to lose its distinctive character and becomes 'reduced' to the natural. The implication is that poor people are a biologically, rather than socially, distinct group. In general, social science does not explain things this way. Instead, social scientists focus on the norms, structures and institutions which order (though never completely shape) how people live. Certainly, their social lives emerge from the natural world. We all have bodies, and when we watch television our eyes, ears and brains are engaged. Still, *how* we watch and respond cannot simply be reduced to physical factors; people interpret messages according to their own values which have been influenced by their social experiences. Rather than being based simply in physical factors, some kind of social explanation is needed.

Table 1 provides a diagrammatic summary of the contrasting theories of disorderly behaviour that we have discussed in this section. The left-hand column shows the theories and the other columns pick out the various factors examined. The arrows indicate influences at work from one factor to another.

Table 1   Theories of the media's relationship to anti-social behaviour

Theory	Social factors	The media	The anti-social in public perception	The anti-social as actual behaviour
Moral panic (Cohen, 1973)	Deep-seated culture of anxiety ⟶	Create folk devils (e.g. mods and rockers) ⟶	Moral panic	Mod–rocker fighting
Policing the crisis (Hall et al., 1978)	Inequality, social crisis and the interest of the state in diverting attention away from these factors ⟶	Take up and develop primary definitions (e.g. muggers) made by the state ⟶	A sense of crisis	Street crime
Media effects research (e.g. Huesmann et al., 2003)		Depict (large amounts of) violence ⟶		Increased violence and aggression among those who have been exposed to media violence

Note that only the media effects approach focuses directly on disorderly behaviour itself. It doesn't have any conception of social factors as causing that behaviour; nor does it consider that public perception might be a significant part of disorderly behaviour.

The other two approaches are more concerned with mediation; that is, ways in which the media generate perceptions of the anti-social. Both also have an account of social factors – the larger context in which the media coverage, public perception and actual behaviour arise. In the *Policing the Crisis* account, the state is seen as concealing the problems of inequality and conflict by dramatising disorderly behaviour ('mugging'). This diverts attention from inequality as a social and political problem to be solved. The state begins the process of mediation and the media then respond to this agenda.

We began this section by suggesting that mediation was a larger process than just what the media do. It is not simply a matter of sensational newspaper headlines or grainy shots of 'hoodies' on the street at dusk. It involves how government mediates social conflict and sets an agenda around it, the forms in which the media take up that agenda, and the ways people respond – not to mention the influences which feed back through the chain. Looked at in this way, the media effects approach is much *less* about mediation than the other two theories we have looked at.

One conclusion to draw from this is that mediation of social problems like anti-social behaviour is complex, and that makes the question of how we might research anti-social behaviour very important. It is to this question we turn in the next section.

Summary

- Mediation of disorder occurs in a number of places: in government, among powerful groups and in everyday ways of thinking.
- The media then play a key role in spreading and amplifying these mediations, so influencing people's perceptions of disorderly behaviour.
- That said, there are varying perspectives among social scientists as to the causes of actual disorderly behaviour and the extent to which the media may contribute to it, ranging from naturalistic to social explanations.

4 Researching disorderly behaviour, its causes and effects

Social scientists vary in their reasons for studying disorderly behaviour. For some the aim is to discover the causes of something that is socially disruptive to enlighten policymakers in their endeavours to reduce or abolish it. By studying statistics of its location and frequency, or by determining the characteristics or motives of offenders, they may be able to identify suitable policies that could be introduced. Other social scientists are more concerned about identifying who has power in society – by looking at behaviour that is criminalised or subject to punishment, and at the penalties that are meted out, they may be able to pinpoint in whose interests rules are made. So key questions they ask concern what, and who, comes to be defined as disorderly.

Graffiti: disorderly behaviour?

These are very broad approaches, but within them we can identify particular groups of social scientists who focus on issues of concern to them. Among the questions they may ask are:

- What are the costs to society of disruption and destruction resulting from anti-social behaviour and of tackling or punishing it?

- Who are the powerful individuals and groups who can influence definitions and policies?

- Can we predict which individuals, neighbourhoods or social groups are most prone to anti-social behaviour?

- How do we find out what motivates seemingly 'ordinary' people to commit such actions?

- What preventative measures or punishments are potentially most effective?

With such questions in mind, how might social scientists go about their research into disorderly behaviour? As we have seen, such behaviour covers a wide range of activities, only some of which at any one time might be considered to be crimes. It is, however, very difficult to study many of these activities, particularly those that involve criminality.

A range of methods and resources is open to social scientists to study behaviour in general, with some of the most prominent being the use of interviews and questionnaires, participant observation, and the use of **official statistics**. Interviews and questionnaires can range from a set of rigid questions that offer a limited number of possible answers to open-ended interviews in which the social scientist has a number of topics to discuss with the people they are researching, with questions flowing freely in response to previous answers. Studies can also vary between large-scale surveys of perhaps several thousand respondents at any one time and smaller samples which trace respondents at various stages over a lengthy period. **Participant observation** involves the social scientist engaging with the subjects of investigation, but this again can vary between the extremes of active and passive participation, and between open observation where the subjects are fully informed that their behaviour is being studied and covert observation where they are not.

Official statistics
Data already produced by agencies such as government departments, international organisations or local authorities, which may involve social scientists in its production. Other social scientists may interpret these statistics and use them as the basis for research.

Participant observation
Participant observation describes the process of studying a social group by taking part in its activities.

The choice of which method or combination of methods to use is dependent upon the topic being studied, the resources at the disposal of the social scientist, the sort of information that is being sought and the ethics of the researcher. Some social scientists seek statistical precision and so prefer to study large numbers of people by way of fixed questionnaires that allow responses to be compared and clear answers reached, while others prefer to obtain a 'richness of detail' of information on a relatively small number of people; they aim to empathise with people to understand their feelings and motivation. The general point is that the choice of methods has a major impact on the kinds of results obtained. So surveys can show numbers and types of cases, say, while interviews and observation may reveal some of the attitudes among the people involved. As a consequence, different methods can lead us to think about anti-social behaviour in different ways.

One interesting example of studying disorderly behaviour was undertaken by the sociologist James Patrick in the late 1960s. Although this research was carried out a long time ago, it still brings out many of the issues and problems involved in such studies.

Activity 5

Read the following extract and note the difficulties/problems Patrick faced with this research.

I was dressed in a midnight-blue suit, with a twelve-inch middle vent, three-inch flaps over the side pockets … My hair, which I had allowed to grow long, was newly washed and combed into a parting just to the left of centre. My nails I had cut down as far as possible, leaving them ragged and dirty. I approached the gang of boys standing outside the pub …

I had not planned to join a juvenile gang; I had been invited. For two years I had been working in one of Scotland's approved schools during my vacations from Glasgow University … I applied for a full-time post as a teacher, was accepted and started work in August 1966. During the Easter and Summer holidays of that year I had met Tim, who had been committed to the school some months previously. Thanks to some common interests, we quickly became friends … In discussion with the boys the topic of gangs and gang-warfare constantly cropped up. … I was sitting on a bench … criticizing boys who got into trouble while on leave. Tim, who had been on the edge of the group … suddenly jumped up and asked me what I knew about boys on leave and how they spent their time. The honest answer was very little … Tim sidled up to me and asked me to come out with him and see for myself.

… At first Tim thought I should be introduced to his mates as an approved school teacher but I soon pointed out the dangers and difficulties of that arrangement. For a start, I would then have been unlikely to see typical behaviour. It was slowly dawning on me that the best solution to the problem would be for me to become a participant observer.

I realised, however, that this method of approach presented its own problems, chief of which was to what extent I should participate. My greatest worry was that incidents might be staged for my benefit, that Tim's behaviour might be radically altered, for better or worse, by my presence … Privately I came to the conclusion that I must be a passive participant …

The situation of my being a middle-class teacher during the
week and a member of a juvenile gang at the weekend
produced a very real conflict for me. In fact it was the internal
struggle between identification with the boys and abhorrence
of their violence that finally forced me to quit.

(Patrick, 1973, pp. 13–14)

Patrick gives a very honest account of his research, pointing to the risks
of the observer influencing the behaviour he is studying, or becoming
so involved that he identifies with the gang. In addition, note the
difficulties that such a researcher might have in gaining access to a
gang, in being accepted by its members, in having the resource of time
to spend with them, and the dangers of committing anti-social or illegal
behaviour himself.

It is important to note the aims of the researcher in this case. A small-
scale study of this sort can produce real insights into what might
motivate people in general, as well as these individuals in particular, to
commit acts deemed to be anti-social. Patrick concluded that, given the
circumstances they were in, it was quite logical for the boys to engage
in violent gang-related behaviour that led to them reoffending while on
leave. He believed his research gave him a real insight into why the boys
behaved in the way they did. Such a study cannot, however, produce
reliable evidence of the extent or geographical distribution of such
behaviour.

There are also ethical questions here. Is it acceptable to study people
without their knowledge or consent? Should the researcher observe
without condemning anti-social behaviour, or even participate in it?

A very different way of studying disorderly behaviour was undertaken at
about the same time as Patrick's study by the criminologist D.J. West
and his colleagues as part of the Cambridge Study in Delinquent
Development (West, 1982). Like the media effects study referred to in
Section 3, this was a longitudinal study. The researchers interviewed
groups of boys aged 8 to 9 in a number of primary schools in a
working-class area of London, gained as much information as possible
about them, and then traced which of them were later convicted of
delinquent behaviour. Comparisons could then be made between those

so convicted and the remainder of the sample to try to identify a series of causal factors:

> We intended to carry out detailed interviews and case studies, as well as make statistical comparisons, so numbers had to be kept down. The study sample was made up of 411 boys and included all the males on the registers of six state primary schools ... in fourth-year classes ... The neighbourhood of the study was chosen because it had a reasonably high delinquency rate ... and because there was a convenient office available ...
>
> All 411 were seen at age 8–9. Repeated visits to schools had to be made in order to catch some persistent absentees. Nearly all were seen at age 10–11 ... and again at their various secondary schools at age 14–15 ... After that, the whole sample was re-interviewed twice more ... at age 16–17 and, more extensively, at age 18–19. The interviews at age 18 ... lasted on average some two hours and were tape-recorded. As well as open-ended enquiries, which encouraged the youth to talk spontaneously, a large number of precise questions were put, the answers to which could be translated into numerical codes. At age 21, in the last systematic coverage, repeat interviews on similar lines to those at 18 were attempted with all of the delinquents and a quota sample of non-delinquents ... Finally, at ages 23 and 24, some particular subgroups were re-interviewed ...
>
> (West, 1982, pp. 12–14)

Delinquents were defined by acquisition of a criminal conviction record in the files at Scotland Yard, but also by self-report enquiries in which they admitted committing offences for which they had not been convicted. On the basis of their research, West and his colleagues concluded that disrupted families were a major cause of this behaviour, with rising family instability since the 1960s having a significant effect.

From this account it can be seen how considerable resources may be required for a longitudinal study. Much time is required in locating the groups to be studied, obtaining permission to do so, and in designing questions to be asked. Interviewers have to be trained and results analysed, with usable findings only resulting at the end of, in this example, fifteen years' work. There is also a danger of the researchers' own views affecting the research. West and his colleagues selected the boys from an area that they believed would be associated with anti-social behaviour, and, although not detailed here, they had their own ideas as to what could be considered 'good' child-rearing practices.

On the plus side, such research avoids looking only at convicted offenders and then examining their past to see if they had things in common before their delinquent acts. Here, the study contains a 'control group' – what West refers to as a 'quota sample of non-delinquents' (that is, a sample made up of individuals who did not have a criminal conviction or who did not admit to criminal offences). This allows the researchers to compare their characteristics with those who did become delinquents.

Activity 6

Put yourself in the role of a social scientist studying disorderly behaviour. What would be the possible methods for studying each of the following (they were all examples cited in a UK Government list of anti-social behaviour)? What might be the significant difficulties involved, and what resources would you require? In each case, consider the possibilities for using large-scale social surveys with pre-coded questions, detailed interviews with a limited number of people, participant observation and official statistics. Jot down your own thoughts before reading our comments.

1   People dealing and buying drugs on the street

2   Nuisance neighbours

3   Begging on the street.

---

1   *Drug-trading:* The key difficulty here is that the illegality of the transactions would make it difficult to recruit a number of willing respondents to be interviewed. Any request in an advertisement for volunteers to come forward is likely to be unsuccessful. Participant observation can also be a problem as participating in criminal activity may lead to legal problems. Official statistics would be of some value, but they could only refer to those individuals who had been cautioned by the police or convicted by courts for their actions. Possibly the best option was that adopted by the sociologist Ned Polsky (1971) in his study of *Hustlers, Beats and Others,* where he used his own pool-playing skills to make contact with some

Begging or relaxing?

individuals who made a living out of conning members of the public into playing pool for money. He then used contacts who trusted him to introduce others engaged in this activity, and so a 'snowball' sample was created. As he put it:

> In my experience the most feasible technique for building one's sample is 'snowballing'; get an introduction to one criminal who will vouch for you with still others ... It is not possible to demonstrate the representativeness of this sample because the universe (all US pool and billiard hustlers) is not exactly known ...

> (Polsky, 1971, pp. 124–9)

2 *Nuisance neighbours:* Trying to identify 'nuisance neighbours' by participant observation might well be a massive waste of time (Where would you observe? How – or in what – would you participate?). Many people accused of this behaviour might not recognise it in themselves and so therefore would not come forward for interview. Probably the easiest way to research this would be to follow up media reports or court records of such behaviour and then to interview the alleged culprits and their victims. With a small sample this could be relatively easy in terms of cost and time, but the representativeness of the sample might be challenged.

3   *Begging:* At street level it may be relatively easy to identify people begging, and the main problem would be to persuade them to answer questions about their activities. Such people might not give an accurate sample of begging as many examples of such activity might not actually be visible on the street. Some 'begging' – or at least asking others for urgent financial assistance – may take place privately within families. It may also be difficult to get honest replies to questions, with people using a range of justifications for their actions. Participant observation is a possible method of obtaining an insight into the experience of begging.

4.1   The use of official statistics

Official statistics can give the impression that a great deal of work has already been done. In the case of criminal behaviour, these statistics have been collated by the police or the government, thereby saving the social scientist who is undertaking research from having to organise questionnaires or arranging to interview large numbers of people.

Crime is of course a subset of disorderly behaviour. That is, crime consists in actions which are expressly forbidden by law, whereas disorderly behaviour is a much larger and necessarily looser category. So, in what follows there is a need to reflect on the fact that while crime figures can provide apparently firm evidence, it is at best evidence about one type of disorderly behaviour.

With these qualifications in mind, we now return to the issue of statistics. The two main sources of relevant statistics are recorded crime data collected by police forces and the British Crime Survey (BCS). Recorded crime figures collected by the police are formed from the records of crimes reported to, and recorded by, police forces throughout the country. The British Crime Survey interviews a sample of adults aged 16 and over who are living in households in England and Wales, and this is paralleled by similar surveys in Scotland and Northern Ireland. It involves asking people about crimes they have been victims of during the previous year.

British Crime Survey offences

England and Wales

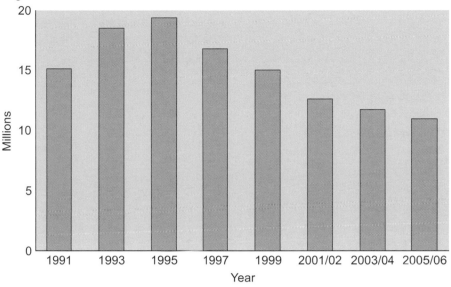

Note: Until 2000, respondents were asked to recall their experience of crime in the previous calendar year. From 2001/02 the British Crime Survey (BCS) became a continuous survey and the recall period was changed to the 12 months before interview.

Figure 2   The experience of crime in England and Wales (Source: ONS, 2007, p. 114, Figure 9.1)

The bar chart shown in Figure 2 indicates that between 1991 and 1995 the number of offences rose from about 15 million to approximately 19.5 million but then fell back to 15 million in 1999 and subsequently to about 11 million in 2005/06.

This particular chart is limited to England and Wales and does not give any indication of the types of crime identified. Table 2 summarises crimes recorded by the police in 2005/06, breaking down offences into various types and providing figures for Scotland and Northern Ireland in addition to England and Wales. Before we examine this more closely, it is interesting to note that the number of recorded crimes in England and Wales in 2005/06 was just over 5.5 million, a figure only about half that for the British Crime Survey.

Table 2   Crimes recorded by the police: by type of offence, 2005/06 (shown as percentages)

	England and Wales	Scotland	Northern Ireland
Theft and handling stolen goods	36	34	24
Theft of vehicles	4	3	3
Theft from vehicles	9	6	4
Criminal damage	21	31	28
Violence against the person	19	2	25
Burglary	12	7	10
Fraud and forgery	4	3	4
Drugs offences	3	11	2
Robbery	2	1	1
Sexual offences	1	1	1
Other offences[1]	1	10	3
All notifiable offences (=100%) (thousands)	5 557	418	123

[1] Northern Ireland includes 'offences against the state'. Scotland excludes 'offending while on bail'.

Source: ONS, 2007, p. 115, Table 9.2

Activity 7

Examine Table 2 and offer an explanation for the difference between the total number of offences in England and Wales in 2005/06 shown in Table 2 and the corresponding number of offences shown in Figure 2.

We will not offer you an answer for this at this stage – think about it now, jot down your answer and then look at it again when you have finished reading the rest of the chapter to see if your answer remains the same. Our answer can be found at the end of the chapter.

4.2   The limitations on the value of official statistics

The availability of official statistics is a major asset for social scientists, avoiding dangers of participant observation and saving immense amounts of time and money needed for longitudinal studies or large-scale questionnaire surveys. They can provide a very useful starting point for research, possibly indicating that a particular area is facing problems on the basis of the number of ASBOs issued or arrests made.

However, great dangers are involved in uncritical usage of official statistics. First, it needs to be remembered that statistics are not unquestionable 'facts' but result from judgements of particular individuals or groups and the processes involved in creating and gathering them. Particular police officers and the crime prosecution services daily take decisions as to whether a possible offender should receive an informal warning or be dealt with more severely. Minor incidents reported to the police require decisions as to whether they should be investigated or not, and any attempt to record and act upon every reported incident would overwhelm the police and the law courts. Similarly, chief constables have some discretion in how to allocate their person power, and this can lead to very different statistics emanating from different police authorities in terms of sexual, drug or road-traffic offences.

In general it has been accepted that there is a **dark figure of crime** that is much larger than the published statistics would indicate. Social scientists have therefore looked to alternative methods, such as **self-report studies** and **victim studies**, which tend to reveal the extent of this dark figure.

Self-report studies may also be misleading in that people may not be honest about what criminal or disorderly acts they have committed, either because they wish to present themselves in a favourable light or possibly because they welcome the image of being the 'rebel' or the 'troublemaker' (Activity 2 in this chapter involved you in a self-report study – consider your feelings when you answered those questions).

Dark figure of crime
The amount of unrecorded or undiscovered crime which does not appear in official statistics.

Self-report studies
Studies that involve confidential questionnaires asking respondents to declare crimes they have committed.

Victim studies
Studies that ask people what crimes have been committed against them over a fixed period of time.

Activity 8

Look at Table 3, which summarises some of the findings of the British Crime Survey, and answer the following questions. Again, the answers will be found at the end of the chapter.

1   What are the annual trends over the period in terms of all crimes reported to the BCS? (Note that the period of time between the columns decreases as the figures become more recent.)

2   Which forms of crime have actually increased between 1981 and 2005/06?

3   In which year was household crime at its highest?

Table 3   Incidents of crime: by type of offence[1]

England and Wales	Millions					
	1981	1991	1995	2001/02	2003/04	2005/06
Vandalism	2.7	2.8	3.4	2.6	2.5	2.7
All vehicle thefts	1.8	3.8	4.4	2.5	2.1	1.7
Minor injuries	1.4	1.8	2.9	1.7	1.7	1.5
Other household theft[2]	1.5	1.9	2.3	1.4	1.3	1.2
Other thefts of personal property	1.6	1.7	2.1	1.4	1.3	1.2
Burglary	0.7	1.4	1.8	1.0	0.9	0.7
Theft from the person	0.4	0.4	0.7	0.6	0.6	0.6
Wounding	0.5	0.6	0.9	0.6	0.7	0.5
Bicycle theft	0.2	0.6	0.7	0.4	0.4	0.4
Robbery	0.2	0.2	0.3	0.4	0.3	0.3
All violence reported to BCS	2.2	2.6	4.3	2.8	2.7	2.4
All household crime	6.9	10.4	12.4	7.9	7.2	6.8
All personal crime	4.1	4.7	6.9	4.7	4.5	4.1
All crimes reported to BCS	11.0	15.1	19.4	12.6	11.7	10.9

[1] Until 2000, respondents were asked to recall their experience of crime in the previous calendar year. From 2001/02 the British Crime Survey (BCS) became a continuous survey and the recall period was changed to the 12 months before interview.

[2] Includes thefts and attempted thefts from domestic garages, outhouses and sheds, not directly linked to the dwelling, as well as thefts from both inside and outside a dwelling.

Source: ONS, 2007, p. 117, Table 9.4

The British Crime Survey is an important example of a victim study. It clearly flags up higher levels of crime than do police statistics, and it avoids dangers of under-reporting or people not wanting to incriminate themselves. However, the accuracy of victim studies is also open to question. There are some crimes where victims may be unaware of their status: that is, they do not know that a crime has been committed against them. The most obvious example is the victim of a confidence trickster, but also shopkeepers may be the victims of small-scale thefts which they cannot identify – this becomes known as 'inventory shrinkage' in the account books. It is also possible that respondents may be too embarrassed to admit to a researcher that they have been victims.

Summary

- Social scientists vary in their reasons for studying disorderly behaviour and ask a wide variety of questions about it.

- A range of methods is available, each with practical, ethical and theoretical considerations that make them suitable/unsuitable for particular research or researchers.

- Some researchers focus on the need for statistical precision while others aim to obtain richness of detail.

- Official statistics of disorderly or criminal behaviour can be very useful resources for social scientists, but they need to be treated with caution.

How do we know?

Methods of social research

Various methods can be used by social scientists in their research, and this chapter has quoted examples and commented upon several of them. Participant observation involves the researcher joining in with the group being studied to gain an understanding of the meaning that participants attach to their behaviour. It involves an emphasis on richness of detail rather than statistical precision, with the researcher endeavouring to empathise with participants rather than making moral judgements about them. It can be very time-consuming, may only be successful if the researcher is accepted by the group, and may involve serious ethical questions. It therefore requires particular social characteristics, connections and skills. In Patrick's case he had to be male and relatively young to gain acceptance and he had to have the support of 'Tim', whom he met in an approved school.

Social scientists using participant observation are generally less concerned with developing general theories of behaviour than with gaining insights into what makes particular individuals and groups behave in apparently unusual ways. On the basis of their studies they may then make more general statements about behaviour that can be compared with the results of other studies.

Longitudinal studies involve the monitoring of research subjects over a lengthy period, often in excess of twenty years. The researcher obtains detailed information on the individuals or groups before monitoring begins, trying to isolate factors that may prove to be significant for future behaviour patterns. In West's case, details on family patterns, parental practices, income and school reports on the perceived sociability of the boys were all collected. Depending on the size of the group being studied, the time span of the research and the number of occasions information is obtained, such studies can be expensive and certainly involve a lengthy time commitment before they provide results.

Social scientists using longitudinal studies are generally aiming to obtain clear statistical information on which theories of behaviour can be based. They endeavour to find links between particular characteristics identified at the outset of their study and future behaviour patterns.

Official statistics are commonly used as a starting point for research, indicating patterns the social scientist seeks to explain. They are produced by a range of agencies, such as governments, international organisations and charities. It is important that any researcher looks critically at the processes through which the statistics have been assembled and they should consider any possible sources of bias. In the case of criminal statistics, some of the potential deficiencies can be reduced by comparing those recorded by the police and the results of the British Crime Survey, which uses victim studies.

It is important to note that official statistics cannot of themselves identify causes of behaviour or provide a richness of understanding in the way that longitudinal studies or participant observation aim to do. Nevertheless, they do provide a starting point for research, and, if studied critically, can give some insights into the assumptions of those who compile the statistics in addition to those whose behaviour is being recorded.

Conclusion

This chapter has examined the nature of disorderly behaviour. It has indicated the ways in which it is not something fixed but is rather determined by society at any time or place. It has also shown that society itself is not a single entity but is divided into different, interlinking and variable groups which will have their own interpretations of acceptable and disorderly behaviour. What is more, society includes the relations (especially of power) between these groups – relations which imply that how the disorderly is defined will often be the subject of dispute. In other words, disorderly behaviour is both socially constructed and contested.

The chapter has also shown that current concerns with 'bad' behaviour or a breakdown in social cohesion are not new but seem to recur throughout history. In this context, the use of ASBOs is seen as just one attempt in a long line of measures to deal with the perceived problem of disorderly conduct and disorderly people. The chapter has particularly focused on the nature of mediation and the particular role of the media in the present era in providing information about the world and giving cues as to how we should understand and react to events and people. We have seen how difficult it is to establish what might be the cause of disorderly behaviour, even in a case, such as exposure to media depictions of violence, when common sense might suggest a straightforward link.

Finally, the chapter has shown how social science can assist in understanding what and how much disorderly behaviour there is. In the examples of how social scientists go about their work, a variety of different kinds of methods was identified. We noted some of the advantages and disadvantages of these, and also how choice of methods can have an impact on the way that disorder is characterised.

Answers to activities

Activity 7

Answer

The police statistics are formed on the basis of people reporting crimes to the police and that report being recorded by the police. Many people may not consider it worthwhile to use their time to report minor crimes when it is likely that little may be done to remedy the situation, or they may fear that the consequences of reporting may be harmful to them (e.g. revenge by those who are accused or prosecuted). The British Crime Survey, on the other hand, is anonymous and involves little commitment on the part of the respondent.

Activity 8

Answer

1   There is an average annual rise in crime of less than half a million between 1981 and 1991, increasing to over a million between 1991 and 1995. The figures then show an *annual* decrease of almost one million between 1995 and 2001/02, with a continuing but slowing reduction to 2005/06.

2   Minor injuries, theft from the person, bicycle theft, robbery and all violence.

3   1995.

References

BBC Action Network (2007) *How Can the Anti-social Behaviour Act Help You?* [online], http://www.bbc.co.uk/dna/collective/A2283824 (Accessed 17 February 2009).

BBC News (2007) *Gordon Brown's Speech in Full*, 24 September [online], http://news.bbc.co.uk/1/hi/uk_politics/7010664.stm (Accessed 18 February 2009).

Becker, H.S. (1963) *Outsiders*, New York, The Free Press.

Brake, M. (1980) *The Sociology of Youth Culture and Youth Subcultures*, London, Routledge.

Burney, E. (2005) *Making People Behave*, Collumpton, Willan.

Cohen, S. (1973) *Folk Devils and Moral Panics*, London, Paladin.

Federal Foreign Office (2007) [online], http://www.auswaertiges-amt.de/diplo/en/Infoservice/Presse/2007/071211-Nook (Accessed 26 March 2008) [Article no longer available].

Hall, S., Critcher, C., Jefferson, T., Clarke, J. and Roberts, B. (1978) *Policing the Crisis: Mugging, the State, and Law and Order*, London and Basingstoke, Macmillan.

Huesmann, R., Moise-Titus, J., Pdolski, C-L. and Eron, L. (2003) 'Longitudinal relations between children's exposure to TV violence and their aggressive and violent behaviour in young adulthood: 1977–1992', *Developmental Psychology*, vol. 39, no. 2, pp. 201–23.

Kennedy, H. (2005) *Just Law*, New York and London, Vintage.

Lodge, M. and Hood, C. (2002) 'Pavlovian policy responses to media feeding frenzies? Dangerous dogs regulation in comparative perspective', *Journal of Contingencies and Crisis Management*, vol. 10, no. 1, pp. 1–13.

Matza, D. (1964) *Delinquency and Drift*, New York, Wiley.

Office for National Statistics (ONS) (2007) *Social Trends*, no. 37, Basingstoke, Palgrave Macmillan; also available online at http://www.statistics.gov.uk/statbase/Product.asp?vlnk=5748 (Accessed 19 February 2009).

Patrick, J. (1973) *A Glasgow Gang Observed*, London, Eyre Methuen.

Pearson, G. (1983) *Hooligan*, London, Macmillan.

Pearson, G. (2006) 'The generation game', *The Guardian*, 8 November 2006 [online], http://www.guardian.co.uk/society/2006/nov/08/youthjustice.comment (Accessed 17 March 2009).

Polsky, N. (1971) *Hustlers, Beats and Others*, Harmondsworth, Penguin.

Quinion, M. (1998) 'Hooligan' in *World Wide Words* [online] http://www.worldwidewords.org/topicalwords/tw-hoo1.htm (Accessed 17 February 2009).

Respect (2008) *What Is Anti-social Behaviour?* [online], http://www.respect.gov.uk/article.aspx?id=9066 (Accessed 17 February 2009).

Shore, H. (2000) 'The idea of juvenile crime in 19th-century England', *History Today*, vol. 50, no. 6, pp. 21–7; also available online at http://www.orange.k12.oh.us/teachers/ohs/tshreve/apwebpage/readings/juvcrime19cbr (Accessed 17 February 2009).

Squires, P. (1990) *Anti-Social Policy: Welfare, Ideology and the Disciplinary State*, Hemel Hempstead, Harvester Wheatsheaf.

Squires, P. and Stephen, D.E. (2005) *Rougher Justice: Anti-social Behaviour and Young People*, Cullompton, Willan.

SureStart (2005) *An Introduction to the Framework: Birth to Three Matters* [online], http://www.surestart.gov.uk/_doc/P0000285.pdf (Accessed 17 February 2009).

Taylor, I., Walton, P. and Young, J. (1973) *The New Criminology*, London, Routledge and Kegan Paul.

Taylor, I., Walton, P. and Young, J. (1975) *Critical Criminology*, London, Routledge and Kegan Paul.

Townsend, M. and Asthana, A. (2008) 'Put young children on DNA list, urge police', *The Observer*, 16 March [online], http://www.guardian.co.uk/society/2008/mar/16/youthjustice.children (Accessed 17 March 2009).

West, D.J. (1982) *Delinquency: Its Roots, Careers and Prospects,* London, Heinemann.

Whyte, T. (ed.) (2008) *Crimes of the Powerful: A Reader*, Maidenhead, Open University Press.

Wikipedia (2009) *Hooliganism* [online], http://en.wikipedia.org/wiki/Hooliganism (Accessed 17 February 2009).

Chapter 9
Making up population

Evelyn Ruppert and Engin Isin

Contents

Introduction

Locating the population

Locating people

Sunday 29 April 2001 was designated census day in the UK. Where were you on that day? In England and Wales over 60,000 **enumerators** attempted to visit every street, rural road and dwelling over a three-week period leading up to that day in order to hand deliver millions of self-completion questionnaires. The questionnaires required individuals to identify themselves and others in their household according to classifications such as age, gender, nationality, ethnicity and occupation. You may well have completed the questionnaire in 2001 and if not it is likely that someone else in your household did so on your behalf, for, unlike surveys and opinion polls, everyone is legally required to be

Enumerator
A person who collects census data by visiting individual homes.

included in a census enumeration. There is a penalty (a fine or six months' imprisonment) for not doing so or for submitting false answers. However, if you were living in other countries of the UK, you may have completed a different questionnaire distributed by enumerators working for the General Register Office for Scotland (GROS) or the Northern Ireland Statistics and Research Agency (NISRA). 2001 marked the first time that the Office for National Statistics (ONS) coordinated the way the census was conducted in all countries of the UK so that the results would be comparable and could be combined to produce population estimates for the union as a whole. And finally, if you lived outside the UK you may have completed a census questionnaire for another country.

So imagine thousands of enumerators walking up and down every street or traversing every rural road in the UK attempting to hand deliver a questionnaire and post-back envelope to every household. How do they know which and how many addresses to visit? They have a record book listing all known addresses based on information collected and provided by local governments. However, despite their best efforts to make contact with a person in every household and ensure a completed questionnaire is returned, in the end it was estimated that only 94 per cent of individuals were included in the returned forms (ONS, 2005).

Activity 1

Can you identify possible reasons for why some individuals might not have been included in the returned forms? What kinds of difficulties might the enumerators have encountered?

We can draw two lessons from this account. First, even with the best efforts of census authorities it is impossible to count everyone. Second, despite many advances in information technologies, a residential address is still the primary means by which a **state** locates people in its territory for the purposes of conducting a census of **population**. But what do we mean by population? In the account above, does it include all the people who live in the UK? Or is it something defined by a state? Actually, it is both. More precisely, it is the people who inhabit a territory because there is an overlapping state authorised to govern that territory. Thus, a population exists only in relation to governing. States use techniques like the census to locate and identify the people who inhabit their territories and make them into a population. As one

State
The political organisation that rules over a given territory and its people.

Population
The people who inhabit a territory governed by a state.

researcher has put it, it is through practices of identification like the census that states make people 'legible' and governable (Scott, 1999).

Population is thus the outcome of the census rather than something out there that already exists. This is what we mean by 'making up population': it is not a fabrication or a fiction but is the product of a number of practices such as the work of enumerators. And one of those techniques involves locating every person through an address. Indeed, it is through an address that governments usually 'address' and govern people. While there are new methods of addressing such as email, none locates people like a street or rural address. On the one hand, an address can be thought of as a form of surveillance and a way that governments can keep track of the location and movement of people. But on the other hand it is also through an address that people get access to government services. Just try to apply for benefits or a driver's license, or register with a doctor's surgery and you will see how an address is necessary. Certainly, this is no better understood than by people who do not have an address, such as rough sleepers. But there are many others for whom a fixed address is not a simple matter; examples being people who are commonly on the move, such as the armed forces and seasonal migrants.

Locating individuals through an address is just one aspect of a census. The second involves *identifying* individuals according to several classifications on a questionnaire.

Identifying people

Activity 2

As an exercise in identifying yourself, complete the questions in Figure 1, an excerpt from the 2001 Census for England and Wales. (The questions for Scotland and Northern Ireland were similar.) Note difficulties or problems you have answering the questions. Were any of the categories unclear? Were you uncertain about which categories fitted you best?

Indentifying yourself by completing the census questionnaire extract in Figure 1 may or may not have been a straightforward exercise for you. In everyday life people are frequently called upon to identify themselves

2 **What is your sex?**

☐ Male   ☐ Female

4 **What is your marital status?**

☐ Single (never married)

☐ Married (first marriage)

☐ Re-married

☐ Separated (but legally married)

☐ Divorced

☐ Widowed

8 **What is your ethnic group?**

Choose ONE section from A to E, then ✓ the appropriate box to indicate your cultural background.

A   White

☐ British   ☐ Irish

☐ Any other White background

please write in

☐☐☐☐☐☐☐☐☐
☐☐☐☐☐☐☐☐☐

B   Mixed

☐ White and Black Caribbean

☐ White and Black African

☐ White and Asian

☐ Any other Mixed background

please write in

☐☐☐☐☐☐☐☐☐
☐☐☐☐☐☐☐☐☐

C   Asian or Asian British

☐ Indian   ☐ Pakistani

☐ Bangladeshi

☐ Any other Asian background

please write in

☐☐☐☐☐☐☐☐☐
☐☐☐☐☐☐☐☐☐

D   Black or Black British

☐ Caribbean   ☐ African

☐ Any other Black background

please write in

☐☐☐☐☐☐☐☐☐
☐☐☐☐☐☐☐☐☐

E   Chinese or other ethnic group

☐ Chinese

☐ Any other *please write in*

☐☐☐☐☐☐☐☐☐
☐☐☐☐☐☐☐☐☐

10 **What is your religion?**

This question is voluntary.
✓ one box only.

☐ None

☐ Christian (including Church of England, Catholic, Protestant and all other Christian denominations)

☐ Buddhist

☐ Hindu

☐ Jewish

☐ Muslim

☐ Sikh

☐ Any other religion *please write in*

☐☐☐☐☐☐☐☐☐
☐☐☐☐☐☐☐☐☐

Source: Office for National Statistics

Figure 1   Excerpt from 2001 Census questionnaire, England and Wales (Source: based on ONS, 2001a, p. 6)

in this manner on questionnaires, passport applications and surveys, and asked to check a series of tick boxes. It has become a rather taken-for-granted practice. But sometimes some people encounter difficulties – what if there is no box to tick? Some people completing the 2001 Census questionnaire had difficulty fitting themselves and others in their household into the tick boxes. For example, some gay and lesbian couples, common law partners, and transgendered people protested that the tick boxes did not include categories that adequately reflected their domestic arrangements or gender identity. It is not that they did not know their domestic arrangements, status or gender but rather that the categories of the census did not recognise their identifications.

The front page of the 2001 Census questionnaire that you completed includes the declaration 'count me in'. The census is often understood as simply the counting of people, as suggested by this declaration. However, the above activity on identifying yourself illustrates how you only count and become part of the population through inclusion in the census and its categories such as gender and religion. That is, the census counts you not only as one person who belongs to the total population, it also counts you as one person who belongs to particular categories or parts of the population (such as males, Hindus or Irish). For this reason the census simultaneously unites people into a population (total) and divides people into different categories or groups (parts).

Recognition and inclusion in the categories or parts of the population is important because the census is used to apportion electoral representation and formulate and distribute government programmes. The extract entitled 'Why we have a census' lists some of the government uses of census data identified by the ONS. It is now hard to conceive of governing without census data on migration, divorce, education, occupation, age, and so on. Data on ethnicity, for example, is used to identify regional disadvantage, monitor policies on equality, and support the allocation of services to particular communities.

Why we have a census

We all use public services such as schools, health services, roads and libraries. These services need to be planned, and in such a way that they keep pace with fast-changing patterns of modern life. We need accurate information on the numbers of people, where they live and what their needs are.

Every ten years the census provides a benchmark. Uniquely, it gives us a complete picture of the nation. It counts the numbers of people living in each city, town and country area. It tells us about each area and its population, including the balance of young and old, what jobs people do, and the type of housing they live in.

Because the same questions are asked and the information is recorded in the same way throughout the UK, the census allows us to compare different groups of people across the entire nation.

The census costs some £255 million for the UK as a whole, but the information it provides enables billions of pounds of taxpayers' money to be targeted where it is needed most. The census gives us invaluable facts about:

Population

An accurate count of the population in each local area helps the Government to calculate the size of grants it allocates each local authority and health authority. In turn, these authorities use census information when planning services within their areas.

Health

Data on the age and socio-economic make-up of the population, and more specifically on general health, long-term illness and carers enables the Government to plan health and social services, and to allocate resources.

Housing

Information on housing and its occupants measures inadequate accommodation and, with information about the way we live as households, indicates the need for new housing.

Employment

The census shows how many people work in different occupations and industries throughout the country, helping government and businesses to plan jobs and training policies and to make informed investment decisions.

Transport

Information collected on travel to and from work, and on the availability of cars, contributes to the understanding of pressures on transport systems and to the planning of roads and public transport.

Ethnic group

Data on ethnic groups help to identify the extent and nature of disadvantage in Britain and to measure the success of equal opportunities policies. The information helps central and local government to allocate resources and plan programmes to take account of the needs of minority groups.

ONS, 2008a

The census is also of interest to social science researchers who depend on census data to analyse and understand the contemporary UK. From the study of demography and migration to identity and consumption, researchers often use census data to study social issues and change. In other chapters of this book and indeed throughout the social sciences you will regularly encounter studies that use or make reference to such census data.

Activity 3

Census data is regularly cited and used as evidence to support an argument in media reports and discussions. Can you think of any recent examples that you have seen in a newspaper, read about on the internet or heard about on the radio or TV news?

For example, see the discussion on urbanisation in Chapter 5 of *Making Social Lives*.

For example, in *The Guardian* newspaper of 8 September 2008 there were two references to census data. One columnist wrote, 'As the last census showed, over 70 per cent of people in this country still describe themselves as Christian' (Bunting, 2008). Another columnist noted, 'What is happening to the UK population at the moment? It is ethnically diversifying, and it is ageing. It is also the case that it is, as of the 2001 Census, marginally more female than it is male' (Bell, 2008).

Because the census is connected to governing, people actively engage in political struggles over the census to ensure that the groups with whom they identify are included in the questions and categories. Inclusion is often necessary for groups to make claims to social resources, services and rights. We will discuss some examples of this throughout this chapter. Therefore, while the census is a particular way that states make up population, it also actively engages people in the process. This requires that people are able know how to identify with the population, where they 'fit' or don't 'fit' in relation to the categories of the census. If you did not understand the questions or the meaning of the categories in the census questionnaire, you would not be able to complete it or understand the results that the census reports and circulates.

While the census involves answering questions and ticking boxes, it is through the translation of responses into numbers that the state produces and then reports on the population; that is, when we 'see' the population it is typically through numbers (like those in the newspaper examples cited above), tables and graphs. For example, a common way that population is visualised is through age–sex population pyramids, as illustrated in Figure 2 and Table 1.

Table 1   Age–sex data, UK 2001 Census

Age range	Total	% of total	Cumulative % of total	Males	% of males	Females	% of females
0–4	3 486 253	5.9	5.9	1 785 688	6.2	1 700 565	5.6
5–9	3 738 042	6.4	12.3	1 914 727	6.7	1 823 315	6.0
10–14	3 880 557	6.6	18.9	1 987 606	7.0	1 892 951	6.3
15–19	3 663 782	6.2	25.1	1 870 508	6.5	1 793 274	5.9
20–24	3 545 984	6.0	31.2	1 765 257	6.2	1 780 727	5.9
25–29	3 867 015	6.6	37.7	1 895 469	6.6	1 971 546	6.5
30–34	4 493 532	7.6	45.4	2 199 767	7.7	2 293 765	7.6
35–39	4 625 777	7.9	53.2	2 277 678	8.0	2 348 099	7.8
40–44	4 151 613	7.1	60.3	2 056 545	7.2	2 095 068	6.9
45–49	3 735 986	6.4	66.7	1 851 391	6.5	1 884 595	6.2
50–54	4 040 576	6.9	73.5	2 003 158	7.0	2 037 418	6.7
55–59	3 339 004	5.7	79.2	1 651 396	5.8	1 687 608	5.6
60–64	2 880 074	4.9	84.1	1 409 684	4.9	1 470 390	4.9
65–69	2 596 939	4.4	88.5	1 241 382	4.3	1 355 557	4.5
70–74	2 339 319	4.0	92.5	1 059 156	3.7	1 280 163	4.2
75–79	1 967 088	3.3	95.9	817 738	2.9	1 149 350	3.8
80–84	1 313 592	2.2	98.1	482 707	1.7	830 885	2.8
85–89	752 035	1.3	99.4	226 520	0.8	525 515	1.7
90+	372 026	0.6	100.0	83 492	0.3	288 534	1.0
Totals	58 789 194	100.0		28 579 869	100.0	30 209 325	100.0

Source: derived from ONS, 2009

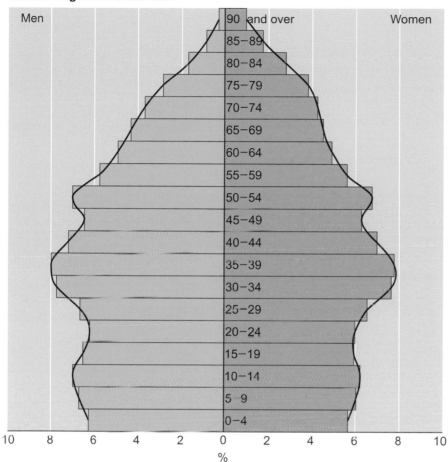

The percentages on the pyramid represent the percentages of 'all males' (to the left) and the percentages of 'all females' (to the right) that are in the age group.

Figure 2   Age–sex pyramid showing data from UK 2001 Census (Source: based on ONS, 2009)

Pyramids represent the percentage or total amount of people broken down by gender and five-year age increments. The shape and distribution of gender and age on the pyramid is then used to compare the relative age and rates of growth or decline of populations, and to see trends in birth and death rates and phenomena like baby booms, wars and epidemics. Another way that population is represented is through tables and numbers such as those in Tables 2 and 3.

Table 2   Marital status (all people aged 16 and over), UK 2001 Census

	Number	Percentage (%)
Single people (never married)	14 186 988	30
Married or re-married people	23 853 128	51
Separated or divorced	4 942 512	11
Widowed	3 947 709	8
Total	46 930 337	100

Source: derived from ONS, 2001b

Table 3   Religion (all people), UK 2001 Census

	Number	Percentage (%)
Christian	42 079 417	71.6
Buddhist	151 816	0.3
Hindu	558 810	1.0
Jewish	266 740	0.5
Muslim	1 591 126	2.7
Sikh	336 149	0.6
Other	178 837	0.3
No religion/religion not stated	13 626 299	23.2
Total	58 789 194	100.0

Source: derived from ONS, 2003

Activity 4

Review Figure 2 and Tables 1, 2 and 3. Can you 'locate yourself' in relation to the population of the UK? One way to do so is to consider what percentage of the UK population shares the same category or group identifications (e.g. age group) as you.

Age: _____

Marital status: _____

Religion: _____

Based on this, write a description about where you would 'locate yourself' in relation to the population of the UK as a whole.

A 48-year-old married woman who doesn't have a religion would locate herself in the same age category as 6.4 per cent of the total population and as relatively older than most others since about 60 per cent of the population is younger than her. This is depicted in the pyramid, where her age group is in the top half of the pyramid. She also has the same marital status as 51 per cent of the population and is part of the 23 per cent not stating a religion. Or we could say that she is relatively older, part of the majority in relation to marital status but in the minority in terms of religious identification. There are many other ways we could express this. The activity underlines how it is through numbers that people usually locate themselves in relation to the whole population and its parts. Because of this we need to think about how population is represented in numbers.

Making up population

The population is usually represented as a whole number such as that reported and illustrated in Figure 3. But, as we have already discussed, it is also represented in its parts. Numbers on income, poverty, literacy, occupation or religion are routinely reported in the UK. The dependence on population numbers is evident in government, business and academia, each of which relies on what could be called an infrastructure of numbers. One author has described this dependence, which took off in the nineteenth century, as the 'avalanche of numbers' (Hacking, 1990), while another has called numbers 'modern facts' because numbers are understood to be descriptive and not interpretations (Poovey, 1998).

Numbers become facts through the assumption that they are **objective**, real and authoritative. Numbers are also concise, precise and easy to circulate. The whole population of the UK can be easily summarised in a few key numbers. Yet, many people are also ambivalent about numbers because they seem to depersonalise everything and oversimplify. Some people argue the seeming precision of numbers hides the assumptions and interests that lie behind them. Still, despite the controversies and challenges about their objectivity there is a dependence on numbers such as population data that is hard to replace or dismantle. Recall the extract on 'Why we have a census' and the government programmes and policies that depend on population numbers.

Objective
Representing things without personal bias, emotion, opinion or interpretation.

409

Figure 3   2001 UK population

Constructivism
The perspective that
individuals and groups
participate in the
creation of their
perceived reality.

See, for example, the
discussion in Chapter 8
of this book of the
construction of
disorder.

This Introduction has introduced how we are going to think about
population in this chapter. We will develop an argument about 'what is
population' from a particular perspective in the social sciences that you
have encountered in previous chapters: **constructivism**. Population is
seen as constructed rather than being an object already 'out there'
waiting to be found, and that is what 'making up population' means. In
Section 1 we discuss how constructivism can help us understand data
on religious identification in the 2001 UK Censuses. We illustrate how
numbering and counting people involve classifying and categorising
them. Questions about the objectivity of numbers and what it means to
be a subject are introduced and the argument that population is
constructed and produced is developed.

In Section 2 we ask the question: how did people come to understand
population this way? We examine the origins of the census from the
early efforts of states to count people to the twentieth century. In
Section 3 we turn to how sampling and surveying techniques, and
government administrative data have started to supplement and replace
censuses as ways of making up population. In Section 4 we bring all of
this to bear on the question of the relationship between being a subject
and being a citizen.

Summary

- A population is the people who inhabit a territory where there is an overlapping state authorised to govern that territory.

- States use techniques like the census to locate and identify the people who inhabit their territories and make them into a population for the purposes of governing.

- Population is the outcome of the census rather than an object that already exists.

- You only count and become part of the population through inclusion in the census and its categories.

- Population is 'seen' when answers on census questionnaires are translated into numbers and represented on graphs, tables and charts.

1   How does a population come into being?

1.1   Becoming an object: classifying and categorising

To begin let's examine one set of population numbers for the UK produced by the ONS. One common interpretation of the data in Table 4 is that it is a measurement of the different religions of people. This is a common interpretation of population data that understands the census as a 'reflection of society' (Goyer and Domschke, 1992). The census is understood as a practice that records actual phenomena: the object to be measured – population – is just as real as physical objects, like mountains and rivers. And just as measuring a physical object faces challenges of accuracy and reliability, so too does the measurement of population. This is an **objectivist** interpretation of population. Understood this way, the challenge of the census is to reflect, as accurately as possible, the real population that exists independent of the census itself.

Objectivist
The perspective that the social world has an existence independent of perceptions.

Table 4   UK 2001 Census results for religion

	Thousands	Percentage (%)
Christian	42 079	71.6
Buddhist	152	0.3
Hindu	559	1.0
Jewish	267	0.5
Muslim	1 591	2.7
Sikh	336	0.6
Other religion	179	0.3
All religions	*45 163*	*76.8*
No religion	9 104	15.5
Not stated	4 289	7.3
All no religion/not stated	*13 626*	*23.2*
Base	*58 789*	*100*

Source: ONS, 2003

In contrast, a constructivist perspective demands that we look more closely at how the data is produced and the underlying assumptions and decisions involved; that is, we critically analyse the proposition that all the census does is record population and that the evidence it produces is objective. We will see that population is not simple and instead is a complex object that censuses attempt to define, delineate, order and reorder.

Not just counting but classifying and categorising people

Table 4 simultaneously represents the total population (the whole) and its division into different religious categories (the parts). In Figure 3 the total population of the UK was cited. However, while the census is often described as the 'counting of noses' or knowing 'how many', it is through the classification and categorisation of individuals that the total population is known. What holds people together as a population is their identification within a classification system that establishes categories of equivalence between them. Religion is one such classification and age, marital status, gender and ethnicity are others. For example, when a person answers the question on religion, they basically establish their equivalence with all other people who may have ticked the same category. Hindu is one such category and Christian and Muslim are others. So, making up population means simultaneously establishing equivalences and differences between individuals. In this way the census encourages and reinforces the view that the social world is composed of distinct groups of people united into a whole people.

The most general equivalence that people share is usually referred to as the 'census population base' (referred to as 'base' in Table 4). In the 2001 Census, the base was defined as individuals who are 'usual' residents at an address in the UK on census day. This definition excludes visitors but includes all resident UK and EU citizens, immigrants, refugees and asylum seekers, even if they are not physically present on census day but spend the majority of their time residing at that address. However, there are other definitions and in 1991 the census counted both usual residents and visitors present on census night. What is important to note here is that the definition of who is counted in the census is not pre-given or fixed but expresses what the state wants to or needs to know in order to govern. The same can be said about other equivalences and differences defined in the census.

Which classifications are included?

Just as the definition of the population base is not given, the other equivalences counted in the census are also not given. Let's continue with religion as an example because the 2001 Census was the first census for Great Britain (England and Wales, Scotland) since 1851 that included a question on religion (a religion question has always been included in the census of Northern Ireland, beginning with the first enumeration in 1926). Much controversy about the question and its meaning had followed the 1851 enumeration, leading to the question eventually being excluded from the census. But during the 150 years when a question on religion was excluded we know that religious identification did not disappear. What this highlights is that what classifications count and get counted and included in the census are matters of political contestation. For while political contestation kept the religion question out of the census after 1851, political contestation also brought it back in 2001. As a result of political lobbying on the part of many faith communities, the ONS established a Religious Affiliation Sub-Group (RASG) to advise on the inclusion of a question in the 2001 enumeration (Southworth, 2005). Members included representatives from nine faith communities and academia. The representatives, and in particular those from Muslim organisations such as the Muslim Council of Britain, stressed the importance of religion being recognised as a fundamental part of their identity. One commentator put it this way: 'The religion question was an issue of strategic importance for the [Muslim Council of Britain] because without it British Muslims would remain statistically invisible' (Sherif, 2003, p. 1). However, others objected and argued that such a question was inconsistent with traditions of freedom and personal privacy about a person's religious beliefs and that 'it is not in the national interest for the census to encourage people to segregate themselves from the rest of the population and to emphasise their differences from each other' (Sherif, 2003, p. 11). In response to these concerns the question was made voluntary, yet some 92 per cent of respondents chose to answer it (ONS, 2003). For some people the recognition of religious identity was a question not only of being officially acknowledged but also of access to government funding and equality rights (see Figure 4) (Sardar, 2000). Indeed, the ONS stated that the information on religion would be used to supplement data on ethnicity, identify areas of disadvantage, monitor policies on equality, and support the allocation of services (see the box on claiming ethnicity: 'Be Irish, Be Counted!').

At last we can stand up and be counted

Ziauddin Sardar is glad that the next census will formally recognise Muslim identity

Figure 4   Muslim identity and the 2001 Census (Source: *New Statesman*, 26 June 2000)

However, while religious identification was included in all three 2001 Censuses in the UK, the question was asked in three different ways as illustrated in Figure 5.

Activity 5

Complete the three versions of the question on religion in Figure 5 and write down your answers. Were your answers for all three the same or different? What accounts for any differences?

One way we can account for the different questions is that each reflects a particular understanding of the meaning of religious identity. For example, the Scottish and Northern Ireland censuses incorporate the idea of belonging to a religion as opposed to having one, as well as the idea that a person's identity is not fixed throughout the course of their life (e.g. 'What religion ... were you brought up in?')

2001 England and Wales Census
What is your religion?

☐ None

☐ Christian (including Church of England, Catholic, Protestant and all other Christian denominations)

☐ Buddhist

☐ Hindu

☐ Jewish

☐ Muslim

☐ Sikh

☐ Any other religion *please write in*

☐☐☐☐☐☐☐☐☐☐☐

2001 Northern Ireland Census
Do you regard yourself as belonging to any particular religion?

☐ Yes   ☐ No

If yes
What religion, religious denomination or body do you belong to?

☐ Roman Catholic

☐ Presbyterian Church in Ireland

☐ Church of Ireland

☐ Methodist Church in Ireland

☐ Other *please write in*

☐☐☐☐☐☐☐☐☐☐☐

If no
What religion, religious denomination or body were you brought up in?

☐ Roman Catholic

☐ Presbyterian Church in Ireland

☐ Church of Ireland

☐ Methodist Church in Ireland

☐ Other *please write in*

☐☐☐☐☐☐☐☐☐☐☐

2001 Scotland Census
What religion, religious denomination or body do you belong to?

☐ None

☐ Church of Scotland

☐ Roman Catholic

☐ Other Christian *please write in*

☐☐☐☐☐☐☐☐☐☐☐

☐ Buddhist

☐ Jewish

☐ Muslim

☐ Sikh

☐ Another religion *please write in*

☐☐☐☐☐☐☐☐☐☐☐

What religion, religious denomination or body were you brought up in?

☐ None

☐ Church of Scotland

☐ Roman Catholic

☐ Other Christian *please write in*

☐☐☐☐☐☐☐☐☐☐☐

☐ Buddhist

☐ Jewish

☐ Muslim

☐ Sikh

☐ Another religion *please write in*

☐☐☐☐☐☐☐☐☐☐☐

Source: Office for National Statistics.

Figure 5   Wording of the question on religion in the 2001 UK Censuses (Source: ONS, 2004)

(Graham et al., 2007). However, in England and Wales a person can only report having a current religion ('What is your religion?'). Graham et al. (2007) also note that how people answer questions on religion or any other identification is very sensitive to the exact question wording. For example, tests of different census questions have shown that minor differences in wording can produce large differences in the proportion of people who say they have no religion (ONS, 2004).

'Be Irish, Be Counted!'

Kevin Howard (2006) provides a case study on the origins of the question on ethnic identity, which was included for the first time in the 2001 UK Censuses. The decision followed nearly two decades of development and political debate. The final approved question ('What is your ethnic group?') included the following categories: White, Black-Caribbean, Black-African, Black-Other, Indian, Pakistani, Bangladeshi, Chinese or 'Any other group'. However, a number of Irish activists argued that the socio-economic disadvantages of the Irish ethnic community were rendered invisible according to this white/non-white binary. They mobilised a political campaign to secure recognition of Irish ethnicity in the 2001 Census. After many years of political debate, lobbying and controversy, the 'White' category was divided into three: British, Irish, and 'Any other white background' which individuals could then write in.

The 'Irish' option was initially advocated to provide benchmark information on Irish relative socio-economic disadvantage in Britain that was not visible in the white/non-white binary categories. Recognition of 'Irish' ethnicity was advocated to address discrimination and to influence multicultural policies. However, it was also taken up by activists to support the claim that the Irish constitute the largest and longest established minority ethnic group in Great Britain. In the run-up to the census a 'Be Irish, Be Counted!' campaign was mounted in the Irish ethnic media combined with a large-scale leaflet distribution around localities of Irish immigrant settlement.

Howard argues that this example illustrates that questions about ethnic identity in censuses are politically motivated:

The implementation of multicultural policies in modern liberal democracies depends on the official institutionalization of ethnic diversity. Ethnic entrepreneurs who consider that their group's needs and identity are excluded from the multicultural framework can be expected to mobilize to secure inclusion. Moreover, it is politicians not census administrators who ultimately decide the format the census takes, what questions will be asked, how they are asked and of whom they are asked. What this means is that systems of ethnic categorization have become sites of contest in contemporary identity politics ... Ad-hoc changes to the ethnic designations used on the census can reflect the outcome of politically motivated compromises rather than considered evaluation as to which ethnic designations are sociologically meaningful.

(Howard, 2006, pp. 105–6)

What Howard is suggesting is that the questions and categories on censuses are the product of political contestation and struggle rather than objective measurements of people's identification.

Which categories of religion are included?

As Figure 5 indicates, each census question also provided a different list of religions. For example, in Northern Ireland the categories included only divisions of Christian (Catholic or Protestant) together with a category for 'other' religion, whereas non-Christian religions were listed on the questionnaires for Scotland and England and Wales.

It is well documented that when a category is included on a form this will influence the number of people identifying with the category; that is, the form itself is active in directing how individuals identify themselves. For example, prior to 1996, the tick boxes on the Canadian census did not include 'Canadian' as a possible ethnic identification (tick boxes included English, Chinese, and so on). However, numerous respondents did indeed write 'Canadian' in the 'other' category and, by 1991, 4 per cent did so. In 1996, when a tick box for 'Canadian' was finally added, the percentage of people identifying as Canadian increased to 31 per cent. By the end of the twentieth century the category became the fastest growing 'ethnic' origin group in Canada (Boyd and Norris, 2001).

Also, the inclusion of a section for individuals to write in an 'any other' category allows people to challenge and assert different categories. This was illustrated in the 2001 UK Census. A group of people launched an email campaign prior to census day and urged people to indicate Jedi as their religion, a belief system at the heart of the *Star Wars* films. Just over 390,000 of the 52 million people in England and Wales wrote 'Jedi' on their census questionnaire. While different motives could be attributed to the campaign and to the individuals who identified as Jedi, the example underscores how individuals can influence the making of population. The responses were coded as 'Jedi Knight' and were included in the 'No religion' category along with responses of people who ticked 'none' and those who wrote 'Agnostic', 'Atheist' or 'Heathen', or who ticked 'other' but did not write in any religion. Indeed, Table 4 reduces the great variability in responses individuals provided. Original entries totalled some 175 different answers! That 'Jedi Knight' was not recognised as a category of religion was not because an insufficient number of people identified as such (more people identified as Jedi than identified as Buddhist, Jewish or Sikh). While people can write in their own categories of religion, this is not sufficient for official recognition as we will discuss later. The extract entitled 'Identifying as "Jedi"' gives more information on the email campaign.

The practice of categorising individuals involves *objectification* – a process that turns people into the *objects* of government. This process reduces the complex meanings and ways that people identify to general categories or classifications; that is, while the meaning of identification with a religion varies, categorisation attempts to reduce this difference to a commonality. Different individuals are thus held together by categories so that they can become *objects* of knowledge and government. Once translated into a category people can then be compared, added up and translated into statistics such as percentages – that is, we are not identified and governed as individuals but as members of categories or groups. However, as discussed previously, to identify requires that people have the capacity to think of themselves as members of a population and are able to identify where they 'fit' within the population through their identification with categories. Just because government categorises people in specific ways, it does not mean that individuals act those categories out as though they are robots. And just because individuals may select the same category it does not mean that they all attach the same meaning to the category. The census thus also involves *subjectification* because it requires that individuals can identify with and recognise themselves and others in categories and thus become **subjects** of knowledge and governing. What this means is that the census does not only construct objects of knowledge and governing; it also produces subjects.

Subject
A person who has the capacity to engage with and participate in governing practices.

Identifying as 'Jedi'

The BBC reported on the 'Jedi' response to the religion question in the 2001 Census for England and Wales in the following article. Consider what the Home Office spokesman's comment says about census categories.

Jedi email revealed as hoax

An email saying that Jedi – the faith in the Star Wars films – will become an official religion if enough people put it down in the forthcoming British census is a hoax. The email has been sent all over the country in the last two weeks stating that if 10,000 people put Jedi on the census form, it will become a 'fully recognised and legal religion'. But the Home Office has said that no matter how many people declare that they follow it, the census counting system means it will not be recognised. A similar thing happened in New Zealand last month when citizens were led to believe they needed 8,000 signatures to make Jedi an official religion. Millions of people worldwide are fans of the Star Wars films, and although they have become something of a cult, very few – if any – can be said to seriously follow Jedi as a faith. But fans are urged to buck the census system in the email, which has become 'viral' – meaning that it is passed on to many different people very quickly. 'As some of you may know there is a census coming around on April the 10th,' it reads. 'If there are enough people who put down a religion that isn't mentioned on the census form, it becomes a fully recognised and legal religion. It usually takes about 10,000 people to nominate the same religion. It is for this reason that it has been suggested that anyone who does not have a dominant religion to put Jedi as their religion.'

Football team

'Send this on to all your friends and tell them to put down Jedi on their census form.' But a Home Office spokesman has said this will not work. Approximately 100 religions are given as options on the form – but Jedi is not one of them. There is an option for 'other', but all those who choose this will be counted as one group and the different 'other' responses will not be counted up individually. 'If 10, 10,000 or 50,000 people put Jedi in the "other" section of the census, it's not going to be reflected in the output,' the spokesman said. The 'other' responses will all be counted up under one code, whereas the other religions have a code each.

'In the last census, where we asked for a religion, lots of people who obviously don't have a religion put their football team,' the spokesman added.

Religious canon

'But it doesn't matter whether you put Jedi, Manchester United, Chelsea, or whatever. It's completely erroneous, it's going to have no impact whatsoever.' The email ended: 'If this has been your dream since you were six years old … do it because you love Star Wars. If not … then just do it to annoy people.' Jedi is the religion that the heroes of the Star Wars films follow, and is supposedly a force created by all living things – hence the phrase 'may the force be with you'.

Sir Alec Guiness as the Jedi Obi-Wan Kenobi in *Star Wars*

'It surrounds us and penetrates us. It binds the galaxy together,' Sir Alec Guinness said in 1977's Star Wars. But some fans are not taking it as a joke, distilling it into a religious canon and taking the film scripts as their scripture. The Jedi Creed is a website operated by fans revelling in such assumed names as Jedi Relan Volkum and Lord Scorn. It addresses such theological questions as 'Should Jedi work for government?' and 'Vomiting: disgusting, or lesson on life?'

BBC News, 2001

1.2 Becoming a subject: acting and engaging

The census would not be possible without people first having the capacity to understand and participate in the practice, and population could not be constructed without their engagement. This capacity also includes the ability to categorise others, since census questionnaires are usually completed by one adult member of a household. Indeed, modern censuses are primarily completed by individual householders who may or may not consult with other adults in the household regarding the completion of a questionnaire (Howard, 2006). We can also assume that parents categorise their children. Through the census and many other practices of classification and categorisation people learn to identify in relation to categories. Indeed, the very legitimacy of the categories listed in the census (and the practice of categorising more generally) depends on the possibility of individuals being able to identify with the categories in circulation. If they cannot, then they must be able to introduce alternatives, as the numerous 'other' responses to the question on religion illustrated. Census categories are thus not just state constructed and imposed, and individuals are not mere respondents but are active participants in shaping their content. As we saw in Section 1.1, while the census imposes a limited number of categories, people do not necessarily limit their identifications to these categories. However, it is state authorities that conduct the census, structure the questionnaire, determine which categories will be included and interpret the results. Although the state engages many individuals and groups, such as social scientists, community leaders and government officials, the final decisions rest with state authorities.

Where do the categories of the census come from if they are not imposed by the state? What is the relationship between the state's census categories, which are officially recognised and therefore 'authoritative', and other categories 'out there'? Authoritative classifications are not separate from practical everyday ones that circulate in different social contexts. Population is not just whatever the state or a census authority wants it to be.

Activity 6

Earlier chapters have discussed different classifications (e.g. ethnicity, criminal) and categories (e.g. White British, Black Caribbean) that are used in different social contexts other than the census. Try writing down a list of everyday classifications and categories that you recall, especially from the previous two chapters.

Categorising is a practice that people do every day as a way of reducing complexity and managing their numerous encounters with other people and situations. The woman at the checkout till is generalised as a cashier, the man collecting rubbish is a dustman, and so on. These generalisations reduce all the unique and individual characteristics of the woman and man to occupational categories. Geoffrey Bowker and Susan Leigh Star (1999) have argued that over time there is usually a convergence between these kinds of everyday and practical classifications and those used by authorities such as census bureaux. They argue that formal classifications and those circulating in our social lives are loosely connected and involved in mutual 'co-construction'. A formal classification system partly makes up a social order; on the other hand, any given social order generates many loosely connected but relatively coherent information resources and tools used to classify. Different classification systems are thus related and are part of making up population. This is an understanding advanced by the nineteenth-century sociologist Émile Durkheim, who argued that practical and everyday social classifications are linked to scientific and government classifications.

What then determines which classifications become authoritative in the census? It happens through the process that we discussed in Section 1.1: classification struggles between many agents in the shaping of the census questions and categories and by individuals who assert alternative categories on census forms. Interpreting the census in this way directs our attention to understanding how particular categories have succeeded over others and have come to be recognised as authoritative, such as the categories of religion. This perspective stands opposed to what is called the objectivist perspective on population that we discussed in Section 1.1: that there is a correct and objective method of identifying and counting people and the task is to ensure this process is not spoiled by politics. Instead, the classifications and categories of the census are a version of the population that has succeeded over

Recall the discussion in Chapter 7 of *Making Social Lives* of how people order and classify people and things in order to 'read' the situation.

others. And succeeding and becoming part of the population has many practical and political consequences: recognition in the census is often the basis of rights claims and influences the allocation of government services.

For example, censuses are sometimes used to demand language rights. In Spain, citizens have used census data on Basque-language speakers to press for more far-reaching protective language legislation (Urla, 1993). In the UK, the Institute for Jewish Policy Research analysed the 2001 Census results on religion for the purposes of future planning and evaluation of public policies for the Jewish community (Graham et al., 2007).

1.3 Becoming a population: constructing and producing

So far we have argued that population is constructed through the census. It is the product of a political process that involves a struggle amongst numerous people to define the classifications and categorisations of the population. David Kertzer and Dominique Arel (2002), for example, document many examples of how this process is quite 'messy' and contingent as it depends on and involves many people. We have also argued that the census must produce population; that is, subjects with the capacity to identify themselves and others as part of the population through the categories circulated by the census. Once produced, the categories of the population survive if they remain useful for governing (objectification) but only if people accept and understand them (subjectification). It is only when a category involves such double identification (state–subject) that it can be said to be authoritative.

Activity 7

Consider again the debate discussed above, in Section 1.1 and in the box on 'Identifying as "Jedi"', concerning the category of 'Jedi' in the classification of religion. Is 'Jedi' an authoritative category? Why or why not?

How did constructing and producing population become a dominant way of governing modern states? In the next section, we trace the origins of the contemporary practice to cast light on what is often taken for granted.

Summary

- An objectivist perspective argues that population is a pre-existing object 'out there' that the census simply seeks to measure and reflect.

- This section puts forward a *constructivist* perspective by building the argument that population is made through practices like the census.

- Population is the product of a social and political process and struggle over the classification and categorisation of people.

- The process of making population involves *objectification* because it reduces the meaning and variety of ways that people identify with general categories.

- Making population also involves *subjectification* because it requires subjects who are able to identify themselves and others as part of the population.

2   What are the origins of population?

A census enumerator at the door for the 1961 Census

2.1   Visiting the street

A census has been taken every ten years in England and Wales since 1801 (except in 1941 during the Second World War), in Scotland since 1861, and in Northern Ireland since 1926 (in 1951 Northern Ireland started to follow the same decennial schedule). For example, for the census that was conducted in England and Wales in 1841, some 35,000 male enumerators (only men could be enumerators at the time) were directed to visit all dwellings in their assigned district on the designated census day. As in 2001, enumerators attempted to hand deliver self-completion questionnaires to every household a couple days before census night. In towns and cities, the main identifier of a dwelling was the street name and house number.

The census is not the only technique that used the house or dwelling as a site to locate and identify people. During the nineteenth century, hitting the streets and conducting door-to-door surveys were techniques through which people were ordered, categorised and then known. Indeed, the data cited in other parts of this book – such as the data on ethnicity and gender – was produced through the technique of visiting each house on a street, interviewing inhabitants and recording and categorising the information collected.

Some notable examples from the nineteenth century, at the time of the first census discussed above, include the social investigations of Charles Booth, Joseph and Seebohm Rowntree, and Beatrice and Sydney Webb (Bulmer and Sklar, 1991). Seebohm Rowntree, for example, carried out a comprehensive survey of streets in York. Charles Booth conducted a large-scale survey investigation of London. Booth and his team of researchers made at least two visits to every street in the city and produced detailed notebooks, surveys and poverty maps, published in the first book of his massive study of the *Labour and Life of the People* (1889). Figure 6 is an excerpt from one of his notebooks. The format consisted of a list of workers living in each house, their occupation and wages, and the other members of their families (wife, children). The notebooks also included many notations and moral commentaries about workers' living conditions, and sometimes about the people themselves. For example, in this excerpt Booth described Simpson Road as 'Dirty tumbledown houses should be condemned. People very poor dirty drinking lot.' On the other hand, he described Harrow Lane inhabitants as 'Respectable working people. Not migratory.'

The format of Booth's notebooks was similar to the census returns that enumerators used to record individual and household information. The census return consisted of a grid of columns covering each question or classification of the population (name, address, age, sex, marital status, and so on) and of rows for categorising individuals in relation to each classification. Unlike Booth's notebooks, the census return included more classifications (e.g. 'where born'), regularised entries into categories and did away with narrative accounts.

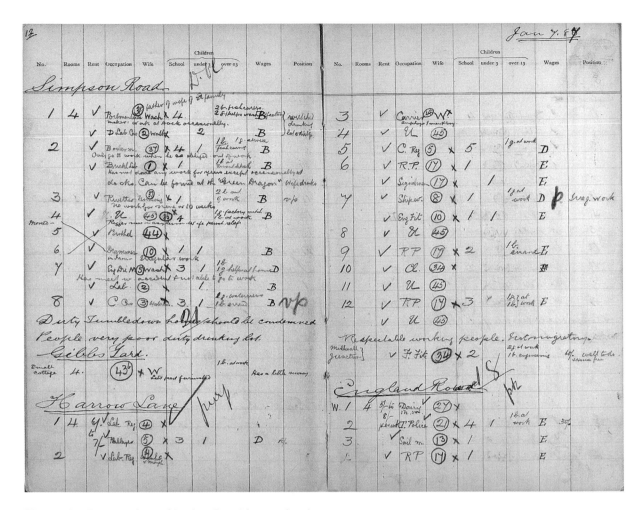

Figure 6   Excerpt from Charles Booth's notebooks

Activity 8

Examine the census return in Figure 7. Can you locate Annie Wood? Based on the handwritten entry, write a description of Annie Wood and others who lived in her household using all of the information recorded on the form. Then locate John Ede and Albert Jones and write similar descriptions for each.

How did you describe Annie Wood's profession? You may have noticed that there are two entries indicated in different handwriting. One states 'Officer Salvation Army' and another 'Preacher.' For John Ede, one entry states 'Baker's Assistant' and another appears to be 'Breadmaker.' And then there is Albert Jones who was originally noted

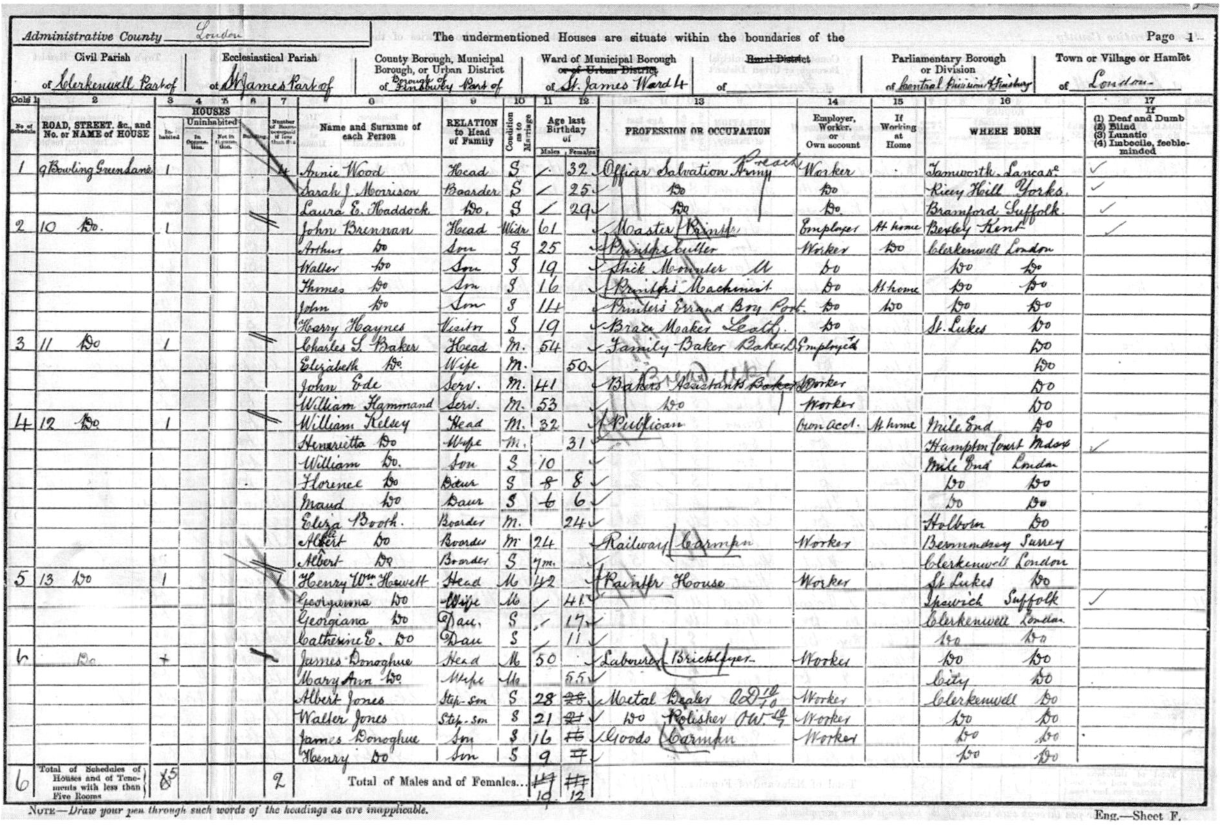

Administrative County London — The undermentioned Houses are situate within the boundaries of the — Page 1

Civil Parish of Clerkenwell Part of | Ecclesiastical Parish of St James Part of | County Borough, Municipal Borough, or Urban District of Borough of Finsbury Part of | Ward of Municipal Borough ~~or of Urban District~~ of St. James Ward 4 | ~~Rural District~~ of | Parliamentary Borough or Division of Central Division of Finsbury | Town or Village or Hamlet of London

1 No. of Schedule	2 ROAD, STREET, &c., and No. or NAME of HOUSE	3 HOUSES Inhabited	4 Uninhabited In Occupation	5 Uninhabited Not in Occupation	6 Building	7 Number of Rooms occupied if less than five	8 Name and Surname of each Person	9 RELATION to Head of Family	10 Condition as to Marriage	11 Age last Birthday of Males	12 Age last Birthday of Females	13 PROFESSION OR OCCUPATION	14 Employer, Worker, or Own account	15 If Working at Home	16 WHERE BORN	17 If (1) Deaf and Dumb (2) Blind (3) Lunatic (4) Imbecile, feeble-minded
1	9 Bowling Green Lane	1				4	Annie Wood	Head	S		32	Officer Salvation Army Preach	Worker		Tamworth Lancas	✓
							Sarah J. Morrison	Boarder	S		25	Do	Do		Ricey Hill Yorks.	✓
							Laura E. Haddock	Do.	S		29	Do	Do.		Bramford Suffolk.	✓
2	10 Do.	1					John Brennan	Head	Widr	61		Master Printer	Employer	At home	Bexley Kent	✓
							Arthur Do	Son	S	25		Printers Cutter	Worker	Do	Clerkenwell London	
							Walter Do	Son	S	19		Stick Mounter	Do		Do Do	
							Thomas Do	Son	S	16		Printers Machinist	Do	At home	Do Do	
							John Do	Son	S	14		Printer's Errand Boy Post.	Do	Do	Do Do	
							Harry Haynes	Visitor	S	19		Brace Maker Leath.	Do		St. Lukes Do	
3	11 Do	1					Charles S. Baker	Head	M.	54		Family Baker Baker D	Employed		Do	
							Elizabeth Do	Wife	M.		50				Do	
							John Ede	Serv.	M.	41		Bakers Assistants Baker	Worker		Do	
							William Hammand	Serv.	M.	53		Do	Worker		Do	
4	12 Do	1					William Kelsey	Head	M.	32		Publican	Own Acct.	At home	Mile End Do	
							Henrietta Do	Wife	M.		31				Hampton Court Mdx	✓
							William Do.	Son	S	10					Mile End London	
							Florence Do	Daur	S	~~8~~	8				Do Do	
							Maud Do	Daur	S	~~6~~	6				Do Do	
							Eliza Booth.	Boarder	M.		24				Holborn Do	
							Albert Do	Boarder	M	24		Railway Carman	Worker		Bermondsey Surrey	
							Albert Do	Boarder	S	7m.					Clerkenwell London	
5	13 Do	1				1	Henry Wm. Hewett	Head	M	42		Painter House	Worker		St Lukes Do	
							Georgianna Do	Wife	M		41				Ipswich Suffolk	✓
							Georgiana Do	Dau.	S		17				Clerkenwell London	
							Catherine E. Do	Dau	S		11				Do Do	
6	Do	+					James Donoghue	Head	M	50		Labourer Bricklayer	Worker		Do Do	
							Mary Ann Do	Wife	M		55				City Do	
							Albert Jones	Step-son	S	28	~~28~~	Metal Dealer	Worker		Clerkenwell Do	
							Walter Jones	Step-son	S	21	~~21~~	Do Polisher	Worker		Do Do	
							James Donoghue	Son	S	16	~~16~~	Goods Carman	Worker		Do Do	
							Henry Do	Son	S	9	~~9~~				Do Do	
6	Total of Schedules of Houses and of Tenements with less than Five Rooms	5				2	Total of Males and of Females	~~14~~ 19	~~17~~ 12					

NOTE—Draw your pen through such words of the headings as are inapplicable. Eng.—Sheet F.

Figure 7 Example of a 1901 Census return

as a 28-year-old female and then changed to a male. We can surmise that a census clerk inferred Albert's sex based on his first name and made this correction. We can also see that the same change was made in other cases and, as a result, the total number of males and females recorded on the form was also corrected. Thousands of these returns were completed in 1901 and many contain changes and additional notations like this one, with erasures and crossed-out entries overwritten in different handwriting. Indeed, when researchers go back to examine original census returns it becomes clear that categorising people was not as straightforward a practice as might be thought. Researchers are not the only ones interested in census returns. Genealogists often use census returns to find their family roots and write family histories, and biographers of famous people use them to locate their subjects.

Typically, the results of the 1901 Census (and others) are presented in numbers and tables like the ones we discussed in the Introduction and Section 1. In such presentations of census data, the processes by which

Annie Wood, John Ede and Albert Jones are named, identified and categorised are no longer visible to us. The original entries such as Annie's identification as an 'Officer Salvation Army' are lost. All individuals are anonymised (names removed) and identifications with categories converted into numbers. Confidentiality laws require that information from a census return can only be used for statistical purposes and that individual identification must be protected for a hundred years. As we have noted, anonymisation and the transformation into numbers is not a straightforward process. The population that was constructed in 1901 was the result of numerous interpretations and translations by people such as individual householders who completed the questionnaires, enumerators who transferred answers onto census returns, and census clerks who checked the enumerators' returns and made changes and corrections.

Recall the discussion, in Chapter 8 of this book, of how crime statistics are not unquestionable facts but result from the judgement of particular individuals or groups.

Fact
A statement that is claimed to be objective and true.

We have spent time thinking through the census return to underscore a feature of numbers that is generally unacknowledged or ignored. Numbers are often represented as descriptive, objective and factual, and separate from interpretation; that is, interpretation is what we do after numbers are produced. For this reason, Mary Poovey (1998) calls numbers 'modern **facts**'. She suggests that if we look at the history of the modern fact – that is, at how different facts were produced – we see that numbers themselves are interpretive because they are based on assumptions about what should be counted and how people should be ordered and categorised. Numbers are thus the product of assumptions, interpretations and judgement. How did governments come to make up population in this way through numbers and statistics? Let's take a further step back in time to understand.

2.2   Census, statistics, knowledge

Prior to modern censuses, counting people began not so much as a means of producing knowledge as one of *registering* people and property, usually for the purposes of tax assessment and military conscription. Such was the purpose of the Domesday Book of 1086, which consisted of a detailed inventory of land and property prepared for William the Conqueror. It is commonly identified as the first count of people in England and the single most exhaustive exercise in information collection by the central state until the taking of the first census in 1801 (Higgs, 2004). Practices before the census are understood as mainly instruments of state power, surveillance and control, and not much to do with apportioning government services and rights. It wasn't until the eighteenth century that producing *numerical* knowledge took hold and it did so as a way to evaluate the well-being and relative prosperity of states. It is for this reason that the word 'statistics' comes from the same root as 'state', and indeed was defined in the early eighteenth century as the systematic collection of numerical and descriptive facts about states. By the end of the nineteenth century, however, statistics became purely quantitative and the connection to the state was loosened.

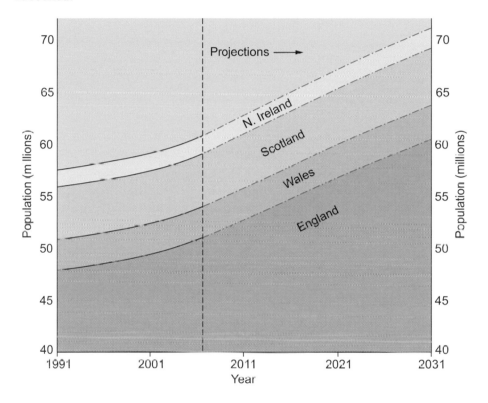

Figure 8   National projections of UK population by 2016 (Source: ONS, 2007)

However, in part it was this original connection to the state that has made statistical data persuasive. It is because statistics have a double reference, to both science and the state, that they have become authoritative. But what is meant by *quantitative*? It is helpful to recall the discussion in Section 1 on classification and categorisation. As we have already discussed, the census does not involve the simple counting of people. It requires the establishing of categories of equivalence between people, a process that involves doing away with individual differences and constructing more general things – objects – that can then be combined and manipulated. Objectification is thus a practice of

Quantitative and qualitative measurement is discussed further in Chapter 4 of *Making Social Lives*.

generalising, whether things or people, and without it statistics would not be possible. Once objectified, people can then be quantified and added up, and patterns and regularities amongst them can be identified. This is what differentiates the simple counting of people from the construction of population. Rates of change, trends and percentages, like those illustrated in Figure 8, are all examples of statistics that are made possible by quantification.

Statistics also made possible another method of making population. Beginning in the mid twentieth century, governments and social scientists increasingly used the statistical method of sampling and surveying a small number of people in order to draw conclusions about whole populations. Later in the century, administrative data was added to the mix of methods. These statistics are the focus of the next section.

Summary

- The census is one of many techniques developed in the early nineteenth century that used the house or dwelling as a site to locate and identify people.
- Categorising people on census returns involves numerous interpretations and translations that are lost when responses are translated into numbers.
- Numbers are interpretive because they are based on assumptions about what should be counted and how people should be ordered and categorised.
- Statistics have a double reference, to both science and the state, and this is one reason why they have become authoritative.
- Quantification involves generalising and categorising people so that they can be combined and added up to produce statistics.

3   What are the new ways of making up population?

3.1   Sampling population

Typically, population statistics produced by government agencies such as the ONS or social science researchers are based on a **representative sample** of a population. In the early twentieth century, surveys based on representative samples began to supplement the census as a way of making up population. In the UK, national sample surveys began in the 1930s in the form of opinion polling, and during the Second World War the Government Social Survey was inaugurated (Osborne and Rose, 1999). Eventually, the number of surveys conducted by the ONS and the agencies for Scotland and Northern Ireland came to far outstrip censuses in constructing population data.

Sampling is a statistical method that identifies a small percentage of a whole population (e.g. 1 in 100) that can be randomly selected and surveyed to make **probabilistic estimates** about the attributes of the whole population. In the early twentieth century, social scientists began advocating and experimenting with sampling as a way of making population. Part of the reason was that it is much easier and less costly than the census and the exhaustive social surveys conducted by Booth and Rowntree that we referred to in Section 2.

However, to choose 1 in 100 or 1 in 1000 at random first requires knowing and locating the total population. Therefore, sampling still depends on a method of knowing the total population or 'how many'. So while sampling has become a preferred method of providing more frequent and detailed population data, a method for knowing the whole population is still necessary. In the UK, the decennial census continues to be that method. However, alternatives such as administrative data are under consideration.

Representative sample
A sample whose characteristics are approximately the same as the population from which it was drawn.

Probabilistic estimates
Numerical assessment of the likelihood that the characteristics of a randomly selected sample are the same as the population from which it was drawn.

3.2   Administrative data

'But how do I know you're you?'

Activity 9

Make a list of all the government identifications that you currently possess (e.g. birth certificate). Which of these (if any) did you apply for yourself?

When Sylvie was born in England on 3 March 1982 her parents were legally required to register her birth within 42 days at the General Register Office, which then issued a birth certificate. Sylvie's parents also filed for a Child Benefit claim with HM Revenue & Customs and registered Sylvie with their doctor's surgery. A few years later, when they were planning a holiday in France, Sylvie's parents applied for and received her first passport. In 1998 Sylvie filled out an application form for a National Insurance number and also for her learner's permit so that she could take driving lessons. In 1999 she completed her first income tax return. Her marriage to Lyle in 2004 was registered with the General Register Office. She also registered with the government's 'identity management' service, which enabled her to do many government transactions online. For each of these transactions with government, various aspects of Sylvie's identity were recorded, such as her father's and mother's names, her date and place of birth, occupation, earnings, marital status, ethnicity, nationality, address, and so on. Throughout the rest of her life Sylvie will continuously interact with government agencies. Each of these can be considered as different measurements of not only Sylvie's identification but also her conduct in relation to government.

All of Sylvie's transactions with government produce administrative data records. During the latter part of the twentieth century, governments started to investigate and develop methods of using this administrative data as a way of making population and possibly replacing censuses. Administrative data could provide a more comprehensive and up-to-date source of knowledge for making population since it could be updated every time someone like Sylvie interacted with government. Modern information technologies have made it possible for computer systems to handle millions of bytes of data and to join up all of a person's identifications and transactions with government. In the UK this is already well developed in relation to a number of functions, such as the joining up of welfare and taxation records.

Several identification technologies have been adopted by the UK Government in the last few years towards making it possible to replace censuses with the use of administrative data. One includes the introduction of a National Identity Register (NIR) to store core personal details of name, address, gender, date and place of birth, date of death, a unique personal identifier, and provide the 'spine' for joining up administrative data. It also contains biometric data on facial, iris and fingerprint measurements to confirm identity, and when linked to other government databases could be used to trace people's movements and transactions. Biometric data is proposed or already being used for passports, visas and driver licensing. Another component includes national identity cards (ID cards), which will have a chip containing the NIR information. Finally, work has started on building a national address register to deal with problems identifying addresses that we described at the beginning of the chapter. The register would cover all properties in England and Wales and could be regularly updated so that the location of every dwelling could be identified centrally.

These identification techniques have in part been justified on the grounds that they will improve government service delivery. Other justifications have included the security imperatives of combating terrorism, organised crime, identity fraud and illegal migration. But the techniques have also been advanced because they can be used to improve knowledge of the population. A population statistical system based on these types of administrative data could replace the census, and the 2011 UK Census may well be the last one according to the most recent recommendations of the UK Treasury Committee (2008). So instead of periodically asking people who they are, population could be constructed based on what people regularly do in relation to government (e.g. visiting doctors, paying taxes, obtaining licenses, crossing borders, receiving benefits).

There are enormous challenges involved in this move, such as public acceptability, legal issues and tensions associated with all of these techniques. In particular, there are concerns about privacy and state surveillance, and technical issues about the compatibility of data sources and the capacity to protect personal data (e.g. see Hier and Greenberg, 2007; Lyon, 2003). For example, in 2007 and 2008 there were several cases of government departments losing or misplacing personal data. Most vocal are the political campaigns against identity cards, which are seen to be a threat to liberty and privacy and indicative of the growth of a 'database' or 'surveillance' state.

The proposals to replace censuses with all or some of these techniques may or may not come about. As you are reading this, they may have not proceeded at all, or not in the form described above. For example, while the NIR and ID cards were approved in 2007, questions remain, for political and technical reasons, as to whether they will be successfully or fully implemented. But for the purposes of this chapter we need to ask: what would be the implications of using administrative data for making up population and for people's engagement in the practice? We turn to this question in the final section.

Summary

- Beginning in the mid twentieth century, governments and social scientists increasingly used the statistical method of sampling and surveying to make up population.
- Sampling is a statistical method that identifies a small percentage of a whole population that can be surveyed to make probabilistic estimates about the attributes of the whole population.

- During the latter part of the twentieth century, governments started to investigate and introduce different techniques such as joined up administrative data to make population.

- Administrative data consists of personal information collected in the course of an individual's transactions with government throughout their lifetime.

4   Census subjects and citizens

So far in this chapter we have discussed how states make up populations by locating, identifying, classifying and categorising people. But we have also emphasised that people do not necessarily accept and conform to the expectations government may have of them in those categories. People actively engage, and are indeed invited to engage, in classification struggles. It is out of these struggles, which involve both objectification (useful for governing) and subjectification (accepted and understood by people), that census categories become authoritative. We now want to argue that if being a subject of the state means being counted and accounted for by government, then being a citizen means not only calling into question how one is being counted and accounted for by the government but also making claims for rights.

When people are able to see themselves as a whole and in parts, we can suggest that they have developed one of the capacities necessary to become **citizens**, for citizenship requires both identification with the whole and differentiation from it. By seeing myself as equal with others (e.g. British) I develop a sense of rights and responsibilities that derives from this identification. By seeing myself as different from others (e.g. Muslim) I also come to recognise myself with certain rights and responsibilities. The modern census has contributed to this understanding of the whole (population) and its parts (peoples).

So far in this chapter we have discussed individuals as subjects of population. However, the rights and obligations of being a citizen of the state differ from those of being a subject, at least in terms of practice. While being a subject involves some rights and obligations, such as the right to mobility and obligations of taxation and conscription, these are often taken for granted. I may travel with my passport, pay my taxes and vote for my political party without having to struggle for these rights (or obligations). While an earlier generation of people may have struggled for these, I now enjoy them by virtue of my membership in the state. Indeed, many rights that I enjoy today are the result of citizenship struggles in the nineteenth and twentieth centuries. This is how citizenship rights and obligations are often defined. But being a citizen of a democratic state such as the UK is to have the right to have rights. What that means is that, as well as enjoying taken-for-granted rights that are given such as those discussed above, being a citizen also involves articulating and claiming rights. Being a citizen involves not

Citizen
A subject who possesses and/or practices rights and duties of citizenship.

only enjoying but also claiming rights, such as access to social insurance, that are acquired through social struggles. It also involves laying claims to rights that currently exist for some citizens but not all, such as marriage rights.

Activity 10

What is the difference between being a subject and being a citizen? When you completed the census questionnaire at the beginning of this chapter did you consider yourself a subject or a citizen? Why?

Understood in this way, therefore, being a citizen involves a different relationship to population. First, being a citizen means being capable of understanding and interpreting numbers and recognising oneself as part of the whole and taking part in making population. But second, being a citizen means not only engaging in and having a critical attitude about the making of population but also making claims for rights. We have argued that population is neither given nor taken; it is made. To approach population and its parts as made entities is a critical attitude that enables subjects to become citizens by articulating and claiming rights. How do subjects become citizens by engaging in making up populations?

4.1   From subjects to citizens: taking part, laying claim

Becoming aware of the consequences of counting and the recognition of identity in censuses has led to many groups taking part in the census and sometimes mobilising to change and influence it. These movements are about people's claims not only to rights and resources but also to the truth about themselves. For instance, in his example of colonial censuses in Bengal, the anthropologist Bernard Cohn (1987) argues that censuses can have a significant influence on the way people understand and look at themselves and their culture. We could also examine the different ways that people in the UK have been able to stand back, look at themselves and understand who they are through the census. Table 5 lists the changes in the questions and content of censuses in the UK since 1801. It illustrates how new classifications were added to the census over time: for example, questions on ethnicity and religion, nationality and language spoken were added over time. We could thus ask what effects the inclusion of these classifications in the census have had on the way people in the UK have come to understand themselves.

Table 5   Census topics, 1801–2001

Subject	1801	1851	1881	1891	1921	1951	1961	1971	1991	2001
Nationality[1]	–	GB	GB	GB	GB	GB	GB	–	–	–
Ethnic group	–	–	–	–	–	–	–	–	GB	UK
Religion[2]	–	GB	–	–	–	–	–	–	–	UK
Language spoken:										
Welsh	–	–	–	W	W	W	W	W	W	W
Irish	–	–	–	–	–	–	–	–	–	NI
Gaelic	–	–	S	S	S	S	S	S	S	S
Infirmity (deaf, dumb, blind, etc.)	–	GB	GB	GB	–	–	–	–	–	–
Long-term illness and disability	–	–	–	–	–	–	–	–	GB	UK
Address one year ago	–	–	–	–	–	–	GB	GB	GB	UK

GB = Great Britain (England (E), Wales (W), Scotland (S)); NI = Northern Ireland; UK = Great Britain + Northern Ireland

[1] In 1851–91 the question was whether British subject or not.

[2] In 1851 the question was asked separate from the census; in 2001 the question was voluntary. There was a question on religion in the Northern Ireland Censuses between 1951 and 1991.

Source: based on ONS, 2008b, pp. 1–2

However, such taking part and laying claim to the truth about various groups is a necessary but not a sufficient condition of acquiring rights. Throughout the twentieth century, various groups have engaged critically in the construction and interpretation of censuses as a means of articulating and claiming rights. That is, they have not only challenged categories but have also made this the basis of rights claims.

In the previous sections we discussed several examples of how subjects have constituted themselves as citizens:

- the inclusion of a question on religion in the 2001 UK Censuses
- the use of census data on Basque-language speakers in Spain
- the inclusion of the ethnic category of 'Irish' in the 2001 UK Censuses.

To end this chapter, let's return to the question on religion in the 2001 UK Censuses. The engagement of census subjects in actively challenging and creating categories was a necessary but not a sufficient condition for engaging in the census as citizens. What is also required is that the categories are the basis of rights claims. For example, the campaign to recognise Jedi as a religion could be interpreted as an ironic act that challenged the categories of the census but did not constitute a claim to rights. However, for many Muslims the recognition of religious identity was a question not only of being officially recognised in census categories but also of claiming equality and social rights such as access to government funding. Indeed, all of the examples above illustrate this point.

4.2 From citizens to subjects?

What then are the implications of new techniques of making population for being a citizen? In Section 3 we discussed developments in making population, such as the joining up of administrative data based on people's conduct in relation to government and their movements rather than asking them questions in censuses. Does the shift towards using administrative data perhaps turn citizens back into subjects since the focus is on the surveillance and monitoring of conduct? Administrative data records what you are doing (being born, getting married, going to the doctor, working, buying a property, immigrating) and tracks and verifies who you are and your movements through biometrics. It is indicative perhaps to note that proposals for joining up government databases refer to people as 'data subjects'.

For citizens it is much more difficult to intervene in the production of data that measure conduct rather than asking people to identify themselves (occupation, ethnicity, religion, nationality, etc.). There are indications that governments consider the data collected via administrative and biometric techniques as being more accurate, reliable and useful than census data and, as mentioned in Section 3.2, the UK 2011 Census may well be the last one. If the collection, interpretation and analysis of data are withdrawn from public contestation and struggle, which this section has argued is essential to being a citizen, what then will be the new relationship between states and citizens in the making of population? If, as we mentioned earlier, the role of the modern census in creating the whole (population) and its parts (categories) has been significant, what means will be available for subjects to constitute themselves as citizens in making up population?

Summary

- Being a citizen of a democratic state means to have the right to have rights. As well as enjoying taken-for-granted rights that are given, being a citizen also involves articulating and claiming rights.

- Population is neither given nor taken; it is made. To approach population and its parts as made entities is a critical attitude that enables subjects to become citizens by articulating and claiming rights.

- Engaging critically in the making of the census is a necessary but not a sufficient condition of acquiring rights. Recognition is not only a question of being officially acknowledged in census categories but also of claiming rights.

- Administrative data raises questions about the capacity of subjects to intervene and constitute themselves as citizens in the making up of population.

How do we know?

Making social science arguments 4: questioning evidence

A lot of what we know about the contemporary UK is gleaned from population data produced by censuses. Population data is often used as evidence to support government policies and political arguments and to make claims about the social make-up of the country, such as its ethnic or religious composition. Whether compiled by governments or social scientists, such evidence, when presented in numbers, charts, tables and graphs, can appear to consist of objective and incontestable facts.

However, social scientists often challenge such evidence and in particular the claim that practices such as censuses produce objective facts. We developed such a challenge from the perspective known as constructivism. We argued that population is made through practices like the census. We examined how evidence and knowledge of the population are constructed by the census, from who to count, to decisions on the questions asked, the wording of those questions and which categories or answers are accepted. We suggested that in the end the census constructs a particular version of population. The basic idea here is that there are other versions possible.

You may or may not agree with the argument we developed. What is important to understand is that to treat evidence critically means to ask questions and enquire about the judgements, assumptions and decisions that go into producing facts.

Conclusion

In this chapter we have used evidence on religious identification in the 2001 UK Censuses to build the constructivist argument that population is made by the census rather than an object waiting to be discovered. We discussed the origins of the census from the early efforts of states to count people through to the twentieth century when the census became a modern and accepted form of making up population. We then turned our attention to how surveys and administrative and biometric data are increasingly supplementing and potentially replacing censuses. In the final section we brought all of this to bear on the question of the relationship between being a subject and being a citizen in the making up of population.

References

BBC News (2001) 'Jedi e-mail revealed as hoax', 11 April [online], http://news.bbc.co.uk/1/hi/entertainment/new_media/1271380.stm (Accessed 24 February 2009).

Bell, E. (2008) 'Selina stokes a diversity debate that needs addressing', *The Guardian*, 8 September [online], http://www.guardian.co.uk/media/2008/sep/08/channelfive.television (Accessed 25 February 2009).

Bowker, G.C. and Star, S.L. (1999) *Sorting Things Out: Classification and Its Consequences*, Cambridge, MA, MIT Press.

Boyd, M., and Norris, D. (2001) 'Who are the "Canadians"? Changing census responses, 1986–1996', *Canadian Ethnic Studies Journal*, vol. 33, no. 1, pp. 1–26.

Bulmer, M., Bales, K. and Sklar, K.K. (eds.) (1991) *The Social Survey in Historical Perspective, 1880–1940*, Cambridge, Cambridge University Press.

Bunting, M. (2008) 'Faith schools can best generate the common purpose that pupils need', *The Guardian*, 8 September [online], http://www.guardian.co.uk/commentisfree/2008/sep/08/faithschools (Accessed 25 February 2009).

Cohn, B. (1987) *An Anthropologist Among the Historians and Other Essays*, Delhi and New York, Oxford University Press.

Goyer, D.S. and Domschke, E. (1992) *The Handbook of National Population Censuses: Europe*, New York, Greenwood Press.

Graham, D., Schmool, M. and Waterman, S. (2007) *Jews in Britain: A Snapshot from the 2001 Census*, London, Institute for Jewish Policy Research.

Hacking, I. (1990) *The Taming of Chance*, Cambridge and New York, Cambridge University Press.

Hier, S.P. and Greenberg, J. (eds) (2007) *The Surveillance Studies Reader*, Maidenhead, Open University Press.

Higgs, E. (2004) *The Information State in England: The Central Collection of Information on Citizens Since 1500*, Basingstoke, Palgrave Macmillan.

Howard, K. (2006) 'Constructing the Irish of Britain: ethnic recognition and the 2001 UK Censuses', *Ethnic and Racial Studies*, vol. 29, no. 1, pp. 104–123.

Kertzer, D.I. and Arel, D. (eds) (2002) *Census and Identity: The Politics of Race, Ethnicity and Language in National Censuses*, Cambridge and New York, Cambridge University Press.

Lyon, D. (2003) *Surveillance as Social Sorting: Privacy, Risk and Digital Documentation*, London and New York, Routledge.

Office for National Statistics (ONS) (2001a) *2001 Census Forms* [online], http://www.statistics.gov.uk/census2001/censusform.asp (Accessed 20 February 2009).

Office for National Statistics (ONS) (2001b) *2001 Census Profiles* [online], http://www.statistics.gov.uk/census2001/profiles/uk.asp (accessed 23 June 2009).

Office for National Statistics (ONS) (2003) *Religion in the UK* [online], http://www.statistics.gov.uk/cci/nugget.asp?id=293 (Accessed 23 February 2009).

Office for National Statistics (ONS) (2004) *Guide to Focus on Religion* [online], http://www.statistics.gov.uk/cci/nugget_print.asp?ID=984 (Accessed 23 February 2009).

Office for National Statistics (ONS) (2005) *Census 2001: The Quality of the Results* [online], http://www.statistics.gov.uk/census2001/stat_methods_qual.asp (Accessed 20 February 2009).

Office for National Statistics (ONS) (2007) *National Projections* [online], http://www.statistics.gov.uk/cci/nugget.asp?id=1352 (Accessed 24 February 2009).

Office for National Statistics (ONS) (2008a) *Why We Have a Census* [online], http://www.ons.gov.uk/census/what-is-a-census/why-have-census/index.html (Accessed 20 February 2009).

Office for National Statistics (ONS) (2008b) *Census Topics 1801–2001* [online], http://www.ons.gov.uk/census/get-data/data-comparability/topics-1801-2001.pdf (Accessed 25 February 2009).

Office for National Statistics (ONS) (2009) *Census 2001: Population Pyramids: United Kingdom* [online], http://www.statistics.gov.uk/census2001/pyramids/pages/UK.asp (Accessed 23 February 2009).

Osborne, T. and Rose, N. (1999) 'Do the social sciences create phenomena? The example of public opinion research', *British Journal of Sociology*, vol. 50, no. 3, pp. 367–96.

Poovey, M. (1998) *A History of the Modern Fact: Problems of Knowledge in the Sciences of Wealth and Society*, Chicago, IL, and London, University of Chicago Press.

Sardar, Z. (2000) 'At last we can stand up and be counted', *New Statesman*, 26 June, p. 24.

Scott, J. (1999) *Seeing Like a State: How Certain Schemes to Improve the Human Condition Have Failed*, New Haven, CT, Yale University Press.

Sherif, J. (2003) 'Campaigning for a religion question in the 2001 Census', London, Muslim Council of Britain [online], http://www.mcb.org.uk/downloads/census2001.pdf (Accessed 23 February 2009).

Southworth, J.R. (2005) '"Religion" in the 2001 Census for England and Wales', *Population, Space and Place*, vol. 11, no. 2, pp. 75–88.

Treasury Committee (2008) *Counting the Population: Eleventh Report of Session 2007–08*, London, TSO; also available online at http://www.publications.parliament.uk/pa/cm200708/cmselect/cmtreasy/183/18302.htm (Accessed 25 February 2009).

Urla, J. (1993) 'Cultural politics in an age of statistics: numbers, nations, and the making of Basque identity', *American Ethnologist*, vol. 20, no. 4, pp. 818–43.

Conclusion: Ordered lives

Simon Bromley and John Clarke

Conclusion: Ordered lives

Now that you have finished your work on these three chapters, do you have some sense of *why social scientists should be so interested in social order and processes of ordering*? You will remember that this was one of the issues that it was suggested you keep in mind as you read the chapters.

Activity 1

Make a quick note of why you think social scientists are so interested in these issues.

For social scientists, there are several linked answers. First, they are interested in social order because it is a fundamental or basic feature of social life. It is difficult to imagine how social life could take place without some form of order that enabled people to interact, live together or engage in all sorts of activities (from shopping to studying).

Second, social scientists might also be interested in the existence of *different social orders*. Although people often write and talk of social order in the singular, it is important to recognise that there are many social orders rather than just one and that social order changes over time and between places. The most obvious way to think about this variation in social order is by linking it to different societies or the same society at different times, and there are other sorts of variation too. A society – like the UK since 2000 – may contain different social orders and different types of social order. So, in Chapter 7, you considered ideas about micro-social orders as well as macro-social order: particular types of interaction (driving, eating in a public place, passing through passport or immigration control) may have their own specific sets of rules and expectations. These particular or micro-social orders exist within the larger macro-social order.

But there may be other variations within a society. Different social groups may have different habits, values, rules and expectations. There may be differences between urban and rural social orders, or between different ethnic, cultural or religious groups. Societies may contain more than one social order – think, for example, about the Amish community in the USA where long-standing religious rules sustain patterns of

449

behaviour, belief and interaction that are different from, but coexist within, the wider social order of the USA. Other sorts of grouping may have their own variations – age groups (as in the idea of youth cultures); specific occupational groups (social order in military settings, for instance); or differences of gender, perhaps. Social scientists might well be fascinated by social order – as they study it they encounter many types of order, which raises questions about how different social orders coexist and interact within one society.

Third, then, an interest in social order leads social scientists to processes and practices of ordering. So they ask, how did this social order come about? How was it made? How is it maintained? Is it shaped by specific social groups and their ideas, values or interests? But if order is being made, then there are also questions about who or what does the social work of ordering – who makes order, who maintains it, who tries to repair it if it breaks? In Chapter 7, you encountered two different sorts of answer to these questions. The first, drawing on the work of Erving Goffman, stressed the 'interactional order' as self-producing and self-sustaining. In the interactions between individuals, order is constantly being produced (sometimes with variations as people find new ways of engaging with one another). The second, drawing on the work of Michel Foucault, stressed the role of authoritative knowledge (especially experts and powerful institutions) in making and changing social order. In Chapters 8 and 9, there was a greater stress on social and political institutions – the media, the police and legal system, governments and the state. Such institutions are expected to take responsibility for maintaining and repairing social order if it seems to be breaking or is troubled by disorder.

This brings us to the other issue that you were asked to think about: *how are social order and disorder connected in social life?* The easy answer is that they are opposites – disorder is the absence of order; order is the absence of disorder. But, as you will have worked out by now, in the social sciences 'easy answers' are often not very helpful. It might be better to think about how order and disorder coexist: most of the time, most societies experience forms of disorder without the society collapsing. Alternatively, we could think of them as interacting – disorderly people or disorderly behaviour strengthen social order by making the rest of society feel orderly. Or social order is maintained (as Chapter 8 suggested) by creating 'folk devils' and turning attention on them to distract from economic, social or political conflicts that might be more threatening. This might even point to questions about how a specific social order produces problems or conflicts – often around inequalities or injustices – that lead to changes in the ordering of that society.

With all these possibilities, you might think that social scientists could not avoid being interested in social order. Like the other two strands that you have encountered, the making of social order is both intrinsically interesting and leads outwards to other social relationships, processes and practices. By now, you may be able to see some of the connections between the three strands.

Acknowledgements

Grateful acknowledgement is made to the following sources:

Cover

Copyright © Peter Cavanagh/Alamy

Introduction: Material lives

Illustrations

Page 4: Private Collection, Courtesy of Thomas Ammann Fine Art, Zurich; Page 8: Copyright © DLILLC/Corbis

Chapter 1

Figures

Figures 2 and 3: Copyright © Kevin Hetherington; Figure 4: Office for National Statistics (2008) 'Expenditure and Food Survey', Office for National Statistics. Crown copyright material is reproduced under Class Licence Number C01W0000065 with the permission of the Controller, Office of Public Sector Information (OPSI); Figure 5: Courtesy of Fosse Shopping Park

Illustrations

Page 16: Copyright © ICP-UK/Alamy; Page 28: Copyright © Image Source/Rex Features; Page 32: Copyright © Sandro Campardo/epa/ Corbis; Page 33 left: Copyright © Time & Life Pictures/Getty Images; Page 33 right: Copyright © Richard Bryant/Arcail/Corbis; Page 35: Copyright © Alex Segre/Alamy; Page 37: Copyright © Stefano Bianchett/Corbis; Page 39: Copyright © Bettmann/Corbis; Page 48: Copyright © Sion Touhig/Corbis

Chapter 2

Figures

Figure 1 bottom and Figure 3 bottom: Copyright © Gerry Mooney

Illustrations

Page 58: Copyright © PA/PA Wire/PA Photos; Page 67: Copyright © Jay Fram/Corbis; Page 83: Copyright © 67/photo/Alamy; Page 88 top and bottom right: Copyright © G M B Akash/Panos Pictures; Page 88 bottom left: Copyright © Fernando Moleres/Panos Pictures

Chapter 3

Table

Table 2: Defra (2007) Municipal Waste Management Statistics, 2006/7, from www.defra.gov.uk/environment/statistics/wastats/archicc/mwb200607, Crown copyright material is reproduced under Class Licence Number C01W0000065 with the permission of the Controller, Office of Public Sector Information (OPSI)

Figure

Figure 6: Copyright © Chris Jordan

Illustrations

Page 113 top left: Copyright © Ian Nicholson/PA Archive/PA Photos; Page 113 centre left: Copyright © Shaun Van Steyn/Stock Collection/Alamy; Page 113 bottom left: Copyright © Alex Livesey/Getty Images; Page 113 right: Copyright © Hans Reinhard/zefa/Corbis; Page 120: Copyright © Maersk/PA Archive/PA Photos; Page 124 left: Stephenson's 'Triumph', woven for the York Exhibition, 1879 (Stevengraph), Private Collection/Bridgeman Art Library; Page 124 right: Courtesy of the Stevengraph Collectors Association; Page 130 left: Copyright © Daniel Berehulak/Getty Images; Page 131 right: Copyright © Toby Melville/Reuters

Introduction: Connected lives

Illustration

Page 155: Copyright © Isabel Hutchison/Alamy

Chapter 4

Figures

Figure 1 top left: Copyright © Kathy deWitt/Alamy; Figure 1 centre left and centre right; Copyright © Flat Earth/Fotosearch; Figure 1 bottom left: and Figure 1 top right: Copyright © Maciej Dakowicz; Figure 1 bottom right: Copyright © Anna Gowthorpe/PA Wire/PA Photos; Figure 3: Courtesy of Stephanie Taylor and Ralph Taylor

Illustrations

Page 175 left: Copyright © Bernard Gotfryd/Getty Images; Page 175 right: Copyright © Morris Engel/Getty Images; Page 183 book cover: Courtesy of the University of Chicago Press; Page 188: Copyright © PA Archive/PA Photos; Page 189: Copyright © Michael Patterson; Page 194: Copyright © Helene Rogers/Alamy

Chapter 5

Figure

Figure 2: Copyright © Sefton Samuels/Rex Features

Illustrations

Pages 207 and 234: Copyright © Steve Hinchliffe; Page 213: Copyright © Hulton Archive/Getty Images; Page 219: Courtesy of Mivan Ltd and The Trafford Centre; Page 220: Copyright © sinopictures/Joerg F Mueller/Still Pictures; Page 223 top left: Courtesy of the Northern Ireland Tourist Board; Page 223 bottom left: Courtesy of This England; Page 223 top right: courtesy of Visit Wales; Page 223 bottom right: Courtesy of Visit Scotland; Page 235 top: Copyright © Birmingham City Council; Page 235 bottom: Courtesy of Community Service Volunteers (CSV)

Chapter 6

Figures

Figure 1 top: Copyright © Andrew Fax/Corbis; Figure 1 bottom left: Copyright © Peter Durant/Arcaid/Corbis; Figure 1 bottom right: Copyright © Angelo Hornak/Corbis

Illustrations

Page 269 top: Courtesy of Ronald Grant Archive; Page 269 bottom: Copyright © ITV Granada; Page 272: Copyright © New York Times; Page 273: Copyright © Mercury Press/Sygma/Corbis

Conclusion: Connected lives

Illustration

Page 293: Copyright © Ace Stock Limited/Alamy

Introduction: Ordered lives

Illustrations

Page 299 right: Copyright © Anthony West/Corbis; Page 299 left: Copyright © Dean Pictures/Rex Features

Chapter 7

Text

Page 334: Glaskin, M. (2004) 'Innovation: The end of the white line', The Sunday Times, 22 August 2004, Copyright © NI Syndication Ltd

Illustrations

Page 328: Copyright © Mary Evans Picture Library/Roger Mayne; Pages 330 and 331: Copyright © Google Earth; Page 332: Copyright © Barry Cawston; Page 336: Copyright © Andrew Buurman; Page 344 left: Courtesy of Colin Buchanan and Partners Limited; Page 344 right: Copyright © Jerry Michalski

Chapter 8

Tables

Table 2: Office for National Statistics (2007) Social Trends, No. 37, Office for National Statistics, Crown copyright material is reproduced under Class Licence Number C01W0000065 with the permission of the Controller, Office of Public Sector Information (OPSI); Table 3: Office for National Statistics (2007) Social Trends, No. 37, Office for National Statistics, Crown copyright material is reproduced under Class Licence

Number C01W0000065 with the permission of the Controller, Office of Public Sector Information (OPSI)

Illustrations

Page 353: Copyright © Picture Post/Hulton Archive/Getty Images; Page 366: Copyright © Image Source/Rex Features; Page 67: Copyright © Alex Segre/Rex Features; Page 371: Copyright © Bettmann/Corbis; Page 383: Copyright © Ashley Cooper/Corbis

Chapter 9

Text

Page 403: Office for National Statistics (2008) 'Why we have a census', Office for National Statistics, Crown copyright material is reproduced under Class Licence Number C01W0000065 with the permission of the Controller, Office of Public Sector Information (OPSI); Page 420: BBC News (2001) 'Jedi e-mail revealed as hoax', 11 April 2001, from BBC News at http://bbc.co.uk/news, Copyright © BBC MMI

Tables

Tables 1, 2, 3 and 4: Census 2001, National Statistics website www.statistics.gov.uk, Crown copyright material is reproduced under Class Licence Number C01W0000065 with the permission of the Controller, Office of Public Sector Information (OPSI); Table 5: Office for National Statistics (2008) Census Topics 1801–2001, National Statistics website www.statistics.gov.uk, Crown copyright material is reproduced under Class Licence Number C01W0000065 with the permission of the Controller, Office of Public Sector Information (OPSI)

Figures

Figures 1, 2 and 5 top left: Office of National Statistics (2001) 2001 Census Form, Crown copyright material is reproduced under Class Licence Number C01W0000065 with the permission of the Controller, Office of Public Sector Information (OPSI); Figure 3: Copyright © 2002 Topham/PA TopFoto.co.uk; Figure 5 right: General Register Office for Scotland (2001) 2001 Census Form, Crown copyright material is reproduced under Class Licence Number C01W0000065 with the permission of the Controller, Office of Public Sector Information (OPSI); Figure 5 bottom left: Northern Ireland Statistics and Research Agency (2001) 2001 Census form for Northern Ireland, Crown copyright material is reproduced under Class Licence Number C01W0000065 with the permission of the Controller, Office of Public Sector Information (OPSI); Figure 6: Courtesy of The London School of Economics and Political Science; Figure 7: Copyright © The National Archives; Figure 8: Office of National Statistics (2006) 'National projections: UK population to rise to 65m by 2016', Crown copyright material is reproduced under Class Licence Number C01W0000065 with the permission of the Controller, Office of Public Sector Information (OPSI)

Illustrations

Page 421: Copyright © Lucasfilm, Picture from The Ronald Grant Archive; Page 426: Copyright © Topfoto www.Topfoto.co.uk

Every effort has been made to contact copyright holders. If any have been inadvertently overlooked, the publishers will be pleased to make the necessary arrangements at the first opportunity.

Index